SUCCESS SIGNS

SUCCESS SIGNS

A Practical Astrological Guide to Career Fulfilment

Marlene Masini Rathgeb

NEW ENGLISH LIBRARY

For Lisa and Amy
who made me believe in everything

First published in the USA in 1981 by St Martin's Press Inc.

Design by Mina Greenstein

First NEL Paperback Edition February 1982

NEL Books are published by
New English Library,
Barnard's Inn, Holborn,
London EC1N 2JR, a division of Hodder and Stoughton Ltd.

Made and printed in Great Britain by
Billing and Sons Limited,
Guildford, London, Oxford, Worcester.

Rathgeb, Marlene Masini

Success Signs.
I. Astrology
133.5 BF1708.1

ISBN 0-450-05353-9

ACKNOWLEDGMENTS

Many people have taken part in making this book a reality. I would like to single out a few of them.

—Susan Zeckendorf, my friend and agent, who planted the seed for this book, and nurtured both it and me as we grew;

—Amy Rathgeb, my daughter, who cheerfully tackled a difficult assignment;

—Janine Hayes, my friend and assistant, whose "success skills" are far greater than she knows;

—Phyllis Rifield, my friend and colleague, whose willing patience is monumental;

—Zoltan Mason, who taught me well, and knew what I could do long before I could do it;

—Anna, Edith, and Nancy, whose interest and loving friendship helped to sustain me; and

—All those others without whom I might never have found my "invincible summer."

CONTENTS

PREFACE

Astrology is such a rich subject that it is unfortunate so much time and talk are devoted to attempting to prove or disprove its validity. But it seems that in our world, such discussions are unavoidable. Since the quest for proof is a characteristic of the scientific age, though, I find the following story relevant. Nobel Prize-winning Danish physicist Niels Bohr was asked by a visitor why he, a man of science, kept a horseshoe over his door. Bohr is said to have replied, "It's a funny thing about horseshoes; even if you don't believe in them they work."

Though astrology and the horseshoe-as-fetish have little in common (partly because there is much evidence both ancient and modern to support the former), this little tale speaks to an important point: In dealing with symbols it is counterproductive to rely solely on the rational function. These days we hear a lot about the left-brain/right-brain distinction. As a symbolic medium, astrology belongs mainly to the right brain—the realm of what is intuitive, unconscious, and hence often undervalued in our "a-plus-b-equals-c" society.

To get to the heart of astrology, one must enter the world of myth and symbol—and the "occult." The real meaning of the term *occult* is "hidden": You have to stretch a little to peer around the corner or over the edge, but when you do the rewards are great. The simple but profound truths that stand behind astrology's symbols can be immensely helpful in sorting out our lives. Some people theorize that the renewed interest in such ancient systems as astrology is a result of the lack of a valid mythology in our time. I agree, but I would go farther. Primitive man "invented" myths to help him make some sense out of the apparent chaos around him.

We are primitives once more, and we need all the help we can get.

This book deals with your horoscope in an effort to help you make sense of yourself in relation to the world around you, to give you an idea of who you are, what you were meant to be, and therefore, how you can become most successful. I like to regard the astrologer as a code-breaker—a trained professional who is able to tell you what clues the universe is giving the individual about how he or she fits into the big picture. One of this century's greatest astrologers, Dane Rudyhar, calls the horoscope "your celestial Name," a beautiful way of reminding us that each person is unique. In ancient tradition, to know the Name of a person, a demon or a force enabled one to control it. It is my hope that by knowing more about your own horoscope—hence your Name—you will be in better control of your life, and your potential success.

Whatever your belief system, I ask you to approach this book with a practical eye, because it is a practical book. As an astrologer and a business woman, I keep one foot in each of two worlds—and manage not to lose my balance. I would like to share with you some of what I have learned from both of these worlds, and, more important, to show you how astrology can help you to become as successful as possible in yours.

ONE

SUCCESS AND ASTROLOGY

1

Career Counseling and Astrology

Listening to the Inner Voice

This is a book about success and how to achieve it. Astrology comes in as a tool—a quite precise tool that can help you carve out your special niche in the world. To be successful you must be a "specialist"; that is, you must have a clear-cut idea of what you want to do in life. The drifter and the failure are often one and the same; the driven soul with a single, burning ambition more often than not makes it big. But most of us fall somewhere between these extremes. With a vague sense of what we are good at and a rather out-of-focus idea of what we are after, we land in careers that seem to suit us well enough. When we see other people become more successful than us, we cite their greater education, better opportunities, greater talent, a rich uncle, luck, or any one of a variety of other factors beyond our control. In reality, the secret of many successful people lies in one simple fact: they know what they want.

Most people want from their careers money and power and those good things that come along with them, like fulfillment and security. Money heads the list because realistically there is no success today that does not include a substantial amount of it. But the goal of success is not the game. The brilliant neurosurgeon with a villa in Spain and a chateau in France has played his life just as skillfully as he has wielded his scalpel. He arrived at success because he knew what route would take him there. It's likely, though not certain, that he would have made a mediocre songwriter, pastry chef, or tax accountant. Acceptable, perhaps—but mediocre. The point is that success is self-realization, and that depends on self-knowledge. The eminent psychologist C. G. Jung put it simply: "Become what you always have been."

In our ultra-competitive world where everyone wants so much, pinpointing your "vocation" is more critical than ever. I have developed a great respect for that humble word *vocation*. It simply means "that to which one is called." When we talk about somebody who has "found his calling," we are usually talking about someone who seems to be "in synch" with himself—and is probably successful at what he does. With vocation so defined, one is tempted to ask who does the calling. Without going beyond the boundaries of this book, let us simply say it is the "inner voice"—and that each of us has one.

Some people can tune into their inner voices quite readily. These are often those enviable types who from infancy just *knew* what they were cut out for. (We all remember a smug kid in school who was teacher's pet because he had some grown-up passion or other.) Sometimes the inner voice is quite faint, but we can make it out clearly enough to have some idea of what we want to do by the time we must decide. For other people the inner voice just whispers for a long time before it shouts and wakes them up. When that happens, look for a career change—or a very unhappy individual.

In the usual career-choice scenario, the vocation signals are weak enough so that the individual follows a career path family members have marked well, a teacher has suggested (perhaps out of his own frustrations), or that circumstance has laid in front of him. That is not to say such passive methods can't bear fruit: Samuel I. Newhouse, one of the most successful publishing magnates of this century, had his first brush with newspapers as a boy when he delivered them during a family economic crunch. But these days it is neither wise nor necessary to depend on such unreliable prods as family pressure, peer pressure, or the winds of chance. Contemporary psychology has given us a bounty of methods for tapping into our "vocation lodes,"—where most of us have riches even our fantasy lives don't reflect. There are many success-oriented career counseling systems in operation now, and most are based on the very sound principle I've been discussing: People achieve the most doing what they like to do. Since most of us are good at what we like to do, it's axiomatic that when you hit on a preference you hit on a talent, latent or undervalued though it may be.

Miracles can be performed sometimes by pointing out such facts as that when you bake a cake or whip up a soufflé, you're performing a chemistry experiment and enjoying it. Obviously this kind of career counseling goes on to use more sophisticated methods of measuring an individual's potential and suggesting compatible fields. But the success-is-being-happy-in-your-work principle is the underlying one. What these systems are really doing is getting people to listen to their inner voices.

Aside from the very obvious goal of success, choosing the career with which you are most in tune has benefits that are far more than "fringies" in these hectic times. When you are doing what comes naturally you work with grace and ease.

That's not to say you don't work hard, but hard work that is invigorating is clearly more rewarding than the kind that is enervating. It just may be that when we find the secret for slotting each person into the right work role, we will have found a powerful preventative for heart attacks, strokes, and other stress-related illnesses. When the work you do goes against your natural grain, it takes a heavy toll. Anyone who feels that the rock he is pushing uphill gets heavier by the day should take a close look at his "chosen" career. Did you choose it, or did it choose you—and do you secretly wish it hadn't?

Since virtually everyone has to earn a living, and since working at the things for which we are best suited is obviously a saner way to live, career counseling should be available to everyone, regardless of age, education level or economic status. Unfortunately such counseling, especially the good kind, is not so easy to come by. And even when it is, people tend to resist. Probing the depths of a human being requires great skill and sensitivity; setting him on a course for life is a great responsibility. There are, of course, excellent people working in the field, and methods of testing, evaluating and advising become more refined by the day. But when the issue is life success or life failure, the seeker after his true vocation would do well to leave no stone unturned.

Astrology As Career Counseling?

Astrology offers a way to get in touch with your inner voice, the wisest career guide of all. Because astrology is so fundamental, and because its principles of personality are basic to all systems of human psychology, its way should be taken very seriously. Astrology is simple, not uncomplex but plain, because it reveals plain truths. Though they may not have "used" astrology to become successful, the realized lives of many successful people are reflections of their specific astrological patterns. The closer you reflect your own, the more successful you will become.

Make no mistake about it; the success that this book is meant to help you find is the best sort, the success that combines material and mental rewards so that each supports the other. In astrological practice, the "house of income" is also the "house of freedom." The underlying astrological significance is more complex than this simple equation indicates, but it does make the point. Material resources are the key to living a full life—to having the freedom and wherewithal to pursue good things. The value of "psychic income" cannot be overestimated in a successful life; but a free cash flow can make it all the more valuable.

Once you accept the fact that people come in patterns, and that these patterns are knowable, you have opened the door to astrology and the concept of an orderly universe. Many people have a hard time with anything that smacks of the cosmic or "divine," though they live according to these principles in one way or another. For example, when you plant a radish seed you don't hold your breath until something comes up. You know you're going to get a radish and not a rose. You "predicted it". Whether or not it will be a prize-winning radish is determined by other factors, including that particular radish's heredity and environment. But the point is that radish seeds produce radishes and rose seeds produce roses.

Human beings are a lot more complicated—both biologically and astrologically—but we can only be what we were meant to be. Though each of us has great latitude, the possibilities are not infinite. The way astrology pinpoints and describes your particular set of possibilities is via your "horoscope." A horoscope is simply a map of the positions of the planets in the sky around you at the moment of your birth. To an astrologer, it is your own "seed pattern"—the potential you that you are free to develop. That pattern, a set of spatial relationships among the sun, the moon, and the planets, never repeats. Your horoscope or your "natal map" is yours alone, like your fingerprints. No one else in the history of the world ever had it or will have it. But, unlike your fingerprints, your horoscope has content: it identifies you in the true sense of the word, describing in detail your particular personality and giving strong clues as to the probable course of your life. The purpose of astrology, rightly understood, is to help you learn that identity by breaking the code of the complex astrological patterns and symbols that your horoscope contains. The role of the astrologer is then that of translator, because astrology is a symbolic language, the earliest and perhaps the most difficult "tongue" in all the world.

With the horoscope so defined, it is easy to see that when it comes to career counseling, astrology has an edge. Because it goes back to first principles—who you are and what you were meant to be—astrology shears away any possible preconditioned ideas (yours or someone else's) about what line of work you should go into. Your horoscope reveals you before anything happened to you. And that is another important point: conventional career counseling that leans heavily on individual preferences presupposes that the person has had the experience that leads to the preference. How can you know you like caviar if you've never tasted it? No such problem with astrology, because it reveals the potential as well as the actual.

Using astrology as a means to the practical end of worldly success is a modern concept, and appropriate to our age. How typical—and how wonderful—to take something rather old (and a little worn), dust it off, shine it up, and recycle it for a utilitarian purpose. The ancients wanted to survive; we want to survive well, and will use whatever means are at hand to achieve our ends.

Throughout the ages astrology has played many different roles, starring roles in certain eras, bit parts in others. It has been "the divine science" that guided kings and emperors in charting their countries' destinies, and the reprehensible outcast of the Church-dominated Middle Ages. The three wise men who sought Jesus were astrologer-kings and greatly revered in their own countries. Personal astrology as we know it was a late development; only the rich and royal were considered worthy of it until the last century.

There are probably as many proofs for the validity of astrology as there are proofs for the existence of God, but all lead back to the "leap of faith." Although he did not intend it as a proof and I do not cite it as an apologia for astrology, C. G. Jung's thinking on the subject deserves a place here.

In his studies, which were geared to elucidating the mystery of the human personality, Jung came to the conclusion that such ancient systems as astrology and the Chinese *I Ching* do in fact operate in our world in a significant way. He decided, however, that the principle upon which they operate is not cause and effect, the relationship the modern rationalist mind expects. Jung—taking a lateral thought-leap characteristic of scientific/philosophic break-throughs—arrived at a new concept: synchronicity or "meaningful coincidence." In brief the idea is that "a" does not *cause* "b," but that "a" and "b" *happen simultaneously*. Of astrology he said: "Whatever is born or begun at a moment in time partakes of the qualities of that moment in time." In effect Jung restated the occult law, "as above, so below"—the ancient principle of correspondences. This means, simply, that the universe is so arranged that what occurs in one sphere occurs in other spheres in different forms. Modern scientists agree. As one physicist puts it: "The whole universe appears as a dynamic web of inseparable energy patterns."

In my opinion as an astrologer, Jung's meaningful coincidence makes a lot more sense in terms of the realities of human existence than the notion that "something out there" is calling all the shots.

Today, astrology suffers from a kind of schizophrenic public image. On the one hand there exists what amounts to mass hysteria among those who follow gossipy, superficial, day-to-day newspaper and radio forecasts. On the other hand there is skepticism, doubt, and even scorn from those who deem it more intelligent to "know better." Between these poles something very exciting is going on. A whole new breed of psychologist/thinker/pragmatist is incorporating the insights of astrology into promising new human disciplines. Astrological research, facilitated by the computer, is rapidly adding contemporary evidence to ancient observations.

Astrology-as-career-counseling falls into this fertile middle ground and—embryonic though it is—rather spectacular results are being achieved. Obviously, however, astrologer/career counselors are at present limited both in number and in geographic areas of operation. This means that a highly promising technique of career counseling is less available than it might be, and for future-oriented "Uranian" types (you'll find out later if you are one) this is a frustrating situation. The purpose of this book's Success System, then, is to give anyone, anywhere, access to the meaning of the most success-significant factors of his own astrological profile.

To follow the Success System all that is required of you is that you know your birth data—the date, year, and time of day (to within one half hour)—and that you have a genuine interest in how that personal information can really shape career decisions. If you have any doubts about whether or not astrology can be of value in choosing a career, it is useful to keep in mind that astrology is the oldest form of psychology. Your approach to it should be like your approach to any modern therapy: what can it tell me about myself and my responses to the world (which may not be ideal) that will help me feel better, function better, achieve more?

2

The Success System

What It Is and How It Works

This book is going to give you a lot of practical information that you can use in deciding upon a career, changing careers, or developing a second one. That information is based on four of your horoscope's most success-significant factors. The one you probably know least about is the one that is most critical: The Midheaven. It is an abstract concept but really no more abstract than those you may be more familiar with—your Sun Sign, your Moon Sign, and your Rising Sign. These are the other three "success points" in your horoscope that will be examined.

In order to bring these abstractions down to earth, a concrete explanation of what a horoscope actually is is necessary. If you know some astronomy, try not to let this metaphoric explanation get in the way.

In astrology the earth, not the sun, is our reference point. Unfortunately a horoscope or "natal map" looks like a confusing mass of signs and symbols to the uninitiated. The problem with getting the picture from a drawn horoscope is that it is two-dimensional, and the actual "map" of the sky at the moment of your birth is a sphere. That's where this image is useful. Think of yourself as a very tiny point at the center of an orange, standing on a slightly less tiny point, the earth. The skin of the orange is the zodiac of signs—the earth's aura or "force field." (Actually the zodiac is a band with a beginning, a middle, and an end that is the beginning, and it goes around the center of the earth; but it is simpler to visualize it as a sphere for our purposes.) That sphere constantly revolves as the earth turns. Beyond the orange are the sun, the moon, and the eight planets, all moving in their orbits. Inside the orange there are twelve even sections. These are the "houses" of the horoscope, each representing a field of human experience. Every planet (remember, the sun and moon are considered planets in astrology) is sending energy to you. Think of that energy in the form of rays—each ray a different color because it emanates from a different planet. At the instant of your birth, each "ray" is striking the orange skin at a specific point that is a degree of a sign of the zodiac; the ray makes a tiny hole, goes through a section of the orange, and eventually reaches the earth—and you.

To give this analogy a bit more content, think of yourself at the central point of the orange, the planets as "activators," the areas of the orange skin as personality characteristics, and the orange sections as different sectors of life experience. When, for instance, the sun's rays strike the area of the orange skin that represents the zodiacal sign Aries, and reach you by going through the orange section that is the "first house" or sector of self, you act (the sun) independently (Aries) in matters that concern you (first house). When the moon's rays activate the orange skin area that is Gemini and reach you via the orange section that represents the home or fourth house, you feel (the moon) restless (Gemini) when you're tied down in a domestic situation (fourth house). These are gross over-simplifications but they should give some indication of how planets, signs, and houses interact. For you, the particular interaction at the instant of your birth forms the horoscope you carry around with you for the rest of your life. The planets move in their orbits, conditions change, you change—but your natal horoscope continues to influence you all your life. It is as if the orange skin were peeled away, the orange sections devoured, the planetary "rays" rendered invisible, still the whole thing has become your own "aura," that which is peculiarly you and will remain so all your days.

The foregoing discussion considered the sun and the moon, but what about those other two vital signs, the Midheaven and the

Ascendant or Rising Sign? Let's refer back to the orange for a minute. You are standing inside it with your left hand stretched out to the east, your right hand to the west. The point on the orange skin your left hand touches at the moment of your birth is the eastern horizon point or your Rising Sun. As the earth rotates throughout a twenty-four-hour period, the sign on the eastern horizon changes, with a new sign appearing about every two hours. The same spatial concept applies to the Midheaven, but instead of its being at your left hand, it is directly above you at the "zenith" of the sky—one of the reasons the Midheaven has traditionally been interpreted as the point of worldly success.

The System

The Success System is a simple one because it is based on a simple equation: Success is finding out who you are and what you were meant to be. Your horoscope contains a multitude of components, but the Success System operates quite effectively around only four. The first three components this book examines—your sun, moon, and rising signs—form the essence of who you are, astrologically speaking. They are the brightest parts of your "aura." Your Midheaven house sign points directly to what you were meant to be in this world, thus filling in the second half of the equation. While your sun, moon, and rising sign are personal points in your horoscope, your Midheaven is the destiny point—in fact it is *the* destiny point.

To start working the system, look up your sun, moon, and rising sign (Ascendant) in the tables in the back of the book. Then read the appropriate sections under the "success skills" of the various zodiacal signs. There is a section for *each* of your personal points. You are going to discover that your familiar (and perhaps beloved) Sun Sign is not the total indicator of personality that so many people believe it is. In fact, it is often the moon that tells all—or at least more about yourself than you ever knew before. And your Ascendant can often explain why you "act out" the way you do.

Once you have thoroughly digested this personality profile

"appetizer," you will go on to the main course: the Midheaven. The Midheaven deals with a segment of life or field of experience, the "career ground" you were meant to occupy in this world. Your Midheaven house sign is based on the time of day you were born, and can be ascertained from the tables. How you specifically fit into your Midheaven "ground" depends on the particular person you are, according to your personal points.

After you examine your Midheaven house, you'll get more information about how you fit into the world of work from your "House of the Sun"—the particular house of your horoscope through which the sun was passing at the time of your birth. Now, theoretically, you've found your calling: the field in which you can be successful. To be most successful, however, you still need more information on how to relate on the job and how to relax off the job. The section on Stress and Success will give you a very clear picture of your own force field and how you "exchange energies" with other people (often the key to getting ahead). It will also tell you how to replenish your own energies in order to have maximum vitality.

Then—because it is more than just a truism that one key to success is timing—you will find a five-year planetary forecast of the influences in effect during that period for both your sun sign and your Midheaven house sign.

There are no fewer than thirteen different sections of this book in which you can find specific information about your own career success, and there can be as many as fifteen (if your sun, moon, and Ascendant are all in different signs). That means you've got some putting together to do. It would be a good idea to make a few notes as you read the sections devoted to you.

What Is Luck?

One final word before you set out to find the road to success. I'd like to make it clear that I believe there really are no "better" or "worse" horoscopes. It is true that different people have different "givens," but I am certain that the degree to which one succeeds is a matter of individual effort. (Need one mention such lives as Helen Keller's?) The horoscope is a map in more ways than one, and *you* choose which routes to travel. You can live out each factor in your horoscope at the higher or the lower level to "shape" your character; and—for better or worse—character is destiny. By who we are (or rather, who we choose to be) we attract what happens to us, or doesn't. It's difficult to focus on any human event that is a matter of pure "luck." Even lottery winners have to have enough faith in life's possibilities to buy tickets. In the end we create our own luck; the purpose of the Success System is to put you in touch with information about yourself that you can use to create as much of your own luck as possible.

TWO

DETERMINING YOUR SUCCESS PROFILE

The Personal Points and the Success Skills

3

Your Personal Points

Sun, Moon, and Ascendant

In the game of astrological one-upmanship, you get extra points for knowing your moon sign or rising sign; in fact if you merely know that you have such things, you are ahead. There is a spreading sophistication among the astrologically aware, and the first indications of it are visible in the popular put-down of the long revered sun sign. However, to disregard the sun sign altogether is to throw the proverbial baby out with the bath water. Sun sign, moon sign, and rising sign (hereafter referred to as the Ascendant) are *all* necessary to consider when defining personality through astrology; you just have to understand which specific facet of personality each represents.

First, let's take all three and look at them together in an analogy based on a home movie of yourself. The sun in your horoscope is what is on the actual reel of film—your "story," as it were. The moon corresponds to the lens and filter through which the beam of projector light passes. The Ascendant is the picture of you others see on the screen.

The Sun

Like the reel of film in the foregoing analogy, the sun is the most important factor in your horoscope: without it, nothing would appear on the screen. Certainly the primacy of the sun sign has been over-emphasized (mainly because it is convenient to write about in magazines and newspapers); but just as the sun is the center of our universe, astrologically speaking your sun sign is your own center. Proponents of esoteric astrology put it this way: the purpose of life is to "become your sun," and the total horoscope shows how to accomplish that. For practical purposes, think of your sun (or sun sign) as your *conscious self* or *your will*. Hence your sun sign should indicate that which you consciously seek and your performance to get it—love, money, fame, control, security. The sun is your basic *identity* as opposed to your surface-level *personality* (that is the Ascendant). The sun is fire, the sun is spirit, the sun is the nucleus of the atom. Likewise, the sun in a horoscope is the animating force—your own.

The Moon

In the sense that it is within your field of consciousness, the sun in your horoscope is a more "rational" factor than the moon. The moon and its sign are the subconscious, the hidden, the unaware, that which is murky and undefined. The sun acts; the moon reacts—to impressions, stimuli, experiences. It is a receiver and our own collective memory bank (some say from past lives as well). The sun "thinks"; the moon "feels"; and just like the filter on the lens, it can color our thinking. The moon is the realm of deep needs and emotions, and can fluctuate just as wildly. But because it can change, the moon can adapt. One convenient way to think of your moon sign is as the manner in which you adapt to things.

The Sun and Moon Together

The relationship between the sun and the moon according to the zodiacal signs is one of the first things an astrologer examines in a horoscope. The sun and the moon interact so closely that it is difficult to separate their influences: the moon literally and figuratively reflects the sun. The ideal combination to have in a horoscope is a "stronger" sun (by sign and house placement) and a "weaker" moon. The reason for this is that the moon "drives" the sun to go out and get what the moon craves. The moon is sheer impulse, and the sun is planned action. Therefore, if the moon "overpowers" the sun, one can be driven by chaotic needs to some rather unpleasant and irrational behavior. You'll find out how to assess the relative strength of the sun and moon in your own horoscope in the sections on elements and zodiacal signs. Keep in mind, however, that each corresponds to a necessary component of the human personality. Without the softening, "feminizing" influence of the moon, the fiery, willful sun could burn everything good away. The moon is our "feeling self," and life without emotional content is empty.

The Ascendant

The sun changes zodiacal signs about once a month, the moon about every two and a half days; the volatile Ascendant can be in one sign or another within the space of minutes. This is why the Ascendant is in many ways the most specific part of your horoscope; it is uniquely you. Unlike the sun and the moon which are there in the sky for all to see, the Ascendant does not have a material form.

A mathematical/astronomical concept, your Ascendant is determined by what sign of the zodiac was on the eastern horizon at the time of your birth. Because you can't see it as you can the planets, you may find it more difficult to believe in its existence and also its efficacy. But like the sun and the moon, the Ascendant is a powerful personal point in your horoscope. You are probably already acquainted with it, since it represents you as you appear to others—your body, your mannerisms, your outward reactions. It is the "you" on the movie screen of our analogy. Unless there is another overwhelming influence in their horoscope (like a block of planets in a single sign), the Ascendant is what you greet when you meet someone. For example, did you ever meet a "poor, pitiful Pearl" who turned out to be a killer? You may have met an Aries sun sign with a Pisces Ascendant. How about that calm, cool, collected character who on further acquaintance turned out to be a mass of seething emotions? My guess would be that he is a Scorpio sun sign with an Aquarius Ascendant. When both sun and Ascendant are in the same sign (often the case with dawn births) or in the same element, you get fewer surprises.

From a more esoteric point of view, the Ascendant signifies the kinds of experiences through which one can discover his own uniqueness. This is an aspect of the Ascendant that becomes clearer to me the more horoscopes I examine, and the more I realize my own. Though my fourth-house sun (Chapter 24 on "Your House of the Sun") should incline me to work out my life in a background slot, my Leo Ascendant keeps forcing me into a more public position. But I no longer fight it, I enjoy it.

Learn To Use All Three

It's important to remember that your Sun Sign, your Moon Sign, and your Ascendant are always in operation. To understand and act upon your sun sign is vital if you are to succeed; the sun is your will and it must have its way—no matter what opposing forces there are. The moon can be your secret weapon or your hidden enemy. The more you know about your moon sign and how it manifests itself in your personality, the better able you will be to control it—and *use* it. Nothing spurs you on to success like a powerful desire *you can define*. As for the Ascendant, take a good long look, because even though it is our surface-level personality, we are not always really aware of how we appear to other people. In the words of Robert Burns, "O Wad some power the giftie gie us to see ourselves as others see us." Astrology gives you the power to do just that by examining your Ascendant sign with an objective eye. To realize your "turn offs" and "turn ons" in relationships with others is to have some mighty effective ammunition always at the ready.

4

The Personal Points As Success Skills

However you may have defined the word "skill" up to now, you must learn a new definition. A skill is usually thought of as something we have acquired, from something as simple as the ability to type to something as complicated as the techniques for restoring fine art. A skill so defined is a specialty that must be learned if you are to succeed in a certain career. But your true Success Skills you always have. These skills are your innate faculties and they are indicated in your horoscope, particularly by the zodiacal signs of the sun, the moon, and the Ascendant.

These all-important factors might be labeled talents instead of skills, because in truth they are natural endowments or "gifts." A talent, by fundamental definition, is something of value, at one time a unit of monetary measure. (Remember the Biblical parable?) By that token, your Success Skills are the talents in your horoscope that you can exchange for cash; in other words, they are the abilities employers are really buying when they hire you. How much income you can exchange for your Success Skills depends a lot on how you use them. With a Success Skill, as with any other gift, you must unwrap the package, examine the contents, and decide how it fits into your life. Remember, too, that we can't use everything we get. Some gifts we don't need; some we just don't want.

According to the zodiacal signs into which they fall in your horoscope, the sun, the moon, and the Ascendant each represents a constellation of skills (no pun intended). That constellation is based on the essential meaning of each Personal Point as cited earlier in this chapter. Again briefly, the sun is your *conscious will*, the moon your *desire nature*, the Ascendant your *out-front personality*. Since very few people are "puries" (all three personal points in the same zodiacal sign), it is extremely important to remember what part of you is being examined when you plunge into the section on Success Skills. Also, it is vital to understand that these skills exist in everyone; but in each person they are colored differently. How the following Success Skills fit together for you is your Success Skills profile.

The Success Skills of the Sun Sign

Some of you may be familiar with the Yin/Yang polarity of eastern philosophy: the female/male or passive/active duality that underlies everything in the universe. The sun in astrology is your Yang or male principle, regardless of your sex. Because the sun represents self-assertion, power, and leadership, the skills of the sun are positive ones—not positive in the sense of desirable, necessarily, but directive, directive of oneself and of others. The skills of the sun are more or less under your conscious control. The sun is then your: *ego strength/self-esteem; goal-directedness; decision-making ability; work ethic; leadership/supervisory ability; risk-taking capability; (conscious) organizational ability; shock resistance/crisis management;* and *self-discipline/capacity for commitment*.

The Success Skills of the Moon Sign

As the sun is your Yang or masculine principle, the moon is Yin—female, adaptive, instinctive. Think of the moon as the female part of an electric connection, of which the sun is the male part. One sends, one receives. Without getting too deep into sexist issues, this might be the place to interject a note about gender. Regardless of the strides toward egalitarianism that have been made in recent years by both women and men, there is still a strong (and unfortunate) tendency in our society for the Yang values to be underrated in women (and by some women); conversely, the Yin side is still repressed in men, usually by men themselves. As a fine balance of Yin and Yang exists in the ideal human, so it does in the ideal career-success candidate. What this means in terms of the Success System is that women should pay special attention to the Success Skills of their sun sign, and men should do the same with their moon sign. Many of us are self-limiting because we have difficulty dealing with the power that springs from the part of us that is opposite to our biological sex. The female, desiring moon, therefore, has to do with these Success Skills, many of which operate in us unconsciously: *power drive/will to win; survival (killer) instinct; sense of timing; ability to sense trends; natural sense of organization; inclination to risk-taking; staying power/patience; adaptability (to people and surroundings); sexual magnetism;* and *mood swings*.

The Success Skills of the Ascendant

For better or worse, your Ascendant can make it or break it for you when it comes to being a total success. For regardless of what is going on underneath, people usually take others at face value. Since the Ascendant comprises the components of your personal style, it is what people meet when they greet you. The Ascendant is the first impression you give and sometimes the only impression people ever get, which is one reason the Ascendant is so important in interview situations. You may have heard that the Ascendant actually determines physical appearance. It does, but since so many other factors enter in—both astrological and genetic factors—detailed "Ascendant portraits" aren't really worth much. The Ascendant is important less superficially. Tall or short, plump or lean, dark or fair, you are your Ascendant in all of these ways: *power of persuasion; presence; personal mannerism (body language); humor/charm; degree of animation;* and *visible responsiveness (how quick on the uptake)*.

Because the Ascendant is the beginning of the first house and a critical point in the horoscope, the qualities of the Ascendant can be altered by a strong planet there. For instance, the most bubbly Gemini Ascendant can be subdued by a powerful Pluto sitting on it. However, for the purposes of the Success System we'll be dealing with "unadulterated" Ascendants.

5

Underneath It All: The Four Elements

That people can be classified is not a popular notion; the very word class has not only undemocratic, but almost anti-human connotations. If you have ever studied natural science, for example, you have met the "classes" that subdivide the animal kingdom. Ironic, then, that humans classify humans virtually whenever they interact (the most obvious form of classifying or stereotyping being the ethnic joke). And when people aren't stereotyping aloud, they are doing it unconsciously, filing others away in neat little compartments of the mind. While fiercely denying it, we are tacitly admitting that certain kinds of people can be classified by certain blocks of characteristics.

One of the most popular and "innocent" kinds of classifying is the game everybody loves to play: "What's my sign?" Even total skeptics play this game—it's neat, it's easy, and it's good clean fun. A major trouble, though, with the game as it is commonly played is that people tend to attribute the good characteristics of any given sign to those they like (particularly themselves) and relegate the bad characteristics to people they cannot stand. So we get such banal statements as: "I'm a Libra, I get along with everyone." "He's a Scorpio, watch out for his stinging tail." It all goes to support the cliché that a little learning can be a dangerous thing—dangerous in this case because most people take the typology of the zodiac signs more seriously than they will admit.

A zodiacal sign, properly understood, is not a laundry list of personality traits; it is a specific kind of "energy." People don't "have" the characteristics of a sign; they are influenced by the kind of energy that sign generates. How strongly or how weakly they are influenced is the result of how many and which planets were in that sign at the time of their birth (the sun and moon being the biggest influencers).

The obvious next question is, "What is this energy and where does it come from?" The concept of energy is more difficult to get a handle on than is a set of "canned" characteristics, but it is essential to understanding the zodiacal signs and to working the Success System. Harnessing the energies that propel you is a must if you are going to utilize them to the fullest in moving toward your success goals. And you will not be able to see your own career ground clearly unless you comprehend the underlying energy of your Midheaven house sign. Once you really know what territory your Midheaven house sign has marked out for you, you should be able to recognize it in any form.

The Four Elements

A zodiacal sign gets its energy from a very fundamental source: the "element" it springs from and that contains it—either fire, earth, air, or water. Before examining the elements to find out what they are and how they affect the signs that affect you, let me give you a handy scorecard:

FIRE SIGNS:	Aries, Leo, Sagittarius
EARTH SIGNS:	Taurus, Virgo, Capricorn
AIR SIGNS:	Gemini, Libra, Aquarius
WATER SIGNS:	Cancer, Scorpio, Pisces

The four elements were once thought to be the basis of all that is; the ancient Greek philosophers called them the components of matter itself. The four elements were really used as the earliest way of defining a human being in his totality, each element being equated to a different facet. Earth was the physical body, its functions, and needs; air was the mind and thought processes; water the emotions or soul; fire, the aspirations and moral character or spirit. In the Middle Ages the elements were redubbed the humors. People were typed as choleric (fiery), melancholy (earth), phlegmatic (watery), or sanguine (air), and treated accordingly by the medical profession (the idea of psychosomatic illness is not new).

That's pretty much the way astrologers still line up the elements: Earth, the solid, practical element, is the body's flesh and bones—its structure. Air, the element of mentality and nervous energy, is the brain and nervous system. Water corresponds to the digestive and lymphatic systems, the glands, the "guts." (Watery people do tend to feel things in the gut.) Fire, as spirit and animation, is the respiratory and circulatory functions—which take the very air we breathe to our most vital part, the heart, and literally give life to the body.

For all practical purposes an element is a mode of perception, a way of seeing the world and responding to it. In short, your basic element determines how you think. Any horoscope is a blend of elements that fight for supremacy in the person, but one element is generally dominant. How can you tell which element dominates your thinking processes? First, of course, you check out your sun, moon, and Ascendant. But that is not necessarily conclusive, since as many as three elements can be involved. I've devised a little psychodrama that can help you pinpoint your dominant element, that is, the way you most often think and respond.

First, the cast of characters. *Earth* is the "solid-state" thinker who operates on sense perception, hence is ultimately practical and realistic. *Air* signifies the rationalist who thinks in the purest sense of the word, logically connecting ideas (and people). *Water* implies the feeling thinker, for whom emotion colors the world and often obscures it. *Fire* stands for the intuitive thinker who sees the future possibilities of the present, leaping mentally forward and sideways, but rarely backward.

What follows is a bit of role-playing to dramatize the different approaches of the people of the four elements.

The scene is a room, empty, except for a table on which is an egg—a white, uncooked egg. Each element's representative is brought into the room and asked, "What do you see before you?" Here are the responses:

EARTH: It is an egg. It is white and I can see it has a brittle shell and a perfect ovoid shape. Eggs are an excellent form of protein, and taste good when properly seasoned. When times get tough, you can live on eggs quite inexpensively; I always have them on hand. Watch out! That egg could roll off the table and get broken; and don't leave it out too long or it will go bad.

AIR: Oh, an egg! Just show me an egg and I have plenty to talk about. Did you know that the ancient Chinese buried them for years until they were thoroughly rotten? They considered them a great delicacy. I was at a party the other night where the hostess served the most marvelous deviled eggs, all beautifully arranged on a platter. Just as I was taking one I spotted a friend I hadn't seen in ages; we're getting together next week to catch up.

WATER: I hate eggs. They have too many associations for me. Whenever I see an egg I remember my mother frying some up for me in our old kitchen where it was so warm and comfortable; I can just smell it. I could write a book about the things eggs remind me of. By the way, I have a funny feeling you didn't get me in here just to talk about eggs; you must have had another reason and I'm not sure I like it.

FIRE: You can't eggs-aggerate about what you can make out of an egg. Ha ha. Seriously, though, just think about it—omelets, soufflés, egg tempera to paint with, crushed eggshells for fertilizer. Hey, I wonder whether the egg could be used as a source of energy? And the shape! So versatile and salable! Somebody is marketing big plastic eggs that come apart to make kiddie boats—one for each kid. Wish I'd thought of it. Do turkeys lay eggs? You see I've got this great idea for a fast-food chain that serves turkey sandwiches called 'The Great Gobbler.' My financing is sure to come through next week.

These are obviously broad-stroke caricatures, not meant to represent real people (though you may recognize someone). But they make the point: To "think like earth" is to have the capacity to handle the physical world, to produce in tangible form; To "think like air" is to be able to bring detachment to a situation, to categorize and structure ideas, to cooperate and communicate; To "think like water" is to absorb and assimilate all the emotional nuances, to go beyond the physical senses and tap the murky subconscious; To "think like fire" means to have unified, immediate perceptions, to view the world with expectancy, often at the expense of details.

When you run into somebody who is a whole-hogger—that is, who always jumps to conclusions off the same side of the bridge—you have probably met somebody who has too much of a given element. Nobody can think in all four modes at once. But anyone can develop the capacity to use another mode. All four are vital to successful thinking, and hence to success itself. To think in a recessive mode or element may never come totally naturally, and you may never do it to perfection, but you can hone your technique to a workable point. For instance, the least poetic among us can be trained to get in touch with our feelings. The mental detachment of air can be cultivated; and even with no earth at all, you can learn to be practical. Intuition—the leaping mental mode of fire—may be the hardest to acquire, but even that is within reach. And it is worth the effort because making use of all four modes is critical to success in the competitive world.

Creativity

Many astrologers associate certain elements with creativity. Usually those elements are fire, because it corresponds more or less to the much-vaunted lateral thinking mode, and water, because the emotions and the subconscious are said to be the source of poetic and artistic vision. But real creative thinking is more complicated, and I don't believe any element can go it alone. All are necessary.

Water and fire are the idea-getters. Water dips back into the past and the subconscious for inspiration; fire raids the future. But once you've got ideas, what are you going to do with them? For one thing, who judges if the ideas are all good? Somebody's got to sift and weigh them, choose some and toss the others out. Air is the logical candidate to do this. Besides objectivity, air has another important talent: that of connecting seemingly unrelated ideas. Once air has done his part, an idea has made a lot of progress; but it is still not fully developed. Somebody has to figure out a way to put that idea to practical use; to make it manifest, so to speak. Earth—good old realistic, solid earth—can do that job.

So you see, without any one of the four element components, no idea has a real chance of making the full trip from a gleam in the eye to a bulge in the wallet. If you are heavily attuned to one element, you probably are a specialist in one of the four idea-producing stages. There is no problem if you are paired with the right complementary work partners; but even then you must tune in sufficiently to the other modes of thinking to be able to get the whole picture. Few people are totally irretrievable "Johnny-one-notes." Those who claim to be are really striking a pose. Don't let them fool you or get away with anything, especially if you are an earth type. It is the real "earthy" thinker who runs the risk of getting dumped with all the details, and therefore most of the work. When you hear an associate wail, "I'm just terrible with numbers," or "I never could learn to do that," learn to say, "There's always a first time."

6

Element Into Sign

The Qualities

The elements are four; the zodiacal signs are twelve. The ancients in their wisdom gave us a neat method for breaking down the four elements among the twelve signs That method is a divisor known as the three qualities—cardinal, fixed, and mutable. You might understand them better if you call them *dynamic*, *static*, and *flexible*, because the qualities signify the movement or direction of a sign. An element is an energy; a zodiacal sign is *kinetic energy*, the "quality," or dynamic, of that sign. We are not speaking literally, of course, but psychologically. (However, some have noted an uncanny correlation between the way a person physically moves and the qualities of the signs that dominate his horoscope.)

These qualities ultimately explain why the three signs in each element are very different, despite their unifying principle. The *quality* of a zodiacal sign is what gives it much of its specificity. For instance, did you ever meet a *flexible* Taurus? Most likely not, because Taurus is the *fixed* or *static* earth sign. In the same element, Virgo, while as practical as Taurus, is able to bend when presented with a viable alternative. Virgo is mutable or flexible.

Will power or determination are associated with the quality of a sign. But it is a matter of type rather than of degree: what kind of will power is intrinsic to a sign can best be understood by looking at the direction in which its quality moves. The energy of the same dynamic signs is directed outward from the center (centripetal), propelling itself headfirst toward its goals. The static sign is directed inward toward the center (centrifugal), hence reinforcing its own energy, or standing firm. The energy of the flexible signs spirals outward, twisting and dodging to get where it is going, much like a running back does on the football field.

Here is how the signs are subdivided by the qualities and elements:

DYNAMIC FIRE: Aries
DYNAMIC EARTH: Capricorn
DYNAMIC AIR: Libra
DYNAMIC WATER: Cancer

STATIC FIRE: Leo
STATIC EARTH: Taurus
STATIC WATER: Scorpio
STATIC AIR: Aquarius

FLEXIBLE FIRE: Sagittarius
FLEXIBLE EARTH: Virgo
FLEXIBLE AIR: Gemini
FLEXIBLE WATER: Pisces

The words dynamic, static and flexible are descriptive in themselves, but because they have to do with movement, the qualities have particular reference to some important on-the-job situations. The *dynamic* signs are the "starter" signs (they literally start the seasons of the year). People with these signs dominant should be self-motivated and have initiative. The *static* signs are "stayers"; an excellent attribute for long-haul projects and positions that require stamina. (A commonly used alternative name for the fixed signs is the "executive" signs.) To be *flexible* is to roll with the punches, a tremendous asset in winning people over to your side, and this is often found in the sales personality). The flexible signs are the "movers" of the zodiac, making job and career changes most easily.

Putting elements and qualities together, you can pretty well "predict" the behavior of a sign—though you will rarely run across it in its purest manifestation. Remember, too, that in the Success System sun, moon, and Ascendant are considered separately. And when it comes to the most critical career issue—to what career field does the Midheaven of your chart point?—the personality aspect of a sign has to be totally rethought. The career ground concept of the Midheaven is another frame of reference altogether. But, to illustrate the zodiacal signs as broad modes of behavior, I will put them to work on a very concrete project—building a house—and "predict" what role each sign would play:

ARIES: DYNAMIC FIRE. *Has idea of house in mind; goes out and scouts terrain to find the right site; retains innovative architect.*

TAURUS: STATIC EARTH. *Gets contractor; walks the property with architect; discusses building materials; helps dig foundation.*

GEMINI: FLEXIBLE AIR. *Investigates the area; introduces self to neighbors; asks about schools and other facilities; makes friends.*

CANCER: DYNAMIC WATER. *Moves into the house, settles down, and makes it a home; starts a family and family traditions.*

LEO: STATIC FIRE. *Creates warm, friendly atmosphere in home; gives lavish parties; adds luxuries to make house a fine place; has more children.*

VIRGO: FLEXIBLE EARTH. *Works with architect and contractor to make sure every detail of house is perfect; makes suggestions to organize space, especially kitchen and closets.*

LIBRA: DYNAMIC AIR. *Handles decorating of house; works so well with interior decorator (and his other clients), ends up going into business with him.*

SCORPIO: STATIC WATER. *Intensifies emotional atmosphere of the home; is center of family interdynamics; has own study in basement; has more children and affair with neighbor.*

SAGITTARIUS: FLEXIBLE FIRE. *Sees the house as only the beginning of a whole development; if there isn't enough space, moves to another area.*

CAPRICORN: DYNAMIC EARTH. *Makes structural improvements in house so it is finest in neighborhood; seeks highest bidder for it.*

AQUARIUS: STATIC AIR. *Friendly with all neighbors though intimate with none; starts community improvement group for benefit of all; becomes pillar of group.*

PISCES: FLEXIBLE WATER. *Thinks about moving but can't decide where; has attic space to write poems about how family is investing house with soul.*

The Sequence of the Signs

When you look up your "vital signs" or personal points in the Success Skills section of this book (Chapters 7 through 10) you will note that they are grouped by element, that is by fire signs, earth signs, air signs, or water signs. The reason for this is that I believe the signs can only be truly comprehended through the elements and qualities. I'm so adamant about it I would prefer that people say, "My sun sign is dynamic air, my moon is static water, my Ascendant, flexible earth" than to tick off their signs by name. However, that is my own idiosyncracy, and it means you may be thrown off by not finding the signs in their usual order. And there is something very significant in that order, because it is literally a restatement of the yearly round of seasons.

Aries is the first sign of the zodiac because spring is synonymous with new life—"creation" itself. And spring begins the moment the sun "enters" the sign of Aries in late March. Taurus follows Aries because new life must have fertile ground and be nurtured to grow. Gemini, the third sign, provides fresh air for life's growth and for it to experience the world around it. The Fourth sign, Cancer, fulfills two roles: it "waters" the fertile earth to promote growth, and begins a whole new season in which that life will come to full flower. Then the round begins again. As with all astrological symbolism, there is both truth and beauty in the cycle of the signs. While it is not necessary to the Success System to go too deeply into the seasonal aspect of signs, it is helpful to be aware of the fact that there is a gradual and logical "growth" from young Aries to the other spring signs, through the flowering signs of summer, to the harvesting signs of fall, and eventually to the "contemplative" signs of winter that wait for spring.

Before going on to the next section where each sign of the zodiac is interpreted in terms of its Success Skills, it would be a good idea to brush up on the Success Skills meanings of the sun, the moon, and the Ascendant as given in Chapter 4. The reason is that each sign manifests itself in a particular way according to which personal point is in that sign.

7

The Success Skills of the Fire Signs

ARIES

Dynamic fire Ruling planet: Mars
Main Martian characteristics: ardent, impulsive, independent

Sun Sign Aries:

There's no question that the typical Aries sun sign person appears to be a born leader. Many are. Unfortunately, however, bossiness does not necessarily a good boss make. What's more, Aries tends to work in fits and starts; in fact, there may be a lot of fits, many starts, but few finishes. Such an erratic work pattern in a leader does not always inspire confidence in those who must follow.

There is passion in the Aries sun sign, however, and a sincere enthusiasm that can make up for many faults. Certainty of purpose (at least for the moment) can get a lot of projects rolling. And if the Aries is backed up by loyal subordinates and associates (which is usually the case), all will go well because they will sustain the momentum.

If you are an Aries sun sign, you must take care that your snap decisions are based on firm foundations. No one is surer than you are when you're sure; but if you plan to stick around to see what happens, you may have to take the consequences. Chances are you will; honor is an Aries strong point and one of those good old-fashioned virtues that can carry Aries sun sign people to the top in an age when such virtues are rare and prized commodities.

One of your on-the-job frustrations will always be that less single-minded, more cautious people than you are unable to comprehend your leap-before-you-look tendencies. You can stand uncertainty, because crisis is your *modus vivendi;* remember that it is not everyone's. The fact that you thrive on risk makes you exciting to work with and for, and I for one would hire you in an instant. I would expect that my day, or at least my week, would be punctuated with your often astounding new ideas; but that one of them might even be workable. Your creativity is unquestioned. No less important would be your sense of adventure and fun. Who says that to be successful you've always got to be serious?

The Aries sun sign person who does not have a steadying moon sign tends to work himself into such a frenzy of disorganization that there is danger of a good idea's coming to naught. If you are such a person, as much as you hate planning ahead, force yourself to do so; or, if you are in a position to, gather more stable forces around you to do the organizing.

The Aries sun sign is dynamic in every sense of the word. In the kinetic sense, Aries always moves forward quite forcefully, rarely losing sight of the mark, clearing obstacles with great leaps (or great lapses). It is not wise to crowd an Aries because you might get elbowed or kneed in the process. But there is one thing for sure; you will never get stabbed in the back.

Moon Sign Aries:

Having an Aries moon is one of those conditions that can be fatal to success if the moon is not harnessed to a rock-of-Gibraltar sun. That may be overstating the case, but there is a problem. When the childlike enthusiasm and blind faith of Aries are not recognized by one's own conscious mind, they can lead you down some pretty thorny garden paths. And little is more pathetic than a child who is badly scratched from simply reaching for a rose. Even more disheartening to you Aries moon signs can be the fact that you know roses are the very thing that will sell like crazy this year. Moon in Aries's timing can be off because you are too far ahead—or more likely because you present your ideas before they are ripe. Without carrying the image too far, moon in Aries can be "green," naive to a fault. The tendency for the Aries moon sign person to be first in line is so strong that it works against itself: To be "firstest with the leastest" is not conducive to making ideas come to fruition.

On the other hand, moon in Aries knows how to survive. The instinct for smelling out danger is sharp; the reactions are instantaneous. There is an incredible alertness that can "wake up" the most slumberous sun (such as Taurus) when anyone or anything threatens. We are, of course, speaking of career situations, but for the Aries moon person, the career terrain might as well be sheer-faced rock.

Regardless of your gender, moon in Aries gives a "tomboy" or comradely character to your personality, which is particularly charming because it is unconscious. This is a fortunate quality because it means that in spite of an inherent selfishness, you with moon in Aries will pull your own weight and cooperate with others when the chips are down.

There is a magnetism about the moon in Aries person that can be felt behind almost any sun sign. Not of a blatantly sexual nature, it is the magnetism of a fire around which people gather for warmth. The pull is strong enough to keep those people around even when the Aries moon person displays his waspish impatience. This impatience can be a stumbling block to lasting achievement, because it seriously interferes with the success drive. If you have an Aries moon sign, observe how easily you can be diverted from your course by petty annoyances (such as slow-witted people). Take the trouble to correct this tendency; it will be worth it because you will be worth more.

Ascendant Sign Aries:

Of all three fire signs, Aries on the Ascendant is the one that gets most visibly "fired up," in both the good ways and the bad ways. First, let's deal with the Aries pop-off temper that has no place to hide when it is hanging out there as the Ascendant. If you have an Aries Ascendant and you recognize the problem, you might try a little trick. Next time someone says or does something you don't like and you feel that famous ire rising, start to cough. (People get red in the face when they cough, too.) Keep on coughing until everyone else in the room has stopped talking (they'll get worried). By that time you should have regained your cool, and have the floor back in the bargain.

On the plus side, Aries's fiery facade could inspire an entire army to go charging into the breach, even when defeat is certain. Behind the "we can do it, men" message may lurk the real truth: that unless there is real staying power behind your Aries Ascendant, what you mean is "*you* can do it." Never mind; high-powered, enthusiastic people almost always get ahead because they make others *believe* in them. And the rare Aries Ascendant who is nothing but "front" soon gets found out. (After the sale is made, however, it's too late—for the buyer, anyway.)

Aries Ascendant people are meeters and greeters par excellence. Though you may lack the gracious charm of the Libra, you make up for it with heartiness and warmth. There is a generosity of spirit that is real. Most Aries people (no matter which personal point is involved) will empty their pockets for another anytime. And when you Aries Ascendant people say, "That's a great idea," you really mean it; you wouldn't discourage somebody for the world (especially if you like him). This direct responsiveness is another chip in the Aries Ascendant pile of winnings. Count on Aries for a visible and audible reaction, however awkward and abrupt it may sometimes be. If you have a "fluent" sun or moon sign, your verbalization may be less choppy. No matter what, however, one can always observe a foot-tapping jumpiness in yourself that betrays a let's-get-on-with-it attitude even the smoothest Aries Ascendant cannot hide. Speaking of smooth, there are some Aries Ascendant people who have never heard the word. The words they know better are "rude," "awkward," and "gauche." If you have an Aries Ascendant, get yourself videotaped in a public situation to find out where you stand.

If you have ever heard that Aries are pushy people, it has probably been from someone who has had experience with an Aries Ascendant. Most Aries sun sign people, by the time they have gotten past high school, are aware enough that they can alienate others. For you Aries Ascendant people, it may be a longer learning process; just make sure you do not let it go on forever.

LEO

Static fire Ruling planet: Sun
Main solar characteristics: vitality, warmth, centeredness

Sun Sign Leo:

Leo sun signs are so proud, they are even proud of being Leos (often without knowing the real reasons they should be). One Leo I know even tries to *look* like a Leo (mane of golden hair, catlike movements) when it is perfectly obvious that her wispy frame comes from a Libra Ascendant. The pride of the Leo sun sign and the ferocity that can arise from it are functions of the flame that burns hot and steady within. You Leos feel your power intensely, because of the thermodynamic power of Leo's planetary ruler, the sun. The Leo sun sign who knows how to deal with that power is sitting in the cat-bird seat (and often has cause to smack his lips). Not that you devour your adversaries and competitors; you simply outshine them. In many ways, the hearty, sincere, passionate, well-organized Leo *is* "the success sign."

Having a Leo sun sign is no guarantee of success, however. When Leo uses his power badly, he does it very badly—alternately growling, preening, snarling, and licking his wounds. (Leo sun signs wound very easily.) A Leo not understood (by himself most of all) can go round in circles without ever getting off dead center, or even believing he *is* the center. You Leo sun signs are—let's face it—self-involved. When this trait manifests itself as enlightened self-esteem, all is well, and you have one very important success skill in your pocket. For the less evolved Leo sun sign, it all comes out as pure childlike selfishness. Leo's dramatic displays in this case can become nasty temper tantrums.

Leos are generally hard workers, though some of your persuasion can be a trifle lazy. What the laziness comes from is a sybaritic love of luxury and pleasure. Leos gravitate toward splendor—in people, places, and things. It goes with your Leo sun sign act, which is really no act at all; there is a magnificence about Leo sun signs that peeks through almost any Ascendant. You Leos make natural bosses—and good ones. With a certain *noblesse oblige*, you beam warmly on subordinates, making them feel loved and comfortable. You can be extremely generous, except when it comes to acknowledging another's opinion. Sometimes dogmatic to a fault, Leo is nonetheless sure of himself, and easily makes others believe in him.

As with all the fire signs, there's a tendency in the Leo sun sign to neglect details (which you consider trifles). But nobody loves danger like Leo. Thrill-seeker that you can be, Leo can even manufacture a crisis situation. It's the ideal opportunity to display your jungle training, hair-trigger responses, and fiercely brave heart. And speaking of hearts, Leo's own can be his downfall. Most of you Leos *are* all heart, and beneath that masterful manner lies a welter of sentimental feelings. You can get to a Leo sun sign, and many craftier types do, with flattery, wheedling, and/or hard luck stories. The Leo sun sign who has got it all together is fairly safe from such strategies, but Leo is a naive sign, and a Leo in the career world should always be alert.

Moon Sign Leo:

Leo moon never stops shining—through thick and thin, on good days and bad. The fixed (static) fire of Leo works splendidly at the unconscious level. You Leo moon sign people generally display a consistent optimism, though it may be naively innocent at times. There is a native ability to persist without losing heart. When a success-bent person has the moon in the sign of Leo, it serves him well in the long haul. He never stops believing—particularly in himself.

You Leo moon people can surprise others by displays of will and temperament that seem to come from nowhere (especially when the sun and/or Ascendant are in more passive signs). The basic drive of your personality is to be, like the sun, the center of everything. Woe to those who slight or ignore a Leo moon sign; the wrath of Leo spurned can be dangerous indeed. But like Leo sun signs, you Leo moon sign people are more often hurt than hurting.

When the Leonine qualities are submerged in the realm of the moon, it is more difficult for the person to understand and hence control them. If you have the moon in the sign of Leo, start checking your reactions. Are they often highly personal? Do you find yourself mentally mouthing childish insults when the situation calls for a much more objective response? Chances are you do so more often than you would like.

Just as Leo moon is personal, it is personable. That very real Leo generosity is now spontaneous, springing from an unconscious source. Leo moon people can be a delight to "brainstorm" with. Their own creative ideas virtually tumble out, articulated well or badly according to the sign of the sun. But even more wondrous is their openness to the ideas of others. Leo moon instinctively senses its own power, hence is secure; there is little need to put others down. You Leo moon people are often the "nice guys" of the zodiac, and many an office popularity contest would put you at the top.

Whereas the Leo sun sign is likely to *tell* you he is a natural born leader, Leo moon sign's leadership abilities can sneak up on you. The magnetism of Leo moon is so strong in every respect that people tend to gravitate toward them and cluster around them. With even the most timid sun sign, many a Leo moon sign person eventually finds himself in a position of power. If you have a Leo moon, it is to be hoped you accept it with humility (not a notoriously prevalent Leo trait); nice guys aren't so nice when they get smug. Without belittling the real abilities of any individual person, I would like to point out that Leo (especially Leo moon) sometimes gets more than he deserves. Though I don't believe in luck as such, there is enough evidence in the form of under-qualified Leo sun and moon signs in higher echelons to warrant the "lucky Leo" superstition.

Ascendant Sign Leo:

There is a young woman I know whom I've dubbed "the golden

cloud," because that is just what I thought I saw the first time she came through my door. Though she has a Leo sun as well as Leo rising, most people with a Leo Ascendant share this resplendence. The description can be purely metaphorical, because Leo Ascendants come in all colors, sizes, and shapes. But nine times out of ten they *radiate*, and that radiation takes the form of good looks, good health, and well-being.

Leo Ascendant people are often con men. Because they look and sound as if they have supreme confidence in what they are selling (whatever it is), they gain yours. Good show, Leo, even if it is pure show. The well-known dramatic flair of Leo comes to the fore most prominently when Leo is on the Ascendant. Gesticulating, posturing, prancing, grandly pronouncing, the person with Leo rising is hard to ignore. You *know* when you've got one around.

And that brings me to a Leo negative point. You Leos (sun and Ascendant signs mainly) can be annoying to others—especially if those others' signs tend toward more discreet mannerisms and a delicate sensory apparatus. Leo is rarely as rude and brash as is Aries on the Ascendant, but sometimes one wishes they would shut up and go away. Being in the presence of a Leo Ascendant in a business situation is like being forced to watch somebody's little darling perform and having to pretend you like it. Most people just grin and bear it, because like Leo sun and moon signs, you Leo Ascendants most often bear no malice. All that sound and fury is an expression of your joy in living, and we all could do with a little more of that. The Leo Ascendant's wit is quick, the manner robust, and there is often an incredible ability to mimic. Leo on the Ascendant always leaves them laughing.

Some of the best dressers have Leo rising, and most often those designer clothes didn't come from the discount store. Extravagance is characteristic of Leo. As the commerical goes, Leo people treat themselves well because they believe they *deserve* it. When Leo is on the Ascendant, look for pure gold. It can literally be the hair color (natural or not), but most often it's the flash of expensive finery. The 14-karat look is a big plus in many business/professional situations. If you look expensive, you must be good. Having a Leo Ascendant can make you a winner all the way—as long as your apparent worth is more than skin deep.

SAGITTARIUS

Flexible fire Ruling Planet: Jupiter
Main Jupiterian characteristics:
expansiveness, truthfulness, optimism

Sun Sign Sagittarius:

Regardless of sex, the Sagittarius sun sign can be the playboy of the western business world. Other horoscopal factors may keep you closer to your desk, but mentally the Sagittarian is very often someplace else—usually a place nobody's been before. Sagittarius, symbolized by the archer with his bow aimed high, tends to shoot for the farthest stars. It's called the sign of the prophet, but I believe the Sagittarian's ability to predict is more properly described as a desire to *make* new things happen.

Maybe it is because Sagittarian sun signs live in the future that you are so full of hope. The cockeyed optimist was surely a Sagittarian sun sign, because you Sags do tend to let your enthusiasms run away with you. If checked by a more sober moon, the tendency is not disastrous. Sagittarians on the job are usually a delight. As bosses you run a loose ship (but can quickly batten down for a storm). As a peer or co-worker you are ultimately friendly and good-natured. Sagittarians are not saints; just philosophers. A natural sense of perspective allows the Sagittarian to put all things in proportion. Letting things roll off your back is very Sagittarian.

Now for the bad news. Honesty may be the best policy, but your bluntness is not always appreciated in the more political circles of the business world. Sagittarians often do not know how to be subtle. The truth must be told—this is most often because the Sagittarian sun sign *knows* he lacks subtlety, and would lose in that kind of contest. However, you Sagittarians can say such outrageous things to others' faces in such a jovial manner that it takes them a while to figure out they've been told off.

Sagittarius is the sign of the promoter, and in your open way the Sagittarius sun sign can promote himself quite well. The problems are: number one, you can promote yourself right out of your area of competence; and number two, you can keep promoting yourself out of one job into the next until you cannot remember who you worked for last week. Stability is not a Sagittarian virtue. Sag's restlessness is not quite as flighty as Gemini's, though, and rather than taking new jobs, Sagittarius takes them on the side. Then you have real problems, because Sagittarius has more of those nasty little things called details to deal with than ever. A typical Sag solution is to drop everything and leave town.

Sagittarius can be creative to a fault, too. Unless you surround yourself with "earth types" to make your ideas become reality (or have a lot of earth in your horoscope), you Sagittarian sun signs can just keep on blowing smoke. Don't get me wrong. There are lots of Sagittarian sun sign success stories; it is just that people may not hear about you because you haven't been successful in one place for a long enough time. Sag is *flexible* fire, and that is hard to hang onto. However, anyone who has had the good fortune to work for or with one of you Sagittarians will probably say it was one of the happiest times of his life—even if it didn't go on very long.

Moon Sign Sagittarius:

Sagittarius is a natural for a number of things, among them teaching. When Sagittarius is the moon sign (and the sun sign allows it) you can exhibit one of several tendencies. The first and least desirable is a propensity to give pompous, if patient, explanations of everything to everyone who will listen. The second is an incredible sense of fairness and impartiality. It is in this case that moon in Sagittarius tends to gravitate to "counseling" positions. If that is not literally your line of work (and it does not have to be), you may find yourself "office philosopher"—the one to whom everyone turns for words of wisdom in difficult situations.

For all the fun that is made of "flaky" Sagittarius, there is a method to your madness. It is not the "greatest good for the greatest number" that is representative of Aquarius. It is the wisdom that says, "See here, life is bountiful and rather short. Therefore, make the most of every moment and let the hard feelings go." To make yourself feel good, the person with moon in Sagittarius may take some pretty wild chances on the job, with more or less success, depending on the sun sign. However, others rarely accuse you Sagittarius moon sign people of playing it safe.

But, like moon in Aries, moon in Sagittarius can get too far ahead of other people. If you have the moon in Sagittarius you would do well to keep your mouth shut once in a while and tuck an idea away for a better time. You have no dearth of ideas, and can certainly find a more appropriate one. Casting pearls before swine may inflate your ego, but it won't earn you much in terms of money or credibility.

I don't have too many worries about you people with moon in Sagittarius, because in the long run the judgment is excellent. The sign of Sagittarius, wherever it falls in the horoscope, comes with natural brakes or (as a Sagittarian boss of mine would say) "landing wheels." Impulsive, impetuous, quick, ready for anything, Sagittarius is rarely foolhardy. The reactions of the moon in Sagittarius are so instantaneous that people often believe they have ESP. You Sag moon people don't really know what somebody is going to say before he says it; you just "get it" so fast it seems that way.

The Sagittarian moon sign person thrives on change, and therefore you should avoid static situations like the plague. Sagittarius (sun or moon sign) can literally get sick if hemmed in or tied down mentally. If there's any new challenge, toss it to a Sag moon sign. Unlike a Taurus, who will groan and complain, the Sag moon sign will laugh with delight and plunge right in.

Ascendent Sign Sagittarius:

Long-legged, loping, a perpetual mover who seems at times to be afflicted with St. Vitus' dance, the Sagittarius Ascendant person just exudes energy. This is not so much the nervous fidgety energy of Gemini as a taut, ready-to-spring-into-action attitude. And that attitude may simply be mental. A double Sag (sun and Ascendant sign) I know could put life and laughter into a convention of morticians. No matter how tense the situation, there is always a smile behind the eyes of the Sag Ascendant person.

That is why people with Sagittarius highly emphasized in their horoscopes are often accused of being nonserious. You can be serious when the occasion calls for it, but you seem to know something the rest of us may not necessarily understand (or agree with): life is a cosmic joke and should be played out as such. With you Sag Ascendant people it may be just a facade, but your air of insouciance is always there—and it can be a tremendous career asset.

Natives getting restless? Send in a Sag Ascendant sign to calm them down and jolly them out of it. Squeeze getting tighter and everyone feeling it? Put Sagittarius rising on the job and see how everyone relaxes—and performs. It is no lightweight we are talking about. Even when Sagittarius is only the rising sign, it lends a depth to the personality that gives substance, but is never heavy.

On a less positive note, you should know that if you have a Sagittarius Ascendant your devil-may-care appearance can make others believe you do not care either. Think about it, especially in interview situations. Do you give the impression that it really does not matter if you get the job or not? When Sagittarius is the sun, moon, or Ascendant sign, there is a tendency to be overly optimistic, as well. Remember, just because you can *visualize* yourself in a certain job situation doesn't mean that you will get the job. Also, while you can easily keep one foot in the "what's to come" and one in the "what is now," does not mean that everyone can. Sagittarius has to occasionally "come on down off that cloud" and face the realities of the world squarely—however boring and mundane they may be. The Sag Ascendant does not give off the wispy, "other worldy" aura that Pisces rising does; there is much more substance as well as fewer "I'm above it all" signals. But you should be wary of the impression you give.

Sag on the Ascendant is the eternal "boy scout"—with honor, truthfulness, loyalty, and courage among the recognized and recognizable virtues. As with other "good" Ascendants, you should check your internal inventory, and make sure you live up to your image.

8

The Success Skills of the Earth Signs

TAURUS

Static earth Ruling planet: Venus
Main Venusian characteristics: comfort-loving, pleasure seeking, hard-working/persistent

Sun Sign Taurus:

It is no accident that Taurus falls among the so-called "executive" signs; Taurus has all the basic equipment to do the job, especially when it is the sun that is in that sign. In Taurus' success pattern fixity of purpose makes up for what can sometimes be an inertia that borders on laziness. Don't get me wrong; you Taurus sun sign people work like crazy. The word laziness here refers to the tendency you have to be satisfied with the status quo, particularly in terms of your own job and goals. Many Taurean sun sign people find themselves getting promoted when they did not ask for it or expect it. (Taureans are not always terribly perceptive about what is going on right around them.) When the promotion occurs, however, you Taureans know you deserve it; the satisfaction Taurus sun sign people feel about their situation often extends to themselves. But your Taurus brand of self-satisfaction is rarely smugness; it is a *certainty* that people working around you usually find highly reassuring. Male or female, a Taurus boss is the staunch, always-there, ever-protective mother everybody has always wanted.

Taurus suns can withstand shocks and stress far better than they can tolerate going out on a limb. "Better safe than sorry" is a Taurus motto, if there ever was one. I am sure that is the reason you Taurus people are often accused of a lack of imagination. It is not that you do not *have* imagination; it just scares you to use it. It's rarely a problem, however, because you patient, coaxing Taureans can draw ideas out of others—and have the grace not to take credit for them.

Taurus' famous stubbornness is the fly in the ointment in terms of ultimate success for this sun sign. The fact that decisions are made slowly is only half the problem. The other, and more potentially disastrous half, is the tendency of you Taurus sun sign people to *stick with* your decisions no matter what—sometimes to an unreasonable extent: "What do you mean that weight of paper doesn't come in green? I said I want green paper. What? Well, maybe you *should* go out and make it. No, I don't care if there's a lovely lemon yellow, I want *green!*" What's going on inside Taurus's head during this scenario is probably something like, "Oh Lord, now I might have to go all the way back to square one and make up my mind all over again, and I'll have to rearrange my schedule and I've got so many other things to do." The deliberative process is slow and painstaking, therefore you do it only once. But at least others cannot accuse you Taureans of snap judgments or flightiness.

When all is said and done, you Taurus sun signs have got a lot going for you on the job—and it is a fact that many of you wind up at the top of the heap. Someone or something else may have pushed you there, kicking and screaming all the way, because you had to leave one nicely broken-in spot for another. But, wherever you land, people recognize your worth, your warmth, and your stability.

Moon Sign Taurus:

Moon in Taurus may seem to slumber at times, but it never really sleeps—at least when it comes to ambition. The drive for material security and possessions is strong. One problem is that you Taurus moon people can be literally bull-headed in attempting to get the things you deeply crave. For all your inherent sweetness and good nature, you power-driven Taureans can be quite crude in your instinctive behavior patterns. What you lack in cleverness you may make up for in sheer weight of influence.

Your judgment is quite sound, however, and a natural sense that things take time to mature will often lend Taurus moon people a degree of patience rarely found. That patience works two ways. On one side, it makes the Taurus moon person a marvelous guide and counselor to the younger and less-experienced. On the other hand, the Taurus moon sign can give a stolidity that is obnoxious. With the patience of Job, a Taurus moon sign will stand firm and eventually thwart any attempts to maneuver him politically. Taurus moon can be virtually oblivious to subtle threats and even not-so-subtle moves on the part of others. You are the one who is still sitting at his desk as the movers arrive to take it out to make room for your replacement. When everyone's patience is exhausted by yours, they finally give up. That's power!

You do not get a picture of someone who adapts and adjusts with lightning speed, do you? That's hardly Taurus moon style, and the lack of it can be a negative. But you Taurus moon people can chalk something possibly better up on your side of the board—sheer animal magnetism. I'm talking about the robust, indolent sexuality of a Moonbeam McSwine rather than the pert cuteness of a Daisy Mae. (For men, use your own images). The earthy quality of the Taurus moon person can be felt through almost any sun sign—and you are pleasant to have around. In times of crisis the Taurus moon person is someone others can lean on and get solace from—rather like comfort food.

Do not ask a Taurus moon person what is going to happen tomorrow; today is the day to be concerned with. That's my polite way of saying that one would be better off reading entrails than asking you Taurus moon people to give creative predictions. Far-sightedness is not a strong point, even though practical foresight is. When the situation calls for a leap of the imagination, you Taurus moon people tend to get your mental feet stuck in the mud. On the other hand, nobody but nobody can play it closer to the vest. When times are tough, one can count on you to conserve, to consolidate, and to organize resources for the long haul—without ever getting flapped.

Ascendant Sign Taurus:

Who is that ever-lovin', pleasure-lovin' character? If you have a hint of padding on your frame, whatever your height or gender, you probably are a Taurus Ascendant. Gourmet, gourmand, connoisseur of life's earthier and sweeter delights, the person with a Taurus Ascendant is almost always a hit among his fellows. There is an affability, a sweetness, and a good nature that is hard to resist. Depending on the rest of your horoscope, you may be more or less talkative, louder or softer in your manner; but there is one thing you probably have—a dulcet, soothing speaking voice that can often sing rather nicely, as well.

In terms of persuasiveness, however, a Taurus Ascendant can give you a bit too much gentleness. Or, what's worse, your all-too-real Taurus stubborn streak can show its face and get other people's backs up. I'm certain most of the salespeople who have most enraged me with their dogmatic unwillingness to accept the fact that truly "I don't *want* any" have been Taurus Ascendant people. Persistence without subtlety is unpleasant, and a bore.

If you have a Taurus Ascendant, you can occasionally seem a bit "slow," both physically and mentally. But in competitive situations, that might be your biggest ace in the hole. Because you seem not to know or care what is going on, you are not regarded as a threat. Great cover! It gives you entrée to all kinds of situations. You can sit quietly—to all appearances thinking about your next good meal or some lovely music—while you are really picking up all kinds of useful information. And the best fact of all is that people trust you. I'm not saying they shouldn't (only you can know that). But it is a quality you should be aware of if you're not. In point of fact, when the sign of Taurus is prominent in a horoscope, you will very often find a person whose career involves being entrusted with the valuables/possessions/money of others. Think of it this way: even though you may occasionally despair about your body's tendency to retain weight, it is better than having a "lean and hungry look" that makes others suspicious. Taurus Ascendant—enjoy!

VIRGO

Flexible earth Ruling planet: Mercury
Main Mercurial characteristics:
discriminating, practical, subservient,
logical, reserved

Sun Sign Virgo:

First things first: let's banish forever that famous mythological virgin, for she is a myth. In fact, if I were writing a different book, I'd elaborate on one of the best-kept secrets of the zodiac—Virgo's intense sexuality. (Technique and experimentation are Virgo hallmarks.) What the virgin image really means is that you Virgo sun sign people seek purity, perfection, and wholeness in everything—particularly yourselves. The fact that no real purity exists in this world is the source of Virgo's dissatisfaction and critical carping, which is again directed mainly inward. A far better symbol than the virgin for Virgo would be the servant; for therein lies your real problem in the world of business/profession. Virgos are missionaries, and they believe their mission is to serve. It is most difficult for the Virgo sun sign person who does not have counterbalancing astrological elements to assume the throne of success. You will assume all the responsibilities and the remuneration that goes with them; but you will tend to believe that kingship and its rewards of ego-inflating obeisance belong to Leo, not to self-effacing Virgo.

There isn't a more self-disciplined worker than the typical Virgo sun sign; your organizational ability is unparalleled in the zodiac; but there are too many Virgos who organize themselves out of existence by valuing the system above the substance.

If you are a Virgo sun sign, believe that I'm not taking pot shots at you without purpose. In my time I've encountered and worked with more than one Virgo I've wanted to shake and wake up to the more daring and rewarding aspects of business life. You have more going for you than a lot of your zodiacal relatives. Use it, and don't succumb to the servile mentality. You can serve others and enjoy the cake as well.

The Virgo sun sign attribute that you can cultivate most

productively is the ability to analyze. No one is master of "take-apartness" like Virgo; and, in any given situation, it is only when all the elements are clear that progress is possible. You do have one big problem: you Virgos are not always willing to take the initiative in putting things back together again in a new way. Virgo's experimentation takes place within very narrow confines; this lack of inspiration can make a lackluster leader.

Another two-edged sword for the Virgo sun sign is your ability to turn emotion on and off quite efficiently (the way you do everything else). There is warmth and sympathy in you, to be sure, (look at Virgo with animals). However, when someone does not live up to your exacting standards, you are capable of giving a critique icy enough to chill a continent—not a popular trait with subordinates, and one of the reasons Virgo more often *is* one than *has* them.

Believe it or not, Virgo humor is a strong point, and one that you should not undervalue. It often takes the form of sardonic wit, but many an executive has used that weapon to slice his way to the top with less equipment than Virgo has behind it. One of the games you success-bent Virgos should play is "let's pretend." Spend a whole day (or a whole week) imitating someone else's style—someone with more flair than you. (Remember, Mercury rules imitators as well.) With your own quite solid substance to back up that style, you could find yourself a formidable force in whatever career milieu you inhabit.

Moon Sign Virgo:

Virgo moon worries whether the sun is going to come up tomorrow (and I speak from personal experience). Virgo moon people operate out of anxiety; and though they are utterly dependable, they can make themselves utterly miserable. They survive because they wouldn't dream of crossing anywhere but at the corner (with the light); heaven forbid they take any chances at all. Maybe that is why it is hard for them to get anywhere higher than midladder in the success business.

If you have a Virgo moon, I'm not recommending that you run out and dive in front of a truck to prove your strength; you've got plenty of that. Just try testing it a little. For instance, instead of skinning your nose on a deadline, miss it—deliberately. You will find that the skies do not fall, and that the reputation you have built up will stand you in good stead. (People may even notice you.)

I'm overstating the case a bit, but with reason. There are probably plenty of you Virgo moon people who don't even recognize the problem (especially if you have a fire sun sign). You probably suffer in silence and pray a lot. The splendid part of having a Virgo moon is that it gives you so many positive qualities. For instance where the Virgo sun sign can consciously suppress his human warmth, it flows naturally from the person with a Virgo moon. You can generally handle people quite gently and quite firmly at the same time. What you Virgo moon people demand of yourselves, you demand of others—but it is justice tempered with mercy. Virgo moon gives patience, too. No needle-in-the-haystack problem is too taxing or too demanding for you. The desire to serve is now unconscious, and it usually serves you well.

Virgo is a flexible sign and when the moon is in Virgo it can stall the power drive because there is hesitancy and uncertainty; (it is really that old anxiety again). Remember that Virgo is earth, which gives a natural gravitational pull toward material rewards. If that desire is thwarted, you Virgo moon people can become bitter and cruel—to yourselves and everyone around you. My advice to anyone with a Virgo moon is to be honest with yourself about your urge for success. When an opportunity arises, don't gloss over your fears with such thoughts as "I wouldn't like that job anyway" or "I'm really not qualified." Live dangerously. Ask for what you want. The worst that can happen is that you will get it, and you will have even more responsibilities to worry about. This is not black humor on my part, just a recognition of the way it is with us Virgo moon people.

While the Virgo sun sign's mania for organization can get in the way of creativity, it is not necessarily so with the Virgo moon person. Your mind automatically and unobtrusively files information neatly away. Then (if your sun sign allows it) you can whip out that information precisely when it is needed. Virgo moon people often think very quickly because your inner filing system is organized so superbly. You should have "instant retrieval."

Ascendant Sign Virgo:

Neat, modest, reserved, critical, fussy, unassuming: all these Virgo attributes apply in spades when Virgo is on the Ascendant. The possessor of such an Ascendant is often a walking caricature of the textbook Virgo, exhibiting all the good points—and all the bad ones. Virgo Ascendant people can make others very nervous because they always feel they are under a microscope. While Virgo sun sign's passion for observation can go on under a more laidback facade, when Virgo is the rising sign it is much more obvious. My nickname for the Virgo Ascendant is "The Inspector," and the inspection can get mighty personal. If you are the type who makes people wonder if they have really washed behind their ears, you've probably got a Virgo Ascendant.

The irony is that most Virgo Ascendant people would be horrified to think their presence was felt at all. Even your physical posture can betray the fact that you are trying to hide. It's really too bad, because the innate tactfulness and warmth of Virgo are much in evidence when it is your Ascendant sign. In situations where someone else is the underdog (for example, is new to the group), the Virgo Ascendant can make the newcomer feel just fine. Virgo will approach him carefully and cautiously, and quietly make him feel at home. You Virgo Ascendants really *care* if people have everything they need. If somebody asks you how to find the rest room, you'll not only show him where it is, but will probably check it first to make sure all the necessities are there.

It is the rare Virgo Ascendant person who ends up in the limelight (though Virgo is a neurotic enough sign that some Virgos may demand it of themselves). Virgo makes the ideal number two man, whether it is the sign of the sun, the moon, or the Ascendant. And if you Virgos can come to terms with this fact, you can flourish in that position. Remember, Virgo is earth, and the earth signs always know how to take care of themselves—particularly in the material sense.

CAPRICORN

Dynamic earth Ruling planet: Saturn
Main Saturnine characteristics: conservatism, seriousness, sense of purpose

Sun Sign Capricorn:

If ever a sun sign should have success written all over it, it is Capricorn. Capricorn is dynamic, giving you drive. It is an earth sign, giving you the ability to bring forth things in material form. Sounds like the perfect set-up for success, and it very often is. However, remember that Capricorn is solid earth, and it can be too, too solid—meaning that you Capricorn sun sign people can lack delicacy and grace. Hardly a tragic flaw? Perhaps, but the desire to accede to the throne of power can be so all consuming that you can become more machine than man in the process. Capricorn is a very materialistic sign in a very materialistic society.

For all the strengths you know you possess, be aware that there is something potentially dehumanizing about the Capricorn sun sign. The approach to everything is often lean and spare; the typical Capricorn only wants to deal with what works. And that goes for people, too. Capricorn often wants them to be as serious and efficient as he is, and will shuck them off like corn husks if they serve no purpose. If you are a Capricorn sun sign, you can avoid this trap. Observe how you deal with other people—particularly peers and subordinates. No one says the boss has to be a mother figure or a crying towel, but your hard-as-nails approach may lose you some good people. And even you need a support system.

You Capricorns can be work horses, and your power comes from industry rather than nervous energy. You are usually so industrious that you keep on going when everyone else has flopped with fatigue. The reason you never stop is that you are never satisfied; there is a self-demand for perfection. It is less obsessive than that of Virgo, however, so it tends to bring you greater benefits.

The benefits may keep on coming, often fast and furious. When they do, ask yourself what makes you run. Is this what it's really all about? How much do I really want money and power? As much as it may work for you in the business world, your Capricorn tunnel vision can cause you personal problems. Scratch a Capricorn sun sign success and you often find an unhappy, unsuccessful individual in private life.

Meanwhile, back at the office, your Capricorn sun sign success skills are superb. Like the mountain goat that is your symbol, Capricorn is shrewd and sure of foot. You plan ahead as no other sign does, knowing exactly where you are putting each foot as you climb steadily (if slowly) to the mountain peak. When you take a risk it is generally a calculated one, and it pays off. Your long-range view applies in every situation, and you can often set a marvelous example by sublimating self to the task at hand.

Let me caution you with one question: Is it possible that your tendency to be all work and no play is oppressive and depressing, to yourself as well as others? Capricorn, ruled by Saturn, is synonymous with melancholy. If they do not have daily substantiation of material progress, some Capricorns can lapse into the doldrums. The Capricorn sun sign without some upbeat elements in his horoscope can cast a pretty black cloud over everything and everyone. When this kind of mountain goat finally gets to the summit, he often finds it's very lonely at the top. This need not be your portrait—especially if you reach out your hand to others as you make your way up.

Moon Sign Capricorn:

When Capricorn is the moon sign, it can be a success-seeker's best friend. The basic drive of Capricorn, like all the earth signs, is to build something of permanence. When that drive translates into instinctive action in the business world, you find a person who is "constructive" in the best sense of the word. Regardless of your sun sign, there is generally a friendly helpfulness about you people with moon in Capricorn—a sincere desire to make things work. Moon in Capricorn is no pushover, however, because what's brewing down there in your subconscious at the same time is a very strong need to achieve.

When the moon is in Capricorn, the success build-up is logical, planned out. There is rarely a skipping of steps, because Capricorn moon instinctively knows the necessity for all of them if the structure is to stand. What this means in terms of on-the-job performance is that you can be a bulwark of stability and organization. A Capricorn moon is great ballast to have, particularly if your sun sign is quite volatile (like Gemini's).

On the minus side, you may find your Capricorn moon can be a drag. Operating at a very low frequency, this moon gives an evenness of temperament. But there are also very few real highs, those creative bursts that result in original thinking and imaginative action.

When presented with fresh ideas, the person with a Capricorn moon often visibly struggles with a basic tendency to see only the practical aspects and not the inherent possibilities. Capricorn moon often desperately wants to be free—to experience ideas and people in a "looser" way. For the person of high intelligence and self-insight, it is possible to use a Capricorn moon brilliantly, recognizing one's limitations and rising above them. Your Capricorn moon works particularly well when it is combined with a fire sun sign—especially Aries or Sagittarius. In these instances, your fiery energy and creativity are firmly harnessed and directed by a moon that always knows where it is going. Many a dynamo who really arrived at success in his career found his way there with a Capricorn moon.

If you have the moon in the sign of Capricorn, my advice is to use it and not let it abuse you. You have super success potential, and the best part is that it can be unobtrusive. The person with a Capricorn moon need never fear coming off as too laidback; it will soon become obvious that you can move mountains if you choose.

Ascendant Sign Capricorn:

The sign of Capricorn is the "natural" sign of the tenth or "authority figure" house of the horoscope. If Capricorn is your Ascendant sign, then you may actually look important and seem to exude power. If there is anything to back up this external statement depends on the rest of the horoscope, of course. Nonetheless, if you've got a Capricorn Ascendant, you've got a great asset; people see you as solid, steady, and *substantial*. In a world where appearances count, that counts for a lot.

It is possible for the person with a Capricorn Ascendant to scare people off, however. Sometimes instead of the all-embracing warmth of a father figure, you have the formidable facade of a taskmaster. Regardless of your sex, you Capricorn Ascendant people can appear stern and forbidding. If you sometimes fear your personal habits leave something to be desired, it may be your Capricorn Ascendant rather than a faulty deodorant. Of course, no one says you have to be likable to be successful; many a rotten personality has a six-figure salary. However, life on the job is much more pleasant when people regard you as approachable, and feel comfortable once they do.

With a Capricorn Ascendant you may lack the more positive qualities of an earthy exterior. Capricorn earth tends to be hard, even "frozen" at times. What this means is that your mannerisms can appear stiff and calculated. No bursts of lusty Taurus enthusiasm for you; and none of the visible sensitivity of Virgo either. Though you may not literally want to get into the field, just keep in mind that any career life is partly a public relations job. Also, there is an increasing trend in the business world to value "people management" over the more old-fashioned "task management." The Capricorn Ascendant who is not wary can easily fall into the trap of exhibiting a management style that went out with the adding machine. If you have a Capricorn Ascendant, you might practice "hanging loose"; start in your personal life, and before you know it you will be a lot more easy-going—and a lot more successful—in your professional relationships.

9

The Success Skills of the Air Signs

GEMINI

Flexible air Ruling planet: Mercury
Main Mercurial characteristics: Quick, mentally dextrous, nervous, humorous, vacillating

Sun Sign Gemini:

It is often the Gemini sun signs who have most difficulty keeping a résumé to one page. Not because you flatter yourself by believing you've done more than you have; you really have. Job-hopping is very Gemini, as is holding down two jobs at once. The motivation is not necessarily ambition, however; it is usually the hyperactivity that arises from restlessness. I often think of the Gemini sun sign as a "willow in a windstorm." As a success skill, restlessness can work two ways. The good side is that when you move fast you can give the appearance of going somewhere. Some employers love a hopscotch career background—if that many people hired you, you *must* be good. The other side of the coin is that when boredom ensues, the learning process stops. Some Gemini sun signs don't stick around long enough to know everybody's name. For you Geminis it is counterproductive in more ways than one, because Gemini loves learning as he loves life itself. Sooner or later the Gemini who has made too many moves will discover gaping holes in his knowledge of a specific field.

Not all Gemini sun sign people are superficial to be sure, especially if your moon sign gives a firm anchor. But since the sun represents willpower and sense of direction, most of you Geminis will have to fight a weakness in that area all your working lives. The obvious remedy is to get into a job or profession where you can use your many talents all at once, and never feel any are lying fallow. That's a tall order, but not impossible.

My epithet for the Gemini sun sign? The *National Enquirer.* No one fires questions at you more rapidly than Gemini (unless it is someone with Mercury on the Ascendant). If you are a Gemini sun sign, you know that it is a great asset. People find it flattering; little do they know your attention span resembles that of a flea. And, face it, you know that your interest in others is often prompted by self-interest. If anything is important to Geminis, it is having all the answers as well as all the questions. You can suck people dry, which is why you make such excellent reporters and writers. Undoubtedly I am underplaying the more positive qualities of the Gemini sun sign, but if you are a Gemini you should be aware that there is more truth than poetry in your legendary changeability. Take care that you manifest it as versatility and adaptability in job situations.

The reasoning powers of the Gemini sun sign should never be undervalued or underrated. Your capacity for detachment and logic give you "coolness" in the best sense of the word. Though Gemini does not seek to create emergency situations, he performs admirably when they arise. When an instantaneous decision is needed, go to a Gemini. That decision may not be the one that Gemini would think of five minutes later, but the prime importance of the executive decision is no myth in business. That is why, almost in spite of yourselves, you Gemini sun signs land in influential spots. In addition, you have verve, a quivering nervous energy, and the capacity to captivate an audience. These are factors that belong on the plus side of what is actually a rather well-balanced Gemini sun sign success ledger.

Moon Sign Gemini:

If you have a Gemini moon, you may have already discovered that it works better for you in your business life than in your personal life. I've warned more than one friend, "Beware of a man with moon in Gemini." (I realize this is a sexist statement, but I *am* female.) What is fickleness and inconstancy in the romantic area can operate as a chameleonlike inventiveness in career situations, however; Gemini moon is creative in the sense that it can make things up on the spot.

Even if a stolid sun sign or Ascendant makes you appear inert, if you have moon in Gemini your mind is never still. It darts hither and yon picking up signals, and playing them back in whatever manner your sun sign dictates: practically, in the case of earth; tinged with feeling, in the case of water; enthusiastically, in the case of fire. Unfortunately, when a Gemini moon is linked with an air sun sign (particularly Gemini), the result can be an "air head." In business terms, that means someone who can never get his act together, no matter how good his ideas are or how quickly they come.

Your Gemini moon should give you a superb sense of timing, and consequently a lightning wit. The "office comic" often has a Gemini moon. If you are a Gemini moon person who prefers cracking jokes to cracking your work, you don't have enough ballast in the rest of your chart to bring you down to earth. Patience is not a moon-in-Gemini virtue. Do people sometimes complain that you are not listening when they're trying to explain something to you? That is your Gemini moon. However, they may get a big surprise a few days later when you act on something they didn't think you heard. The memory of the Gemini moon person is often phenomenal, and the radar receptivity is so strong it can operate almost on its own.

You moon in Gemini people can *think* yourselves into really wanting to move ahead. Whether you do or not in any substantial way depends on how strong the will and self-disciplinary powers of your sun sign are. You may simply talk about what you're going to do to further your career; be aware that talking and thinking don't make it so. If you have the moon in the sign of Gemini, it is wise to make a tight game plan for reaching your career goals. The plan will undoubtedly be very logical, quite precise, and include some rather clever moves. Just make sure you take out that plan and look at it once in a while to see how many of those maneuvers you have really acted upon. Gemini moon can unfortunately be all talk and no action unless a lot of force is applied—by himself or others.

Ascendant Sign Gemini

If someone flashes by so quickly that it is difficult to make out who it was, it was probably a Gemini Ascendant. If Gemini is your rising sign, you probably have lots of flash and dash. And if your sun and/or moon sign is strong enough, it can help prevent your having a flash-in-the-pan career life.

The Gemini Ascendant comes on not with a bang but a hustle. Everything about you is fast, from your walk to your most likely incessant chatter. A less nimble sun or moon sign can slow your pace considerably but not your degree of animation. The person with a Gemini Ascendant is the fast-talker who can talk his way both into and out of a lot of tight spots. The tendency of Gemini to invent on demand comes to the fore when that sign is on the Ascendant. Promises, promises can gain you entrée almost anywhere; but if the goods aren't delivered, you can just as quickly get ushered out.

This superficiality prevails rarely, however, and most people with a Gemini Ascendant find their glibness a super "extra" to have in both interview and on-the-job situations. It is a sheer delight to encounter someone in the business world who possesses charm as well as the more solid virtues. Gemini's excitability and high-strung nerves can be a great asset when they come across as vivacity and enthusiasm. You Gemini Ascendant people are usually highly memorable, and it is tough to keep a bump-on-a-log in mind when you are casting about for likely job candidates or thinking about who should get the promotion. Suave, urbane, fond of intellectual pleasures, the person with a Gemini Ascendant is impressive without being oppressive. Even if a situation requires a heavy hand, you can wield it with a light touch.

There is one cautionary note I would pass along to Gemini Ascendants (or those who may hire such): make sure the job has enough variety to keep your happy feet and mobile mind occupied at all times. The biggest potential threat to Gemini in the career world is boredom—and that goes for both Gemini sun sign and moon sign, as well.

LIBRA

Dynamic air Ruling planet: Venus
General Venusian characteristics: sybaritic, amiable, romantic

Sun Sign Libra:

With this complex sign, it is best to deal immediately with that word "dynamic" (cardinal, to you astrology buffs). Libra's reputation for being a shillyshallying pushover has little basis in fact—at least the facts of the business/professional world. In my day I've met many a Libra sun sign (male and female) with a will of iron and an often dangerous degree of single-mindedness about personal goals. I said dangerous, and I mean it. "Dynamic" energy, astrologically speaking, can cut through anything and anyone. The reason you Librans can surprise people with the strength of your inner determination is that there is always a slightly "ethereal" character to the air sun signs; and it comes through virtually any Ascendant. Also, never forget that Libra is ruled by that gracious lady Venus, who can make almost any kind of behavior seem acceptable.

I have no intention of making you Libra sun sign people out to be monsters—far from it. In fact, the potential ruthlessness of your sun sign is often a source of unhappiness to you, because there is nothing that Libra desires so much as (you have it!) peace and harmony. The extraordinary *conscious* need of the Libra sun sign to please everyone is much more than an astrological cliché. Libra's ego needs and goal-directedness are in conflict with Libra's equally strong necessity to refrain from battle. That may be the reason so many of you gravitate toward the arts, where there is (theoretically at least) less dog-eat-dog competition. No one suffers more than Libra yourself from the consequences of your self-seeking actions.

Primarily for the above reasons, you Libra sun sign people do not make the best of all possible leaders and supervisors. Head-on confrontation comes with the executive territory, so you gun-shy Librans tend to stay away from it. As with all the air signs, your nerves suffer under stress. With Libra, even a hint of ugliness can cause trauma. Libra sun sign people function best in positions where your native refinement and impartiality allow you to pour oil on the troubled waters of others. Librans can be arbitrators without peer—as long as they are not involved in the dispute.

I've probably alienated quite a few of you Libra sun sign readers by now, but I'm afraid I must go farther. Like a man without a woman, a Libra without a partner is the proverbial ship without a sail. Independent action does not come easily or naturally to you. It is when you are forced to function on your own (possibly even believing you can) that you run into problems. Feeling only "half there," the solo Libran tends to grab all the marbles and dash in a mad panic toward the executive suite (smiling politely and murmuring apologies to those who get bowled over).

There are certain kinds of one-person jobs that you Libra sun signs do consummately well, however—sales, for instance (preferably under a good, strong sales manager). Your brand of pleasant amiability laced with Libra's native smarts can win over the toughest customers. The bottom line of my message is this: Libra sun signs of the world, for lasting success, unite with a partner. You do it often enough in marriage; why not in business?

Moon Sign Libra:

When Libra is the moon rather than the sun sign, a great deal of that dynamic goal direction turns to mush. It sinks down into the unconscious where it often prompts dilettantism rather than drive. It's you people with moon in Libra rather this Libra sun signs who get the indecisiveness award. I find there is a lack of concentration and a tendency for your minds to wander. Moon in Libra's motto is, "Get it done quickly so I can get on to the next thing that strikes my fancy." The creative leanings of you Libra moon people are strong, as is the sex drive—or, more properly, the flirt drive. Just as Libra's famous (and real) impartiality wants to see all possible sides, you with the moon in Libra may want to merge with all possible partners. I know this is a book about careers and success; but, let's face it, sex in the office is an issue. I'm enough of a romantic not to regard your flirtatiousness negatively. In fact, so long as your inconstant moon tends to business, it can lend a lot of charm to your personality—and liven up the dreariest commercial atmosphere.

No matter what your sun sign is, if you have moon in Libra, you have taste—and could actually utilize that taste to make a living. You have a love of beauty and symmetry that goes beyond externals; it is actually a sense of harmonious balance that is a tremendous asset in many careers. Moon in Libra instinctively knows when there is something not quite right, something slightly off kilter—be it in a piece of copy, a marketing plan, an interior design, or a stock portfolio.

Moon in Libra almost invariably gives you neatness and orderliness, in every respect. However, when it comes to getting ahead, these attractive qualities are no substitute for the will to win. The moon in Libra person can be, quite frankly, a bit lazy about keeping an eye on the main chance. You are easily diverted, particularly by anything of beauty that comes into your highly receptive field of vision. The aesthetic powers of the Libra moon work most positively when your sun is in a fire sign. In this instance, Libra's airy creative imagination fans the fires of ego, and you can move forward in a constructive direction.

The famous scales that are the classic symbol of Libra point up a most desirable attribute of the moon in Libra. If you have one, you may not give yourself enough credit for the fact that you are, in the main, even-tempered. Libra is the "peace at any price" moon. There can be outbursts, of course—particularly if the rest of the horoscope indicates irascibility. However, when the shouting is over, so is the anger. You moon in Libra people have an incredible ability to forgive and forget. In fact, you may tend to fraternize with and even seem to lick the very hands of those who have wounded you (which is incredible to more grudge-holding types). It's not masochism—just sociability. The moon in Libra person will choose pleasure over business any day. Why mess up your after-hours life just because of some office-hours unpleasantness? This is eminently rational, eminently moon in Libra.

Ascendant Sign Libra:

When the sign of Libra is on the Ascendant, you are a class act all the way. You may possess actual physical beauty; you undoubtedly have a beautiful manner and gentle mannerisms. Some people with a Libra Ascendant are "poetry in motion." One of my favorite images for Libra on the Ascendant is the welcoming, smiling host or hostess who *assures* you that you haven't come too late or too early—even though the dinner may be thoroughly ruined or not even in the oven yet. And when you spill your wine, she will pretend she has always wanted a rose cast to the carpet anyway. A Libra Ascendant is a great social asset, but heaven help the unwary if your Libra Ascendant is covering up something quite mean and ugly. You could then give some of the ruder shocks of the business/professional world.

Libra on the Ascendant bestows the ideal external qualifications of the counter-spy. When butter won't melt in your mouth, you can hardly be suspected of having a knife up your sleeve. Libra Ascendants, always remember you possess great protective coloring (and it's usually damn attractive camouflage). When you decide to use it actively, you can always conjure up your quite remarkable powers of sweet talk. Depending on other factors, you may be more or less articulate, but you sure can be persuasive. Yours is the "honey" of a manner so many others would be wise to cultivate.

No matter what your specific physical characteristics, you are probably considered "decorative." Libra Ascendant people are often found in out-front positions—and there are a lot more of those than just manning the reception desk. For the males with this Ascendant, you could slap on the labels "chivalrous" and "courtly." Keeping to the old-fashioned terminology (which is somehow appropriate), the females often have an air of delicacy. For both sexes, civility, tact, and polish are generally in evidence. And those last two words are the key: remember, the Ascendant is a veneer. If yours is Libra, you might take pains to be sure you live up to your look.

AQUARIUS

Static air Ruling planet: Uranus
Main Uranian characteristics: inventive, original, rational

Sun Sign Aquarius:

People often have difficulty remembering Aquarius is an air sign and not a water sign. Rather than the obvious fact that Aquarius' symbol is the water bearer, I attribute the confusion to the very un-airlike dogmatism of you Aquarians. Really pushing it, one can generally swing a Gemini or a Libra over to the other side. Not so with Aquarius—when you're right, you're right. Because it is usually some supra-personal cause you are stuck on, it is hard to fault you humanitarian Aquarians. When commercial interests are paramount, however, the tendency can be quite annoying—and counterproductive to your own success. You may find yourself fighting for a cause that got lost when you weren't looking, while your rivals have gone speeding on ahead of you.

On the positive side, Aquarians really *believe* in what they believe in. No one can be more impassioned and more detached at the same time than you Aquarius sun signs. Your moral passion may be great, but it is very difficult for the typical Aquarius to zero in on another individual and form an intense relationship. Toward groups you are terrific, and as bosses you are eminently fair and rational, but you're rarely particularly sympathetic.

In fact, the air element's detachment is at its strongest when the sun is in the sign of Aquarius. Aquarians are often loners. You can be amusing, to be sure, and are often fond of intellectual rapport and "head games." But somehow or other it is difficult to believe that such a clear-thinking individual who never stoops to pettiness or suspicion is really human. If others sense a chill in the presence of Aquarius, they should shrug it off and remember one of your best qualities: you value the liberty and privacy of others as much as you do your own.

You Aquarian sun signs are just loaded with success skills, the kind that employers really go for. You are inventive, often iconoclastic in your break-through concepts; yet, at the same time, you unconventional Aquarians will follow every rule in the book. (By the time the Aquarian is an adult, he has become merely an armchair revolutionary.) One problem you typical Aquarius sun signs may encounter on your trip to the top is fixity of purpose. You may plan all your moves with absolute clear-headedness; but you may find yourself hard-pressed to change course when circumstances dictate it. Flexibility is not necessarily an Aquarian virtue. Reasonableness is, however, so when it becomes obvious that a certain road is leading nowhere, you will probably abandon it. If that bothers you, others may never know, however. You would *never* lie, but you'll always keep your messier emotions to yourself. Aquarians are not paragons of virtue, but they do have a lot of good basic equipment to make it in just about any field. Your scientific bent may be strong; Aquarius is almost as good at seeing all the components as Virgo, yet never loses sight of the whole. As therapists Aquarians are highly competent, if a little cool. In fact, for total success, your Aquarian sun signs would do well to warm up to life and feel how the other half lives.

Moon Sign Aquarius:

When the independent, rebellious spirit of Aquarius gets lodged in the moon (or subconscious) it can last a lifetime—with variable consequences. In youth, the Aquarius moon keeps pushing for freedom; and unless there is a great deal of stability in the person's sun sign, he can drift indefinitely. In adulthood, an Aquarius moon generally imparts a liveliness and spirit to the personality that is sheer delight in the business/professional world.

If you have an Aquarian moon, you never want to hear "that's just the way it is. Those are the rules; those are the limitations." Ever inventive, ever seeking to improve the quality of your own lives as well as the lives of others, you Aquarian moon people are never satisfied with pat answers. The "show me" challenge Aquarius moon puts forth is reminiscent of Taurus, which is also a static or fixed sign.

When the moon is in Aquarius, the intelligence is usually clear, because the emotions do not cloud it. Sometimes the person will *try* to let his reason be swayed, however, and it's almost perverse (but very Aquarian). Many moon in Aquarius people long to "feel" more than they do, and would really like to be swept away by emotions. You rarely are, however, and that is one of your greatest strengths in the career world.

The humanitarian nature is powerful when the moon is in this sign. Everyone is equal, so everyone is equally deserving of help and support. You Aquarian moon people make terrific administrators, especially when your decisions affect the emotional lives of your employees. Fair is fair, and you never let anyone forget or deplore that fact. Others should not try to do special pleading with an Aquarian moon. They may get a stern, if kindly, lecture.

Curiosity may have killed many a cat, but to my knowledge it's never done any harm to those with the moon in Aquarius. You are the curiosity seekers of the zodiac. You seek out not only the curious, but the frankly bizarre as well. It is hard to shock a person with this moon; aberrations are simply a delight. It all goes back to your scientific bent, and unless too analytical, it serves you well in business. Taking risks is a piece of cake for you, and (unless your own independence is threatened) virtually nothing appears too dangerous.

I must touch on the tendency of this moon to exhibit eccentricity. It sometimes comes out in rather peculiar ways, like strange manners of speech and dress. When Aquarius is under control—as in the sun sign—it rarely gives a need to shock. That is the province of moon in Aquarius. If this is one of your personal points, I suggest you check yourself carefully in the mirror each morning to see if some subconscious hostility may be showing on the outside.

Ascendant Sign Aquarius:

Sociability marks all the air signs, to a greater or lesser degree. With Aquarius, this trait is most pronounced when the sign is on the Ascendant. You Aquarian Ascendant people tend to spring along, so full of energy and life others can almost smell it. There is a flashiness to all your movements, though they are generally tempered with grace. Your voice is probably warm, your manner hearty—and sometimes just plain loud. It is rare for you to go too far in that direction, however, because the rational quality of Aquarians gives you moderation in all things when it is on the Ascendant.

The desire to be different is always a latent possibility with

Aquarius. With Aquarian Ascendant people it comes out in a special way. Though their "shticks" may vary widely, they are originals, and their originality is almost always a mark in their favor. They can exhibit some very unique success skills that are powerful career assets. If Pisces is your sun sign, for instance, humor may be your overall modus operandi, and it can be delightful. If it is Gemini, you may be a walking encyclopedia who entertains with interesting knowledge. The point is that Aquarius Ascendant is rarely a bore.

This Ascendant does extremely well in group activities. Never bland, the person with Aquarius Ascendant is able to make his presence felt, yet he will not attempt to hog the limelight. The fairness and honest good nature of this sign often resembles that of Sagittarius. Your Aquarian Ascendant will take you farthest when it is hitched to a powerful sun sign like Scorpio, Capricorn, or Leo. It is a marvelous veneer to put over the most ruthless kind of ambition. With more "laissez-faire" sun and or moon signs, the Aquarian Ascendant in itself will not make up for a lack of drive, however.

In spite of your surface flashiness (or maybe because of it) you Aquarius Ascendant people are often singled out for sober assignments—that is, for missions where something delicate and difficult is to be accomplished, and the stakes are high. You usually can with gentle humor and/or refreshing candor take on the most hostile opponent and mollify him. You Aquarian Ascendant people also seem to be virtually indefatigable. Your strength is not like that of Capricorn, who seems impossible to wear down. It is more as if you possess an inexhaustible well of good spirits. A little like Libra on the Ascendant, you Aquarian Ascendant people rarely let it be known that your feet are hurting like crazy and you desperately want this to be over.

Prehaps the biggest bonus Aquarius on the Ascendant bestows on you is an air of acceptance. You have an unflappable quality that comes off as calm, collected interest in anything or anyone new and different. It is cool, in the best sense of the word.

10

The Success Skills of the Water Signs

CANCER

Dynamic water Ruling planet: The Moon
Main lunar characteristics: sensitivity, compassion, fearfulness

Sun Sign Cancer:

To me it is one of the great anomalies of the zodiac that Cancer, the quintessential stay-at-home sign, is superb out there in the business world. Cancer is often called fearful, timid, retiring, and there is some truth in these descriptions. However, what one tends to forget is that Cancer is a *dynamic* or starter sign. But that is only part of the story: I see the real clue to Cancer's career success in the claws of the crab that symbolizes the sign. You Cancer sun sign people *grab hold*, and it is virtually impossible to get you to let go.

On the one hand you snatch at responsibility and details, therefore making a conscientious, reliable worker. On the other hand, don't let others take their eyes off anything they want (like a job)—you will be clutching it to your breast before they know it. Cancers are just highly acquisitive and *personal* to a fault. They want everything to belong to *them*. This mine-all-mine tendency arises from the deep-seated need for emotional security that is typical of Cancerians. In business, the more you Cancer sun signs can amass, the less you feel like crying for your crib blankets.

You Cancer sun sign people are the pack rats of the world—literally collecting and *keeping* everything. (Home and office are often cluttered.) What this means to Cancer's career performance is that you are bad at delegating authority. Though Cancer sun signs are very often found in leadership or supervisory positions, you function there more as sympathetic, nurturing mother figures than as efficiently organized overseers.

The emotional receptivity of Cancer is legendary, though I see more of it when it is the moon rather than the sun sign. Nevertheless, you Cancer sun sign people can "feel out" situations marvelously well, and generally know how to act. (Cancer sun sign people are fairly well in control of their rampant sensitivity.) On the other hand, your extraordinary capacity to feel can be a heavy burden—to yourself and others. Nothing is blacker than a Cancer's black mood, because it arises from both fear and imagination, each feeding the other until the problem seems monumental. Then, such brooding, such wailing, such expectations of disaster!

In this respect the Cancer sun sign's saving grace is that you are so resilient—water is fluid. You can bounce back quickly and deal with *real* crises much better than one might expect. The Cancer sun sign can be as efficient as a machine and as decisive as a computer, as long as he is not threatened with looking foolish. Of all the Cancerian fears, the greatest is fear of ridicule. That is why you supposedly sensitive Cancers can fool others by appearing hardhearted at times. It is not the real thing, just self-protection. Otherwise you might cry. On balance the Cancer sun sign has a terrific collection of success skills. If you use all of them and do not leave some on the shelf to get dusty, you have it made.

Moon Sign Cancer:

When the moon is in the sign of Cancer it is "at home," so to speak. Cancer is the natural sign of the moon, so the two should work together beautifully. They do, but because all Cancerian traits are thereby heightened, the combination can be a bit much—both for you with Cancer moon and those with whom you come into contact. Operating at the subconscious level, the person with a Cancer moon is free to dream—and often does so, both day and night. This may sound like an exaggeration, but you Cancer moon people can give the impression of being sound asleep with your eyes wide open. Maybe if I had a kaleidoscopic Cancer moon I'd like to spend a lot of time daydreaming in beautiful patterns too; but the tendency to "moon" (literally) is very hard on your success drive. For one thing, your ultimate career goals get rather hazy and can seem more like a mirage than a real objective. In fact, the person with the moon in Cancer is so extremely impressionable that his goals keep shifting all the time. Suggestibility runs so high that all the Cancer moon person has to hear about is a friend or co-worker's ambitions, and he has incorporated those into his "wish book" as well.

With your incredibly active imaginations, you Cancer moon people can spin the most beautiful webs of multicolor gossamer threads. The problem is in untangling them before they break. If you have a reality-oriented sun sign (like earth) you can do the organizing job yourself and put your ideas to work. Without such a strong ally, you had better take care you get into the right job milieu, where creativity really counts.

In spite of everything (or perhaps because of it) the Cancer moon person knows how to survive. Unfortunately, some of your survival techniques may be less than desirable—for instance, "creating" excuses in order to avoid blame. This is not really a moral lapse, but rather a manifestation of the typical Cancer moon person's desire to be left alone. "Don't hassle me" is very moon in Cancer.

When a Cancer moon is brought under control—either by maturity or a strong sun sign—it has many good things going for it. Creativity is one of these, without question, but there are some other highly desirable success skills as well. A particularly good one in the career world we live in is your ability to adapt to changing circumstances without getting rattled. Another moon-in-Cancer asset is a sympathetic ear that is firmly attached to a very large heart. You moon in Cancer people instinctively react to the needs of others—and respond with both kindness and practical support.

There is nothing like your Cancer moon to make others feel wanted and needed.

Ascendant Sign Cancer:

When a Cancer Ascendant enters the room, you may think you have just heard the command, "Lights, camera, action." There is a star quality about Cancer Ascendant people. Male or female, you are probably sexually magnetic, with a voluptuousness about the body and face (which can tend to fat in older years). In spite of a dreamy quality (which is also very attractive), you generally react visibly to all kinds of stimuli, and tend to seek them out.

When Cancer is on the Ascendant, the famous changeability of the sign becomes a desire for novelty and excitement. That is one reason you Cancer Ascendant people are often considered exciting, even if you are fairly low key. You are most likely action-oriented. Though you might move slowly, you get around a lot, accomplishing a great deal without seeming frenetic.

There is a bit of the actor about the way you people with Cancer rising can hold an individual or a group in the palm of your hands. You do it with less dash and flamboyance than Leo or Sag, but you do it consummately well. Here is that Cancerian anomaly again: the most domestic of types, Cancer is a natural for public life. (In studying the Houses of the Midheaven, you'll find out that Cancer/the moon does "rule" the public.)

Cancer Ascendant people can be very "arty" types, not just fond of but often obsessed by the arts—music particularly. This has its place as a success skill because you seem cultured. It is rarely an affectation; there is usually a genuine love of the finer things in life. All the sensory equipment of you Cancer Ascendant people works quite well, right down to the manner of speech, which is usually pleasantly dulcet.

Unfortunately, with Cancer on the Ascendant you always have the drag of Cancer's moodiness to deal with. In fact, it is when Cancer is rising that you tend to do the most complaining. You may be so sensitive to the workings of your own body that every little twinge becomes a chronic disease. If you have a Cancer Ascendant, you should really make an effort to keep your medical records to yourself. Remember, *you* are feeling the pain, and it's unfair to pass it on to others. And that goes for emotional pain as well as the physical kind.

SCORPIO

Static water   Ruling planet: Pluto
Main Plutonian characteristics: reserve,
depth of insight, power

Sun Sign Scorpio:

If still waters run deep, they run their deepest in Scorpio. The static or fixed water sign, Scorpio's force is that of dammed-up water—applying mega-pressure to everything it touches. I for one do not shy away from you Scorpios. In fact, I believe you have been much maligned out of misunderstanding.

The first thing to understand about your sun sign—in your business or personal life—is that Scorpio possesses a power that is different in kind as well as degree. Scorpio power is the power of Pluto, Scorpio's ruler and the planet that is associated with nuclear energy. Fortunately, in most cases no one knows better than Scorpio that this power must be controlled. Most Scorpios sense that out of control they can be dangerous beyond belief—both to themselves and to others. Therefore, your famous Scorpio reserve is usually an outward manifestation of your efforts to master yourself. Scorpios can be secretive, it is true. But again, the source of your secrecy is the tight lid you probably keep on your maelstrom of powerful emotions.

People usually don't meet the truly destructive kind of Scorpio in the career world (he's long since been in jail, or the graveyard). In business or professional life, typical Scorpios are often achievers without peer. When they turn their incredible willpower onto almost any situation, they are able to master it and win the day.

Intensity is the key word for you Scorpio sun signs. You channel yourselves totally into whatever the task at hand may be. You are intense of speech, as well, and it often comes out as the most biting, most hurting kind of sarcasm. Someone else could say it more gently, but not Scorpio, because you are so *intent* on making your meaning felt.

Scorpio is a highly physical sign, particularly in the sexual sense. This is relevant here because the blatantly sexual nature of Scorpio is a great component of your power over either sex. But Scorpio is physical in other ways, too. There is tremendous energy, both of body and of mind—not the scurrying of Gemini or the leaping of Sagittarius, but strong, sure movements that always reach the mark. Mentally and physically, you Scorpios calculate every move you make. In short, Scorpio, you are shrewd.

I may have made it sound as if every Scorpio who walks through the door of a company will end up owning it. This is not true, for a number of reasons. First, Scorpios can be easy to hate. And even if people would rather avoid a head-on confrontation with a Scorpio, there are other ways of getting at him—like refusing to promote him. But a second and more common reason for Scorpio failure is diffusion of energy. A Scorpio who can't get a handle on himself can be all over the place, operating ineffectually wherever he lands. Instead of the calculated risk, his modus operandi can be the daring impulse that just misses the mark.

If you have a Scorpio sun sign, I hope you will take my words kindly. People have done you a lot of dirt. I cannot undo it, but at least I will try to help. Scorpio sun signs: *relax,* and get into your power.

Moon Sign Scorpio:

Putting a Scorpio moon with a "light" sun sign is like operating a kiddie car with an eight-cylinder engine. The word drive could have been coined for Scorpio moon. But since all that drive is at the subconscious level, it can take its owner nowhere—very fast. If you have a Scorpio moon, here is how to handle it.

First of all, keep reminding yourself you have one of the best of all possible success skills—an intense *desire* to make it. You simply have to find out what "it" is so you don't cause chaos all around you. Another thing is you, above all people, can bring confusion to your enemies. There is an air of mystery about you that can make you *seem* very important—even if your deepest thought at the moment is, "When is lunch?"

When your Scorpio moon isn't pushing you around, it can give you some excellent on-the-job traits. For instance, when the moon is in Scorpio the person is generally cool in more ways than one. Cool means practical and self-confident, able to operate efficiently in high-danger situations without losing one's head. However, a negative aspect of Scorpio moon's cool is that he'll take care of "number one" every time, sometimes to the detriment of others. Just try imposing on someone with a Scorpio moon and you will see what I mean.

Sex—the real, roll-in-bed kind—is very important when the moon is in Scorpio. Exciting as it is, such a tendency can be very distracting. Also, once sexually engaged, the Scorpio moon person (more so than the Scorpio sun sign) requires dynamite to extricate himself from the situation. I mention this because more than one heavy Scorpio has come a cropper in business because of sex.

The office cynic often has a Scorpio moon. It is hard for you with moon in Scorpio to trust; and unfortunately some of you are not to be trusted. Left to your own devices, you can make tremendous contributions to whatever career or job you bring your talents. It is when you run into political situations that the trouble can start. To get what you want, the Scorpio moon person will often do anything. By now you are convinced that your Scorpio moon will do you in. Before you get carried away, remember that disloyalty is not inevitable in Scorpio moon people. It can and does happen—just as it does with many another moon or sun sign.

A final positive note is if you have moon in Scorpio, you are the ideal investigator—and not just of the light stuff. The courage of the Scorpio moon person to face the unknown is invaluable. Make sure you appreciate it.

Ascendant Sign Scorpio:

If Capricorn on the Ascendant has any rival in the zodiac for coming off as a stiff, it is Scorpio rising. Scorpio's natural bent toward self-control and secrecy are all too obvious when it is the Ascendant sign. Whereas sun sign Scorpio can more or less *use* these tools, the Scorpio Ascendant person is at their mercy.

To get a reaction from you Scorpio Ascendant people, others could try taking their clothes off—but even that might not alter your impassive exterior. I am exaggerating, of course, but it is true that it requires a bit of effort to relate to some people with the sign of Scorpio rising. Once people get to know you, your facade can come tumbling down. But at first it seems impervious.

I have elaborated this point because the rigidity of this Ascendant can be a valuable asset in another connection. Scorpio rising has true grit, and may love nothing more than to test it. In the most stressful situations—both physical and mental—the person with a Scorpio Ascendant is often observed not to turn a hair. Push him, pull him, harass him, send the furies down on him, the Scorpio Ascendant person will appear to remain in control.

If I have given an "iron-man" image to the Scorpio Ascendant, I'll take some of it back. There is a tremendous subtlety to you with this sign rising, and the capacity to utilize it at will. Some of the most skillful manipulators have Scorpio on the Ascendant. You can be a master of persuasion, and not the least of this talent comes from your intense, penetrating way of looking at people, *concentrating* on them. It can happen that a few minutes under your compelling gaze can leave people mesmerized. Your voice goes along with it, too—emphatic and convincing, no matter how soft.

The sign of Scorpio—wherever it falls in the personal points—is a mixed blessing for the possessor. Regardless of sex, the Scorpio often resembles the little girl with the little curl—alternately very, very good and just plain horrid. This is reflected in the fact that there are two symbols for Scorpio—the hideous scorpion with the stinging tail and the Phoenix that rises from its own ashes. I must conclude that duality has marked the sign of Scorpio since time immemorial.

PISCES

Flexible water   Ruling planet: Neptune
Main Neptunian characteristics:
vagueness, mysticism, adaptability

Sun Sign Pisces:

When you mention the sign of Pisces, a lot of people smile knowingly. But they probably don't know a thing, because of all the signs, Pisces is the most difficult to comprehend. At the tail end of the zodiac, Pisces partakes a bit of all the signs that come before it, but not enough to give Pisces real definition. And therein lies your problem: Pisces is a vague sign in more than one sense of the word. Not that all Pisceans are absent-minded, though it is a recognizable trait in some. Pisces tends to walk around in a cloud—the romantic and nebulous haze cast by Neptune, its ruler.

It is this aura of mystery that gives you Pisceans much of your famous charm. The problem is, just as others cannot tell what you are thinking, you often don't know either. Life is too full of possibilities for the Piscean, and you want to experience and encompass them all—often all at one time. What Pisces really lacks is a sense of direction (remember those two fish swimming in opposite directions?). When you find it (as most do with maturity), you can achieve as much as any other sign. Well, almost as much.

Many Pisceans really do not *care* about material success. Even if you sense it only dimly, you probably are in touch with the spiritual dimension that marks this sign. In his search for the absolute, the Piscean can decide to merge with that dimension completely and enter the spiritual life. The vast majority of you, however, function in the workaday world with more or less success. You can achieve the heights when you put your talent for empathetic understanding to good use, as in therapeutic situations. This super-insight is a powerful tool in the commercial world as well. Talk about being able to psych people out—Pisces is the master, and therefore the consummate salesman. The quality of compassion is almost always in evidence when Pisces is the sun sign, and there is generally a hearty good nature. However, though I may alienate a few people, I must say that I believe most Pisceans do better as supervisees than as supervisors. (They joke with their employees too much.)

So far I hope I've painted a fairly attractive portrait because, on the whole, Pisces has excellent human qualities and not a few positive success skills. However, there are two breeds within this sign, and I must mention the second. That is the parasite, the uncertain Piscean who *knows* he needs support, and will insinuate himself into the good graces of others to get it. No one can control people and/or situations more subtly than a Pisces when the goal is to save himself. The underdog figures big in the Pisces sun sign's scheme of things. When the particular Pisces is on the track, he'll fight like crazy to help a fellow who's down. But when Pisces *feels* like the underdog, others should watch out. They can get taken to the cleaners.

If you are a Piscean who learned self-control at a decent age, you will have little trouble in your career life (however, you may transfer your scattery tendencies to your love life). But all Pisces sun signs should take that word self-control seriously. It is no fiction that drugs and alcohol have helped many of your sign bear the pain—and lose a job.

Moon Sign Pisces:

Rather than pity the poor working girl, pity the poor Pisces moon! With your subconscious cast adrift on a sea of shifting emotions, you Pisces moon people often have more trouble getting it together than anyone. The situation can be quite different, of course, with strong support in the rest of the horoscope. But in general, when the moon is in Pisces there is an irresolute quality to the personality. Easily discouraged, you people with moon in Pisces can suffer from a kind of cosmic dissatisfaction—and not be able to get in touch with what would sate your hunger.

Many of you Pisces moon people "feed yourselves" by taking care of everybody and everything. I call it the "sucker moon," and one does find many bleeding hearts with this astrological configuration. People with moon in Pisces make good vets; you generally cannot even bear to see a pet white mouse suffer from a hangnail. It is usually the human variety of "sick puppies" you support, however.

If you don't fall into this trap, you are free to use some of the most potent success skills in the zodiac. The mystical sense of Pisces operates like a form of ESP when the moon is in this sign. You moon in Pisces people tend to arrive at creative concepts and solutions that often defy logic. It is the "poet's moon" that can astonish by the beauty and clarity of what comes from it.

Even more than the Cancer moon, the Pisces moon has a radar that ranges far and wide, picking up all manner of sensations and dumping them into the subconscious for later creative use. However, it is a mixed blessing; no one suffers like you with moon in Pisces from discordant sights and sounds, which are the norm in many business and professional situations. If you have a Pisces moon, use it well, and keep analgesics handy at all times.

The changeable character of the sign Pisces becomes a love of diversity when the moon is in this sign. Pisces moon people don't need to change their jobs every time they get restless; they can simply redecorate their offices. On a more serious career note, your love of change can be translated into an ability to deal with all types of people. Moon in Pisces people don't fear the unfamiliar or the eccentric; you thrive on it. You have a kind of timidity, but it simply goes away when somebody or something fascinating presents itself.

Pisces is—believe it or not—organized. And when Pisces is the sign of the moon, you possess a natural penchant for order. It makes for clear thinking and a clean desk at the end of the day. Ambition does not run high when the moon is in Pisces because your desire is not for power but for peace. You Pisces moon people are lovely to have around.

Ascendant Sign Pisces:

Pisces on the Ascendant is like an Impressionist painting—all light and color, but easier to discern when you step away from it. However, most people want to get closer to a Pisces Ascendant—you're so fascinating. Part of the fascination you hold for others is your capability to change with the wind, or at will. Pisces rising is the sign of the actor, the true actor whose physical body is only a vehicle for the many different roles he must play. In fact, Pisces rising usually has an incredibly mobile face.

You can see that having a Pisces Ascendant can work two ways in real life. It is an ideal position for certain kinds of work, especially where a great deal of versatility is required. On the other hand, people don't seek out the Pisces Ascendant person when they are looking for a stability symbol. Your whimsical quality may be purely external, depending on the rest of your horoscope, but it is too true that we are most often taken at face value.

You Pisces Ascendant people don't *seem* to mind if you aren't taken seriously; as a matter of fact you probably don't remember it very long. When Pisces is rising, it really does work to make the mind more absent than present—except when it comes to turning on the charm. And the Pisces Ascendant person can turn it on and off at will. Most of you are irresistibly romantic figures. Part of the romance comes from a wispy, wistful quality that your physical body may even deny. (A lot of Pisces Ascendant people are on the stout side.) You just seem to *need* somebody, and no matter who gets close, they generally get hooked. Pisces rising will return the favor in kind, giving lots of attention, affection, and compassion. For as long as it lasts.

This may sound like a sexual/romantic reference, but actually the scenario is often played out in the business world when Pisces rising is one of the principals. The person with Pisces rising rarely has trouble getting hired; and—unless he really screws up—he won't actually get fired. What will happen is his frustrated superiors and co-workers will keep asking, "What went wrong? What did we do that made you lose interest? Why aren't you happy? What can we do for you?" And on, and on.

Some of you with a Pisces Ascendant are rather indolent—*lazy* to put it bluntly. You often put so much effort into your act that there's little energy left for anything else. But, all in all, it's not the worst rising sign to have. Somebody will always buy your violets.

THREE

FINDING YOUR OWN CAREER GROUND:

The Planets and the Midheaven

11

The Midheaven

You should now have a pretty clear picture of the astrological forces that work to make you who you are. But this is only the first part of your "success story": fortunately, astrology is a multilevel discipline that deals not only in the psychology of the individual, but in the probable shape of his life as well. Your horoscope quite plainly maps out where you belong on this increasingly complicated earth—not the actual geographic location, but something more pivotal: your career ground.

Enter the Midheaven, perhaps the richest astrological symbol of them all. To put it to use in planning your career, an explanation of the astrological house system is necessary. You met the houses briefly as the sections of that orange in the description of a horoscope. Now think of the houses as twelve segments of a 360-degree circle, or as twelve even slices of the great pie of life. That is what the houses are, dimensions or "departments" of human experience. The house that falls at the Midheaven of your horoscope indicates in which of life's departments your career lies.

As the twelve zodiacal signs proceed logically and naturally from younger-than-springtime Aries through old-and-wise Pisces, there is also a logic and a sequence to the twelve astrological houses. That round also begins with the first, House of Aries, and ends with the twelfth, House of Pisces. However, it is important to understand that the signs and the houses are not the same. They do correspond to each other in certain respects, but a sign and a house are two entirely different concepts. A zodiacal sign is an *energy force;* an astrological house is a *place*. A house doesn't do anything; it must be acted upon—or rather acted in. The zodiacal sign Aries and the House of Aries have things in common, but the first signifies how one acts, the second, where one acts.

The Midheaven in your horoscope marks off the slice of pie or house that was directly overhead as the great wheel of the zodiac was "stopped in time" at the moment of your birth (in the place of your birth). That Midheaven house represents your apportioned share in the world of work or profession. It is your career ground; it is unique to you and you were "meant" to occupy it. Like the Ascendant, the Midheaven is an elusive point in that it changes signs quickly in a twenty-four-hour period. Understanding the "slice of life" at which the wheel stopped is vital to your success. In the next chapter each career ground or House of the Midheaven is translated into career fields—both broadly and more specifically. To "find your ground," look up the position of your Midheaven in the tables at the back of this book. Since that position is based on the time of day you were born, do everything possible to ascertain that time as closely as you can, to within one hour. (In the tables in the Appendix of this book you will find tips for getting your birth time accurately. However, if all attempts fail, you can gain some useful information by reading the career ground sections that correspond to your sun sign and rising sign.)

Unlike the sun, the moon and the Ascendant, which are personal points in a horoscope, the Midheaven is most often described as a destiny point—*the* destiny point. This reputation derives, like all other astrological conclusions, from observations, thousands of observations by thousands of people over thousands of years (one of the reasons astrology is called the "observed science"). At a very early point in time, astronomical (hence astrological) calculations became quite precise: Stonehenge, for example, has been described as a giant astrological "computer." Therefore, the elusive Midheaven—the highest point the sun reaches in its daily path through the sky—got a lot of attention right from the beginning. And right from the beginning astronomers/astrologers noticed that the Midheaven had an uncanny connection to a person's role in life.

Until fairly recently most people didn't have much choice about roles or what they could do to earn their keep; kings produced kings, shoemakers bred shoemakers. That you have a career—let alone a choice of career—is quite a modern notion. As times changed, the significance of the Midheaven in earthly life became better defined. The fuzzy, generalized view of it as the destiny point took more concrete shape, and the Midheaven was reborn as the point of profession, the point of status, the point of public performance. Your Midheaven is you in the open—exposed, you might say, for all the world to see. It doesn't make much difference how "private" your life or your career is; you are judged by what you do and how well you do it. Those who judge you may be few in number, but they nevertheless represent your world.

Since the Midheaven is at the top of the chart or horoscope, you might think of it as the top branches of a tree, a tree in full flower. The Midheaven's opposite point—the Nadir—is the roots—your roots, the comfortable, memory-soaked place from which you came. The Nadir in your chart tells a lot about the kinds of things you need to relax and feel at home, and will come into play later on in your Success System. Now it is important for what it represents in terms of polarity (what a lot of astrology's symbols are all about). As the Nadir in your chart is your private sector, its opposite pole—the Midheaven—is your public sector.

Despite the fact that I have defined the Midheaven as a destiny or life-path point rather than a personal point in your horoscope, there is one way in which the Midheaven is an indicator of personality or, more properly, of character. The Midheaven sign embodies qualities that we admire, however unconsciously. The Midheaven is what is important to us, what we respect, and therefore what we hope to incorporate into our own lives. Ideally we incorporate the Midheaven's qualities through the life work or career route we choose. When you think about your real aspirations in terms of the person you would like to become, you are reflecting the influence of the Midheaven in your horoscope.

The Midheaven is the starting point of the tenth house of the natural or archetypal horoscope. The tenth house is the natural House of Capricorn, the sign that is associated with the planet Saturn. Saturn, about which you'll learn more later, is (among many other things) the planet of adulthood. (Some say Saturn-influenced people are "old" at birth.) We each have to deal with the Saturn of our own horoscope according to the particular sign and house in which it falls in our chart. But in terms of anyone's horoscope, the saturnine character of the Midheaven means that the Midheaven is something to be achieved through time and maturity. Many people never achieve their Midheaven, no matter what chronological age they achieve; others reach for the Midheaven and arrive at it (and success) when they attain emotional maturity, which can be at any age.

One of the goals of the Success System is to help you "grow into" your Midheaven naturally—and in good time. "Naturally" means by choosing the career space you were meant to occupy; "in good time" means without the aimless sideways movement that can delay success—and maturity. The bottom line in terms of the Success System is that you would do well to have a healthy respect for your Midheaven and what it is telling you about a very important part of your life.

Like all transcendant symbolic languages, astrology resists translation—particularly by imperfect humans using an imprecise human language. In dealing with the zodiacal signs as indicators of personality, one is still in reasonably shallow water, because it is simply substituting abstraction for abstraction. What is more imprecise than calling a Gemini capricious? How capricious? About what? Where capricious? And when? Pinning that same Gemini principle down to the specifics of a desk, an office, and a paycheck is quite another matter. The water suddenly gets very deep, and the shore looks farther away.

I have given each Midheaven house a solid structure, possibly too solid. Before describing that structure, therefore, I must tell you that when you have reached your Midheaven house you've gotten to the very heart of the Success System. And it's time to spell out the fact that the system is a process—a process in which you participate. However many fields are "assigned" to your career ground, and however many specific jobs are listed therein, they are still only possibilities—and of necessity limited in number. Your House of the Midheaven gives you guidelines, and it is *you* who must put those guidelines to work, bringing your practical intelligence to bear on them. There is magic in the system to be sure, but it is magic of a cooperative nature. Not to understand this point is to fall into the ultimate absurdity: "What do you mean I'm not right for this job? My astrologer said I was." So don't let the structure your friendly astrologer has given your Midheaven house get in the way of your own imagination—or your own logic. If you can't draw, you can't draw and that's that. To run out and apply for an illustrator's job because it happens to turn up as one possibility in your "success profile" would be like going after a small straw in a high wind.

12

The Planets

Keys to the Midheaven Houses

Up to now you have been looking at the signs of the zodiac as energies, modes of perception, and patterns of behavior—in short, as symbols of personality. Now, in looking at the Houses of the Midheaven, you have to make a switchover to thinking about those same signs as symbols of space, as different career fields. The planets are the key here. Those very substantial and very real heavenly bodies unlock some of the most fundamental meanings of the signs of the zodiac—especially as they relate to the houses.

Every planet in our solar system (including the sun and moon) embodies a wealth of myth, tradition, and legend. The riches are so great, it would be impossible to do them justice here. However, in the next section you will find that each Midheaven house description leads off with a specific planet's "résumé." Even a quick glance at that résumé will give you new insight into the sign of your Midheaven house—and light up your own career space quite clearly.

You may have heard that each sign of the zodiac is ruled by a planet. The planet that rules a sign has been assigned to it by tradition—but not arbitrarily. Very briefly, here's how it happened. Earliest man observed that some things in the sky stood still and other were "wanderers" (the root meaning of the word planet). It became clear that the wanderers took regular routes—that is, had cycles—and that phases in those cycles corresponded to events on earth, as well as to human behavior. After having compacted several thousand years of discovery into a couple of sentences, I'll compound the insult to history by saying that people/astrologers simply began to put earth and sky together. Finally, since certain planets "acted" in a similar fashion to certain signs, it seemed not only logical, but inevitable, that they should be matched up.

At one point in time the planets were actually believed to be gods—gods with real power to intervene in human events. This factor played a large part in the eventual planetary assignments. Because Jupiter (Jove) seemed wise and fair, he was a natural companion to Sagittarius. Mercury (Hermes) moved fast and pulled some fancy tricks in his orbit—like Gemini. The Moon Goddess, by whatever name she was known, seemed as mysterious as the process by which people reproduced themselves, and thereby became associated with the fertile, female-related sign of Cancer.

And so it went, through the signs and planets. In essence what it all means is that certain planets partake of the same qualities as certain signs; a planet is a "concentrate" or distillation of a sign.

Up until Uranus (first of the three "modern" planets) was discovered in the 1700s, there were only seven planets and twelve signs; so five planets had to double in brass. Now, with Uranus, Neptune, and Pluto up there to do their work, only two planets rule more than one sign (Venus and Mercury). Some astrologers believe there are two more planets out there and that when we finally discover them there will be the neatest possible line-up: twelve planets and twelve signs. For now, we'll work with what we have. As you explore the Midheaven house of your career space, I think you will find the information about the planet that rules that space a real eye-opener.

The planets are also the key to the sequence in which the Houses of the Midheaven are treated in the next section. Obeying the order of the solar system, I have started with the house the sun rules—the House of Leo—and followed the planets outward from the sun. The houses of Mercury, whose orbit is closest to the sun, come next; the House of Scorpio, which is ruled by Pluto, comes last, as that planet's orbit is farthest from the sun. The orbit of the earth is of course represented by the moon and the House of

Cancer. Most everyone has seen a model or a drawing of the solar system—with the sun at the center of more or less concentric circles. That is the picture to keep in mind when you locate your Midheaven house. It is important, because the closer planets in general rule the earlier and more primary concerns of man, and the more distant planets, the later or more "sophisticated" concerns.

13

The Midheaven and the System

Your Midheaven house is a whole which is greater than the sum of its parts, a "gestalt" to be comprehended in toto before it can be parceled out into specific jobs. If you diagramed a Midheaven house chapter you would get an inverted pyramid—a broad spectrum of general principles at the top, career areas in the middle, specifics at the bottom. Arriving at the job that is meant for you is therefore a deductive process (from the general to the specific), and as in all deductive processes, if the general premises are not thoroughly assimilated, the conclusions can be weak. That is why the *concept* of your Midheaven house is so important. Once you understand that concept completely, you will be able to recognize your calling, no matter what specific job guise it is wearing.

You get your first clues to the gestalt of your Midheaven house from the description of the planet that rules your space. Next, you will find out what kind of ground your Midheaven house is—"open ground," "solid ground," "far ground," etc. Quite obviously these are not literal descriptions. Your career ground is a conceptual idea: the fact that the House of Virgo is "partitioned" underscores its connection with specialization. To give each Midheaven house's ground more definition, I've listed some of the integrating ideas that form the common career themes.

Next come the IPT clusters that belong to your Midheaven

house: I for ideas, P for people, T for things/materials/substances. These IPT clusters are called such because in all careers one is dealing with ideas, people, and/or things. An IPT cluster is more inclusive than a specific career or profession, and can embrace many. For example, in the diagnostic/healing arts any given IPT cluster can (and often does) turn up in more than one Midheaven house. There is crossover because different phases of a cluster belong to different Houses of the Midheaven. I've given indications of those differences by breaking down the IPT clusters into some of the more specific careers and professions that are most often connected with that house.

Astrology has given us some quite clear indicators of which careers belong to which house in the things ruled by the sign/planet of that house. The principle of rulership, or the universal law of correspondences, extends to just about every detail of our world, both large and small. It is through these details, selected for their relevance to career, that you will find some of your most valuable information about where you belong. It is worth more than cocktail party conversation, for instance, to know that Gemini/Mercury rules transit and traffic, while Jupiter/Sagittarius rules scientific publications. (I will admit, however, that I've thrown in a few rulerships just for fun.)

Specific Jobs

The personal points (sun sign, moon sign, and Ascendant) now enter the picture—and the system. Just as the personal points show your success skills, they can be used to indicate where you belong in a particular field. Therefore, each Midheaven house is sectioned off into the twelve zodiacal signs, and within each of these sections I've "assigned" jobs. Those that fall under the signs of your personal points belong to you.

Two things become immediately obvious. The first is that these job assignments are given as guideposts or benchmarks rather than as hard-and-fast conclusions. The second thing you will quickly see is that since personal points can fall into as many as three signs, you may have quite a few job assignments. That is true, and they do not carry equal weight. That is why I've devised a simple job-rating system:

- If it is your sun sign that is assigned to a specific job, give that job three stars.
- If it is your moon sign, give that job two stars.
- If it is your Ascendant, give the job one star.
- If both sun and moon are in the same sign, the job earns six stars.
- If both sun and Ascendant are in the same sign, give five stars.
- If both moon and Ascendant are in the same sign, it's a four-star job.

If by some chance you are one of those rare birds who has all three personal points in the same sign, you can stop counting stars and start adding up salary figures. (Although you might just be too much of one thing for your own good.)

Double Destiny

Within each House of the Midheaven, one zodiacal sign is noted as "double destiny"—the sign that corresponds to that particular house (i.e., the sign of Aries within the House of Aries). This is relevant if you have the sun or the moon in the same sign as your House of the Midheaven. In astronomical terms it means that at the moment of your birth, the sun or the moon was at the very zenith of the sky, and therefore at the top of your natal horoscope. The ancients believed that the child with such a horoscope was no ordinary mortal; in actual practice it sometimes happens that this configuration does actually correspond with fame and/or fortune (equally often, infamy). If you have the sun or the moon in your Midheaven house sign, it is possible you are "destiny's child"; with both planets there, you have a double whammy. (The Ascendant obviously can never coincide with the Midheaven since by their nature these two points fall approximately 90 degrees apart in the wheel of the zodiac.)

At this point some of you are probably depressed. You've got nothing assigned to you higher than three-star jobs (your sun sign jobs) and none of them appeal or apply to you. Rejoice! Think of it this way: you've got more latitude than a lot of other people, and there's plenty of room to move around within your space.

A Final Note

One of the greatest virtues of such an ancient and transcendental system as astrology is that it can be applied to human affairs at any point in time. The world turns every day, and takes a few lurches about every other day. Since the job/career market is more like shifting sand than solid rock, the effects on it are pronounced. About the most steadying prop anyone can take along on a trip across those sands is the confidence that you know what you were meant to do.

Since the span of our active, productive years gets longer and longer, more can happen during the time we still have to do something. In fact, historians and social scientists tell us the most significant (and disturbing) factor about our era is how fast things change. If you look at a time line, you will observe we appear to be approaching hyper-speed. What does that mean in terms of individual achievement? Just this: to be successful you have to be virtually shock-proof. In fact, the secret of success that I put right at the top of the list is readiness for the new. True, some of us are more flexible than others (both astrologically and psychologically speaking); but the capacity to react quickly and make fast turn-arounds when conditions change is not unavailable to anyone. The security of purpose your astrological profile—particularly your Midheaven—can give you is worth more than any pension plan the most generous company can offer. And it is the most valuable insurance against ever being out of work, a phrase that to me simply means one is temporarily not on a payroll (including one's own).

If you interpret your Midheaven house correctly and understand what you're really all about, you'll never be out of work, but only out of phase, a temporary condition in which one is preparing for the next leap forward and the next adventure. Your operative principle can be put to work at anything, anywhere. Not that your choice of career fields is unlimited; quite the opposite, in fact, because the boundaries of your Midheaven house are there for the purpose of defining the broad career fields and IPT clusters you belong in. But some of the most successful people in the world have created their own jobs. They have sensed a need, spotted a trend, and then applied their operative principle to it. I'm not recommending that you walk in off the street to a major company and tell them their troubles are over because you can do "job x" if "job x" doesn't exist. It's more subtle and complicated than that, as you'll see.

Now, on to the Houses of the Midheaven.

14

Midheaven House of Leo

The Sun, the Ruling Planet

In the Egyptian Book of the Dead, there is a passage that reads like the beginning of Genesis, with "Ra," the sun, substituted for "God." To the Egyptians Ra *was* God, creator of heaven and earth and all things. The sun, either as God made manifest or as the God principle, was chief deity to many early people. Brahma to the Hindus, Mithra to the Persians, Adonai to the Phoenicians, Sol and Helios to the early Romans and Greeks, respectively, the sun was literally and figuratively the center of life on earth. It was both feared and revered for its power—to create, to heal, to destroy.

It would have been difficult for early man to ignore the fact that the sun called all the shots, marking off the day from dawn to sunset, causing darkness and fear when it vanished. Even today we are all but powerless in the sun's presence, as in times of drought. We know now that the sun affects earthly life in other ways, as well, from causing cancer to interfering with radio communications.

In astrology, the omnipotent sun is the little bit of God in each of us. Its symbol—a circle with a dot in the middle—is a shorthand way of describing this. The circle is the one, the endless, the everything; the dot is the atom of divinity in the individual, which permits growth. The sun's rulership of Leo gives that sign great force. Yes, the sign of Leo as a personality indicator is often associated with egotism. But when Leo is connected with the Midheaven and the destiny, that self-centeredness translates into centralized energy. Leo at the Midheaven means a calling where one is the nucleus—a career or profession where it is possible to put one's personal stamp on the work. Fidel Castro, Johnny Carson, and Sigmund Freud are diverse but prime examples of House of Leo destinies. If you have Leo at the Midheaven, you are meant to be a source of power—a steady generator of heat and energy that turns everything on, and sheds light all around it.

That sounds like a tall order for any human; but many people with Leo at the Midheaven do it every day unconsciously, almost effortlessly. Fame does not necessarily follow, nor does a six-figure salary; but the principle applies at every level of operation. There are specific careers associated with House of Leo to be sure, and though they vary, there are common "solar" themes. However, as you examine those careers, keep this in mind: you are not actually meant to play God, but others may ask it of you. If it is any consolation, remember that with the sun behind you, you can cast a tall shadow.

Characteristics of House of Leo Career Ground: Central, Bright, "Hot."

Integrating Principles of Leo Career Ground: Vitalization • • • self-expression • • • being at the heart • • • externalization • • • personalization • • • grandiosity • • • pleasures • • • inherited power • • • aspiration • • • organization • • • confidence • • • creativity • • • pride • • • ambition • • • generosity • • • individuality • • • humanity • • • gilding • • • autocracy • • • showmanship • • • buttressing • • • determination • • • possessiveness • • • sense of drama • • • stability • • • the territorial imperative.

The Major IPT Clusters/Careers of the House of Leo

Public administration/Public life: all levels of government.
Amusements/Pleasures: all phases, including speculation.
Concerns of children: especially the very young.
Corporate Management: all types of businesses and industries.
Diagnostic/Healing arts: big-money specialties, including surgery; counseling.

Luxury trades: all phases, particularly fashion and retailing.
Money and finance: all phases earning and purchasing.
Performing arts: all specialties, particularly the theater.
Philanthropy: all paid positions.
Visual arts: both fine and decorative.

A Selection of Things Ruled by the Sun/Leo

theaters • • • thrones • • • sun rooms • • • sporting events • • • children • • • arenas • • • the spinal column • • • stock speculation • • • lovers • • • playgrounds • • • impresarios • • • organizers • • • parties • • • games of chance • • • golf courses • • • the heart and circulatory system • • • directorates • • • cinemas • • • things of gold and gold mines • • • castles • • • schoolrooms • • • high society • • • showboats • • • pregnancy • • • holidays • • • ovens • • • lion tamers • • • money changers • • • furs • • • autobiographies • • • showy buildings • • • lighting specialists.

Some Specific Jobs for Each Sun, Moon, and Ascendant Sign with House of Leo at the Midheaven

Aries

Heart surgeon; dancer/choreographer for theater or movies; director of playground programs in a large city; professional gambler.

Taurus

Head of day nursery or preschool program; head of fund-raising for charity; dress designer; throat specialist.

Gemini

Editor-in-chief, theater arts book club; nightclub entertainer or owner; scriptwriter; personnel director for a large corporation.

Cancer

Chief of pediatrics in a large hospital; obstetrician/gynecologist; financial officer for movie studio; owner of fast-food chain.

Leo (Double Destiny)

Actor/actress in legitimate theater; president or chairman of the board of corporation; mayor, governor, or high government official; gold trader.

Virgo

Head dietician in a public school system; internist; financial secretary for a charity; owner of fine crafts shop; high position in Health and Welfare Department.

Libra

Public relations for charitable organization; designer clothes merchandise manager or fine retailer; kidney specialist; art teacher for young children.

Scorpio

Chief financial officer for an insurance company; sex-change surgeon; child psychiatrist; owner of a chain of fashion boutiques.

Sagittarius

Venture capitalist; owner/manager of a gambling casino; chief of imports for a fur manufacturer; dance teacher for young children.

Capricorn

Chief of orthopedic surgery; purchasing agent for fine jewelry manufacturer; museum-quality sculptor; owner of a dating service.

Aquarius

Founder and administrator of a charitable organization; solo instrumentalist; owner/operator of a flight school; chief of radiology in a major hospital.

Pisces

Actor/actress in theater or movies; museum-quality painter; display director for luxury retailer; amusement park owner/operator.

15

Midheaven Houses of Gemini and Virgo

Mercury, the Ruling Planet

Hottest, quickest-moving of the planets, the planet closest to the sun, Mercury has been intimately involved in human affairs since it was first observed early in human prehistory. Probably because humans identified with this planet that followed the sun as closely as they did, they assigned it rulership over two "human" signs. Did it ever occur to you that the Gemini twins and the Virgo virgin are people symbols rather than animal symbols like the ram, the crab, the lion? I am not implying that Geminis and Virgos are any less bestial than the rest of us, but the human concept is important to understanding Mercury—and your career space.

Mercury represents the most important single faculty that separates man from the other animals: reason. Mercury is the principle that distinguishes between thinking and instinct, organizing the impulses the mind receives from the universe into realized projects on earth.

All of the legends about Mercury associate him with information, learning, and wisdom in some form. The Egyptians called Mercury Thoth, and gave him the job of scribe to the gods—"keeper" of the divine books. In order to get his information, Mercury had to move around a lot and move fast. No surprise, then, that to the Hindus he was son of the wind god, and could by his airy nature get into any nook or cranny. There are connections between Mercury and the Buddha as he represents divine wisdom, the ancient principle of *budhi* or enlightenment. By the time the Greeks latched on to Mercury it was obvious he had a lot to say, so they dubbed him Hermes—god of the persuasive tongue. As Zeus's messenger, he had wings on his head and his heels to allow him to move with all deliberate speed when carrying his lord's wishes and words. Mercurius, the Roman name, is the root of the one we use today. In Rome, Mercury was given all due honors and recognized as a consummate orator and teacher.

Through their common rulership by Mercury, the signs Gemini and Virgo share the principle of active intelligence brought down to earth and applied to the affairs of men. In Gemini that intelligence is used in reacting to experience, recording or relating it, connecting ideas with ideas and people with people. Some examples of House of Gemini "connectors" are Rona Barrett and Walt Disney on the light side, naturalist Rachel Carson with a more serious message.

In Virgo the Mercury principle works itself out in the analyzing of ideas and circumstances in order to improve them. In career terms, Mercury in Gemini is the transmitter of earthly ideas and things; Mercury in Virgo implements them. From this it follows that House of Gemini careers often involve the spoken and written word, while House of Virgo careers are more geared toward experimentation and practical application, as in the cases of Eleanor Roosevelt, Gloria Steinem, and est founder Werner Erhard.

Since in the House of Gemini one enlightens people and in the House of Virgo one serves them, both are indicators of quite earthly destinies. By "earthly" I do not mean dull, but rather having to do with the here and now: that is why Gemini's destiny is near ground, Virgo's narrow ground. If you have either of these houses at the Midheaven, you are meant to be concerned with this world, not some other. In case the more soulful among you find this destiny less than inspiring, let me remind you of a few things about Mercury. He is swift of foot, silver of tongue, nimble and dextrous, clever (often brilliant), and always on the move. Of all the gods the human mind ever invented, Mercury probably got the most exciting jobs of all—and thoroughly enjoyed them.

Midheaven House of Gemini

Characteristics of House of Gemini Career Ground: nearby, neighboring, interconnected.

Integrating Principles of Gemini Career Ground:
Linking • • • connection • • • dissemination • • • this versus that • • • reasoning • • • bridging • • • nervousness • • • cause and effect • • • joining • • • association • • • articulation • • • adroitness • • • cunning • • • dexterity • • • distribution • • • questioning • • • responding • • • trading • • • swiftness • • • the herald • • • jargon • • • novelty • • • the ephemeral • • • curiosity • • • sending • • • moving • • • distinguishing • • • intellectualism.

The Major IPT Clusters/Careers of the House of Gemini

Commerce: retailing in all phases.
Communication of news message: information in all phases, all media.
Entertaining or role playing: particularly comedy and mimicry.
Language arts and trades: writing and speaking.
Numbers: primarily accounting and bookkeeping.
Persuading arts and trades: public relations; sales (direct and indirect); advertising; politics.
Scholarship, especially teaching: all phases, particularly languages and elementary and secondary education.
Technology: computer field, primarily software.
Travel and transportation industry: all phases.
Visual arts: primarily graphic and decorative.

A Selection of Things Ruled by Mercury/Gemini

Air mail • • • ambidexterity • • • buses • • • broadcasters • • • pulmonary area • • • respiratory system • • • books and bookstores

• • • court reporters • • • train conductors • • • editors • • • gossip • • • handwriting • • • letters • • • libraries • • • merchants • • • nervous system • • • novelists • • • things that come in pairs • • • printers • • • photoengravers • • • primary and secondary schools • • • traffic • • • typewriters • • • visiting • • • speech impediments • • • reporters • • • repair men • • • storytelling • • • shipping and receiving.

Some Specific Jobs for Each Sun, Moon, and Ascendant Sign with House of Gemini at the Midheaven

Aries
Sales manager for a computer manufacturer; test pilot for aircraft manufacturer; high school physical education teacher; editor, textbook publisher.

Taurus
Preschool or kindergarten teacher; musical comedy writer or performer; soft goods merchandise manager for a department store; menu planner for a cruise ship or airline.

Gemini (Double Destiny)
Ventriloquist or voice-over specialist for radio or television commercials; society news editor for newspaper; book distributor or bookstore owner; foreign language teacher.

Cancer
Graphic designer at an advertising agency; cost accountant for paper manufacturer or printer; political news analyst; food editor.

Leo
News bureau chief for a newspaper or wire service; drama teacher/coach at a high school or college; chief financial officer in a computer firm or airline.

Virgo
Drama or film critic for a newspaper or magazine; head of computer programming; speechwriter at a political public relations firm; philology teacher.

Libra
Fashion editor for a newspaper or magazine; interior decorator at a motel chain; speech or voice coach; public relations for luxury retailer.

Scorpio
Obituary writer at a newspaper or magazine; novelist; classical languages teacher; head of internal audit for a retail chain.

Sagittarius
Head of air traffic control; independent sales representative in a computer firm; resident scholar in foreign university; singer/dancer in musical theater.

Capricorn
Editor/publisher of a newspaper or magazine; administrator of tour programs; department store president; political candidate.

Aquarius
Radio or television announcer; head of shipping for export manufacturer; lung specialist; science fiction writer.

Pisces
Teacher of English literature in high school or college; creative director of an advertising agency; speech therapist/counselor; film or television comedian.

Midheaven House of Virgo

Characteristics of House of Virgo Career Ground:
narrow, concentrated, partitioned.

Integrating Principles of Virgo Career Ground:
Specialization • • • craftsmanship • • • ministering • • • taking apart • • • studiousness • • • categorizing • • • refining • • • making

better • • • dedication • • • separating • • • criticism • • • caretaking • • • purifying • • • serving • • • observation • • • effacing of self • • • intellectualism • • • precision • • • obedience • • • perfectionism • • • microscopic vision • • • invention • • • pragmatism • • • detail • • • health • • • exactingness • • • discrimination • • • duty/responsibility • • • realism • • • what works • • • sanitizing.

The Major IPT Clusters/Careers of the House of Virgo

Agricultural resources: many phases.
Animals: care and breeding.
Diagnostic/healing arts: most types of medical practice and research, nursing, paramedical services, and therapy.
Education and educational institutions: most phases.
Inspecting and improving arts and trades: primarily health and safety.
Manual arts and trades: all types of craftsmanship.
Numbers: accounting and bookkeeping.
Research and lab work: all types, particularly chemical.
Service arts and trades: particularly food and lodging.
Technology: primarily engineering.

A Selection of Things Ruled by Mercury/Virgo

The abdomen • • • animals in general • • • the bowels • • • chemists • • • closets • • • clerical work • • • dental hygiene • • • desks • • • critics • • • dry cleaners • • • gardens • • • poultry • • • groceries • • • the harvest • • • public health and health in general • • • relief • • • societies • • • draftsmen • • • inspectors • • • crafts • • • mathematics • • • medicine • • • nutrition • • • pantries • • • dispensaries • • • restaurants • • • sanitation • • • satire • • • sewing • • • the spleen • • • nursing • • • teachers • • • locked rooms • • • physical culture • • • the hands • • • libraries • • • maps • • • menus • • • working people • • • laundries • • • the intestines • • • inferiors • • • weaving • • • filing • • • defects.

Some Specific Jobs for Each Sun, Moon, and Ascendant Sign with House of Virgo at the Midheaven

Aries
Head of elevator safety inspection of a large city; abdominal surgeon; chief draftsman for civil engineering firm; technical director for the legitimate stage.

Taurus
Pianist or piano teacher; biochemical research; chief accountant at a factoring firm; domestic services administrator for a hotel or motel chain.

Gemini
Information officer in a public health program; teacher of writing techniques; lung specialist; actor or comic.

Cancer
Financial administrator of a welfare program; restaurant health inspector; writer of prose; oceanographic research.

Leo
Fine jewelry design and manufacture; head of medical records for a hospital or nursing home; government agricultural program; drama teacher or coach.

Virgo (Double Destiny)
Inventor; nutrition expert; editor-in-chief of a technical publication; head of cancer research program.

Libra
Drama or art critic; technical advisor in a fashion manufacturing firm; actress; stylist for food photography.

Scorpio
Sanitation engineer; veterinary surgeon; history professor; professional athlete.

Sagittarius

Owner of a dog training school; research in language learning techniques; mapmaker; dancer for ballet or musical theater.

Capricorn

Geologist or geology professor; sculptor; chief administrator in a city school system; orthopedist.

Aquarius

Head of library services at a university; electrical engineering and research; project planner for a public housing program; instrumentalist.

Pisces

Occupational therapist; literary critic; podiatrist or shoe salesman; songwriter.

16

Midheaven Houses of Taurus and Libra

Venus, the Ruling Planet

It's not just because the arithmetic doesn't work out right (ten planets and twelve signs) that Venus has two roles to play. There are and have always been two faces to the lovely planet: one sacred (Libra), one profane (Taurus). This is not to say that all Librans are saints and all Taureans are gross. The problem is that we have abused the words sacred and profane so that their real meanings are obscured. The sacred side of Venus as manifested in Libra refers to the ideal cosmic marriage of the male and female principles in the universe. Perfect balance—completeness, if you will. The profane (Taurus) aspect of Venus might better be described as mundane, because it is the basic nurturing quality of Mother Earth that permits all natural things to grow in this world. In some mythologies Venus is the daughter of the moon, and symbolizes much of what issues from the great Mother, love, kindness, patience, and beauty.

All of the legends about Venus rank her high on the cosmic scale. To the Hindus as *Laksmi* and the Greeks as Aphrodite, she sprang forth from the sea and is bathed in the profound symbolism of primordial water. (You may be familiar with Botticelli's painting of "Birth of Venus" with Venus skimming the surface of the sea.) The beauty of Venus is usually defined as the beauty of generosity; she is the unselfish giver of life's pleasures and bounties. (When Venus is especially prominent in an individual horoscope, you have a knockout—either male or female).

The Romans, with their penchant for passing out duties, made Venus patroness of the arts in addition to her more ancient rulership of the "creature comforts" of earthly existence, such as food, clothing, and the home. Though Venus is hardly two-faced (a more genuine planet you won't meet), she does have two complementary roles. Venus in Taurus stands for material growth and prosperity; Venus in Libra stands for spiritual and aesthetic progress.

Sexually speaking, Venus is the perfect man or woman; that is, Venus is both the charm and grace that attract, and the lusty physical desires that hold. Since Venus is a "feminine" planet, let's stick with that concept to see how it elucidates the career spaces of Taurus and Libra. The dependable, mothering role of women belongs to the House of Taurus, and with it all things and activities that comfort, promote growth, tend to basic needs and material well-being. The extended meaning of the Venus/Taurus principle includes the enrichment of life on earth. Some of this house enriched it in very different ways: Marilyn Monroe, Margaret Sanger, and Mies Van Der Rohe.

In the House of Libra we meet Venus, the courtesan (a perfectly respectable calling, by the way). It is the Venus who welcomes, smiles, entertains graciously—sharing her perfectly balanced and aesthetically beautiful world with all who enter. She is not without sex, but it is subordinated to her more social charms. Though Venus/Libra has exquisite taste, she is actually quite democratic. In Greece one of Venus/Aphrodite's titles was "Pandemos" or "of all the people." Venus/Libra exemplifies the principles of negotiation, beautification, social consciousness, and entertainment. Many entertainers, among them Jackie Gleason and Mickey Rooney, have House of Libra at the Midheaven. Jurist Earl Warren and feminist leader Betty Friedan illustrate quite different dimensions of the same space.

Within these two broad-stroke pictures of Venus there are many nuances, hence many callings; Venus is a subtle planet. Oddly enough, though Taurus is the "feminine" sign ruled by Venus and Libra the "masculine" sign, I reverse them somewhat when I think in terms of career space. This is probably because the House of Taurus is a quite solid, earthy domain and House of Libra seems like "lighter" space. At any rate, as you explore your Midheaven house, be it Taurus or Libra, remember that Venus is a very well-rounded cosmic lady—beautiful in every sense of the word. She will be only too happy to show you around, and will probably fix you a great meal as well, complete with candlelight and sweet music.

Midheaven House of Taurus

Characteristics of House of Taurus Career Ground: personal, basic, warm, and comfortable.

Integrating Principles of Taurus Career Ground

Fundamentals • • • physical senses and sense pleasures • • • nurturing • • • indulgence • • • comforts and comforting • • • personalizing • • • building up • • • gathering in • • • leniency • • • things of value • • • possessions • • • using • • • security needs • • • growing • • • the voice • • • fertility • • • eroticism • • • unification • • • kindness • • • attachment • • • the material • • • stabilization • • • perpetuating • • • patience • • • indulgence • • • warmth • • • tenacity • • • affability • • • calmness • • • conservation • • • luxury • • • relaxation.

The Major IPT Clusters/Careers of the House of Taurus

Building arts and trades: all phases of construction.
Buying/selling/collecting: things of value (art and jewelry); real estate.
Diagnostic/healing arts: nursing; counseling (especially children); diseases of ear, nose, and throat.
Domestic arts and sciences: all phases of food and clothing.
Environment/natural sciences/trades: agriculture; horticulture; farming; animal husbandry.

Life-sustaining, life-promoting professions.
Managing/earning money (for self and others): all phases of banking and finance; stocks, bonds, and all types of securities.
Performing arts, both individual and group: music, all phases, especially vocal.
Personal adornment: all phases of fashion and beauty trades.
Public service: federal, state, and local administration.
Visual/decorative arts: painting, interior design, and decoration.

A Selection of Things Ruled by Venus/Taurus

Acoustics • • • birds • • • botany • • • cabinetmakers • • • delicacies • • • art stores • • • banks • • • cash and checks • • • pastel colors • • • confectioners • • • the throat and neck • • • the thyroid gland • • • the cervical vertebrae • • • landscape gardeners • • • loan companies • • • pianos • • • stables • • • precious stones • • • florists • • • vocal cords • • • pigs • • • sense of taste • • • fragrances • • • wheat • • • music • • • shoes • • • storerooms • • • rings • • • emeralds • • • dairies • • • pastures • • • suitcases • • • maypoles • • • love/passion • • • furniture polish • • • bread • • • linen.

Some Specific Jobs for Each Sun, Moon, and Ascendant Sign with House of Taurus at the Midheaven

Aries

An independent real estate dealer; director of public safety program in city or state government; administrator of nursing services for a hospital or nursing home; investment counselor to widows and orphans; throat surgeon.

Taurus (Double Destiny)

Dairy farmer or stock breeder; bank president; vocalist or speech teacher; otiolaryngologist; head of construction firm; fashion designer.

Gemini

Editor/writer for fashion or art magazine; lyricist or singer; owner of flowers- or candy-by-wire service; publicity director for mutual funds company.

Cancer

Bakery owner or administrator; pediatrics nurse or physician; financial officer for major firm; art collector or dealer; owner of jewelry or fashion boutique.

Leo

Musical comedy star; administrator of food and food/service programs for city or state school system; owner of fashion manufacturing firm; real estate mogul.

Virgo

Senior draftsman for construction firm; perfume chemist or tester; senior tax accountant for a loan company; voice or music critic.

Libra

Public relations representative for singer, musical group, or theater; head of modeling or cosmetics firm; legal counselor to investment group; florist or landscape gardener.

Scorpio

Senior partner in a securities firm; genetics research or livestock breeder; individual instrumentalist on piano or violin; child psychiatrist.

Sagittarius

Head of securities investment for multinational firm; administrator for state or federal agriculture department; supervisor of airport construction; legal advisor to nursing home or food processor.

Capricorn

Securities and investment analyst; real estate tax assessor for city or state; financial administrator for a theater group or opera house; building materials purchasing agent in a construction firm.

Aquarius

Music composer or conductor; director of urban renewal projects; contemporary jewelry designer; director of youth agricultural projects.

Pisces

Fine artist or sculptor; scenic designer; director of correctional or mental health facilities for city or state; fashion model or fashion photographer.

Midheaven House of Libra

Characteristics of House of Libra Career Ground: shared, balanced, ornamental.

Integrating Principles of Libra Career Ground:

Sharing • • • relating • • • marrying • • • partnering • • • adjusting • • • comparing • • • reasoning • • • give and take • • • harmony • • • equilibrium • • • cordiality • • • peacemaking • • • idealism • • • pliancy • • • sociability • • • beautification • • • gratification • • • pleasing • • • justice • • • romance • • • cooperation • • • equity • • • adjudication • • • discrimination • • • objectivity • • • refinement • • • impressionability • • • finesse • • • negotiation • • • acceptance.

The Major IPT Clusters/Careers of the House of Libra:

Advocacy and the persuasive arts: most phases of law; selling (mainly indirect); public relations; politics.
Communications arts: writing; advertising in the creative phases.
Cultural activities: teaching, especially liberal arts.
Diplomatic arts: foreign service, labor relations and arbitration.
Entertaining and role playing: all phases of acting.
Evaluating and adjusting arts and trades: insurance; quality control; appraising.
Fine arts: all phases.
General and personal aesthetics: fashion and beauty fields; decorating; graphic arts; retail buying.
Group improvement: social work.
Hospitality and the leisure arts and services: travel; hotel and resort management.

A Selection of Things Ruled by Venus/Libra

Actors and actresses • • • alliances • • • beauty salons and beauticians • • • bedrooms • • • boutiques • • • contracts • • • dressmakers • • • kidneys and the urinary tract • • • fashion • • • tailors • • • ovaries • • • receptionists • • • social functions • • • dilettantes • • • divorces • • • furniture • • • jugglers • • • lawsuits and litigation • • • love and affection • • • musicales • • • negotiation • • • poetry • • • the internal reproductive system • • • dressing rooms • • • scales • • • lumbar region of spine • • • vasomotor system • • • veins • • • vines • • • wigs • • • sororities • • • sachets • • • ornaments.

Some Specific Jobs for Each Sun, Moon, and Ascendant Sign with House of Libra at the Midheaven

Aries

Trial lawyer for accident claims; psychiatric social worker; slapstick comedian; merchandise manager for furniture.

Taurus

Fashion illustrator; chef or maitre d'hotel at a restaurant or resort; public relations expert for a singer or musical group; history or art teacher.

Gemini

Press attaché at a foreign embassy or consulate; information office work for a legal aid society; jingle writer in an advertising agency; book buyer for a department store.

Cancer

Birth control adviser to young people; quality control at a food processing plant; fashion designer; politician.

Leo

Courtroom litigator for divorce and tax cases; actor in movies or legitimate theater; fashion merchandise manager; chief of staff in foreign service.

Virgo

Insurance adjuster; interior designer specializing in use of space; stand-up satirist or comic; case worker in a social service agency.

Libra (Double Destiny)

Press relations for high government official; movie star; travel agent or tour director; museum director or art teacher; decorative artist.

Scorpio

Political party chief; trial lawyer for criminal cases; history teacher; life insurance adjuster.

Sagittarius

Foreign ambassador; head of tour planning, travel agency, or airline; dancer; judge or chief magistrate.

Capricorn

Sculptor; chief of quality control for beauty products firm; hotel or resort manager; merchandise manager for hard goods.

Aquarius

Performing musical artist; project planner in a social services agency; novelist; civil rights lawyer.

Pisces

Poet; layout designer in an advertising agency; actor in legitimate theater; public relations officer for a hospital.

17

Midheaven House of Cancer

The Moon, the Ruling Planet

One of the semantic issues with which some scientists are concerned is whether the moon should be called earth's satellite or its "other half." Of all the satellites in our solar system, the moon is the largest relative to the size of its parent planet. Also, the two are interdependent. Earth's gravitational pull keeps one side of the moon hidden from us. And even the most pragmatic earthling will agree that the moon controls our tides and has an uncanny correlation with the menstrual cycle. From the beginning, therefore, the silvery "inconstant" moon has been the object of careful observation.

The moon is also inextricably linked to the sun, the source of its light and thus the cause of its very visiblity. So, as the sun was god, the moon to many ancient peoples was "The Great Mother" who gave form to the Divine Seed. (In Catholicism Mary is a mother/moon symbol.) The moon has long been seen as a great matrix or protective covering that both gives life and protects it: As Ceres to the Romans and Diana/Demeter/Proserpina to the Greeks, she ruled fertility, crops, and child-bearing. The other aspect of the moon/sun relationship is "receiving and reacting." As the moon receives the light of the sun, it reacts instinctively and changes accordingly.

The House of Cancer's main career connections follow quite naturally from the moon's two roles—one is biological and life-supporting, the other is impressionable sensor and rhythmic reactor. In the one batch of careers the moon translates the will of the sun into concrete realities, many connected with survival needs. In the other, the moon's extreme sensitivity gives it rulership over the public's wants and wishes—in effect the public consciousness. These two aspects are seen in the lives of Albert Schweitzer on the one hand, Nelson Rockefeller, John F. Kennedy, and Jimmy Carter on the other.

There is a primitive, tribal quality to some House of Cancer concerns; it is the home of Jung's collective unconscious—the reservoir of man's ancient memories. Within the lunar/House of Cancer domain falls the integrating of people into tribal units, or from a contemporary point of view, political and social factions.

Two images help to clear the mists from House of Cancer careers: one is Proust's *Remembrance of Things Past*, probably the most famous collection of sense memories in all literature. The other is the famous Cancer crab which—as Hamlet said—can go backward. The crab is elusive, self-protective, determined to survive.

Though the moon is theoretically the most knowable of the heavenly bodies in our system, much of her remains mysterious—like the Woman she represents. In Egypt the moon was Isis, ruler of magic. There is much creative magic in the moon, and it can be put to good earthly use in many House of Cancer careers.

Characteristics of House of Cancer Career Ground: enclosed, secure, sensitive.

Integrating Principles of Cancer Career Ground:

Belonging • • • surrounding • • • conserving • • • nurturing • • • protecting • • • caring for • • • the past • • • dreams • • • fluidity • • • endings • • • heredity • • • instincts • • • security • • • turning inward • • • containingness • • • the matrix • • • enveloping • • • integrating • • • managing • • • adaptability • • • changeableness • • • emotions • • • fertility • • • fluctuation • • • growing • • • the imagination • • • instincts • • • the personality • • • sensations • • • sentimentality • • • softness • • • the subconscious.

The Major IPT Clusters/Careers of the House of Cancer

Affairs of women: all phases, especially biological and sociological.
Cultural resources and activities: especially with regard to tradition.
Diagnostic and healing arts: many phases, especially concerns of women and children; nursing; counseling; in-depth psychology.
Domestic arts and sciences: especially survival needs, i.e., food, shelter, and clothing.
Finance: especially commodities.
Fine arts: many phases, especially creative writing.
Human resources: especially personnel work.
Natural resources: especially the soil, the sea.
Politics and public affairs: all phases, including trend analysis.
Real estate and housing: all phases.

A Selection of Things Ruled by the Moon/Cancer

The public • • • history • • • biography • • • antiques • • • tears • • • midwives • • • the ocean/water/all liquids • • • museums • • • everyday affairs • • • the stomach • • • bakeries • • • bathrooms • • • boats • • • caterers • • • crops • • • the esophagus • • • gastronomy • • • groceries • • • crops • • • houses • • • kitchens • • • dining rooms • • • shellfish • • • ulcers • • • the uterus • • • women in general • • • collectors • • • night-blooming flowers • • • farmer's markets • • • buried treasure • • • glass • • • introverts • • • lakes and marshes • • • motels • • • obstetrics • • • shopkeepers • • • milkmen.

Some Specific Jobs for Each Sun, Moon, and Ascendant Sign with House of Cancer at the Midheaven

Aries

Land developer; militant in the cause of feminism; surgeon specializing in stomach disorders; independent commodities trader.

Taurus

Pediatric nurse or pediatrician; pattern maker for clothing manufacturer; soil scientist or agronomist; birth control counselor.

Gemini

Real estate salesman; political pollster; rare books curator; antique dealer.

Cancer (Double Destiny)

Personnel director; politician or political trend analyst; novelist or poet; restaurant owner.

Leo

Holder of political office; financial officer for a construction materials firm; child psychiatrist; women's rights leader.

Virgo

Dietician in an old age or nursing home; fertility researcher; library administrator for a museum; market researcher.

Libra

Historical landmarks preservation; publicist for day-care center fund-raising; painter; gynecologist.

Scorpio

Head of political party, local or national; owner of mining concern; specialist in reproductive problems; psychoanalyst.

Sagittarius

Oceanographer; international commodities specialist; women's rights or child welfare lobbyist; international famine relief fund-raiser.

Capricorn

Head of acquisitions for a museum or library; financial advisor to political candidate; geologist; real estate trader.

Aquarius
Natural resources conservationist; public housing administrator; political news analyst or broadcaster; family counselor at a public agency.

Pisces
Creative writing teacher or poet; play therapist for retarded children; public school lunch program coordinator; political speech writer.

18

Midheaven House of Aries

Mars, The Ruling Planet

In contrast to the generally excellent reputation of Venus, Mars has had a rather checkered career. This masculine planet has always been recognized as a powerful, virile force; but that force has been eyed differently by different civilizations. The Egyptians called Mars Ptaz and made him god of man's creativity. Later on Mars was elevated to the rank of primal spirit in human form. That is the thing to remember about Mars: he's always been human, sometimes all too human. The Hindus called the planet Mars Kartikeya and said he was created out of the sweat of Shiva the Destroyer—a very humanlike origin.

The Greeks had a real problem with this aggressive planet, which they christened Ares. The more civilized of them gave Ares the cold shoulder because he crashed his way into their polite society by way of the barbarians; but naturally the Spartans literally worshiped Ares for his toughness. The Ares-shy Greeks named his sister Strife and two sons Fear (Phobos) and Fright (Deimos). But Ares' most famous child is Eros, and I think that is what gave the Greeks trouble—they were, after all, a little light on good old-fashioned heterosexuality.

Mars is sex in the sense of active procreation. You don't have to be sexually obsessed to notice that the symbol for Mars is topped by an erect penis. The lusty warlike Romans welcomed Mars with open arms, giving him lots of new duties. In Rome Mars ruled nature, fertility, new projects, and ideas. The ultimate honor for

Mars was to be made lord of the beginning of earthly creation: when the sun reaches zero degrees Aries in its yearly path through the zodiac, spring begins.

To associate Mars and the sign of Aries merely with war and sex would not be giving the devil his due, and it would be giving your career space short shrift. War, aggression, courage, physical stamina, passion, strife, and divisiveness all do fall within the province of Mars. But the cosmic principle behind these things is the real clue to Mars: and that is generative power. It is not so much the power of spirit as the power of matter. There are no constructive beginnings on earth without it. As Mars is fire, Mars is heat, and the heat of passion has started a lot more things in this world than battles and babies.

If Mars rules your Midheaven, be prepared for a primal calling—something very basic, perhaps even in connection with human survival. It may require risk and daring. The dangers, if there be such, need not be physical. They are the dangers that confront people whenever they challenge limits and seek to overcome them. Mars is man alone with only himself to rely on. You may never actually be in your own business, but with Mars ruling your career space, your calling should be characterized by independence of mind and spirit. Some mere mortals who personify House of Aries career lives are Pablo Picasso, Salvador Dali, Jane Fonda, and Truman Capote.

Characteristics of House of Aries Career Ground: free, open, challenging

Integrating Principles of Aries Career Ground

Exploration • • • beginnings • • • self-interest • • • essentials • • • the physical body • • • temerity • • • competition • • • surmounting obstacles • • • breaking new ground • • • turbulence • • • impulse • • • emergencies • • • eagerness • • • vigor • • • incitement • • • enthusiasm • • • penetration • • • propulsion • • • independent action (mental and physical) • • • never-beforeness • • • the now • • • being on the scene • • • immediacy • • •

ambition • • • pioneering • • • go-aheadness • • • maleness • • • being in the vanguard • • • conquest • • • desire • • • controversy.

The Major IPT Clusters/Careers of the House of Aries

Animal and natural resources: veterinary medicine; stock breeding.
Diagnostic and healing arts: all phases of surgery, especially neurological; psychiatry; physiotherapy; forensic medicine.
Exploring, building, creating new spaces, products, or opportunities: all phases of architecture; surveying; engineering, especially civil and metallurgical; research and development for an industrial product.
Entrepreneurial activities.
Figuring and then playing the odds: commodities and futures, all phases.
Investigative arts and trades: journalism and reporting, especially high-risk phases; insurance investigation.
Motor activity: competitive sports; pro and amateur athletics; acrobatics.
Performing and visual arts: highly individual phases, including dance.
Social sciences: psychology, especially behavioral and industrial; marketing research.
Regulatory services: law enforcement.
Strategic, combative, and competitive arts and trades: the military, all phases; (direct) sales; litigation, especially criminal; new-product advertising and promotion.

A Selection of Things Ruled by Mars/Aries

Skin disorders and rashes • • • burns • • • violent crimes • • • red blood cells • • • lumberjacks • • • cadets • • • pugilists • • • sheep • • • hardware manufacturers • • • fractures • • • tournaments • • • wreckers • • • gymnasts • • • adrenalin • • • machinery • • • demolition • • • all cutting instruments • • • diamonds and diamond cutters • • • drilling (dentistry) • • • contagious diseases • • • the common people • • • the genitals/urogenital system • • • rock music • • • metals • • • satire • • • rebellion • • • tobacco • • •

millinery • • • the head • • • the brain • • • opticians and optometrists • • • physical coordination.

Some Specific Jobs for Each Sun, Moon, and Ascendant Sign with House of Aries at the Midheaven

Aries (Double Destiny)

Residential and institutional architect, with innovative firm; investigative reporting, muckraker, war correspondent; commodities customers man or lone trader; military, non-desk job; pro athlete, non-team; brain or eye surgeon or neurosurgeon.

Taurus

Landscape architecture; purchasing agent for an architectural/construction firm; animal husbandry involving breeding and selling; ear/nose/throat doctor.

Gemini

Sports or crime reporter; public relations for architectural firm in heavy industry; writer/reporter for house organ in similar fields; court reporter; advertising sales person for newspaper or magazine.

Cancer

Obstetrics and gynecology physician or surgeon; food or housing manager; military or law enforcement in the industrial fields; head of industrial psychology department; interior designer; commodities analyst.

Leo

Performer in legitimate theater; courtroom litigator, both criminal and civil; chief of surgery or administrator of surgical services; venture capitalist; athletic coach in high school or junior high.

Virgo

Civil engineering, in technical phases; microsurgeon; records supervisor for law enforcement agency, the military, or surgical/

medical profession; draftsman for architectural firm; health and safety inspector.

Libra

Labor relations in industry; public relations specialist in medical field; insurance claims adjuster; plastic or cosmetic surgery, or public relations job related to same.

Scorpio

Courtroom litigator; criminal investigation or apprehension; surgery that is reconstructive or exploratory; commodities sales or trading; institutional architecture; pro sports, individual.

Sagittarius

College athletics coach or administrator; architect or engineer for an international firm; foreign correspondent; veterinarian for larger animals; trainer of race horses.

Capricorn

Financial officer for a manufacturing or engineering firm; corporate lawyer; government contracts negotiator for architectural firm; investment analyst for insurance firm.

Aquarius

Civil rights litigator; urban renewal projects work as surveyor or architect; professor of social psychology; head of research and development in electronic engineering firm.

Pisces

Dancer on stage or film; alcohol or drug rehabilitation counselor in industry or law enforcement agency; fine artist, specializing in new techniques; medic or chaplain in the military.

19

Midheaven House of Sagittarius

Jupiter, The Ruling Planet

In astrology, Jupiter (with Saturn) marks the dividing line between the so-called "personal planets" and those that are considered more generational—Uranus, Neptune, and Pluto. In this role, Jupiter is the planet that links God and/or the universe with man, communicating universal principles to him. As Mercury connects man with man and thus rules the "lower" or more mundane mind, Jupiter is lord of the "higher mind"—i.e., religion, philosophy, and ideologies.

Everything about the planet Jupiter is prodigious, from its size (318 times that of earth) to the tremendous luminosity of its ever-changing bands of color. Far from ignoring this spectacular sight, early man connected Jupiter with a wisdom and power far beyond his own. Many myths place Jupiter higher than, or at least equal to, the sun. A descendant of the first-of-all-gods, Ouranos, and Gaea the earth goddess in early Greek mythology, Jupiter has always kept one foot in heaven and one planted firmly in this world. If the sun was god, Jupiter was the temporal lord. To the Hindus he was Vishnu, the preserver, the second person of their creator/preserver/destroyer trinity. In Greece as Zeus, Jupiter sat atop Mount Olympus holding both a thunderbolt and the staff of life; in other words, he was a single divine personage with power to create or destroy at will. Almost as if to prove his partial humanity, Zeus came down from the top quite often to mate with earthlings. (His real soulmate was Hera, however, called Juno in Rome.)

In his role as intermediary between the temporal and the divine, Jupiter is said to be both an Abraham figure (all-forgiving, compassionate father) and the "mouthpiece"/interpreter of cosmic laws on earth. With a reputation like this it is no wonder Jupiter/Sagittarius rules spiritual quests, prophecy, and all reaching for the beyond. In everyday terms this often translates into long-distance travel and other peripatetic activities; but equally often the trips are purely mental. As Mercury darts hither and yon carrying messages and ideas, Jupiter travels more slowly and surely, bearing with him the basic principles behind information and ideas. Jupiter represents a human faculty beyond the purely rational (which is one reason intuitive leaps are typical of Sagittarian-influenced individuals). Jupiter is not a rebel (unlike Uranus); he is a traditionalist, a preserver of right and justice.

The careers of the House of Sagittarius range from the sublime to the quite mundane, the common thread being one of reaching and stretching. As a huge but gaseous planet, Jupiter has breadth without density. What you should look for in a House of Sagittarius career, therefore, is substance without strictures. No matter what zodiacal signs your personal points fall in, if you have House of Sagittarius at the Midheaven and your job holds you too close to earth, you will feel the frustration of the caged bird who is unable to fly. Some who ventured far and wide with House of Sagittarius at the Midheaven are Alfred Hitchcock, Alexander Solzhenitsyn, W. H. Auden, Benjamin Spock, and Linus Pauling.

Characteristics of House of Sagittarius Career Ground: faraway, free, abstract.

Integrating Principles of Sagittarius Career Ground

Projecting • • • aiming • • • anticipating • • • the future • • • synthesizing • • • educating • • • expanding • • • developing • • • mobility • • • locomotion • • • aspiration • • • opportunity/opportunism • • • optimism • • • buoyancy • • • creative change • • • boldness • • • truth • • • magnanimity • • • excess • • • duality • • • impersonality • • • indulgence • • • eagerness • • • higher values • • • versatility • • • non-linear thinking • • • preaching • • • didacticism • • • abundance • • • logic • • • speculation • • • mercy • • • joviality • • • idealism • • • advising.

The Major IPT Clusters/Careers of the House of Sagittarius

Abstract or futuristic studies and activities: space and astrology, for example.
Communications and language arts: particularly publishing; inspirational or didactic writing; foreign languages and translation.
Diagnostic and healing arts: some phases, larger animal veterinary medicine; counseling or advising.
Figuring the odds: all forms of speculation.
Finance: particularly international.
The law: most phases, particularly codification and adjudication.
The physical body and motor arts: all sports and physical activities, including the dance.
Religion and the religious life: all phases, including theological scholarship.
Teaching, scholarship, and higher education: all phases.
The sciences: particularly research, both organic and inorganic worlds.
Transportation and import-export: all phases, particularly air trades.

A Selection of Things Ruled by Jupiter/Sagittarius

Altars • • • airline travel • • • higher education • • • hunting • • • jockeys • • • the hips and thighs • • • all voyages • • • sciatic nerves • • • professors • • • social migrations • • • the law • • • lumbago • • • theologians • • • foreign agencies • • • game animals • • • the blood • • • liver and hepatic system • • • corpulence • • • casinos • • • black sheep • • • the aristocracy • • • ambassadors • • • senators • • • shoes • • • regalia • • • Puritans • • • restitution • • •

philosophic societies • • • popes • • • profiteers • • • parole • • • ordinances • • • mercy • • • passports • • • pedigrees • • • luck.

Some Specific Jobs for Each Sun, Moon, and Ascendant Sign with House of Sagittarius at the Midheaven

Aries

Professional athlete; military attaché at foreign embassy; trouble-shooter in import/export business.

Taurus

Financial officer for multinational company; magistrate; simultaneous translator at the United Nations.

Gemini

Publisher of race track tout sheet; philologist; chief of ground-to-air communications for airport; religion editor.

Cancer

Pastoral priest or teaching nun; paleontologist; manager for a cruise line or shipping firm; publisher of food magazine.

Leo

Professional dancer; owner of gambling casino or resort; president of university; senator or ambassador.

Virgo

Research chemist for new synthetic materials; court reporter or legal researcher; nutrition adviser for sports figures; chief accountant of international publisher.

Libra

Publisher of fashion or beauty periodical; judge or litigator; aesthetics professor; multilingual tour guide or operator.

Scorpio

Veterinary surgeon; gym owner or athletic coach; church historian or theologian; atomic physicist.

Sagittarius (Double Destiny)

Semanticist or foreign language teacher; newspaper or magazine publisher; chief executive of airline; international investment counselor; philanthropist.

Capricorn

Head of religious order; owner of race horses or baseball/football team; head of futurology research group; circuit or supreme court judge.

Aquarius

Astrologer; publisher or writer of religious- or future-oriented periodical; drafter of civil rights legislation; head of political science or international studies department of university.

Pisces

Member of contemplative religious order; philosophy scholar or professor; director or publicist for charity; legal aid adviser.

20

Midheaven House of Capricorn

Saturn, The Ruling Planet

There is a tendency to divide the planets into the "good guys" and the "bad guys"; but this is not surprising, since astrologers have long done so. However, as traditional astrology continues to blend with modern psychology and both disciplines become more sophisticated, the lines get more and more blurred. Saturn—the chilly, leaden planet who has always been the real "baddie"—is now considered a mixed blessing. Saturn was called "the greater malefic" by the ancients because he was known to bring restrictions and limitations. But in this fact lies Saturn's strength: to work with Saturn correctly is to have dominance over one's passions, and often over the material world. Astrologers now consider Saturn "badly placed" in a natal horoscope if it does *not* give structured parameters to the personality, and they advise that the only way to be free of Saturn is to learn his stern lessons. Saturn is the teacher, the tester, the tempter.

When Saturn rules the Midheaven, as it does with the House of Capricorn, he is a little like Santa Claus. If you are bad, you don't get a thing; but if you are good, the rewards can be almost unlimited. Saturn's history shows that the greatest deterrent to personal power is untrammeled ambition. He started as Kronos, the son of Ouranos and Gaea in early Greek mythology. However,

Kronos became an usurper, castrating his father and ascending to the throne of heaven and earth. He was so fearful of competitors, he swallowed his children—all except Zeus who was miraculously saved. Zeus then taught his father Kronos a lesson by sending him into exile, where he has been the shadowy figure of Father Time ever since. Because he knows the pitfalls, Saturn keeps his scythe at the ready to cut down those who delude themselves and try to grab too much. Saturn is the ultimate realist.

Saturn ruling the Midheaven can mean a career of obligations and responsibilities—a setting of limits for self and others. The House of Capricorn, which is the natural tenth or Midheaven house of the horoscope, is synonymous with The Establishment. It requires active, responsible social participation—and often brings the honors and status to go with it. Many of the Saturnian virtues may be called into play in your career: economy, control, practicality, patience, perseverance. You may not literally be an authority figure, a public administrator, or a titan of industry; there are many "lighter" careers within the House of Capricorn. Nonetheless, underlying everything there will be a seriousness of purpose. I call the House of Capricorn the house of "true grit."

If it all sounds very grim, it isn't really. Consider the House of Capricorn careers of Stavros Niarchos, Elizabeth Arden, Dwight Eisenhower, Douglas MacArthur, and long-time favorite Lawrence Welk. Whatever you do, if you do it well, your career should reflect the rewards of the steady energy that is Saturn. And one of the very best things about a Saturn-ruled destiny is that Saturn is connected with longevity and staying power. In career terms, it means that if you persevere to the top of the heap, no one can push you off.

Characteristics of House of Capricorn Career Ground: solid, defined, very real.

Integrating Principles of Capricorn Career Ground

Controlling • • • limiting • • • substance • • • status • • • realism • • • reputation • • • directing • • • experience • • • delegated authority • • • setting in stone • • • dominating • • • structure • • • achievement • • • outermost limits • • • "office" • • • the functional • • • integration • • • responsibility • • • duty • • • security • • • discipline • • • public performance • • • emergence • • • contraction • • • coolness • • • the material • • • ambition • • • condensation • • • building • • • convention • • • the economical • • • fortitude • • • inflexibility • • • necessities.

The Major IPT Clusters/Careers of the House of Capricorn

Banking and finance: many phases, especially mortgage work.
Big business or industry: many phases, particularly management.
Bureaucracy: all levels of government, federal, state, local.
Diagnostic and healing arts: many phases, especially dentistry, orthopedics, and geriatrics.
Education: mainly administrative phases.
Labor: most phases, especially management.
Numbers: mainly economics, mathematics.
Performing and visual arts: individual phases, particularly sculpture.
Physical sciences: many phases, particularly earth studies.
Property, real estate, construction: all phases.
Regulatory and correctional services: all phases.

A Selection of Things Ruled by Saturn/Capricorn

Watches and clocks • • • cement • • • rules and regulations • • • sculptors • • • the bones • • • reliability • • • ores and ore mines • • • economics • • • mortuaries • • • efficiency • • • experts • • • credit • • • depression • • • leather goods • • • the hair • • • chambers of commerce • • • arthritis • • • archeology • • • bankruptcy • • • ceramics • • • common sense • • • constipation • • • dogmas • • • the elderly • • • industry • • • fallow fields • • • frostbite • • • granaries • • • hardware • • • jailors • • • junk dealers • • • lumber • • • mortgages • • • mountainous places • • • property • • • slums.

Some Specific Jobs for Each Sun, Moon, and Ascendant Sign with House of Capricorn at the Midheaven

Aries

Burial plot salesman; probation officer; land speculator; athletic administrator in high school or college.

Taurus

Real estate tax assessor for city or state; comptroller in a major corporation; geologist; economist.

Gemini

Stand-up comic or musical comedy star; mathematics professor; head of public relations firm with industrial accounts; labor lobbyist.

Cancer

Director of women's correctional facility; water conservation administrator; head of construction firm; dean of women at college or university.

Leo

Labor leader; president or chairman of the board of a major company; coal mine owner or operator; director of public preschool programs; mortgage administrator at a bank.

Virgo

Registrar at college or university; sanitation commissioner; economic trends analyst; tax accountant; dental hygienist.

Libra

Director of recreation for prison or house of detention; administrator of fine arts program at college or university; labor relations expert; geriatric counselor; sculpture curator, museum.

Scorpio

Prison warden; orthopedic surgeon; real estate owner or landlord; sales manager at major insurance firm.

Sagittarius

Game warden; head of engineering for an aircraft manufacturer; president of college or university; international economist; lead dancer on stage or films.

Capricorn (Double Destiny)

Dentist or head of university dental program; chiropractor; bureau chief of F.B.I. or attorney general's office; purchasing agent of major construction firm.

Aquarius

Director of urban renewal programs for state or city; head of science department at college or university; individual instrumentalist; administrator of nursing home complex.

Pisces

Geriatric counselor; sculptor; water supply commissioner; customer relations for bank or major manufacturer.

21

Midheaven House of Aquarius

Uranus, The Ruling Planet

When you get to the orbit of Uranus, you step over the line into the outer limits—the realm of the "higher octave" planets. The discovery of Uranus in 1781 (with a Uranian instrument, the telescope) turned the astronomical/astrological world upside down. No one (except some astrologer-priests of the ancient world) even suspected its existence. To most, the solar system—in fact, the universe—ended with the orbit of Saturn. However occultists, metaphysicians, and others attuned to its vibrations saw that Uranus's discovery was necessary to man's mental and spiritual evolution. The physical world, even with its Jupiterian connection to the divine, was limited and limiting. As the higher octave of Mercury, Uranus demanded the development of man's sixth sense—nonverbal knowing that goes beyond logic and the purely material.

Uranus is difficult for most people to get in touch with. Some individuals are able to "use" the Uranus of their natal horoscopes quite handily; they tend to be the geniuses, revolutionaries, and sometimes anarchists of our world. When Uranus rules the Midheaven, however, it "works" for any mere mortal, driving him onward and upward almost against the will.

Uranus, the high-voltage "electric" planet, tends toward two main career paths: the iconoclastic and the humanitarian, and sometimes both rolled into one. When Uranus was named, astronomers and astrologers alike had in mind the great mythic figure of Ouranos, the "solar force" and father of all gods to the ancient Greeks. Although there is no real "Uranus story" on the books, two myths connected with Aquarius, the sign ruled by Uranus, may serve to elucidate. One concerns Deucalion, a kind of cosmic Noah to the later Greeks. Angry Zeus sent a great flood to destroy the world. Deucalion, warned by his father Prometheus, built a wooden chest and took his wife aboard. Safely landed after nine days of rain, husband and wife went straight to Delphi and got instructions about how to repopulate the world and start a new race. I call this the dawning of social consciousness.

Uranus/Aquarius's other dimension—the quirky one—is illustrated in the Ganymede myth. Ganymede was such a pretty little boy Zeus wanted him for his own, and so whisked him off to Mount Olympus to serve as cupbearer (among other things). Lest Ganymede's father be too shocked and disconsolate, Zeus gave him a brace of immortal chariot horses in exchange. A fair trade, and a rational solution that satisfied everyone. With Uranus, all things are acceptable—and within reason.

For those of you with Aquarius at the Midheaven, rest assured that all this usually translates into much smaller (and less bizarre) dimensions; but in Uranian careers there is always a touch of individual style, responsible daring, and/or a desire to improve things/conditions. There is also often a degree of invention or independent action. Aquarius's rational component sometimes surfaces as a capacity to put distance between self and subject—as in psychotherapy or sociological research.

With Uranus as the ruler of your destiny, you can expect a career life that is far from dull—that is, if you accept the challenge of this revolutionary, rule-breaking planet. Many have, and their acceptance has taken them more than one step beyond the ordinary in both their work and their rewards. Some House of Aquarius rule-breakers are Henry Kissinger, George Bernard Shaw, Isaac Asimov, Julia Child, and Cole Porter.

Characteristics of House of Aquarius Career Ground: new, unique, improved.

Integrating Principles of Aquarius Career Ground

The unconventional • • • experimentation • • • association • • • innovation • • • helping • • • combining • • • breaking through • • • coolness • • • humanitarianism • • • searching • • • networking • • • caring • • • observing • • • progress • • • inspiration • • • visions • • • rationality • • • liberalism • • • absence of bias • • • reform • • • the occult • • • freedom • • • suddenness • • • originality • • • the unexpected • • • abruptness • • • extremism • • • thrills • • • awakenings • • • paradoxes • • • freethinking • • • obliqueness • • • the intellect • • • higher consciousness • • • fanaticism.

The Major IPT Clusters/Careers of the House of Aquarius

Amusement arts: many phases, including pop-writing, cartooning, films.
Communications arts: mainly broadcasting, all phases; all media.
Diagnostic and healing arts: some phases, especially nervous disorders and mental health; radiology.
Entrepreneurial activities: all, including free-lance work.
Futuristic studies and activities: all forms; all phases of occultism.
Human rights and humanitarian causes: all phases, including legal work connected with associations, civil rights, feminism, philanthropy.
Musical arts: most phases.
The physical sciences and technologies: most phases, especially nuclear physics; meteorology; electronics.
Scholarship and teaching: especially technical and higher studies, such as metaphysics.
The social sciences: all phases.

A Selection of Things Ruled by Uranus/Aquarius

Earthquakes • • • refugees • • • associations • • • fireworks • • • sudden changes • • • deviation • • • stunts • • • patents and patent attorneys • • • divorce • • • aviation • • • rock and electronic music • • • computers • • • elevators • • • astrology • • • blizzards • • • bachelors • • • the ankles • • • contortionists • • • electricity • • • eviction • • • geniuses • • • magnetism • • • highways • • • hydraulics • • • liberators and libertines • • • brotherly love • • • mutinies • • • remoteness • • • schisms • • • service stations • • • seismology • • • telephones • • • thresholds • • • the weird • • • zealots.

Some Specific Jobs for Each Sun, Moon, and Ascendant Sign with House of Aquarius at the Midheaven

Aries

Free-lance inventor; trouble-shooter for telephone company; neurological specialist or surgeon; field supervisor of census or polltakers.

Taurus

Rock vocalist or instrumentalist; family mental health counselor; radio or television announcer; head of civic improvement organization.

Gemini

Recording or broadcasting engineer; computer designer or programer; liaison officer of a social work agency; songwriter; reform journalist.

Cancer

Director of public maternity and child-care information center; women's rights lawyer or counseler; film writer or director.

Leo

Radio or television performer; director or administrator of philanthropy; chief of radiology; performing psychic.

Virgo

Instrumentalist or sound technician; psychiatric social worker; cartoonist; metaphysics professor.

Libra

Marriage counseler; movie star or set designer; architect for public housing; free-lance artist.

Scorpio

Sexual dysfunction counseler; director of public mental health facility; head of major radio or television network; trends analyst for market research firm.

Sagittarius

Astrologer; professor of meteorology; radiation therapist; science fiction writer.

Capricorn

Owner or operator of an independent telephone and telegraph communications company; director of development for nuclear research; patent attorney.

Aquarius (Double Destiny)

Musician, either group or individual; researcher for space technology; chief attorney or advisor for civil rights group; professor of aerodynamics; astronomer.

Pisces

Hypnotherapist; medium; position in radio, television, film acting; administrator of social services for the underprivileged.

22

Midheaven House of Pisces

Neptune, The Ruling Planet

Neptune is the planet of sleep and the mysterious dreams that come with it. The ultimate purpose of the Neptunian/Piscean destiny is to turn dreams into reality. The medium through which this occurs is emotion rather than thought.

Because Neptune is a higher octave planet, the emotions it inspires are of a very high order. And since Neptune is the higher octave of Venus, the two main themes of those emotions are love and beauty. But while Venus's love is personal, Neptune's is universal. Venus asks for love in return, but Neptune asks for nothing. Similarly, the beauty Venus sees is clearer, sharper, easier to define. With Neptune it is almost beyond the grasp, which is why those who grasp it are often supremely creative artists.

Hazy Neptune (a billion miles farther away than Uranus) is synonymous with the ineffable, the indefinable. It is connected, then, with all that is glamorous and fantastic, as well as all that is deceptive. Casting a mist over everything, Neptune is the master of illusion. Those who respond to its vibrations can be either consummate actors or reprehensible tricksters. Likewise, in elevating love to the suprapersonal, Neptune can shape human lives of great service or formless Utopian dreams. Extremism is a Neptunian characteristic.

From whence comes all this creative power and all this formlessness? From the seas that cover most of the earth's surface, from the dissolving and cleansing properties of water, at once the universal solvent and the grace-giving agent of baptism. Neptune is, of course, Poseidon, Lord of the Deep—by the Greeks granted rulership over most of the world. While Jupiter maintains contact with God, Neptune or Poseidon reaches beyond Him to the source: the one, the everything. For most people with Pisces at the Midheaven this transcendental dimension will operate more personally than professionally; but it is important for you to know it is there.

Since the prongs of Neptune's purifying trident spear all three phases of the human person—physical, emotional, and mental—the paths to achievement in the House of Pisces can lead in many directions. On many of these paths, "involvement" is a watchword. The helping careers of House of Pisces differ from those of Aquarius in that there is more humanness than strict, objective humanitarianism. Escape is another Piscean theme. (In fact, many with this sign emphasized in their horoscopes try to dodge reality with drugs and alcohol.) As a career motif in this house, however, escapism takes the form of movies and all illusional entertainments. High creativity in all art forms, the spiritual and occult, motivational management, and sales are also among the top-of-the-list House of Pisces career possibilities. A single binding concept is dealing effectively with intangibles. If you get nothing else from Neptune, his rulership should mean a professional life where you can exercise graceful control and mental agility. These examples of House of Pisces destinies may make your own a bit clearer: Vincent Van Gogh, heart surgeon Christiaan Barnard, Pope Paul VI, Glenn Miller, and Albert Einstein all fall within the boundaries of this house.

Characteristics of House of Pisces Career Ground: boundless, beautiful, within.

Integrating Principles of Pisces Career Ground

Understanding • • • dissolving barriers • • • ambiguity • • • confidentiality • • • giving solace • • • universalizing • • • disguising

• • • pretending • • • confinement • • • unselfishness • • • paying dues • • • hallucinations • • • sensory awareness • • • asceticism • • • retreating • • • the insubstantial • • • manipulating • • • merging • • • sensualism • • • resourcefulness • • • flowing • • • persuading • • • soaking up • • • glamor • • • dualism • • • change • • • insight • • • perceptivity • • • imagination • • • the immeasurable • • • flexibility • • • flimsiness • • • enchantment.

The Major IPT Clusters/Careers of the House of Pisces

Business and the professions: all creative phases, including many managerial facets.
Caretaking and custodial services: all phases related to places of confinement.
Counseling and guiding arts and sciences: all forms of advising, including pastoral work; some phases of teaching.
Diagnostic and healing arts: some phases, particularly abnormal psychology, faith healing, and other unorthodox methods.
Drugs, chemicals, and liquids: all levels, at all related businesses, including pharmaceuticals, alcoholic beverages.
Entertaining and role playing: most phases.
Fine or creative arts: particularly fiction and poetry; music; painting and sculpture; photography.
Illusional arts and trades: particularly filmmaking; set design; undercover work.
Performing arts: especially the dance and the theater.
Persuading arts and trades: all forms of selling; the advertising business.
Religious, spiritual, and occult higher studies and activities: all phases, including some aspects of physics and higher mathematics.

A Selection of Things Ruled by Neptune/Pisces

Makeup • • • melodrama • • • liquids and fluids • • • drugs • • • anesthetics • • • cameras • • • magic • • • the feet • • • fictitious names • • • confidence men • • • alibis • • • asylums • • • the ballet • • • bigamy • • • the drama • • • the navy • • • forecasting • • • eyeglasses • • • harps • • • imprisonment • • • insanity • • • lavatories • • • mob psychology • • • mythology • • • paint • • •

pharmacologists • • • potions • • • private investigators • • • romance • • • seduction • • • secret societies • • • sleep • • • submarines • • • swimming • • • false teeth • • • automobile tires • • • fog • • • holy water • • • chiropodists • • • barrooms • • • fish.

Some Specific Jobs for Each Sun, Moon, and Ascendant Sign with House of Pisces at the Midheaven

Aries

Chief of decoy services for police department; advertising space or time salesman; mimic or mime; foot surgeon.

Taurus

Head of religious retreat home; bar or restaurant owner; therapist in speech disorders; composer.

Gemini

Copy chief at an advertising agency; sales manager for a pharmaceutical company; scriptwriter in a film company; communications specialist for church group or religious organization.

Cancer

Owner or sales manager for a boat manufacturer or distributorship; gourmet chef; professor of church history or comparative religion; novelist or biographer.

Leo

Stage actor or actress; manager of home for retarded children; film producer or head of studio; psychiatrist specializing in personality disorders.

Virgo

Head dietician in prison, hospital, or nursing home; chemist; graphic designer for advertising agency; priest or nun.

Libra

Painter or art photographer; spokesperson or fund-raiser for religious group or mental health charity; instrumentalist on harp or piano; personnel director of major firm.

Scorpio

Undercover agent for F.B.I. or C.I.A.; head of religious order or canon lawyer; head of psychiatric services in a major hospital; sales manager for alcoholic beverage manufacturer.

Sagittarius

Head of new product development in pharmaceutical or soft-drink bottling firm; legal counsel to entertainment union; ballet dancer; distributor of foreign films.

Capricorn

Sculptor or head of art ceramics firm; financial administrator for mental institution; top management of cosmetics or fragrance firm; agent or manager to top movie or theater star.

Aquarius

Director of community mental health program; poet or lyricist; professor of higher mathematics; owner or manager of string of movie theaters.

Pisces (Double Destiny)

Nuclear physicist; theologian or philosopher; dramatist or creative writer; magician or illusionist; art therapist for the mentally retarded; clairvoyant; personnel manager in hydroelectric plant or oil refining company.

23

Midheaven House of Scorpio

Pluto, The Ruling Planet

There is a heaviness or density about everything connected with Pluto. Astronomically speaking, density is the main physical characteristic of this remote planet, that is so distant that from its surface the sun would appear as merely a bright star. Pluto's discovery in 1930 (the result of some spectacular space detective work) was based on the premise that something quite big must be causing the disturbances in Uranus's eccentric orbit. When this something was found to be Pluto, that planet's small size relative to its gravitational pull was an amazement to scientists.

Pluto's power is the power of compressed energy; when that energy is released, it can blow with the force of a nuclear explosion. (Ask any Scorpio.) Pluto is the higher octave of Mars, and as such is connected with war and force. But Mars's destruction is light stuff compared to Pluto, which can not only break things, but also change their very atomic structure. The sexual connotations of Pluto are more intense, as well; Mars may perform the act, but Pluto plants the seed and causes conception.

In legend the Pluto principle is one of death and transformation. In myth, underworlds abounded, and each had a god to rule it. Pluto's kingdom for the early Hebrews was the Cave; for the Hindus Kamoloki—"where desires are worked out." The Norse called it Hel. What is important about these Pluto/Hades/Satan-ruled netherworlds is that they were transitional—places for waiting and purification before a new and more glorious birth. Pluto only destroys to create anew; think of the snake shedding its skin or the caterpillar turning into a butterfly.

The Greeks added another and brighter leaf to Pluto's book by making him lord of buried treasure. Pluto may use force to bring to light what is hidden, but it is often of great value. This explains Pluto/Scorpio's connection with depth psychology and its plumbing of the subconscious for buried neuroses.

The sex/birth/death/rebirth cycle of Pluto makes for strong career themes in the House of Scorpio. Some Pluto/Scorpio destinies involve transforming things and people, forcing them to grow. The growth Pluto brings about may not always be painless, but the purpose is to exalt. Most people with House of Scorpio destinies will not live them out at anything like the exaltation level; that is reserved for the few. The more common motifs in this house are discovery, redirection, clearing away, creative change. The supervisory role is often played out, too, and sometimes in areas others do not choose to tread. For maximum success, look for a career involving intensity. Some intense destinies that fall within the House of Scorpio are those of Chiang Kai-shek, David Ben-Gurion, Jonas Salk, Mao Tse-tung, Ralph Nader, Margaret Mead, and Pope John XXIII. Some lighter but noteworthy careers are those of Billie Jean King, Dustin Hoffman, and Paul Newman.

Characteristics of House of Scorpio Career Ground: hidden, compressed, dangerous.

Integrating Principles of Scorpio Career Ground

Probing • • • eliminating • • • regeneration • • • will • • • endurance • • • permanence • • • aggressiveness • • • courage • • • dynamism • • • positiveness • • • force • • • controlling • • • patience • • • solitariness • • • release of blockages • • • growth • • • continuity • • • anonymity • • • compulsion • • • demolition • • • exploration • • • metamorphosis • • • mortality • • • procreation • • • preservation • • • purging • • • rejuvenation • • • severity

• • • renewal • • • purification • • • submergence • • • turning points • • • the unknown.

The Major IPT Clusters/Careers of the House of Scorpio

The body: all forms of strenuous physical activity.
Death and dying: all related phases, including burial.
Detection, undercover, and investigative arts and trades: especially criminal work.
Diagnostic and healing arts: especially surgery, intensive psychotherapy.
Finance, taxes, and insurance: most phases, especially in connection with heirs.
Military/industrial complex: all phases related to war and defense.
Managment of people, services, countries: all phases.
Politics: all phases, including international.
Removal, sanitation, and purifying trades: including all waste products; demolition.
Research and exploration arts and sciences: many phases, including all aspects of organic and inorganic world.

A Selection of Things Ruled by Pluto/Scorpio

Reptiles • • • the anus • • • cemeteries • • • bill collectors • • • the sex organs • • • legacies • • • espionage • • • rubbish dumps • • • autopsies • • • bombs • • • brothels • • • organized crime • • • executions • • • fertilizers • • • inscrutability • • • juvenile delinquents • • • nuclear physicists • • • pornography • • • passion • • • pest control • • • poisons • • • pollution • • • puzzles • • • satire • • • septic systems • • • suicide control • • • venereal disease • • • viruses • • • wars • • • alimony • • • the excretory system • • • life insurance • • • the muscles • • • the mortality rate.

Some Specific Jobs for Each Sun, Moon, and Ascendant Sign with House of Scorpio at the Midheaven

Aries

Coroner; military liaison, munitions manufacturer; owner of demolition firm; field researcher for endangered species.

Taurus
Surgeon specializing in throat cancer; cemetery or mortuary administrator; estate-tax specialist; sanitation commissioner.

Gemini
Crime reporter or racket-exposé journalist; public relations specialist for defense department; editor for house organ of major firm; life insurance salesman.

Cancer
Gynecologist/surgeon; high position in state department; water supply pollution expert; birth defects prevention research.

Leo
Head of state; professional athlete; chairman of the board or president of firm with government contracts; sex-change surgeon.

Virgo
Health and safety violations inspector; manager of death records department; behavioral psychologist; life insurance actuary.

Libra
Labor arbitrator for steel or aircraft manufacturer; family death counselor; public relations or press liaison for F.B.I. or attorney general's office; cosmetic or reconstructive surgeon.

Scorpio (Double Destiny)
General or military strategist; psychoanalyst; owner of rubbish removal or trucking firm; evangelist.

Sagittarius
Explorer or professor of natural history; litigator in accident or death claims cases; international politician or professor of political science; long-distance runner.

Capricorn
Head of big-city detection department; geologist or earth-resources

researcher; mortician or owner of funeral home; top management position in big business.

Aquarius

Astronaut or space researcher; director of relief services for widows and orphans; political platform writer; head of conservationist group.

Pisces

Counseling or research for terminal patients; competitive swimmer; oceanographer; manager of out-patient center in psychiatric hospital.

24

Your House of the Sun

Just as the time of day you were born pinpoints your House of the Midheaven, it also tells you into which house of the horoscope your sun falls. This is a simple formula with no charts required. Each of the twelve sectors or slices of the horoscope wheel has a fundamental meaning. How that meaning relates to your career field has already been spelled out, according to which *sign* is on your tenth or Midheaven house (the top of your chart). But the *sun*—your will and basic life orientation—can and probably does reside in a different house of your horoscope. That house says a lot about you and what makes you run; you might say it indicates just how brightly your sun does shine.

Here is a list of catch-phrases and a brief sum-up of each house of the sun. (In locating yours, remember we are dealing in "real" or sun time, corrected from daylight savings and/or war time. Also, if you were born far east or west of the meridian of a time zone, there can be as much as a half hour's difference in clock time from sun time. Check how to find true local time instructions in tables at the back of this book.)

Born four A.M. to six A.M.: Sun in first house

You are an "I am" person who must impose his individuality on a work situation in order to feel fulfilled. Regardless of the rest of your astrological profile, if you are relegated to a background or "rubber stamp" position, you will suffer psychologically. Your sun sign, whatever it is, is a particularly strong influence on your personality. The sun-in-the-first-house person rarely has a severe inferiority complex; the reverse is often the case.

Born two A.M. to four A.M.: Sun in second house

The keynote of your personality drive is "I must have." Possessions, whether of a material or a psychic nature, are extremely important to you. In your career, you will make strong efforts to amass money and/or power, for they are essential to your emotional security. Your basic life orientation is more toward self than others.

Born midnight to two A.M.: Sun in third house

"I observe" is the label that can be slapped on you. Even if you are an emotional water sun sign, this house placement of the sun will give you a certain amount of objectivity. You thrive in a social environment, and must have a great deal of personal interaction in any job situation if you are to be happy. The sun sign is only moderately important.

Born ten P.M. to midnight: Sun in fourth house

The subconscious of the person with sun in the fourth house says "I need/I want" throughout his entire life. The drive for closeness and emotional security is strong, and the ability to venture beyond the nest is rather weak. Fourth-house-sun persons tend to stay in jobs for quite a while, equating the office with home. Ambition is not marked, and self-esteem is low. However, the sun sign has great influence.

Born eight P.M. to ten P.M.: Sun in fifth house

The words for this house placement of the sun are either "I project" or "Here I am." Take your pick; both mean that by nature the person wants to be a superstar, and will attain that goal or shrivel up and die. This is not to be taken literally; one can be a superstar virtually anywhere, and physical death does not actually threaten. But for the fifth-house-sun person, lack of recognition can feel like the same thing.

Born six P.M. to eight P.M.: Sun in sixth house

"I must" is the unfortunate running theme of the sixth-house-sun person. Here you find your workaholics, those who must produce at top capacity at all times, or suffer the tortures of the damned. If you have a sixth house sun, watch out for nervous tension, and be sure to take vacations—even if you don't feel you deserve them. A strong sun sign can be somewhat obscured in this house.

Born four P.M. *to six* P.M.*: Sun in seventh house.*

"I can if . . ." is the phrase that marks the tentative seventh-house-sun person. There is always a reason to delay or avoid independent action; the necessity for support is paramount (or so the person believes). The sun falls smack in the sector of others, and unless the person is on guard, those "others" can make all his life decisions for him.

Born two P.M. *to four* P.M.*: Sun in eighth house*

Here are born the "I will" people of the world. No matter what namby-pamby elements may dominate the horoscope, this house placement of the sun gives an extraordinary drive for power and dominance. The sphere of action may be limited, but the degree of willpower is usually not.

Born noon to two P.M.*: Sun in ninth house*

Ninth-house-sun people are often content if they can simply say "I see." This is the house of understanding, and if that need is satisfied, the person can often feel fulfilled. Many academics and philosophers have a ninth house sun. If you have one and your ambitions are more worldly, take note and rectify.

Born ten A.M. *to noon: Sun in tenth house*

These are the "double destiny" people who often achieve fame and/or notoriety in spite of themselves. The key words are "I do," and it is sometimes just as simple as that. More often, those with sun in the "house of ambition" have to and do put in a great deal of effort, but even that can come effortlessly. The sun sign is powerful.

Born eight A.M. *to ten* A.M.*: Sun in eleventh house*

The people with sun in this house can be characterized by "I wish/I hope." Those hopes and wishes often go beyond their own personal life goals, and there is a high degree of idealism and altruism. Sometimes they live for their friends, and often cannot live without them. Since those friends are usually in high places, it works well for life success.

Born six A.M. to eight A.M.: Sun in twelfth house

This is the house often called "prison" by the ancients, and to console himself, the person so confined often says "I believe"—in whatever. There is a philosophical tendency often forced upon those with an "eclipsed" sun in the twelfth house. The ego has difficulty asserting itself, and frustration can occur if the necessity to be recognized is too strong. Remember, they also serve who have twelfth house suns.

FOUR
STRESS AND SUCCESS

25
The Elemental Energies

The concept of energy reenters the Success System at this point, because it is at the heart of your career performance. We are talking about astrological or universal energy, of course, not the physical kind that can be measured in caloric units. It is this energy that underlies personal stress. Learning to *use* stress is a good plan for anyone, and virtually a prerequisite for the person bent on making it in the professional world.

The human being as an energy field is not a new idea. In recent years a number of medical/psychological therapists have been thinking in terms of "blocked energies" or "misdirected currents" as the cause of physical or emotional illness. Bio-Energetic Therapy actually measures the magnetic energy that emanates from a person. The Russian-developed Kirlian camera can photograph this energy. The idea of interchanging energies with another person is also the foundation of much psychic and faith healing.

For our purposes, your own particular energy field is the "aura" you received from the universe at the instant of your birth, "programmed" by the zodiacal positions of the planets. The energies of that aura can make you or break you in the professional world because they are the key to how you can use stress successfully.

Stress is inevitable in interpersonal relationships; but whether that stress is creative or destructive is determined by how you exchange energies with other people. And you are bound to meet plenty of them in a working lifetime. Anyone who has had an intense love affair knows that positive stress is blessedly real. By the same token, when you get uncomfortable vibes (or no signals at all) you are probably in the presence of hostile or incompatible energy. The Success System provides you with two ways to deal with interpersonal stress constructively in your career life: the first, by understanding your own force field, the second, by learning how your sun sign element interacts with the other elements.

The stress for which people pop all kinds of pills and take extended vacations is really depleted energy. (If that sounds obvious, remember we are not just talking mentally or physically.) No matter how brightly your aura glows, it is not inextinguishable. Complete extinction is, of course, death—but even a severe depletion can feel like it. Most of us get moderately drained of our psychic energies on a regular basis. In order to function at success level, it is vital to learn how to rev up those energies to the maximum whenever you feel the need.

Once again your horoscope gives clear instructions about how to do just that. The zodiacal sign that is directly opposite your Midheaven house sign indicates the things and activities that make you feel loved and secure—the perfect antidote to feelings of anxiety and tension. The Nadir of your chart, as it is called, represents your home, your roots, your foundation. It is the province of the moon and therefore the subconscious; so your Nadir may be a revelation. You may learn some tricks you never thought of to get you through the night—and to wake up smiling.

How to Use Stress on the Job: Your Force Field

Many a potentially successful career has foundered on the rocks of interpersonal relationships. Depending on your orientation, you may rejoice in or despise the fact that you have to share your career space with other people. But it is a fact, possibly the central fact of professional life. Fortunately, those other people are products of the same universe as you, so astrology can offer some important insights into what makes both you and them run.

The main roles anyone plays in the workaday drama are boss, employee, counselor, seller, and buyer (also known as prospect, client, or customer), and most one-on-one exchanges involve some combination of them. Possibly the most important role, however, is that of peer, because it is in this area that most difficulties arise. You hear a lot about competition being not only healthy, but even necessary to getting ahead; but the word cooperation generally gets short shrift. It is possible, of course, to both compete and cooperate, and those who do have mastered one of the more potent success skills.

The first thing to consider is that you are the pivot point in any interpersonal relationship. That aura you walk around with enters every room with you, goes on every appointment, creates a magnetic field around any desk, chair, or podium you occupy. It is your force field, the energies you give off to other people that condition what they give you back.

Taking sun sign, moon sign, and Ascendant sign into account, there are eight force fields. They are based on two groups of elements: fire and air, which are considered positive, and earth and water, which are considered negative. I find the electricity symbols preferable to the masculine/feminine distinction that is often used. Either works, though, because the point is polarity.

To decide which of the following force fields is yours, determine the elements of your sun sign, moon sign, and Ascendant sign. (If you have forgotten, go back to Chapter 5, "Underneath It All: The Four Elements.") Translate the air and fire signs into pluses (+), and the earth and water signs into minuses (−). Jot the three down in this order: sun, moon, and Ascendant, and match up your results with the appropriate force field description that follows.

FORCE FIELD #1. *Sun+ Moon+ Ascendant+*

With all three personal points in positive signs you probably come on strong and stay that way. If all three are fire signs, the situation is intensified; air is not quite so threatening. But that is what you are—a threat, and a triple threat at that. This can work for you or against you. Unless there are compensations (i.e., earth and water signs) in other parts of your horoscope, you may come across as abrasive and unfeeling in the case of fire or frankly chilly in the case of air. If you are all or predominantly fire, you might prove exhausting in your tendency to generate high enthusiasm at a steady and even noisy level. If you are mostly air, you could chatter and push yourself right out of someone's favor with your nervous energy. If you are aware of and can correct these possible flaws, your potential is quite marvelous. In the world of getting and spending, the positive qualities (astrologically speaking) are valued very high. You will exude interest, energy, and alacrity, and never seem to need a break. Your aura is particularly bright, so what you say and do (whatever it is) is generally impressive. The one other potential negative in this all-positive combination is that some people (especially superiors) may secretly fear you are out to take over the world—and everyone else's job along with it.

FORCE FIELD #2. Sun+ Moon+ Ascendant–

There is an aspect of the sneak thief about you. Not literally, of course, but you do tend to disarm people and then take them by surprise with your forcefulness. The disarming quality comes from your water or earth Ascendant, which will make the first impression you give a fairly "soft" one. If it is earth, you will have all the earmarks of a reliable, conscientious, and fairly serious person who puts business first, personal concerns second. With a water Ascendant, your positive and more aggressive sun and moon signs are masked with a kind of sweetness. That sweetness need not be all surface, but (especially if your sun or moon is in fire) you can get mighty charged up and temperamental when the occasion trips you off. Once people catch on, you've blown your cover—but it's still good cover to have. In general, this force field is an excellent combination. Underneath your relatively pliable exterior, you are quite commanding, and can assume and maintain a position of dominance. Your performance can be positive in the best sense of the word. Do take the trouble, however, to integrate some of the more desirable qualities of your earth or water Ascendant into your total personality, particularly in dealing with subordinates. In self-defense against your own docile front, you might, more often than not, turn hard as nails.

FORCE FIELD #3. Sun+ Moon– Ascendant+

You are a curious paradox. You have the will to win, and all the basic equipment necessary to do so, but somehow or other you lose heart—and your nerve—when push comes to shove. It's that old devil moon, which is in a negative earth or water sign. Don't get the impression that everybody with such a moon is in trouble; what it really amounts to is that your subconscious drives are out of whack with the rest of you. In general, the earth and water signs tend to want to draw within (even Capricorn does), while fire and air project outward. In effect this means that you will give the impression of being hard-headed, and may even believe you are. But, at the critical moment, you retreat. You may even beat yourself up for this tendency, which only intensifies the "downer" influence of your moon. The solution is to work with it. Become familiar with that core of influence, and sense when it is about to let you and your "active" sun down. When you are on the line, let your fire/air sun and Ascendant go on automatic and do the talking or hawking for you. Meanwhile, your moon can lay back and play strategy games—earth perceiving just what is going on, water feeling it. In some ways this is one of the best force field combinations: It is excellent in therapeutic situations, for instance, giving the possessor a nice balance of objectivity and sensitivity. In any encounter, it enables you to temper force with feeling.

FORCE FIELD #4. Sun+ Moon− Ascendant−

This force field may cause much frustration. Your sun sign is ready for action, but your Ascendant doesn't show it and your moon doesn't know it. Your frustrations most probably will arise from slow recognition of your worth by peers and superiors. And it is difficult for you to summon up the drive to do something about it. This is an excellent "creative" combination, however—and by this I mean the word as it is loosely thrown around in such businesses as advertising and publishing. This will be particularly true if your moon is in one of the water signs. With that sensitive base, you can form some nice creative concepts. With a fire or air sun sign, you should also have the determination and ego strength to get them across to others. With an earth moon you can lay practical plans, and implement them quite easily. It's the water or earth Ascendant that causes the real difficulties here. It might cause you to come off as a little too sober or serious for your own good. No matter how lightly you may patter when the subject is trivia, when the talk turns to business, your spark may seem to go out. Again, without the positive proddings of an active or positive moon, you could easily chalk it all up to things as they are—and miss out on opportunities. If this is your force field, think this one over: next time you feel unappreciated, take a look in the mirror. Do you really reflect the certainty and enthusiasm you feel about your ideas? You certainly can, if you try.

FORCE FIELD #5. *Sun– Moon+ Ascendant+*

This force field generates a success profile to about the same degree as force field #4, but the situation is somewhat different. Here you've got the name, but you really don't know how to play the game. Your fire or air Ascendant makes for a "brilliant" exterior, and having your moon in a positive sign as well puts some push behind it. Where this force field goes astray is in consciously putting all the pieces together with either logic (air) or inspiration (fire). Your moon is operating at a very high frequency, and your Ascendant can reflect it. However, when the sun must do its implementation work, something gets lost. If you have this force field, you undoubtedly feel at times that you are misunderstood, and it is not unlikely that you are. That hot idea that surfaced from your moon and that you presented so well may quickly turn cold when you try to plan its implementation. What happened? Simply this: your sun has put a damper on things—either by being too practical (earth) or too negative (water). And in this case I am using the word negative to mean pessimistic. What baffles people is why you seem to lose enthusiasm for your own good ideas. Your challenge in business or the professions is to develop the courage to make your convictions work. Remember, the sun in anyone's horoscope is the vitalizing force. Without a "vital" sun, the most passionate plans run the danger of coming to naught.

FORCE FIELD #6. *Sun– Moon+ Ascendant–*

This is a force field other people should approach with caution—and so should you. If you haven't found out already, you will discover at some point that when pushed too far you can act like a raving maniac. Your earth or water sun and Ascendant—no matter how "sturdy"—give the impression that you are a relatively docile creature. You don't push and shove; if you want something, you go about getting it in your own quietly forceful manner. However, just let someone lean on you too much, and you become "all moon"—that is, all instinct. Then, almost without conscious thought, you can tear your opponent to shreds with icy, biting logic, or practically burn him away with a tongue of fire. I worked with someone in business who had this force field, and I can tell you it's a wonder to watch. First the impassive face, then the slow boil, then the eruption! The person who has this force field is especially explosive if people try to take advantage, or to get away with something. In spite of this volatile tendency (which can be controlled to a degree), this combination works quite well. It is better when you work with others or for them, however. In a leader, force field #6 leaves something to be desired (unless Capricorn is dominant). But even in an administrative position, there is a quiet strength that is real, because it has a positive moon to back it up.

FORCE FIELD *#7. Sun– Moon– Ascendant+*

This is a difficult force field, more so for you than for other people. It is not pleasant to be told with regularity, "Gee, you're a lot different than I thought." It makes you start to wonder what people take you for. They probably take you for someone who is very outgoing and quite self-confident, which is not altogether true. In social and personal situations you make out very well. You have the spark and/or wit to attract (air/fire), and the emotional depth to relate nicely later on (earth/water). In business, however, this force field can have its drawbacks. For one thing, you may often be called upon for more "out front" work than you really care to do. In actuality, though you seem perfectly at ease in any situation, you are not really comfortable in groups of people you do not know well. Nor are you happy taking on brand new challenges—though you look the part. The tried and true is your most compatible area of operation. Many people not only survive but thrive beautifully with this force field. It is no contraindication to success. What you should be aware of, however, is your own level of anxiety. If you choose a career where your apparent breeziness puts you often in the path of challenge and risk, you could end up with a problem. You may well be up to it, but the question is, will you be happy doing it? Yours is a force field where the degree of material reward should be carefully balanced against the personal side of the scale.

FORCE FIELD *#8. Sun– Moon– Ascendant–*
This is the force field of the person who may be "always a bridesmaid, but never a bride." A dismal prospect? In the private sector, perhaps, but in the business world it is doubtful that you would ever really want the starring role anyway. Especially if your personal points are mainly in earth signs, you are well aware that attaining material security is the real purpose of one's work life. And you are by nature quite basic and tuned into the more personal side of things, both in your public and private worlds. Don't take me wrong if I say you are the "strong, silent type." You can and probably do make considerable verbal contributions in whatever field you operate—and very practical and/or perceptive ones at that. But somehow that's not where you live. The "low frequency" vibrations you give off reflect your values, and most people respect you for them. Unless you are mostly "solid" earth or "hard" water, there is a pleasant suppleness about you. But because you "handle" well, you might easily be suckered—that is, appear to be a dumping ground for everyone else's problems. Chances are you know that, and protect yourself against it. In fact, self-protection is one of your outstanding success skills. From that point of view—and many others—this is a force field to be reckoned with. In the commercial or fine arts or wherever you land, you'll stay around for a long time, and slowly but steadily reach the top.

26

How the Elements Interact

Synergy is an unfortunately overused word that in one sense means "energies working together," a smooth and mutually beneficial interchange. It can be regarded as the ideal way for people to act upon each other. In the haphazard world of business, though, where it is more often expediency than preference that pairs people off, synergy is not always the resulting mode. Whether this is a fortunate or an unfortunate state of affairs depends on your point of view. The words friction, tension, and stress have generally negative connotations—but in fact they are productive ways in which materials interact. You couldn't make a building stand very long without the physical principle of stress, for example. The same goes for people in the professional world. When you toss two incompatible characters together, you may not get a fine or a lasting romance, but chances are they will produce the unexpected. And in business, the goal is not harmony but progress.

That is why I am giving you both the good news and the bad news about how the four astrological elements and energies act upon each other. Of course you want to get along, but you also want to get ahead. In effect, that means you can't dodge anybody.

You have found out about your own force field; now I'll be dealing just with your sun sign element. There's a practical reason for this: For the most part that is all you will be able to find out about your opposite number in business. If you know the person well, you may be able to get full birth date and time, and if this is the case, look up their other personal points and adjust these readings accordingly. There will also be plenty of times when you won't have the faintest idea of what sun sign you're dealing with at the outset; but I promise you, before long you'll be able to accurately spot an element. You will of course meet "turntypes," as one psychologist and astrologer calls them. But (especially if you become interested in this crazy game) they will serve to sharpen your perceptions.

In the following dialogues, I have more than once stepped over the line into parody. My excuse is that I have used exaggeration for emphasis: the colors here are so bold, that you should be able to match anyone against them. And the purpose is for you to be able to "predict" the probable course of any on-the-job interchange.

DIALOGUE 1 *Fire/Fire*

This will not be love at first sight, because the competitive component is very strong. But fire and fire will at least understand each other, and understanding fire types can be a big problem for other people. It is that intuitive mode of thought fire people habitually use, almost deliberately obscuring present evidence in order to build future castles. And, even more disconcertingly, they get from A to Z by leaping over the entire middle of the alphabet.

FIRE A: We really have to put our minds to the Smith affair. Jones says the whole thing might fall apart.

FIRE B: He always looks on the dark side. I'm confident.

FIRE A: So am I. Say, won't it be great when the thing is operating and our profits are doubled?

FIRE B: Right—then we can start test marketing the Smitholater number 2.

FIRE A: Glad you mentioned that. I've had some great ideas. For instance, we could add a few . . .

FIRE B: Of course, and then it would be easy to make them optional at a higher price.

FIRE A: Especially when the packaging I have in mind is . . .

FIRE B: Like that, huh? Just what I was thinking, but maybe it needs more pizzazz, like . . .

FIRE A: Yeah, I can just see it. Why is everyone getting so nervous about the initial deal when you and I know that . . .

FIRE B: Right. There are so many pessimists in the world.

FIRE A: Speaking of them, maybe we better ask Jones what he thinks we should do about the immediate problem.

DIALOGUE 2 *Fire/Earth*

Far from dumb, fire knows only too well he's got a practical bone missing. That's why he has a grudging admiration for earth. Earth, for his part, would love to soar above the obvious, but doesn't know how. Hence his fascination with fire.

FIRE: You've always got all the answers. Tell me how we're going to handle this one.

EARTH: If you look at the facts, it's pretty clear what we have to do.

FIRE: I don't care what we *have* to do; I want to know what we *can* do to make it better for us. You're usually pretty good at that.

EARTH: This time I think we need some of your creative thinking.

FIRE: Okay. What I suggest is that we take a flyer and go for broke.

EARTH: I wish I could agree with you, but I'm afraid . . .

FIRE: Oh, come on, you're always worrying about things like next year's tax audit.

EARTH: We may not be around to see it the way you carry on.

FIRE: As a matter of fact, let me tell you confidentially about this fantastic job I'm after.

EARTH: I'd love to hear it, but I really should get back to my desk.

Earth, ever the realist, turns away with a mixture of envy and relief thinking, "Maybe if he leaves, I can get his job. It's a little more money, and I need it." Meanwhile, fire is on the phone with his broker investing the increased income he hasn't earned yet from a job he may not get. Or will he?

DIALOGUE 3 *Fire/Air*

If you have ever fanned glowing coals into flame, you'll get this picture immediately. Though he would prefer to work within a structure he comprehends, air is delighted with the way fire responds to his ideas. Fire usually finds air a blessed relief from some of the more soggy people around him.

AIR: I've been thinking about how we can improve relations between all the departments.

FIRE: More parties? Great!

AIR: No, I had something a little less noisy in mind. A company newsletter.

FIRE: Oh, ho! The Daily Cruise—a great name for a firm like ours.

AIR: No, not daily. People would get bored with it too quickly. One must keep in mind how people are.

FIRE: Well, I've got some suggestions for who we could put on the personals—births and deaths and all those things.

AIR: I hadn't thought of that kind of news. But it would be a nice adjunct to the business reportage and thought pieces I had in mind. Got any idea about clever ways to distribute it?

FIRE: Sure. I'll have my department mock up a special company newsstand we can put in the lobby. The building might object, but we'll worry about that later.

AIR: Thanks. It's always a pleasure to shoot the breeze with someone who shoots back.

DIALOGUE 4 *Fire/Water*

This is usually a case of instant antipathy because both feel threatened—fire by water's obvious dampening properties, and water by his suspicion that fire doesn't like him and would rather deal with someone else. Fire would, and another reason is that fire just doesn't feel comfortable with water's emoting, dire premonitions, and longing for the good old days.

FIRE: Look. I've been trying to explain that it's all very simple. Positive change. And no one's going to suffer.

WATER: I don't know. I just don't like the smell of it.

FIRE: Well I do. At least it's a new way of doing things.

WATER: I've got letters in my files about what happened last time we thought about making a change. Must have been '48. Or was it '51?

FIRE: Look. You don't have to worry about a thing. I'll take all the flak. It doesn't bother me. (And I'm going on vacation anyway.)

WATER: You just don't know how it can be. I do, oh, do I ever!

FIRE: Well, if you feel that strongly about it . . .

WATER: Now don't get me wrong. I wouldn't want anyone to think I'm not cooperative. It's just that I've got this feeling . . .

FIRE: Let's continue this later; I've got to get some fresh air.

DIALOGUE 5 *Earth/Earth*

When element meets element, there is quite naturally a degree of understanding, so the exchange is reasonably pleasant. But when two earth types try to get together, the conversation rarely leaves the ground. Most of the time neither one of them ever gets a glimpse of the forest, either, they are both so absorbed in details. This interchange is supposed to result in a whole new floor plan and a boost to company morale.

EARTH A: The way I see it, if we move Smith into Jones' office, that will free up space for Roberts.

EARTH B: But he really doesn't need that much space. We should leave him where he is and build shelves.

EARTH A: Why spend money on carpentry? I say we move him and make him double up with the photocopier.

EARTH B: Good point. Now, what are we going to do about the bathrooms?

EARTH A: They're quite adequate. Good solid facilities. Need a coat of paint, but forget magazine racks.

EARTH B: Agreed. But have you seen the condition the cleaning people leave that ladies' room in?

EARTH A: Not recently, but the men's room is a disgrace. Maybe we should recommend a new brand of detergent. My wife's been using Brand X—one of those no-name cheapies.

EARTH B: Terrific product. I use it, too. Hey, at this rate we may come in under budget.

EARTH A: Hand me a piece of paper. While we're finishing this up I want to make up my shopping list—wheat germ, yogurt, vitamins . . .

EARTH B: Let's not rush through this. We haven't even started to talk about the really important things yet. Now, last time I looked around the wastebaskets looked a little shabby.

EARTH A: Let 'em shove them farther under the desks.

EARTH B: Brilliant.

DIALOGUE 6 *Earth/Air*

These two get along almost famously. Their orientations—one practical, one logical—come from roughly the same place. But there is a big difference, and that lies in the fact that earth is closer to home base than air. Earth really does care a lot; air might like to, but he is by nature too lofty.

AIR: I think this program meets everybody's needs, and I'm delighted you've agreed to undertake its implementation.

EARTH: It's good, and it works. Everything is so clearly laid out, anyone should be able to understand it.

AIR: I notice you've made some notes, however. What do you mean by "insufficient extras"?

EARTH: It strikes me that instead of just orange juice and milk, the kids might like some cookies now and then. And shouldn't we build in some space for classroom pets?

AIR: I don't understand why those things are important. This program is meant to feed their minds, not their stomachs. And animals require extra personnel time.

EARTH: What's the matter? Don't you like kids and animals?

AIR: Of course I do. I get upset just thinking about the dreadful conditions underprivileged kids live with. And *Lassie* is a fine motion picture. But the answer is "no" on the extras.

EARTH: Just as well. Wait until I tell you how much this thing is going to cost, anyway.

AIR: Pass me the Kleenex.

DIALOGUE 7 *Earth/Water*

It would be stating the obvious to point out that when you mix these two elements you literally get mud. In the end earth and water people may have to pry themselves apart, but they know it's better for both of them.

WATER: I just can't seem to get anywhere with this project. Thought you could help me out.

EARTH: I'll try. But I don't seem to have the feel for these things that you do. Have you thought about putting the septic tank farther away from the house?

WATER: That's not my problem. What I really need is some advice about how to handle this couple. I think they're out to get me—have been hassling me ever since I've been on the job.

EARTH: Gee, that's too bad. I know how it is to get uptight about things like that. Let's go out for a bit and talk it over. There's a terrific little restaurant that just opened up.

WATER: I'd love it; they've got great cheesecake. But I'd better not. Been watching my diet. Old ticker, you know.

EARTH: By the way, did you hear about what happened to Jones? Real shame.

WATER: I feel bad, too, but I'd rather not talk about it. Think I'll go see Johnson. He always cheers me up.

DIALOGUE 8 *Air/Air*

What a pair of butterflies is here! They can keep circling a subject for hours and never figure out where to land. But neither of them usually minds because discussion is their favorite form of exercise. It's so ultra-civilized.

AIR A: When you consider the possibilities, it might be better if we chose Plan A.

AIR B: It has definite merit, but have you also thought about the potential of Plan B?

AIR A: Most certainly, and there are advantages. But one must take into account the contingencies.

AIR B: Are you using the word in the sense of likelihood—or with its less desirable connotations of the unforeseen?

AIR A: The latter, of course. One must consider every angle.

AIR B: Quite true. Plan A might be a safer course. But, then again, the unpredictable can have its charms. Did I tell you about the woman I met at a party who dresses herself each day by reaching into a dark closet and putting on whatever she touches? Most amusing.

AIR A: Does she look outside first to see if it's raining?

AIR B: Didn't ask, but I'm glad you did. It will give me an excuse to call. She and her husband look like good people to know.

AIR A: You could ask them about Plan A versus Plan B.

AIR B: Excellent thought. Let's kick that around for a while.

AIR A: Don't mind if we do.

DIALOGUE 9 *Air/Water*

One of the rules of element interchange is that people generally admire what they lack. Their awareness of the deficiency may be dim, but it can operate like a magnet. This is often the case with air and water. One thinks he would like to feel; the other feels he would like to think. Both feel at a disadvantage.

AIR: I just can't understand how you get along with all those people down in production. I can't talk to them about anything.

WATER: I don't know; I guess I just sort of sense it when somebody needs a friend. But you do so well with the boys upstairs. What's your secret?

AIR: That's easy; we either talk business or chat about our golf games. I must admit it makes me nervous when one of them asks me how I'm feeling. I never quite know what they're getting at.

WATER: Most days I'd have plenty to say if anyone asked me that. Like today, I have this funny pain in the back . . .

AIR: There was an interesting article in the paper the other day about the connection of lower back pain with alcohol consumption.

WATER: I almost never drink too much. Did someone say I do? You always know what people are talking about.

AIR: Then why don't I have as many friends in this company as you do?

WATER: Aaaah, everybody likes you. You're smart.

AIR: You really think so?

WATER: I don't know, but you see I get this feeling . . .

DIALOGUE 10 *Water/Water*

The natural milieu of water is the emotions. Because their capacity for empathy is almost inexhaustible, many people with water emphasized in their horoscopes gravitate toward psychiatry and the counseling professions, both as practitioners and as patients. Here's what can happen when water meets water on that marshy ground.

WATER A: You say you've felt this way since you were a child.

WATER B: I think so.

WATER A: You're not sure?

WATER B: Well, you've got me all confused.

WATER A: I'm sorry. I didn't mean to. I think you may be confusing yourself.

WATER B: What makes you say that? Am I not doing things the way you want me to?

WATER A: I just want you to be comfortable. Would you rather not talk about your childhood today?

WATER B: I'd rather not, but you know best.

WATER A: No one can be wise for someone else. But maybe we should wind it up for today.

WATER B: That means you don't give a damn about me, doesn't it?

WATER A: On the contrary; I think I care too much.

WATER B: If you care so much, why do you keep trying to make me miserable?

WATER A: I'm trying to do the opposite. But if you're so miserable why do you keep coming back?

WATER B: I need you.

WATER A: That makes me feel good.

27

Stress Relief: The Nadir

There are any number of theories about how the harried, uptight executive can turn off his workaday mind, relax his body, and restore his strength. Most of the recommended methods—like meditation—are valid. What they do, in effect, is to make the person feel whole again by putting fragmented body and soul back together. This is the principle at work in the astrological method of relaxing. The Nadir of your chart is the "other half" of your Midheaven; as the Midheaven is the public you (your body), the Nadir is the private you (your soul). Like the Midheaven, the Nadir is an indicator of the atmosphere or environment a particular person can thrive in rather than the personality itself. In the case of the Nadir, this environment is the original or primal one that represents the "womb" from which you came and is therefore, the "safest" place for you to retreat in times of stress. Although it sometimes does, the Nadir will not necessarily reflect your childhood milieu. It does indicate what for you would have been the ideal—regardless of your sun, moon, or Ascendant sign.

These suggestions for the activities, entertainments, and "goof-offs" most suited to help you really relax are given for your Nadir sign, which is opposite your Midheaven house sign.

Libra at the Midheaven: Aries at the Nadir

There is an edge to the activities that go with Aries at the Nadir—a fairly sharp edge. What works best is a combination of vigorous activity, competitive sports, and being where the action is. That is, rather than needing the peaceful pause that refreshes, the person with Aries at the Nadir relaxes by doing. Doing something physical is at the top of the list, and it can be free-fall parachute jumping, downhill skiing, hang-gliding, or a fierce game of tennis or racquetball. The point is, with Aries at the Nadir, one thrives on competition—with oneself and/or others. A few rounds on the golf course or turns at the parallel bars might do; and if that's all there is available, it will have to. However, with Aries at the Nadir the person feels most alive when there is an element of risk—of mind or body. Likewise, when he is a spectator, Aries at the Nadir needs a lot of action and noise. A rock concert, a fast game like hockey, or a day at the races are all typical turn-ons.

When at home base, the Aries Nadir person is most comfortable with fairly spare surroundings—lots of white walls, clean edges, and little clutter. It's a very "modern" sign. He should make room for a super stereo system and a creative hobby, however, such as woodcarving, the drums, or drawing.

Scorpio at the Midheaven: Taurus at the Nadir

If you could re-create the field of flowers in which Ferdinand lolled so happily, it would be the ideal milieu for Taurus at the Nadir. There is an extreme need for peace and quiet, and a predilection for all natural things.

What this means is that the Taurus Nadir person should slip away to the country as often as possible, even for day trips. Most cities have at least one oasis of green, so he should seek out nature walks there. Even spending a few minutes under some trees or near a fountain can be refreshing when Taurus is the Nadir sign. Music truly does soothe the savage breast that can rage inside the person born with this Nadir. All forms of music are pleasing, but especially the classical. Regardless of your personal taste, if this is your Nadir, savor chamber music. You may be surprised. Its beautiful structure re-creates the world in which you were meant to live.

Art, too, is high on the list of Taurus Nadir relaxers—either the viewing or the doing. Museum trips from time to time are a must. Stimulation of the other senses brings blessed relief, too. In addition to the obvious, Taurus at the Nadir should indulge in comfort food when the stress is severe (as long as the "ice cream moments" don't become too frequent). The ideal surroundings are warm and comfortable with lots of plants, plump pillows, and soft colors. The home of the Taurus Nadir person is incomplete without a piano; and for stress relief the possessor should polish it as well as play it.

Sagittarius at the Midheaven: Gemini at the Nadir

While the individual with personal points in Gemini might tend to become over-stimulated, the person with Gemini at the Nadir requires mental activity to really get it together. This Nadir loves company, and can be in misery without it. Group activities can include cocktails and conversation, bridge, or a game of chess.

Obviously there are times when everyone wants to be alone. Ideal Gemini Nadir solo pursuits are reading and watching "head stuff" on television; an inane sitcom could be worse than nothing. Speaking of the tube, here's a little trick for Gemini Nadir people who may have a horror of solitude. No matter what you are doing, leave on the television image and turn down the volume; the effect is of activity in the room.

Of course, a movie or a play is good relaxation fodder for Gemini at the Nadir, too. However, even if it is anathema, you Gemini Nadir people should move your bodies as well as your minds, and in some structured way. Brisk walks at a fast clip work wonders; deep breathing of fresh air should go along with them. With Gemini at the Nadir, you will undoubtedly share living quarters. Regardless of your partner's preferences, you should make sure you have a room of your own. Pile it high with books and records; decorate with prints and drawings; keep it as cluttered as you like. That way it will be a real Gemini retreat.

Capricorn at the Midheaven: Cancer at the Nadir

If you have Cancer at the Nadir you know those yearnings for a dark, quiet place. Symbolically, your "home" is really the womb. Even if it isn't the actual thing, you can create a like atmosphere to achieve the peace that you desire.

The prime requisite is filling your home base with all the things you love—the memorabilia that recall to you the times you have been happiest. Cancer at the Nadir thrives on the past. That also means traditional furnishings are the most compatible for you. However, if you can afford it, avoid ersatz antiques. Cancer at the Nadir calls for the real thing, in whatever you surround yourself with. And that includes people. For the Cancer Nadir person, a cozy evening with one old friend is preferable to the most scintillating gathering of strangers, or even acquaintances. For the person with Cancer at the Nadir, home is where the heart is, and the central point is the kitchen. In fact, cooking should be learned as a survival skill, as a hedge against those moments when disaster threatens to overwhelm. To the lists of things the Cancer Nadir person collects, should be added all forms of kitchen utensils.

Water in all forms is the natural milieu of this person. That means physical and outdoor activities should center around it. Swimming is the most truly relaxing form of exercise; sailing and all water sports are marvelously refreshing.

Aquarius at the Midheaven: Leo at the Nadir

The person with Leo at the Nadir should bathe himself in light—real sunlight as often as possible; substitute forms when it is not available or when he is indoors. While Cancer prefers subdued colors and soft lighting, the natural Leo atmosphere is bright in every sense of the word. Reds, oranges, and golds should dominate the decorating scheme; windows should be as bare as possible. Although the Leo Nadir person responds beautifully to a night on the town, entertaining at home is equally restoring. The most effective gatherings when Leo is at the Nadir are those in which no expense is spared. Lavishness is truly comforting, and spending money can be worth a month in the country. Leo at the Nadir marks the person who is a natural host or hostess. Whatever the childhood may have been, he seeks to create an atmosphere where generosity and genuine warmth abound. Speaking of warmth, if you have Leo at the Nadir, try to put a working fireplace in your future if you do not already have one. An evening of fire-gazing can set you up to withstand anything that occurs the next day. Travel is a Leo Nadir pursuit, as it is when any fire sign is on this point in the chart. The obvious places to head for are beaches, tropical islands, or the "sun" countries. Because Leo is a fire sign, fairly strenuous sports and physical activities are the most beneficial.

Pisces at the Midheaven: Virgo at the Nadir

The greater the chaos in his public world, the more the person with Virgo at the Nadir will need order in his private one.

Virgo Nadir people (like Virgos) can find that sharing living quarters with another person causes great tension. This is especially so if that other person is the slightest bit sloppy, and that goes for his tastes in music, art, and food, as well as his personal habits. The best way for the Virgo Nadir person to relax is to get away from everyone—including his one and only. Solitary vacations are a great prescription, but the hotel service had better be flawless. Like Gemini at the Nadir, Virgo here calls for a sequestered spot within the home. In his very own place, the Virgo Nadir person should be free to pursue whatever hobby he likes. There are many that would suffice, such as stamp-collecting, model-building, jewelry-making, etc. The common threads are mental and manual dexterity and concentration. The person needn't be proficient; the absorbing nature of the work is what brings about the relaxation of tension. Unless the person is also a Virgo sun or moon sign, the necessity for perfection won't be so strong. However, when it comes to the state of his overall environment, this is not quite the case. A home base that does not have a place for everything and everything in its own place can make a person with this Nadir literally ill. If this is your Nadir, recognize this tendency, and make your partner aware of it. If all else fails, take a walk or visit a health food store.

Aries at the Midheaven: Libra at the Nadir

Libra at the Nadir means that you are most renewed by "civilized" pleasures. They do not necessarily have to involve others, but you do feel most alive when least alone. In general loud bashes are out, however. Libra Nadir thrives on the soft tinkle of ice in cocktail glasses, cultivated conversation, and tasteful surroundings.

Under the rulership of Venus, Libra at the Nadir derives

immense benefit from all that is beautiful—it can be music, art, a good read, or a night at the ballet. But Libra Nadir's need for harmony and structure goes even deeper, and is more subtle. It extends to every detail of his environment, both physical and emotional. Not only should the person with Libra at the Nadir have something lovely to look at wherever he turns; he should also avoid like the plague any after-hours relationship that is even the least bit unsightly. This sensitivity can be mitigated by a "tough" sun or moon sign; but it can never be totally eradicated.

Male or female, the Libra Nadir personality should indulge in sports or physical activity where graceful movements count more than sheer strength. Golf is an ideal unisex sport; and more and more males are finding that some form of dance as exercise is a great way to unwind. This is the Nadir of the Sunday painter, but any creative hobby can do wonders to brighten Monday's back-to-work mood.

Taurus at the Midheaven: Scorpio at the Nadir

Scorpio at the Nadir is an indicator of active relaxation, as is Aries: strenuous sports of all kinds are high on the list. The Scorpio Nadir person should go so far as to get into organized amateur competitions. Long-distance ocean racing, with its intense endurance requirements, would be an ideal Scorpio Nadir pursuit. However, much more available activities like handball or squash will do quite nicely. For the less competitive, tough workouts at a gym should be considered.

Though he may not know it, the person with Scorpio at the Nadir revs up much better in solitude than in company. Groups sap his energy, because his natural environment is the inner rather than the outer world. If you have a Scorpio Nadir, you could find meditation most rewarding. Most meditative techniques require strong concentration on a single object or word, so the very intensity of the discipline would have its effect on you.

The purpose of the Scorpio Nadir person's efforts at relaxation should be to remove his mind from himself. Besides meditation, other good techniques are reading something that requires concentration, doing crossword puzzles, or playing other mind games.

Scorpio Nadir surroundings should be anything but flimsy or trendy. Good leather furniture, woven textures in subdued colorings, gleaming woods are some of the components that should be in a Scorpio Nadir decorating scheme. And the company Scorpio Nadir keeps should be as solid as his surroundings.

Gemini at the Midheaven: Sagittarius at the Nadir

The dream home of the person with Sagittarius at the Nadir is full of people and activity—that is, if he ever stays home. There is a natural urge to travel, and it is not likely that his childhood experiences include changes of residence. It doesn't much matter where the Sagittarius Nadir person goes, as long as there's plenty to do. Inactivity is death.

In addition to all kinds of sports, you with Sagittarius on the Nadir should consider getting involved in amateur athletics in your spare time. Little League teams now welcome coaches of either sex. The great outdoors always beckons. Like Taurus, you should get out of town as often as possible—but you should choose more rugged terrain. City-side, keep up with all that is current. The Sagittarius Nadir, even more than Gemini, signals the need for newsy things. That will give the Sagittarius Nadir person plenty to talk about when he takes out his natural gregariousness at home. Large, sprawling parties are like balm for his soul. There, he can be peripatetic right on his own ground.

There is a more serious side to this Nadir as well. Law and politics will be of high interest; the Sagittarius Nadir person might even get involved in local political organizations for the sheer joy of it. With this Nadir, the person is most comfortable when most involved. There are quiet times necessary, of course, and the person should fill them with mental pursuits.

Cancer at the Midheaven: Capricorn at the Nadir

The Capricorn Nadir person often has a natural affinity for concrete—that is, the big city. Not that he doesn't enjoy nature; in fact, rock-climbing is a suggested sport. However, when all is said and done, Capricorn Nadir doesn't want to get too far away from all that is civilized and structured. He might find his leisure time filled up with things others do not find at all relaxing; he might enjoy being a member of the Chamber of Commerce or performing some other voluntary civic duty. The trappings of security make him feel secure. That goes for his own home, as well. Regardless of sun or moon sign, the Capricorn Nadir person will want the best of everything in his surroundings, because that is where he comes from, symbolically at least. The home need not be showy, but it should always look ready to be shown. There is not the compulsion for neatness that there is with a Virgo Nadir; but the person with a Capricorn Nadir feels best when all's right with his domestic world. On the physical side, Capricorn Nadir goes in for "establishment sports"—anything from golf to riding to hounds, depending upon what the local establishment dictates. In books, art, and literature, the tastes will be high, or again, at least at the top level of the particular community.

For true relaxation, the person with a Capricorn Nadir should get close to the earth and earthier things sometimes, either actually gardening, or pursuing a hobby where he builds with his hands.

Leo at the Midheaven: Aquarius at the Nadir

Sky diving, solo flying, and/or spending a lot of time above the timber line are the ideal ways for Aquarius Nadir people to "turn off" and tune into themselves. Less physically lofty things can turn the trick, but they, too, should be at a high level. This is the Nadir of the person who thrives on being an activist, particularly in the area of community improvement. Unlike Capricorn, Aquarius Nadir will gravitate not toward what is best, but toward what could be better. He thrives in the pure air of good neighborship. In more private moments, the person with an Aquarius Nadir takes naturally to "curiosities." Science fiction, pornography, electronic music, and other such far-out delights can absorb his interest. He might even be a collector of such things. The home he makes for himself will be open to all, but only at his invitation. In spite of his concern for others, the Aquarian Nadir type is a private person. He might even choose the house on the highest ground, being most secluded from view. The "Aquarian nest" that represents his original environment might have been a touch chilly. At any rate, what the person with an Aquarius Nadir needs now is to be left alone—not all the time, but more often than you might expect. Modernism is reflected in his personal tastes; but in his need for contemplative solitude, there is more of the monastery and the Middle Ages.

Virgo at the Midheaven: Pisces at the Nadir

Everything the Pisces Nadir conjures up is soft, cloudy, and a little nebulous. This goes not only for music and colors; it can characterize the person's very modus operandi in his leisure hours. Having things in a state of flux could drive most other types wild; the Pisces Nadir person thrives on it. That is why, even though sun or moon sign might dictate otherwise, the person with this Nadir does best when he hangs loose about his after-hours activities. That doesn't mean he should do nothing; it means he should try not to structure that part of his life too tightly. The natural propensity is for spur-of-the-moment decisions that suit his particular mood. Those moods can vary, of course, depending on what signs the personal points fall in. But what satisfies those moods best are typically Piscean pursuits—for instance, liquid refreshment of all sorts, but swimming and water sports are the most highly recommended. This is the Nadir of the person who becomes obsessed with the idea of a long, warm bath right in the middle of a busy day. Of course, it is a natural relaxer. Actual poetry and everything poetic fall under this Nadir as well. It is as if the Pisces Nadir person keeps trying to recapture the feeling of being soothed by lullabies. Other things can soothe too, though, like genial company. Unlike the Aquarian Nadir, this is the sign of the "drop in" home. It may not always be the neatest, but Pisces Nadir likes it that way. Clutter is one of life's greatest comforts.

FIVE

TIMING YOUR SUCCESS

28

Five-Year Planetary Forecast for Each Sun Sign and Midheaven House Sign

Those who mistake their good luck for their merit are inevitably bound for disaster.

A man gazing on the stars is proverbially at the mercy of the puddles on the road.

No comment is necessary on the two quotations that begin this chapter. I do hope their intent is clear enough to sum up my point of view on astrological prediction.

In the predictions that follow, you should look at both your sun sign and your Midheaven house sign. They indicate two different ways of looking at planetary cycles, that is, the "transits" or actual paths of the planets in the sky during the next five years. The cycles with which I have dealt are those of Neptune, Uranus, Saturn, Jupiter, and Mars.

In terms of timing, Neptune represents a kind of permanent

condition that will be in effect for some years to come. Uranus is a similar case, but does move more quickly. Saturn is the "hour hand," Jupiter the "minute hand," and Mars the "second hand." Pluto moves too slowly to be of any real use as a timer; the planets faster than Mars do no more than bring "good" or "bad" days.

The planets affect the individual in two ways. In the first they form "aspects" or geometric angles to his natal sun—that is, the degree of the sign into which the sun falls in his natal horoscope.

Some angles (90-degree squares and 180-degree oppositions, for instance) bring stressful periods. Harmonious aspects, like 60-degree sextiles and 120-degree trines, in general herald good times. The second way in which the planets affect the individual is by traveling through various sectors or houses of the horoscope, indicating which areas of his life will be affected. In this case, the Midheaven is the reference point.

When you look at how the "decans" of each sign are divided, it should remind you that the sun does not pass from one sign to the next on the same day each year. It varies from year to year. If you are born on the "cusp" between two signs, be sure to check out your birthday in Table 1, "Sun Sign Changes," in the back of the book.

Sun Sign Aries

First decan: March 22–March 31
Second decan: April 1–April 10
Third decan: April 11–April 21

From now through January 1984, Neptune in the sign of Sagittarius will be trine to your sun, bringing benefits of creativity, but a touch of confusion regarding ultimate goals. Those born in the third decan of Aries will be most affected.

Of great importance to all Aries sun signs, is the fact that in mid-November 1981—after a few months of hesitantly dipping its toes in the sign—Uranus enters Sagittarius, and remains there until February 1988. This has a great energizing effect, stimulating first-decan people through 1982 and 1983, those born in the second decan are affected in 1984 and 1985, third decan people later on. Uranus can bring "explosions" and "earthquakes," loosely translated as unexpected career changes.

Throughout 1981 and until the end of 1982 (and also mid-1983) Saturn moves through the sign of Libra, strongly affecting Aries sun signs. Its effects vary, but they usually involve frustration. Under Saturn transits, things do not move swiftly. However, the good news is that it is the right time to seek relatively permanent career ground. In 1981 Jupiter moves right along with Saturn in Libra, mitigating his less pleasant effects. In fact, with Jupiter in Libra, Aries sun signs can look for opportunities to expand. The next big Jupiter year for Aries sun signs starts in December 1982 and goes on till mid-January 1984, a most beneficial period. Things are not really "Jupiter-great" again until February 1985 when the planet moves into Aquarius.

Midheaven Sign Aries

Through most of the next few years (until late November 1984), Neptune hovers in your sector of hard work, softening the long hours you may be putting in. This same sector begins feeling the effect of Uranus in February 1981, and will be affected for years to come. This could mean an erratic job pattern, but if it does, you can look for relief to Jupiter, which comes along in late 1982 and stays throughout 1983. He should ease your tensions, and bring some profits, too.

When Saturn makes his pass through this work sector from mid-November 1985 through February 1988, you'll really be able to put it all together. Meanwhile, throughout 1981 and until the end of 1982, Saturn resides in your private sector of domestic life. Because Jupiter is with Saturn in 1981, this should be an excellent year in that area, if a trifle somber. In 1984 and most of 1985 Saturn brings you the possibilities of some solid and possibly even lasting creative work. Chances are you will begin in these creative ventures under Jupiter in 1982.

If you have ever thought of going into partnership, make your move in 1984, when Jupiter is in your sector of "others." (You might consider marriage, too.) In 1985 and 1986 Jupiter continues to climb toward your Midheaven, arriving there in early 1987. With Saturn still making you concentrate, this could be a time of considerable achievement.

Sun Sign Aries/Midheaven Sign Aries

For Aries sun signs, a fast-moving Mars brings its fiery push-aheadness, and for Aries Midheaven people, a very energetic Mars (in its own sign) touches your Midheaven and gives you a shove during the following periods: mid-March to late April 1981; late February to early April 1983; early February until mid-March 1985. Stumbling block times for Aries sun sign and Aries Midheaven people are: mid-December 1981 until early August 1982; late November 1983 through mid-January 1984; late October until mid-December 1985.

Sun Sign Taurus

First decan: April 22–May 1
Second decan: May 2–May12
Third decan: May 13–May 21

Neptune has no great effect on Taurus sun signs until the end of 1984 when it enters Capricorn, a compatible earth sign, and could "glamorize" things. Uranus, which has been troubling Taureans for years, gives its last gasp in Scorpio from mid-March to mid-November 1981, affecting only third-decan people. All of you can look for relief after that.

Saturn, which won't do much in the meantime, will begin opposing Taurus in December 1982 when it enters Scorpio, to stay until mid-November 1985 (with a brief respite from May to August 1983). First-decan people will start to feel it right away at the end of 1982, and others later on in the period of Saturn's stay in Scorpio. As in all things, when Saturn opposes he can be a blessing or a curse. My advice to you is to utilize the period to examine your true career goals, and test every opportunity that comes along for its solidity.

Jupiter will have just left Scorpio when Saturn enters, so at least through 1982 you should be able to feel Jupiter's beneficial rays and put them to work for you. Use the time wisely, because Jupiter doesn't do much for you again until January 1984, when he enters Capricorn and should bring a blast of good things until he leaves in early 1985.

Midheaven Sign Taurus

Neptune has been affecting your "creative" sector for some time and will give you a touch of the poet until it leaves Sagittarius completely in late November 1984. (He might bring confusion in matters concerning children, too.)

If you have begun to feel as if your home life will never be settled and secure again, take heart. Uranus leaves that sector when it leaves Scorpio forever (or at least for eighty-four years) in mid-November 1981. (Many divorces and residence changes happen under that transit.) Then for a good long time you'll have Uranus prodding you to do something very special—particularly in the area of independent work.

Saturn is crawling toward the Nadir of your chart and will reach it in early 1983; then you will really get settled, in home and career. However, this is not peak achievement time. Saturn here begins a building process that will culminate fourteen years from now. However, in the meantime plenty of good things are going to happen. Jupiter will be swinging through your communications house, giving you excellent on-the-job ammunition. And when it gets to your home base in early 1982, it will brighten it considerably. Then in late 1982 Jupiter starts beaming in the area of "public performance," meaning you can shine, too. Throughout 1984 Jupiter will make you accept hard work gracefully; in 1985 your personal relationships and partnerships get his benefits. By early 1986 your joint finances should begin to feel his effects.

Sun Sign Taurus/Midheaven Sign Taurus

For Taurus sun signs, there will be bursts of Martian energy; and for Taurus Midheaven people, these are the times you should shoot for the moon: Late April until early June 1981; early April to mid-May 1983; mid-March to late April 1985. For both Taurus sun signs and Taurus Midheaven signs, these are the times that will try your souls, and your patience: early August till late September 1982; mid-January through mid-August 1984; mid-December 1985 till early February 1986.

Sun Sign Gemini

First decan: May 22–June 2
Second decan: June 3–June 12
Third decan: June 13–June 21

I don't want to imply that Gemini sun signs have their wits easily scattered, but Neptune hasn't been making it any easier. He will continue to try to mess up clear career thinking for third-decan people until 1984—so take note.

Some real excitement begins for Gemini sun signs in mid-February 1981, when Uranus enters Sagittarius, and continues on for seven years. Change is in the air, and all decans should be on the alert. First-decan people will feel it from 1981 to 1983, second decan mainly in 1984 and 1985, third decan after that. Uranus is bringing an opposition aspect, so the surprises may not all be pleasant, however.

Saturn is "friendly" to Geminis, as friendly as he can be, until about December 1982, when he assumes a more or less neutral position—except for another good spell from May through August 1983. Take advantage of Saturn's good points now. He may really start to put the brakes on you in mid-November 1985, for a two-year period, in which you could feel hemmed in.

1981 is a great Jupiter year for Geminis. He will both push you and pull you from December 1982 until January 1984, when Jupiter will be in Sagittarius, your opposite number sign. You will not feel the full force of friendly Jupiter again until February 1985, but it will be in effect throughout that whole year.

Midheaven Sign Gemini

Neptune continues to "bless" your home sector until 1984.

Remembering that Neptune both clouds things and makes them lovelier; do your own interpretation.

It is important, because Uranus—sometimes called the "great destroyer"—begins to affect that sector in February 1981. It is a seven year transit, and you will get the full effects at some time during that period. Think positively: a beneficial relocation could be on the agenda.

From early 1981 through December 1982 (and again between May and September 1983) you will be experiencing the dubious pleasure of having Saturn in your sector of earned income. He has a very bad reputation for the ills he can bring here in terms of restricted finances, etc. However, as one astrologer says, people have been known to win the lottery under this transit. Don't take any chances, however; lock your discretionary income cash box for the duration, and throw away the key. Saturn will continue to affect you very personally when he is in Scorpio (mainly 1984 and 1985); you get him out of your own hair and into your sphere of others starting around the beginning of 1986. At that time, Saturn "opposes" your Midheaven, and you could make a job change—either voluntary or involuntary.

Since Jupiter is in your "money house" as well in 1981, you will probably be in reasonably good shape. In 1982 Jupiter has good effects on your immediate surroundings (including your job); then in 1983 he drops in at your home and does his good work there. In 1984 and 1985 Jupiter should both expand your creative thinking and ease up any job tensions you have. In 1986 your personal relationships and partnerships will experience a Jupiter boon.

Sun Sign Gemini/Midheaven Sign Gemini

Gemini sun signs are affected quite actively by Mars (fire planet stimulating air sign); and for Gemini Midheaven signs, these Mars to Midheaven transits should be acted upon: early June to mid-July 1981; mid-May till end of June 1983; late April through mid-June 1985. Times when "hyper" Gemini sun signs could come a cropper, and when Gemini Midheaven people should take care not to falter are: late September until early November 1982; mid-August through early October 1984; early February until late March 1986.

Sun Sign Cancer

First decan: June 22–July 3
Second decan: July 4–July 13
Third decan: July 14–July 22

Neptune more or less "leaves you alone" until January 1984, when this planet enters Capricorn, the opposing sign to Cancer. Mark the date well, because you will have Neptune with you for many years to come. Since Cancer is a highly creative sign, I like to think Neptune will do its work constructively. Neptune brings indecisiveness, however, so all decans should be watchful.

Third-decan Cancer sun signs will still have Uranus in friendly aspect during much of 1981. Positive changes are the general rule under this transit. Use them well, because Uranus leaves you, for all intents and purposes, for quite a while.

All Cancer sun signs will undergo a "square" aspect of Saturn to the sun during the period January 1981 to December 1982. The first decan will feel it mainly during the first year; the second and third decans in 1982. This kind of Saturn transit can be a bit heavy. It will be a period of reevaluation at the least. Think of it as a time to lay sturdy foundations that will hold when Saturn opposes in about seven years. During some of 1983, all of 1984, and most of 1985, Saturn gets cozier for Cancer sun signs—so the strain will not last.

Anyway, Jupiter holds hands with Saturn during 1981, so things won't be too "saturnine" for first-decan people. 1982 is a "good Jupiter year" for all Cancers; 1984 is another one, and particularly significant with Jupiter in Capricorn. A lot of good can happen; you won't really find Jupiter doing his best for you again until 1987.

Midheaven Sign Cancer

Lucky you, the great Jupiter/Saturn conjunction (with both planets in the same sign) of 1981 (a once-in-twenty-years event) takes place in your house of "self." To give specifics is not possible, but there will undoubtedly be a significant "benefit consolidation" for you. Depending on where you are in your career life, it could be a promotion, a beneficial change, or recognition of you as an individual.

Take advantage of it, because Neptune continues to haunt all your communications, and Uranus may start to cause you problems in that area when it enters Sagittarius in early 1981 to stay for some time. However, Uranus's presence in this "neighborly" house could mean a great stimulation of your social and job connections.

When Saturn moves on to Scorpio in 1983, to stay intermittently until November 1985, you will have to tolerate the frustrations he brings to your house of personal income and possessions. Do not fear, however, because this is often simply a realignment of values. You may do some soul-searching about what is really important to you.

Throughout 1982 Jupiter will be in Scorpio, affecting this possessions sector, so it is possible you will go out on a limb of overexpansion during that period, and will want to pull back. Jupiter revs up communications during 1983, sends good rays to your home during 1984, moves on to your creative sphere in 1985 (could mean a birth), and lightens up your work load in 1986.

Sun Sign Cancer/Midheaven Sign Cancer

Mars doesn't have tremendous force when it is in the sign of Cancer, but it does give initiative to Cancer sun signs, and touches the top for Cancer Midheaven people during these periods: mid-July through end of August 1981; end of June till mid-August 1983; June tenth through end of July 1985. All of you should watch out for aggravations and obstacles from: November first until December tenth 1982; early October until mid-November 1984; late March until early October 1986.

Sun Sign Leo

First decan: July 23–August 2
Second decan: August 3–August 14
Third decan: August 15–August 23

Third-decan Leo sun signs will continue to have the marvelously glamorizing rays of Neptune shine on them until January 1984.

That can mean they will do great things, or just dream about them.

All Leo sun signs, easily stimulated anyway, will be receiving a lot of Uranian energy when that planet enters Sagittarius in early 1981 to stay until 1988. First-decan people will start "freaking out" during late 1981 and 1982; the second decan feels it during 1983 and 1984, and the last decan later on. Don't worry; it's all very positive, and very exciting.

Saturn is a nice steadying influence to Leos until late 1982 and during parts of 1983. When the "testing planet" is in Scorpio during 1984 and 1985 it "squares" Leo, causing people of that sun sign to think things over. It may even hurt a bit; but when Saturn enters Sagittarius in mid-November and stays there until 1988, things not only ease up, they take a big turn for the better.

During 1981 Jupiter will be with Saturn in Libra, making things reasonably cushy for Leos. When Jupiter does its "square thing"—as it does to Leos in 1982—the effects are generally expansive. Jupiter in Sagittarius during 1983 is even better for Leos; 1984 is problematical; and in 1985 Jupiter will be in Leo's opposite sign, Aquarius. Leos in general are optimistic enough to get something positive out of this, and even to get their due from the benefic planet when it is in Pisces in 1986.

Midheaven Sign Leo

From now until early 1984 Neptune remains in your money house—and that can bring mixed emotions. There is a tendency to be careless, but it is not fatal to the income unless the whole chart shows such tendencies. After January 1984 it moves on to cloud up communications for a number of years.

Uranus, which has been stimulating your house of individuality for some time, moves into the income house in early 1981. The presence of these two planets here makes caution advisable, especially in investments. Uranus can bring swift reversals of fortune.

Saturn "hides away" in your twelfth house, causing some psychological "downers," until the end of 1982. Then it makes a dramatic pass over your Ascendant into your first house, bringing with it a change of heart and blessed relief. You reap the benefits until it moves into the income sector in mid-1985, but by that time you should have it all together.

Jupiter spends 1981 in your twelfth house, taking the bite out of Saturn. It reaches your Ascendant sometime in 1982, but until Saturn crosses over a while later, all the expansion you feel may be in your waistline. Early in 1983 Jupiter does the nicest thing possible by moving into your income and values sector. From then until February 1985, Jupiter prepares you for all the nice things that will happen when it enters the sign of Aquarius and your home sector. It contacts your Midheaven (by opposition) at the same time; so, in spite of Saturn, you should be fairly well off.

Sun Sign Leo/Midheaven Sign Leo

Mars in Leo is a natural for stimulating things (fire planet in fire sign). It gets Leo sun signs going and touches Leo Midheavens with exciting effect at these times: September until late October 1981; mid-August until October first 1983; late July until mid-August 1985. The times when Mars for you has least force and most potential career dangers are: January 1981; December tenth 1982 through January eighteenth 1983; mid-November until late December 1984; October ninth until late November 1986.

Sun Sign Virgo

First decan: August 24–September 3
Second decan: September 4–September 13
Third decan: September 14–September 23

Neptune continues in Sagittarius until 1984, affecting the third decan of Virgo not altogether pleasantly. Analytical Virgo might find his usual clear thinking a bit difficult.

Uranus enters Sagittarius, and therefore goes into a "tense" aspect for Virgos, in early 1981; it takes a breather back in Scorpio through part of the year, then goes back in full force until February 1988. Usually energizing, Uranus to Virgo can be enervating; it will affect the first decan until early 1984, then the second and third decans in the four years following. Saturn is in your neighboring sign, Libra, in 1981 and 1982. For the next two years it resides in Scorpio, which is fairly friendly to your sun. However, in mid-November 1985 Saturn enters Sagittarius for a two-year stay that might not be an altogether harmonious period for Virgo sun signs. If you are a first-decan Virgo, test the waters for your later-decan friends, and give them some tips as Saturn comes to square their suns.

Jupiter stays alongside Saturn in Libra during 1981, and brings positive things to Virgo while in Scorpio in 1982. In 1983 Jupiter travels through Sagittarius, which could be an "upper" for Virgos. In 1984, when Jupiter is in Capricorn, Virgo earth people should have a heyday buttoning everything down. There is not much Jupiter action in 1985, but 1986 could be feast or famine when Jupiter goes into Pisces, Virgo's opposite sign. It all depends on how Virgo plays it. This is one time caution is not advisable.

Midheaven Sign Virgo

Neptune continues to hover around your Ascendant and first house—a not altogether clear-cut time in one's life. It will be in this sector until 1984 when your second house of income and values gets this dubious visitor.

Uranus is the big one to watch in coming years. When this change-maker planet goes into Sagittarius in early 1981, it begins to get close to your Ascendant, and you get close to a big life transition. Depending on the degree of your Ascendant, the change could come at any time during this five-year period.

Virgo Midheaven people have just experienced two of the best years of their career lives, when Saturn was in Virgo.

It is not all over, though, because Jupiter in Libra throughout 1981 and 1982 means this beneficial planet is still high in your chart, and should work well for you. The picture may change in 1983 when Saturn goes into Scorpio and your twelfth house. Sometimes it just hides there, bringing only mild psychological grief; but outward manifestations are not unknown. Sometime from late 1985 until early 1988, Saturn will pass over your Ascendant, and you will feel like a new person. You may get a new career, too.

Jupiter has been right at the top of your chart, too, and will stay there while it is in Libra in 1981. In 1982 it goes into your twelfth house sector of privacy, and should prepare you for anything to come. In 1983 you get Jupiter's full benefit in your house of self, always a good time. It may take the edge off Saturn. In 1984 it brings economic blessings in your second house. In 1985 and 1986 respectively, Jupiter will be in your third (communications and neighbors) house, and your fourth. Since Jupiter in 1986 is in the very compatible sign of Pisces, you should enjoy "harvest" in your private sector.

Sun Sign Virgo/Midheaven Sign Virgo

Mars works rather well in Virgo, so when Mars is in your sun sign during the next few years, you should strike while it is hot. For Virgo Midheaven people, these are the periods when Mars reaches the career pinnacle of your chart: October twenty-second through mid-December 1981; October first through late November 1983; mid-August until late October 1985. Mars is generally negative for both groups at these times: February until mid-March 1981; January eighteenth until late February 1983; late December 1984 until early February 1985; late November through the end of 1986.

Sun Sign Libra

First decan: September 24–October 3
Second decan: October 4–October 14
Third decan: October 15–October 23

Neptune will continue to do rather nice creative things to the last decan of this sign until early 1984, when it goes into Capricorn and into the square (not so pleasant) aspect of the first decan. Second and third decans follow, but it takes years.

Uranus going into Sagittarius should mean a pickup in the life tempo for Librans. It starts for first-decan people in early 1981, begins affecting second decan in early 1984, the third a few years after that.

Saturn will be in the sign of Libra until December 1982 (as well as mid-1983). All of this sign please note that you should use this transit wisely by taking only calculated risks. It can bring spectacular results later on, though the present circumstances might not be ideal. Saturn resides in Scorpio from 1983 through 1985, doing very little for or against you. At the end of 1985 it enters Sagittarius and brings more steadiness and concentration than anything else to Libra.

Librans in 1981 reap the once-in-twenty-years benefits of the great Jupiter/Saturn conjunction; the importance of this period cannot be overemphasized. In 1982 Jupiter moves into neighboring sign Scorpio, and in 1983 into Sagittarius, its home sign, and a very friendly position for Librans. In 1984 the picture is not quite as bright with Jupiter in Capricorn, but in 1985 Jupiter moves into Aquarius—another air sign, and a good place for Librans.

Midheaven Sign Libra

If nothing really spectacular happens in 1981—the year of the great Jupiter/Saturn conjunction—maybe you just aren't looking. The big event takes place very close to your Midheaven, and that is nothing to take lightly. As Saturn moves on in the three following years, he moves slowly and majestically through your public sector, bringing stature and status if all goes well. Hope it does, because in November 1985 Saturn begins a more-than-two-year stay in your twelfth house, and normally doesn't bring much good there.

However, Jupiter stays up on top during 1982 in the sign Scorpio, and should give you a chance to make it big before it gets temporarily eclipsed in your twelfth house in 1983. The big "coming out" is 1984, when Jupiter goes into Capricorn and passes over your Ascendant into your first house of self. You have to watch this one, because it may be so smooth, all you notice is that you are gaining weight. Use the period to put some fat on your career.

Meanwhile Neptune ruffles your unconscious in Sagittarius, and will not be noticed too much until early 1984 when it starts to affect your Ascendant—and your objectivity.

Uranus, meanwhile, goes creeping into your twelfth house as well and stays there for a long while. This could usher in a period of underlying tension. Watch for it.

Sun Sign Libra/Midheaven Sign Libra

Mars generally loses some of its "oomph" in Libra, but for you Libra sun signs it is a prod to action. When Mars hits Libra and it is your Midheaven sign, you should use the time well. These are the times for both groups: mid-December 1981 through early August 1982; November twentieth 1983 through January twelfth 1984; late October 1985 until mid-December. The "down times" for Mars vis-á-vis you Libras/Libra Midheavens are: mid-March until late April 1981; late February until early April 1983; early February 1985 until mid-March.

Sun Sign Scorpio

First decan: October 24–November 3
Second decan: November 4–November 13
Third decan: November 14–November 22

Neptune really isn't too much of a factor for Scorpios in this period, though it does mildly nice things to the first decan from early 1984 on for a few years.

Uranus has been the nemesis—or the champion—for Scorpio sun-sign people for some time, bringing swift, dramatic changes. Last-decan people will continue to feel Uranus until it goes definitely into Sagittarius in mid-November 1981.

Your "Saturn time" (that is, Saturn in the sign of Scorpio) is coming up. It creeps up on you during 1981 and 1982 while Saturn is in Libra, then Saturn starts hitting first-decan Scorpio people in early 1982. Saturn turns around for a few months, then comes back with a vengeance in late August 1983 to stay until mid-November 1985. Saturn hits anyone's sun only once in about thirty years, so don't waste time moaning about the possible hardships. Be assured that good will come of it.

Jupiter, which spends 1981 in Libra, makes sure those good things will come by entering Scorpio in 1982 and staying the entire year. When it moves "next door" into Sagittarius in 1983, it will still be somewhat of a benefactor. Then, in 1984, you get a nice "sextile" when Jupiter moves into Capricorn for the year. While in Aquarius in 1985, Jupiter will be somewhat neutralized for you; but in 1986 while Jupiter stays in Pisces (its "best" sign), you get some splendid rays that should be a relief after Saturn's effects.

Midheaven Sign Scorpio

Neptune continues to affect your area of hopes and wishes until early 1984. Let's hope it doesn't lead to wishful thinking. If that is the case, you will get a jolt when Uranus enters this sector in early 1981, upsetting applecarts and possibly bringing about a revision of friendships and on-the-job relationships.

Saturn spends 1981 and 1982 in your ninth house; if you use it well, you will gather the knowledge and learning necessary to strike it big when Saturn hits your Midheaven—the career pinnacle—sometime between late 1983 and late 1985. Saturn will move on through this prestigious area of your chart until early 1988, so there is plenty of time to make sure you make it.

Jupiter is in your ninth house helping Saturn to help you learn throughout 1981, and moves up to Scorpio and to your Midheaven in 1982. You could be holding all the marbles. Jupiter brings powerful friendships in 1983, then sinks into relative obscurity in 1984, emerging triumphantly in 1985 to make its once-in-twelve-years pass over your Ascendant. In 1986 the benefit-bringer enters your house of income. With this planetary line-up, it would be hard to lose. Just make sure you don't.

Sun Sign Scorpio/Midheaven Sign Scorpio

Mars and Scorpio do very well by each other, so these should be good perids for Scorpio sun signs. If your Midheaven is Scorpio, these are the times to take best advantage of the very positive period coming up: early August until September twenty-second 1982; January twelfth through mid-August 1984; mid-December 1985 through early February 1986. The times to watch for pitfalls are: late April until early June 1981; early April until mid-May 1983; mid-March through late April 1985.

Sun Sign Sagittarius

First decan: November 23–December 3
Second decan: December 4–December 13
Third decan: December 14–December 22

If you are a third-decan Sagittarius, you still have Neptune with you until 1984. For your sign, however, the nebulous planet can mean just more creativity than usual. However, it can also mean a dangerous spur to your gambling spirit.

Adventure-loving Sagittarians should be eagerly anticipating the entrance of Uranus into their sign. It starts stirring up the first decan in early 1981, but really gets going in November. Second-decan people can expect it in early 1984, third decan not until early 1986. Happy major life changes to you all.

While Saturn is in Libra during 1981 and 1982, Sagittarians should make the most of its friendly, if stern, aspect. Saturn will come creeping up on you during 1984 and 1985 in Scorpio, and will hit Sagittarius in early 1986. Saturn brings reality, and with it a touch of humility, not at all a bad prescription for Sagittarians.

The Jupiter years coming up are great ones for Sag sun signs. In 1981 Jupiter is in Libra and causes a lovely sextile. In 1982 the benefactor planet is warming up in Scorpio. When it enters its home sign of Sagittarius in 1983, it means good things for everyone, but especially Sag sun signs. The glow will keep on glowing throughout 1984, when Jupiter is in Capricorn, and flare up again when it goes into Aquarius in 1985 and Pisces in 1986.

Midheaven Sign Sagittarius

For the next five years, all of the major planets are in the upper or public sector of your chart. Make hay while they shine on you! The first one to touch your Midheaven (besides Neptune, which has been hanging out there for some time) is Uranus, starting in early 1981 and continuing through the sign of Sagittarius for a number of years. Almost anything can happen, almost all of it positive if you keep your eye on the ball.

Saturn started to climb up from obscurity for you a few years ago when it was in Virgo. In 1981 and 1982 it moves higher up in Libra, then into Scorpio, and reaches the pinnacle of your chart—the sign of Sagittarius—in late 1985. The two-year period after that is your time to shine as never before.

Meanwhile, Jupiter will make the same swing, reaching Sagittarius and your Midheaven in 1983, then continuing on in your powerful friends sector in 1984. In 1985 you won't see much of Jupiter, but in 1986 he will reemerge, pass over your Ascendant, and make you expand all over the place. That is just about the time Saturn will be at the apex. Make the most of these transits; you will not get another chance like this for many years to come.

Sun Sign Sagittarius/Midheaven Sign Sagittarius

Mars and Sagittarius do just fine together. If you are a Sag sun sign, these are the times Mars will help you make a move; and if you have a Sagittarius Midheaven, these are the peak times during a generally peak period: late September through November first 1982; mid-August through early October 1984; early February until late March 1986. If anything can go wrong, it will be during these priods: early June to mid-July 1981; mid-May till the end of June 1983; late April until June tenth 1985.

Sun Sign Capricorn

First decan: December 23–January 1
Second decan: January 2–January 11
Third decan: January 12–January 20

Capricorn sun signs begin to "get theirs" from Neptune in mid to late 1984—but only the first decan will feel it for several years. Neptune could give a nice imaginative touch to this sign.

Uranus doesn't really have much to do with the sign of Capricorn until 1988. But last-decan people will still be feeling a friendly sextile (energy) from Uranus until late 1981.

Stern Saturn gives a stern aspect to all Capricorns during 1981 and 1982. Don't let it get you down. By early 1983 things will lighten up when Saturn goes into Scorpio and throws friendly vibes to Capricorn. When Saturn enters Sagittarius in late 1985, there are only a bit more than two more years to wait until Saturn hits its home sign of Capricorn. 1988 and 1989 are the "Capricorn years," and even the soberest of that sign will have something to smile about.

Closer to the present, Jupiter takes the weight off the effect of Saturn in Libra during 1981. In 1982 Jupiter in Scorpio is a boon to all Capricorns. 1983, when Jupiter is in Sagittarius, is a warm-up year for the big event when the "sugar daddy" planet goes spinning into Capricorn in 1984. The effects should last through 1985 and 1986, when Jupiter moves through neighboring Aquarius and hits ultrafriendly Pisces.

Midheaven Sign Capricorn

This Midheaven is sitting pretty in the coming years. Neptune is currently giving a touch of "idealism" to learning and on-the-job preparation; it will reach Capricorn and the Midheaven in early 1984. Though there can be confusion about career aims at that time, there is also a "romancing" effect. Uranus is in an excellent spot (the house of studies) to stimulate the mind throughout the entire five-year period starting in early 1981.

With all that going on, Saturn should cause no problem as it transits the partnership and marriage house in 1981 and 1982. For the next four or five years it keeps climbing up toward the Midheaven, bringing consolidation first to joint finances, and then all that study and preparation you will be doing. Finally Saturn reaches Capricorn and your career high spot in early 1988, and you should be ready for it.

Jupiter, meanwhile, starts out in your house of others in 1981, transits your eighth (joint monies) and ninth (learning) houses during 1982 and 1983. In January 1984 Jupiter enters Capricorn and will touch your Midheaven sometime during that year. It can only mean beneficial things—a kind of preparatory step for the big Saturn "hit" that comes in 1988.

Sun Sign Capricorn/Midheaven Sign Capricorn

Mars is called "exalted" in Capricorn because it works so well in that sign. It will work for Capricorn sun signs and at the same times it will be touching and energizing in the Midheaven for those with Capricorn there: November first until December tenth 1982; early October until mid-November 1984; late March until early October 1986. The times when Mars will not work too smoothly for either group are: mid-July until September first 1981; end of June until mid-August 1983; June tenth until July twenty-sixth 1985.

Sun Sign Aquarius

First decan: January 21–January 31
Second decan: February 1–February 10
Third decan: February 11–February 18

Neptune continues to cast a rosy, if hazy, glow over third-decan Aquarians. This will stay in effect until early 1984.

Uranus is moving into a good sign to do good things for Aquarians. When it reaches Sagittarius in early 1981 (for good in late 1981), Uranus will be "turning on" Uranian Aquarians for years. But only the first decan will feel it until the end of 1983, then the second decan begins to be affected, the third in early 1986.

Saturn's transit through Libra is a highly positive one for Aquarians. This continues until late 1983 when Saturn enters Scorpio for real, making a few passes before then. Saturn's message to Aquarians becomes a bit sterner at that time. If they heed it, they will be in good shape for Saturn's move into Sagittarius at the end of 1985. This can be a time of more than moderate achievement for Aquarians.

Jupiter in Libra in 1981 makes Saturn's good vibes all the better. 1982 sees Jupiter in Scorpio, a rather neutral sign position for Aquarians. When Jupiter moves into its own sign of Sagittarius in 1983, it brings excellent things Aquarius's way—that is, if the exuberant people of this sign don't get too exuberant. In terms of Jupiter's effects on Aquarius, 1984 is a lie-low year; but 1985 is quite another story, when Jupiter hits the sign of Aquarius itself. Let's hope you Aquarians can keep the lid on.

Midheaven Sign Aquarius

Neptune continues to mess up your house of joint finances, taxes, etc., and won't move out until 1984. However, for those who may have experienced a tedious, tense period in partnerships and marriages, the good news is that Uranus is moving out of this sector in early 1981. Then it still can bother your financial picture, but at least your relationships will have some calm.

For Aquarius Midheaven people, Saturn starts out in the work house, where it will bring lots of extra assignments (but hopefully extra money as well) during 1981 and 1982. Then it passes into Scorpio, your sector of others, during 1984 and most of 1985. Here it may cause some difficulties, but unless you are in business with a partner, your professional life should be unaffected. Then Saturn moves on into the house of joint finance until late 1987, not an altogether unwelcome presence.

Jupiter lightens your work load somewhat in 1981 when it is in Libra. Jupiter enters your house of partners in 1982, benefiting relationships of all kinds. In 1983, Jupiter starts its climb toward your Midheaven, first helping out your financial picture, then in 1984, expanding your learning horizons. In early 1985 Jupiter enters Aquarius and approaches your Midheaven. The big moment could be anytime during that year. What is likely to happen is a "small break" that paves the way for a much bigger one later on, when Saturn finally gets to the top (early in 1991).

Sun Sign Aquarius/Midheaven Sign Aquarius

Mars will be in Aquarius, and therefore a strong influence on Aquarius sun signs, and Mars gives its shot of adrenalin to Aquarius Midheaven people's career strategies during: January 1981; December tenth 1982 until January eighteenth 1983; mid-November until late December 1984; early October until late November 1986. Mars is more or less neutralized or even hostile during these periods: September first until October twenty-second 1981; mid-August until October first 1983; late July until mid-August 1985.

Sun Sign Pisces

First decan: February 19–March 2
Second decan: March 3–March 12
Third decan: March 13–March 21

Confusing Neptune continues to bring confusion to third-decan Pisceans until early 1984, something to be watched carefully.

When Uranus moves into Sagittarius in 1981 (for sure in mid-November), first-decan Pisceans begin to feel the not altogether pleasant square aspect. Second- and third-decan people will feel it later on during the next seven-year period. Since both Uranus and the square aspect are energizing, it is to be hoped these factors will get the affected Piscean moving in a constructive direction.

Saturn is neither here nor there for Pisceans during 1981 and 1982. Saturn in Scorpio—in full force by late 1983—is quite another matter. It is an excellent steadier for Pisceans, and a good time in their lives to seek security. Late November 1985 Saturn moves into Sagittarius, and things get tighter. It is to be hoped they do not get too tight, because the gains of the previous several years should be consolidated during this period.

Jupiter spends 1981 in Libra, then moves into Scorpio in 1982, throwing a lovely trine to Pisces sun sign people. The problem with Jupiter smiling on Pisceans is that they tend to relax too much. When Jupiter moves into Sagittarius in 1983, there is a bit more push and it's quite positive, too. When Jupiter hits Capricorn in 1984, Pisceans may not be ecstatic; and 1985 could be a fairly neutral year. However, it is best for Pisces to lie low and rest up for 1986, when Jupiter enters their sign and brings benefits almost to a fault.

Midheaven Sign Pisces

This should be the beginning of a far more positive period than you have experienced in recent years. Saturn reached your Nadir a few years ago, and in 1981 started its climb toward the top, your Midheaven. It will still take a while, but there are lots of good things along the way.

Neptune continues to bring either confusion or the glow of romance to interpersonal relationships. It is wise to check out all business partnerships carefully during this period (until 1984). Uranus, which has been a constant irritation to you in work matters, moves into Sagittarius in early 1981, where it could either liven up or break up some relationships.

Saturn spends 1981 and 1982 giving a solid base to all your creative efforts. By late 1983 it has moved into the work sector, where it may bring some rather tough discipline into your life until the end of 1985. At that point, it crosses over into the public sector and starts upward toward the Midheaven.

During Saturn's long journey, Jupiter will take up the slack and give you lots to work well with. In 1981 the beneficent planet gives you creative inspiration. In 1982 it takes the edge off any overtime efforts you may have to put in. In 1983 it brings expansion and joy to all kinds of relationships—both business and personal. In 1984 your joint finances may get a real boost. If you study something job-related, 1985 may find you adding to your assets. It will all pay off in 1986, when Jupiter moves into Pisces and reaches your Midheaven. That's the time your career can really take off.

Sun Sign Pisces/Midheaven Sign Pisces

Mars in Pisces doesn't have the edge it does in some other signs, but for Pisces sun signs it will give a special push at these times. If Pisces is your Midheaven sign, these are the periods when extra career-furthering efforts are most likely to pay off: February until mid-March 1981; January eighteenth through late February 1983; late December 1984 through early February 1985; late November 1986 through the end of the year. When Mars is not at its best for you is: October twenty-second until mid-December 1981; October first until November twentieth 1983; mid-August until late October 1985.

APPENDIX
THE TABLES

How to Use the Tables in This Book

Abbreviation of Zodiacal Signs

In all of the following tables the zodiacal signs are indicated as follows:

A = Aries	T = Taurus	G = Gemini
C = Cancer	L = Leo	V = Virgo
Li = Libra	S = Scorpio	Sg = Sagittarius
Cp = Capricorn	Aq = Aquarius	P = Pisces

Finding Your Birth Time

Since the time of day you were born determines both your Ascendant and your Midheaven house sign, it is important that you know that time within one half hour in order to use this book to best advantage. It is not wise to rely on the memories of parents or other family members; sometimes, however, the correct time has been recorded in a family memory or baby book.

Very often your birth time is given right on your birth certificate, though the situation varies widely from state to state. If you want to obtain your birth certificate—or if you have it and it does not give birth time—write to the Bureau/Office of Vital Statistics/Records in the capital city of the state in which you were born. In some states birth time information is recorded on a separate and confidential medical document signed by the birth attendant. That information is obtainable, but only by the individual himself or a parent. In writing for any birth certificate or birth time record, you must state that it is your birth time you are seeking to ascertain. This is the information you must provide:

- Full name of the person whose record is desired
- Day, month, and year of birth

- Place of birth (city or town, county, and state, and hospital if known)
- Full names of both parents, including mother's maiden name
- Your relationship to the person whose record is requested

Most states charge a nominal fee for this service. Check in advance and send the amount required along with your request to avoid a delay.

ADJUSTING YOUR BIRTH TIME FOR DAYLIGHT SAVINGS OR WAR TIME

(Applicable to all tables)

Before the Uniform Time Act of 1966 standardized the observation of Daylight Savings Time for the entire country from the last Sunday in April until the last Sunday in October, regulations varied widely from state to state and from community to community. If you have any questions about whether Daylight Savings Time was in effect when you were born, be sure to check with a local library or other community agency.

There is no doubt about War Time. During the following periods, the entire country observed War Time:

March 31 to October 27, 1918
March 30 to October 26, 1919
February 9, 1942 until September 30, 1945

If you were born when either Daylight Savings Time or War Time was in effect, you must subtract one hour from your recorded birth time.

ADJUSTING YOUR BIRTH TIME FOR TRUE LOCAL TIME

(Applicable to all tables)

Unless you were born right on the meridian of a time zone, your recorded birth time is not True Local Time. True Local Time (or sun time) differs from clock time, which is the same throughout the entire time zone. The difference depends on how far the longitude of your birthplace is from the meridian of the time zone in which you were born. Zones are measured in 15 degrees of longitude, the distance the sun "travels" in approximately one hour. Each degree of longitude represents four minutes.

To find the True Local Time of your birth, first look up the nearest full degree of longitude to your birthplace (any atlas will show it). Determine the number of degrees the birthplace longitude differs from the longitude of the time zone meridian.

The meridians of the United States time zones are as follows:

- Eastern Time Zone: 75 degrees
- Central Time Zone: 90 degrees
- Mountain Time Zone: 105 degrees
- Pacific Time Zone: 120 degrees

Next, multiply the difference between the longitude of your birthplace and the time zone meridian by four (minutes). If your birthplace is *east* of the zone's meridian, *add* the result to your recorded birth time. If your birthplace is *west* of the zone's meridian, subtract it. The result is True Local Time.

For example:

1. Pittsburgh is in the Eastern Time Zone.
2. The nearest degree of longitude to Pittsburgh is 80 degrees.
3. The meridian of the Eastern Time Zone is 75 degrees.
4. The difference between these two is five degrees.
5. Five degrees multiplied by four minutes equals twenty minutes.
6. Pittsburgh is west of the Eastern Time Zone meridian, so the twenty minutes should be subtracted from the recorded birth time.

The easiest way to understand this concept is to say that when the clock reads 5:00 in Pittsburgh, the sun still has twenty minutes to "travel" before reaching Pittsburgh. Therefore, the True Local Time is 4:40, even though the clock reads 5:00.

ADJUSTING YOUR BIRTH TIME FOR TIME ZONE

(Applicable to Moon Sign and Sun Sign tables only)

The times given in this book (except for Ascendant and Midheaven times, which are universal) are for the Eastern Standard Time Zone. To adjust the times given in these tables, the following corrections should be made if you were not born in the Eastern Time Zone.

- If you were born in the Central Time Zone, subtract one hour from recorded birth time.
- If you were born in the Mountain Time Zone, subtract two hours.
- If you were born in the Pacific Time Zone, subtract three hours.
- If you were born anywhere in Great Britain, *add* four hours during the winter months and five hours during British Summer Time.

When to Use the Sun Sign Changes Tables

Contrary to popular belief, there is no standard day of the month on which the sun changes from one zodiacal sign to the next. Both the day and the time of day for the sun's change vary from year to year. If you were born between the nineteenth and the twenty-third of any given month, it is wise to check these tables for your sun sign. You may be in for a surprise. (In my own case, my late-night birth time on November twenty-second makes me a Sagittarius rather than the Scorpio I believed I was before getting interested in astrology.) As for being born on the cusp, it is my conviction that one is either one sign or another, not a blend of the two.

How to Use the Moon Sign Tables

The moon changes signs approximately every two to two and one half days. To ascertain the zodiacal sign of the moon at the time you were born, look up your birthday in the table for the year of your birth. If there is only one sign abbreviated, the moon was in that sign for the entire twenty-four-hour period beginning at midnight Eastern Standard Time on that date. If the moon changed signs on the date, there will be two signs listed, one in the upper left-hand corner, one in the upper right-hand corner. Below the two signs listed will be a time, either A.M. or P.M. What this means is that the moon was in the sign indicated by the abbreviation in the left-hand corner from midnight on that date until the time listed, at which point it moved to the next sign—indicated by the abbreviation in the right-hand corner.

For example: If the entry for your birthday looks like this,

C		L
	6:56 P.M.	

it means that the moon was in the sign of Cancer until 6:56 P.M. Eastern Standard Time, at which point it moved into the sign of Leo.

If the entry for your birthday looks like this,

Li

it means the moon was in the sign of Libra for the entire day, beginning at midnight.

How to Find Your Ascendant and Midheaven House Signs

This is a simple method for determining your Ascendant and Midheaven house signs with a high degree of accuracy (after you have carefully adjusted your birth time).

The first step is to convert your birth time, corrected for Daylight Savings or War Time as well as True Local Time, into time on the 24-hour clock. (Do not correct for time zone.) That simply means expressing your birth time as time is noted in the armed services: that is, for birth times after noon, add twelve. For example, 3:00 P.M. becomes 15:00. If you were born at 11:59 P.M., your birth time on the 24-hour clock is 23:59. If you were born one minute after midnight, it is 0:01.

The next step is to find your Base Time. (Base Time is midnight at the Greenwich Meridian or zero degrees latitude.) In the following tables you will find Base Times given for each day of the year. Jot down the Base Time for your birthday. To it add your birth time expressed in 24-hour terms. If the result is over 24, subtract 24. What you now have is your Sidereal Birth Time (from *Sidus,* Latin for star). This is a "universal" time, so do not take time zone into consideration.

To find your Ascendant, in Table 4, Ascendant House Signs for Sidereal Birth Times, locate the span of time in the Ascendant section that includes your sidereal birth time. Your Ascendant sign is the sign indicated for that span of time.

To find your Midheaven house, follow the same procedure in Table 5, Midheaven House Signs for Sidereal Birth Times.

For example:

1. You were born at 6:35 A.M. True Local Time on April 26.
2. The Base Time listed in Table 3 for April 26 is 14:13.
3. Your birth time on the 24-hour clock is 6:35.
   14:13 + 6:35 = 20:48, your Sidereal Birth Time

Your Ascendant Sign is Gemini; your Midheaven House Sign is Aquarius.

1. You were born at 10:15 P.M. True Local Time on December 24.
2. The Base Time listed in Table 3 for December 24 is 6:08.
3. Your birth time on the 24-hour clock is 22:15.
   6:08 + 22:15 = 28:23
   Since the result is over 24, subtract 24:
   28:23 − 24:00 = 4:23, your Sidereal Birth Time

Your Ascendant Sign is Virgo; your Midheaven House Sign is Gemini.

(When calculating times, remember you are dealing in minutes and seconds so that anything over 59 in the minutes column becomes a whole hour and should be added to the hour column.)

NOTE: Latitude makes a difference in the Ascendant sign. The times given for Ascendant signs are for 41 degrees north latitude, the approximate latitude of New York. If you were born more than 200 miles to the north of that latitude, your Ascendant could be the preceding sign; born more than 200 miles to the south, it could be the following sign.

Table 1 SUN SIGN CHANGES 1910 – 1970

	Jan	Feb	Mar	Apr	May	June	July	Aug	Sept	Oct	Nov	Dec
1910	Cp Aq Jan 20 4:59p	Aq P Feb 19 7:28a	P A Mar 21 7:03a	A T Apr 20 6:46p	T G May 21 6:30p	G C June 22 2:49a	C L July 23 1:43p	L V Aug 23 8:27p	V Li Sept 23 5:30p	Li S Oct 24 2:11a	S Sg Nov 22 11:11p	Sg Cp Dec 22 12:12p
1911	Cp Aq Jan 20 10:52p	Aq P Feb 19 1:21p	P A Mar 21 12:55p	A T Apr 21 12:36p	T G May 22 12:19p	G C June 22 8:36a	C L July 23 7:29p	L V Aug 24 2:13a	V Li Sept 23 11:17p	Li S Oct 24 7:59a	S Sg Nov 23 4:57a	Sg Cp Dec 22 5:53p
1912	Cp Aq Jan 21 4:29a	Aq P Feb 19 6:56p	P A Mar 20 6:29p	A T Apr 20 6:12a	T G May 21 5:27a	G C June 21 3:26p	C L July 23 1:14a	L V Aug 23 8:02a	V Li Sept 23 5:08a	Li S Oct 23 1:50p	S Sg Nov 22 10:48a	Sg Cp Dec 21 11:45p
1913	Cp Aq Jan 20 10:19a	Aq P Feb 19 12:45a	P A Mar 21 12:18a	A T Apr 20 12:03p	T G May 21 11:50a	G C June 21 8:09p	C L July 23 7:04p	L V Aug 23 1:48p	V Li Sept 23 10:53a	Li S Oct 23 7:35p	S Sg Nov 22 4:36p	Sg Cp Dec 22 5:45a
1914	Cp Aq Jan 20 4:12p	Aq P Feb 19 6:38a	P A Mar 21 6:11a	A T Apr 20 5:54p	T G May 21 5:38p	G C June 22 1:55a	C L July 23 12:47p	L V Aug 23 7:35p	V Li Sept 23 5:35p	Li S Oct 24 1:18a	S Sg Nov 22 10:21p	Sg Cp Dec 22 11:24a
1915	Cp Aq Jan 20 10:00p	Aq P Feb 19 12:23p	P A Mar 21 11:51a	A T Apr 20 11:28p	T G May 21 11:10p	G C June 22 7:29a	C L July 23 6:27p	L V Aug 24 1:16a	V Li Sept 23 10:24p	Li S Oct 24 7:10a	S Sg Nov 23 4:14a	Sg Cp Dec 22 5:16p
1916	Cp Aq Jan 21 3:54a	Aq P Feb 19 6:18p	P A Mar 20 7:47p	A T Apr 20 5:25a	T G May 21 5:06a	G C June 21 1:25p	C L July 23 12:21a	L V Aug 23 7:09a	V Li Sept 23 4:15a	Li S Oct 23 12:58p	S Sg Nov 21 9:58a	Sg Cp Dec 21 11:45p
1917	Cp Aq Jan 20 9:37a	Aq P Feb 19 12:05a	P A Mar 20 11:37p	A T Apr 20 11:17a	T G May 21 12:59p	G C June 21 7:15p	C L July 23 6:08a	L V Aug 23 12:54p	V Li Sept 23 10:00a	Li S Oct 23 6:44p	S Sg Nov 22 3:45p	Sg Cp Dec 21 4:46a
1918	Cp Aq Jan 20 3:24p	Aq P Feb 19 5:53a	P A Mar 21 5:26a	A T Apr 20 5:06p	T G May 21 4:46p	G C June 22 1:00a	C L July 23 11:52a	L V Aug 23 6:37p	V Li Sept 23 3:45p	Li S Oct 24 12:33a	S Sg Nov 22 2:38p	Sg Cp Dec 22 11:42a
1919	Cp Aq Jan 19 10:21p	Aq P Feb 19 11:45a	P A Mar 21 11:19a	A T Apr 20 10:59p	T G May 21 10:39p	G C June 22 6:54a	C L July 23 5:45p	L V Aug 24 12:28a	V Li Sept 23 9:35p	Li S Oct 24 6:21a	S Sg Nov 23 3:25a	Sg Cp Dec 22 4:27p
1920	Cp Aq Jan 21 4:05a	Aq P Feb 19 5:29p	P A Mar 20 5:00p	A T Apr 20 4:39a	T G May 21 4:22a	G C June 21 12:40p	C L July 22 11:35p	L V Aug 23 6:22a	V Li Sept 23 3:25a	Li S Oct 23 12:13p	S Sg Nov 22 9:16a	Sg Cp Dec 21 10:17p
1921	Cp Aq Jan 20 8:55a	Aq P Feb 18 11:21p	P A Mar 20 10:51p	A T Apr 20 10:32a	T G May 21 10:17a	G C June 21 6:36p	C L July 23 5:31a	L V Aug 23 12:15p	V Li Sept 23 11:20a	Li S Oct 23 6:03p	S Sg Nov 22 3:21p	Sg Cp Dec 22 4:08a
1922	Cp Aq Jan 20 2:48p	Aq P Feb 19 5:16a	P A Mar 21 4:49a	A T Apr 20 4:29a	T G May 21 9:11p	G C June 22 12:27a	C L July 23 11:20a	L V Aug 23 6:04p	V Li Sept 23 5:10a	Li S Oct 23 11:53p	S Sg Nov 22 8:55p	Sg Cp Dec 22 9:57p

SUN SIGN CHANGES 1910 – 1970

	Jan	Feb	Mar	Apr	May	June	July	Aug	Sept	Oct	Nov	Dec
1923	Cp Aq Jan 20 8:35p	Aq P Feb 19 11:00a	P A Mar 21 10:29a	A T Apr 20 10:06p	T G May 22 9:45p	G C June 22 6:03a	C L July 23 5:01p	L V Aug 23 11:52p	V Li Sept 23 9:04p	Li S Oct 24 5:51a	S Sg Nov 23 2:54a	Sg Cp Dec 22 3:53p
1924	Cp Aq Jan 21 2:29a	Aq P Feb 19 4:51p	P A Mar 20 4:20p	A T Apr 20 3:59a	T G May 21 3:41a	G C June 21 12:00n	C L July 22 11:58p	L V Aug 23 5:48a	V Li Sept 23 2:58a	Li S Oct 23 11:44a	S Sg Nov 22 8:46a	Sg Cp Dec 21 10:45p
1925	Cp Aq Jan 20 8:20a	Aq P Feb 18 11:43p	P A Mar 20 11:13p	A T Apr 20 10:51p	T G May 21 10:33p	G C June 21 5:50p	C L July 23 4:45a	L V Aug 23 11:33a	V Li Sept 23 8:43a	Li S Oct 23 5:31p	S Sg Nov 22 2:36p	Sg Cp Dec 22 3:37a
1926	Cp Aq Jan 20 2:13p	Aq P Feb 18 4:35a	P A Mar 21 4:01a	A T Apr 20 3:36p	T G May 21 3:15p	G C June 21 11:30p	C L July 23 10:25a	L V Aug 23 5:14p	V Li Sept 23 2:25p	Li S Oct 23 11:18p	S Sg Nov 22 8:28p	Sg Cp Dec 22 9:34a
1927	Cp Aq Jan 20 8:12p	Aq P Feb 19 10:35a	P A Mar 21 11:59a	A T Apr 20 9:32p	T G May 21 9:08p	G C June 22 5:21a	C L July 23 4:17a	L V Aug 23 11:06p	V Li Sept 23 8:17p	Li S Oct 24 5:07a	S Sg Nov 23 2:14a	Sg Cp Dec 22 3:18p
1928	Cp Aq Jan 21 1:57a	Aq P Feb 19 4:20p	P A Mar 20 3:44p	A T Apr 20 3:17a	T G May 21 2:53a	G C June 21 11:07a	C L July 22 11:02p	L V Aug 23 4:53a	V Li Sept 23 2:36a	Li S Oct 23 10:55a	S Sg Nov 22 8:00a	Sg Cp Dec 21 9:04p
1929	Cp Aq Jan 20 7:42a	Aq P Feb 18 10:07p	P A Mar 20 9:35p	A T Apr 20 9:11a	T G May 21 8:48a	G C June 21 5:01p	C L July 23 3:54a	L V Aug 23 10:41a	V Li Sept 23 7:52a	Li S Oct 23 4:41p	S Sg Nov 22 1:48p	Sg Cp Dec 22 2:53a
1930	Cp Aq Jan 20 1:33p	Aq P Feb 19 4:00a	P A Mar 21 3:30a	A T Apr 20 3:06p	T G May 21 2:42p	G C June 21 11:53p	C L July 23 10:42a	L V Aug 23 4:27p	V Li Sept 23 1:35p	Li S Oct 23 11:25p	S Sg Nov 22 7:34p	Sg Cp Dec 22 8:40a
1931	Cp Aq Jan 21 7:18p	Aq P Feb 19 9:40a	P A Mar 21 9:06a	A T Apr 20 8:40p	T G May 21 8:15p	G C June 23 4:28a	C L July 23 3:21p	L V Aug 23 10:10p	V Li Sept 23 7:23p	Li S Oct 24 4:15a	S Sg Nov 23 1:25a	Sg Cp Dec 22 2:30p
1932	Cp Aq Jan 20 1:07a	Aq P Feb 19 3:29p	P A Mar 20 2:54p	A T Apr 20 2:28a	T G May 21 2:07a	G C June 21 10:23a	C L July 22 9:18p	L V Aug 23 4:06a	V Li Sept 23 1:16a	Li S Oct 23 10:04a	S Sg Nov 22 7:10a	Sg Cp Dec 21 8:14p
1933	Cp Aq Jan 20 6:53a	Aq P Feb 19 9:16p	P A Mar 21 8:43p	A T Apr 20 8:19a	T G May 21 7:57a	G C June 21 4:12p	C L July 23 3:06a	L V Aug 23 9:53a	V Li Sept 23 7:01a	Li S Oct 23 3:48p	S Sg Nov 22 10:53a	Sg Cp Dec 22 1:58a
1934	Cp Aq Jan 20 10:37a	Aq P Feb 19 3:02a	P A Mar 21 2:28a	A T Apr 20 2:00p	T G May 21 1:35p	G C June 21 9:48p	C L July 23 8:42a	L V Aug 23 3:32p	V Li Sept 23 10:45a	Li S Oct 23 9:35p	S Sg Nov 22 6:44p	Sg Cp Dec 22 5:49p
1935	Cp Aq Jan 20 6:29p	Aq P Feb 19 8:52a	P A Mar 21 8:19a	A T Apr 20 7:50p	T G May 21 7:25p	G C June 22 3:32a	C L July 23 2:33p	L V Aug 23 9:24p	V Li Sept 23 6:38p	Li S Oct 24 3:29a	S Sg Nov 23 12:35a	Sg Cp Dec 22 1:37p

SUN SIGN CHANGES 1910 – 1970

	Jan	Feb	Mar	Apr	May	June	July	Aug	Sept	Oct	Nov	Dec
1936	Cp Aq Jan 21 12:12a	Aq P Feb 19 2:33p	P A Mar 20 1:58p	A T Apr 20 1:31a	T G May 21 1:08a	G C June 21 9:22a	C L July 22 8:18a	L V Aug 23 3:11a	V Li Sept 23 12:26a	Li S Oct 23 10:18a	S Sg Nov 22 6:25p	Sg Cp Dec 21 7:27p
1937	Cp Aq Jan 20 6:01a	Aq P Feb 18 3:21p	P A Mar 20 7:45p	A T Apr 20 7:20p	T G May 21 6:57a	G C June 21 3:12p	C L July 23 2:07a	L V Aug 23 8:58a	V Li Sept 23 6:13a	Li S Oct 23 3:06p	S Sg Nov 22 12:17p	Sg Cp Dec 22 1:22a
1938	Cp Aq Jan 20 11:59a	Aq P Feb 19 2:20a	P A Mar 21 1:43a	A T Apr 20 1:15p	T G May 21 12:51p	G C June 21 9:04p	C L July 23 7:57a	L V Aug 23 2:46p	V Li Sept 23 12:00n	Li S Oct 23 8:54p	S Sg Nov 22 6:06p	Sg Cp Dec 22 7:13a
1939	Cp Aq Jan 20 5:51p	Aq P Feb 19 8:10p	P A Mar 21 7:29a	A T Apr 20 6:55p	T G May 21 6:27p	G C June 22 2:40a	C L July 23 1:37p	L V Aug 23 8:31p	V Li Sept 23 5:50p	Li S Oct 24 2:46a	S Sg Nov 22 11:59p	Sg Cp Dec 22 1:06p
1940	Cp Aq Jan 20 11:44p	Aq P Feb 19 2:04p	P A Mar 20 1:24p	A T Apr 20 12:51a	T G May 21 12:23a	G C June 21 8:37a	C L July 22 7:34p	L V Aug 23 2:21a	V Li Sept 22 11:46p	Li S Oct 23 8:39a	S Sg Nov 22 5:49a	Sg Cp Dec 21 6:55p
1941	Cp Aq Jan 20 5:34a	Aq P Feb 18 7:59p	P A Mar 20 7:21p	A T Apr 20 6:51a	T G May 21 6:23a	G C June 21 2:33a	C L July 23 1:26a	L V Aug 23 8:30a	V Li Sept 23 5:33a	Li S Oct 23 2:22p	S Sg Nov 22 11:38a	Sg Cp Dec 22 12:44a
1942	Cp Aq Jan 20 11:16a	Aq P Feb 19 1:39a	P A Mar 21 1:03a	A T Apr 20 12:30p	T G May 21 12:01p	G C June 21 8:08p	C L July 23 6:59a	L V Aug 23 1:50p	V Li Sept 23 11:10a	Li S Oct 22 8:01p	S Sg Nov 22 5:23p	Sg Cp Dec 22 6:31a
1943	Cp Aq Jan 20 5:20p	Aq P Feb 19 7:41a	P A Mar 21 7:03a	A T Apr 20 6:32p	T G May 21 6:03p	G C June 22 2:13a	C L July 23 1:05p	L V Aug 23 7:55p	V Li Sept 23 5:12p	Li S Oct 24 2:09a	S Sg Nov 22 11:22p	Sg Cp Dec 22 12:30p
1944	Cp Aq Jan 20 11:09p	Aq P Feb 19 1:28p	P A Mar 21 12:49p	A T Apr 20 12:18a	T G May 20 11:51p	G C June 21 9:03a	C L July 22 6:55p	L V Aug 23 1:47a	V Li Sept 22 11:02p	Li S Oct 23 7:57a	S Sg Nov 22 5:09a	Sg Cp Dec 21 6:15p
1945	Cp Aq Jan 20 4:55a	Aq P Feb 18 7:15p	P A Mar 20 6:38p	A T Apr 20 6:08a	T G May 22 5:41a	G C June 21 1:52p	C L July 23 12:48a	L V Aug 23 7:36a	V Li Sept 23 4:50a	Li S Oct 20 1:45p	S Sg Nov 22 10:56a	Sg Cp Dec 22 12:04a
1946	Cp Aq Jan 20 10:44a	Aq P Feb 19 1:10a	P A Mar 21 12:34a	A T Apr 20 12:03p	T G May 21 1:34a	G C June 21 7:45p	C L July 23 6:37a	L V Aug 23 1:23p	V Li Sept 23 10:41a	Li S Oct 23 7:37p	S Sg Nov 22 4:47p	Sg Cp Dec 22 5:54p
1947	Cp Aq Jan 20 4:32p	Aq P Feb 19 6:53a	P A Mar 21 6:13a	A T Apr 20 5:40p	T G May 21 5:04p	G C June 22 1:19a	C L July 23 12:12p	L V Aug 23 7:09p	V Li Sept 23 4:29p	Li S Oct 24 1:27a	S Sg Nov 22 10:38p	Sg Cp Dec 22 11:44a

SUN SIGN CHANGES 1910 – 1970

	Jan	Feb	Mar	Apr	May	June	July	Aug	Sept	Oct	Nov	Dec
1948	Cp Aq Jan 20 10:18p	Aq P Feb 19 12:37p	P A Mar 20 11:57a	A T Apr 19 11:25p	T G May 20 10:58p	G C June 21 7:11a	C L July 22 6:08p	L V Aug 23 1:03a	V Li Sept 22 10:22p	Li S Oct 23 7:19a	S Sg Nov 22 4:29a	Sg Cp Dec 21 5:33p
1949	Cp Aq Jan 20 4:11a	Aq P Feb 18 6:27p	P A Mar 20 5:49p	A T Apr 20 5:18a	T G May 21 4:51a	G C June 21 1:03p	C L July 22 1:58p	L V Aug 23 6:49p	V Li Sept 23 4:05a	Li S Oct 23 1:04p	S Sg Nov 22 10:17a	Sg Cp Dec 21 11:24a
1950	Cp Aq Jan 20 10:00a	Aq P Feb 19 12:16a	P A Mar 20 11:36p	A T Apr 20 11:00a	T G May 21 10:27a	G C June 21 6:37p	C L July 23 5:30a	L V Aug 23 12:24p	V Li Sept 23 9:44a	Li S Oct 23 6:48p	S Sg Nov 22 4:03p	Sg Cp Dec 22 5:14a
1951	Cp Aq Jan 20 3:53p	Aq P Feb 19 6:10a	P A Mar 21 5:26a	A T Apr 20 4:49p	T G May 21 4:15p	G C June 22 12:25a	C L July 23 11:29a	L V Aug 23 6:22p	V Li Sept 23 3:38p	Li S Oct 23 12:37a	S Sg Nov 22 9:52p	Sg Cp Dec 22 11:01a
1952	Cp Aq Jan 20 9:38p	Aq P Feb 19 11:57a	P A Mar 20 11:14a	A T Apr 20 10:37p	T G May 20 10:04p	G C June 21 6:13a	C L July 22 5:05p	L V Aug 23 12:03a	V Li Sept 22 9:24p	Li S Oct 23 6:22a	S Sg Nov 22 3:36a	Sg Cp Dec 21 4:44p
1953	Cp Aq Jan 20 3:22a	Aq P Feb 18 5:41p	P A Mar 20 5:01p	A T Apr 19 4:26a	T G May 21 3:53a	G C June 21 12:00n	C L July 22 10:53p	L V Aug 23 5:46a	V Li Sept 23 3:07a	Li S Oct 23 12:07p	S Sg Nov 22 9:23a	Sg Cp Dec 21 10:22p
1954	Cp Aq Jan 20 9:14a	Aq P Feb 19 11:33p	P A Mar 20 10:54p	A T Apr 20 10:20a	T G May 21 9:48a	G C June 21 5:55p	C L July 23 4:45a	L V Aug 23 11:37a	V Li Sept 23 8:56a	Li S Oct 23 5:58p	S Sg Nov 22 3:14p	Sg Cp Dec 22 4:25a
1955	Cp Aq Jan 20 3:03p	Aq P Feb 19 5:19a	P A Mar 21 4:36a	A T Apr 20 3:58p	T G May 21 3:25p	G C June 21 11:32p	C L July 23 10:25a	L V Aug 23 5:19p	V Li Sept 23 2:42p	Li S Oct 22 11:44p	S Sg Nov 22 9:02p	Sg Cp Dec 22 10:12a
1956	Cp Aq Jan 20 8:49p	Aq P Feb 19 11:05a	P A Mar 20 10:21a	A T Apr 19 9:44p	T G May 20 9:13p	G C June 21 5:24a	C L July 22 4:20p	L V Aug 22 11:15p	V Li Sept 22 8:30p	Li S Oct 23 5:35a	S Sg Nov 22 2:51a	Sg Cp Dec 21 4:00p
1957	Cp Aq Jan 20 2:43a	Aq P Feb 18 5:01p	P A Mar 20 4:17p	A T Apr 20 3:45a	T G May 21 3:09a	G C June 21 11:21a	C L July 22 10:13p	L V Aug 23 5:07p	V Li Sept 23 2:27a	Li S Oct 23 11:33a	S Sg Nov 22 8:45a	Sg Cp Dec 21 9:49p
1958	Cp Aq Jan 20 2:20p	Aq P Feb 18 10:49p	P A Mar 20 10:06p	A T Apr 20 9:28a	T G May 21 8:52a	G C June 21 4:57p	C L July 23 3:51a	L V Aug 23 10:47a	V Li Sept 23 5:10a	Li S Oct 23 5:12a	S Sg Nov 22 2:30p	Sg Cp Dec 22 3:40a
1959	Cp Aq Jan 20 2:20p	Aq P Feb 19 4:38a	P A Mar 21 3:55a	A T Apr 20 3:17p	T G May 21 2:38p	G C June 21 10:50p	C L July 23 9:45a	L V Aug 23 4:44p	V Li Sept 23 2:09p	Li S Oct 23 11:12p	S Sg Nov 22 8:23p	Sg Cp Dec 22 9:35a

SUN SIGN CHANGES 1910 – 1970

	Jan	Feb	Mar	Apr	May	June	July	Aug	Sept	Oct	Nov	Dec
1960	Cp Aq Jan 20 8:11p	Aq P Feb 19 10:26a	P A Mar 20 9:43a	A T Apr 20 10:06p	T G May 20 8:33p	G C June 21 4:43a	C L July 22 5:38p	L V Aug 22 10:35p	V Li Sept 22 8:00p	Li S Oct 23 5:03a	S Sg Nov 22 2:19a	Sg Cp Dec 21 5:27p
1961	Cp Aq Jan 20 2:02a	Aq P Feb 18 6:27p	P A Mar 20 5:27a	A T Apr 20 2:33a	T G May 21 1:51a	G C June 21 10:12a	C L July 22 9:12p	L V Aug 23 3:46a	V Li Sept 23 1:26a	Li S Oct 23 10:46a	S Sg Nov 22 8:10a	Sg Cp Dec 21 9:25p
1962	Cp Aq Jan 20 7:49a	Aq P Feb 18 10:16p	P A Mar 20 9:30p	A T Apr 20 8:51a	T G May 21 8:17a	G C June 21 4:24p	C L July 23 3:19a	L V Aug 23 10:13a	V Li Sept 23 7:35a	Li S Oct 23 4:41p	S Sg Nov 22 2:02p	Sg Cp Dec 22 3:15a
1963	Cp Aq Jan 20 1:55p	Aq P Feb 19 4:09a	P A Mar 21 3:20a	A T Apr 20 2:37p	T G May 21 1:59p	G C June 21 11:04p	C L July 23 9:00a	L V Aug 23 3:58p	V Li Sept 23 1:24p	Li S Oct 23 11:30p	S Sg Nov 22 7:50p	Sg Cp Dec 22 9:02a
1964	Cp Aq Jan 19 7:43p	Aq P Feb 19 10:25a	P A Mar 20 9:43a	A T Apr 19 9:00p	T G May 20 8:33p	G C June 21 4:43a	C L July 22 3:38p	L V Aug 22 10:35p	V Li Sept 22 8:00p	Li S Oct 23 5:03a	S Sg Nov 22 2:19a	Sg Cp Dec 21 3:27p
1965	Cp Aq Jan 20 1:30a	Aq P Feb 18 3:49p	P A Mar 20 3:05p	A T Apr 20 2:27a	T G May 21 1:27a	G C June 21 9:56a	C L July 22 8:49p	L V Aug 23 3:43a	V Li Sept 23 1:06a	Li S Oct 23 10:11a	S Sg Nov 22 7:30a	Sg Cp Dec 21 8:41p
1966	Cp Aq Jan 20 7:21a	Aq P Feb 18 9:39p	P A Mar 20 8:53p	A T Apr 20 8:12a	T G May 21 7:33a	G C June 21 3:33p	C L July 23 2:24a	L V Aug 23 9:18a	V Li Sept 23 6:43a	Li S Oct 23 3:52p	S Sg Nov 22 1:15p	Sg Cp Dec 22 2:29a
1967	Cp Aq Jan 20 1:05p	Aq P Feb 19 3:25a	P A Mar 21 2:37a	A T Apr 20 1:56a	T G May 21 1:19p	G C June 21 4:23p	C L July 23 8:16a	L V Aug 23 3:13p	V Li Sept 23 12:38p	Li S Oct 23 9:44p	S Sg Nov 22 7:05p	Sg Cp Dec 22 8:17a
1968	Cp Aq Jan 20 6:54p	Aq P Feb 19 9:11a	P A Mar 20 8:22a	A T Apr 19 7:42p	T G May 20 7:07p	G C June 21 1:13a	C L July 22 2:13p	L V Aug 22 9:52p	V Li Sept 22 6:26p	Li S Oct 23 1:30a	S Sg Nov 22 12:59a	Sg Cp Dec 21 2:00p
1969	Cp Aq Jan 20 12:30a	Aq P Feb 18 2:47p	P A Mar 20 2:08p	A T Apr 20 1:18a	T G May 21 12:41a	G C June 21 6:55a	C L July 22 8:05p	L V Aug 23 2:35a	V Li Sept 23 12:07a	Li S Oct 23 9:03a	S Sg Nov 22 6:23a	Sg Cp Dec 21 7:44p
1970	Cp Aq Jan 20 6:25a	Aq P Feb 18 8:43p	P A Mar 20 7:59p	A T Apr 20 5:16a	T G May 21 6:32a	G C June 21 2:43p	C L July 23 1:38a	L V Aug 23 6:35a	V Li Sept 23 5:59a	Li S Oct 23 3:05p	S Sg Nov 22 12:25p	Sg Cp Dec 22 1:36a

Table 2 MOON SIGNS 1910 – 1969

1910

	1	2	3	4	5	6	7	8	9	10	11	12	13	14	15	16	17	18	19	20	21	22	23	24	25	26	27	28	29	30	31
Jan	V	V Li 7:37a	Li	Li S 8:18p	S	S	S Sg 8:19p	Sg	Sg Cp 5:39p	Cp	Cp Aq 11:52p	Aq	Aq	Aq P 3:49a	P	P A 6:45a	A	A T 9:38a	T	T G 12:57p	G	G C 5:02p	C	C L 10:23p	L	L	L V 5:51a	V	V Li 4:05p	Li	Li
Feb	Li S 4:32a	S	S Sg 5:04p	Sg	Sg	Sg Cp 3:02a	Cp	Cp Aq 9:13a	Aq	Aq P 12:12p	P	P A 1:40p	A	A T 3:19p	T	T G 8:18a	G	G C 11:02p	C	C	C L 5:28a	L	L V 1:40p	V	V Li 11:58p	Li	Li	Li S 12:15p			
Mar	S	S	S Sg 1:09a	Sg	Sg Cp 12:11p	Cp	Cp Aq 7:22p	Aq	Aq P 10:32p	P	P A 11:09p	A	A T 11:14p	T	T	T G 12:38a	G	G C 4:30a	C	C L 11:03a	L	L V 7:56p	V	V	V Li 6:45a	Li	Li S 7:06a	S	S	S Sg 8:05a	Sg
Apr	Sg Cp 7:55p	Cp	Cp	Cp Aq 4:31a	Aq	Aq P 9:00a	P	P A 10:05a	A	A T 9:32a	T	T G 9:26a	G	G C 11:33a	C	C L 4:55p	L	L	L V 1:34a	V	V Li 12:43p	Li	Li	Li S 1:12a	S	S Sg 2:13p	Sg	Sg	Sg Cp 2:11a	Cp	
May	Cp Aq 11:45a	Aq	Aq P 5:49p	P	P A 8:23p	A	A T 8:32p	T	T G 8:02p	G	G C 8:49p	C	C	C L 12:31a	L	L V 7:59a	V	V Li 6:45p	Li	Li	Li S 7:26a	S	S Sg 8:16p	Sg	Sg	Sg Cp 7:56a	Cp	Cp Aq 5:32p	Aq	Aq	Aq P 12:30a
Jn	P	P A 4:36a	A	A T 6:16a	T	T G 6:39a	G	G C 7:15a	C	C L 9:51a	L	L V 3:52p	V	V	V Li 1:41a	Li	Li S 2:07p	S	S	S Sg 2:56a	Sg	Sg Cp 2:13p	Cp	Cp Aq 11:14p	Aq	Aq	Aq P 5:58a	P	P A 10:43a	A	
Jly	A T 1:47p	T	T G 3:37p	G	G C 5:08p	C	C L 7:43p	L	L	L V 12:53a	V	V Li 9:41a	Li	Li S 9:35p	S	S	S Sg 10:25a	Sg	Sg Cp 9:39p	Cp	Cp	Cp Aq 6:05a	Aq	Aq P 11:56a	P	P A 4:07p	A	A T 7:26p	T	T G 10:19p	G
Aug	G	G C 2:53a	C	C L 4:39a	L	L V 9:57p	V	V Li 6:12p	Li	Li	Li S 5:33a	S	S Sg 6:26p	Sg	Sg	Sg Cp 6:04a	Cp	Cp Aq 2:29p	Aq	Aq P 7:39p	P	P A 10:41p	A	A	A T 1:01a	T	T G 3:52a	G	G C 7:13a	C	C L 11:48a
Sep	L	L V 5:56p	V	V	V Li 2:22a	Li	Li S 1:28p	S	S	S Sg 2:21a	Sg	Sg Cp 2:38p	Cp	Cp Aq 11:52p	Aq	Aq	Aq P 5:11a	P	P A 7:29a	A	A T 8:28a	T	T G 9:48a	G	G C 12:36p	C	C L 5:25p	L	L	L V 12:21a	
Oct	V	V Li 9:28a	Li	Li S 8:44p	S	S	S Sg 9:36a	Sg	Sg Cp 10:25p	Cp	Cp	Cp Aq 8:50a	Aq	Aq P 3:21p	P	P A 6:05p	A	A T 6:26p	T	T G 6:17p	G	G C 7:24p	C	C L 11:07p	L	L	L V 5:53a	V	V Li 3:29p	Li	Li
Nov	Li S 3:11a	S	S Sg 4:06p	Sg	Sg	Sg Cp 5:00a	Cp	Cp Aq 4:18p	Aq	Aq	Aq P 12:25a	P	P A 4:42a	A	A T 5:46a	T	T G 5:11a	G	G C 4:52a	C	C L 6:41a	L	L V 12:07p	V	V Li 9:16p	Li	Li	Li S 9:12a	S	S Sg 10:14p	
Dec	Sg	Sg	Sg Cp 10:56a	Cp	Cp Aq 10:16p	Aq	Aq	Aq P 7:19a	P	P A 1:21p	A	A T 4:12p	T	T G 4:38p	G	G C 4:11p	C	C L 4:48p	L	L V 8:24p	V	V	V Li 4:10a	Li	Li S 3:35p	S	S	S Sg 4:40a	Sg	Sg Cp 5:13p	Cp

1911

	1	2	3	4	5	6	7	8	9	10	11	12	13	14	15	16	17	18	19	20	21	22	23	24	25	26	27	28	29	30	31
Jan	Cp	Cp Aq 4:01a	Aq	Aq P 12:49p	P	P A 7:32a	A	A T 11:59p	T	T	T G 2:15a	G	G C 3:02a	C	C L 3:49a	L	L V 6:30a	V	V Li 12:48p	Li	Li S 11:06p	S	S	S Sg 11:53a	Sg	Sg	Sg Cp 12:29a	Cp	Cp Aq 10:56a	Aq	Aq P 6:54p
Feb	P	P	P A 12:56a	A	A T 5:35a	T	T G 9:02a	G	G C 11:27a	C	C L 1:33p	L	L V 4:39p	V	V Li 10:22p	Li	Li	Li S 7:39a	S	S Sg 7:52p	Sg	Sg	Sg Cp 8:36a	Cp	Cp Aq 7:17p	Aq	Aq	Aq P 2:49a			
Mar	P	P A 7:48a	A	A T 11:20a	T	T G 2:22p	G	G C 5:24p	C	C L 8:44p	L	L	L V 1:04a	V	V Li 7:18a	Li	Li S 4:20p	S	S	S Sg 4:04a	Sg	Sg Cp 4:52p	Cp	Cp	Cp Aq 4:11a	Aq	Aq P 12:12p	P	P A 4:50p	A	A T 7:13p
Apr	T	T G 8:48p	G	G C 10:52p	C	C	C L 2:14a	L	L V 7:22a	V	V Li 2:36p	Li	Li	Li S 12:06a	S	S Sg 11:46a	Sg	Sg	Sg Cp 12:33a	Cp	Cp Aq 12:32p	Aq	Aq P 9:39p	P	P	P A 3:01a	A	A T 5:11a	T	T G 5:38a	
May	G	G C 6:06a	C	C L 8:08a	L	L V 12:50p	V	V Li 8:26p	Li	Li	Li S 6:35a	S	S Sg 6:32p	Sg	Sg	Sg Cp 7:20a	Cp	Cp Aq 7:39p	Aq	Aq	Aq P 5:52a	P	P A 12:38p	A	A T 3:46p	T	T G 4:11p	G	G C 3:37p	C	C L 4:03p
Jn	L	L V 7:13p	V	V	V Li 2:07a	Li	Li S 12:21p	S	S	S Sg 12:37a	Sg	Sg Cp 1:27p	Cp	Cp	Cp Aq 1:43a	Aq	Aq P 12:25p	P	P A 8:30p	A	A	A T 2:13a	T	T G 2:44a	G	G C 2:19a	C	C L 1:54a	L	L V 3:35a	
Jly	V	V Li 9:17a	Li	Li S 6:25p	S	S	S Sg 6:39a	Sg	Sg Cp 7:31p	Cp	Cp	Cp Aq 7:33a	Aq	Aq P 6:03p	P	P	P A 2:33a	A	A T 8:32a	T	T G 11:40a	G	G C 12:28p	C	C L 12:24p	L	L V 1:26p	V	V Li 5:32p	Li	Li
Aug	Li S 1:45a	S	S Sg 1:23p	Sg	Sg	Sg Cp 2:08a	Cp	Cp Aq 2:01p	Aq	Aq P 11:59p	P	P	P A 8:01a	A	A T 2:10p	T	T G 6:22p	G	G C 8:41p	C	C L 9:53p	L	L V 11:26p	V	V	V Li 3:06a	Li	Li S 10:16a	S	S Sg 8:48p	Sg
Sep	Sg	Sg Cp 9:36a	Cp	Cp Aq 9:34p	Aq	Aq	Aq P 7:16a	P	P A 2:29p	A	A T 7:48p	T	T G 11:46p	G	G	G C 2:46a	C	C L 5:17a	L	L V 8:05a	V	V Li 12:22p	Li	Li S 7:16p	S	S	S Sg 5:20a	Sg	Sg Cp 5:38p	Cp	
Oct	Cp	Cp Aq 5:55a	Aq	Aq P 3:58p	P	P A 10:54p	A	A	A T 3:11a	T	T G 5:55a	G	G C 8:11a	C	C L 10:54a	L	L V 2:41p	V	V Li 8:40p	Li	Li	Li S 3:36a	S	S Sg 1:34p	Sg	Sg	Sg Cp 1:36a	Cp	Cp Aq 2:13p	Aq	Aq
Nov	Aq P 1:10a	P	P A 8:48a	A	A T 12:52p	T	T G 2:27p	G	G C 3:10p	C	C L 4:38p	L	L V 8:05p	V	V	V Li 2:04a	Li	Li S 10:27a	S	S Sg 8:57a	Sg	Sg	Sg Cp 8:55a	Cp	Cp Aq 9:39p	Aq	Aq	Aq P 9:31a	P	P A 6:34p	
Dec	A	A T 11:41p	T	T	T G 1:16a	G	G C 12:54a	C	C L 12:39a	L	L V 2:27a	V	V Li 7:35a	Li	Li S 4:08p	S	S	S Sg 3:08a	Sg	Sg Cp 3:23p	Cp	Cp	Cp Aq 4:05a	Aq	Aq P 4:17p	P	P	P A 2:34a	A	A T 9:29a	T

1912

	1	2	3	4	5	6	7	8	9	10	11	12	13	14	15	16	17	18	19	20	21	22	23	24	15	26	27	28	29	30	31
Jan	T G 12:26p	G	G C 12:24p	C	C L 11:17a	L	L V 11:24a	V	V Li 2:43p	Li	Li S 10:07p	S	S	S Sg 8:57a	Sg	Sg	Sg Cp 2:21a	Cp	Cp Aq 10:06a	Aq	Aq P 10:05a	P	P	P A 8:40a	A	A T 4:14p	T	T G 9:40p	G	G C 11:13p	C
Feb	C L 10:46p	L	L V 10:23p	V	V	V Li 12:13a	Li	Li S 5:53a	S	S Sg 3:35p	Sg	Sg	Sg Cp 3:51a	Cp	Cp Aq 4:32p	Aq	Aq	Aq P 3:52a	P	P A 2:15p	A	A T 10:24p	T	T	T G 4:13a	G	G C 7:29a	C	C L 8:41a		
Mar	L	L V 9:13a	V	V Li 10:54a	Li	Li S 3:26p	S	S Sg 11:44p	Sg	Sg	Sg Cp 11:12a	Cp	Cp Aq 11:49p	Aq	Aq	Aq P 11:27a	P	P A 8:59p	A	A	A T 4:15a	T	T G 9:36a	G	G C 1:20p	C	C L 3:53p	L	L V 5:58p	V	V Li 8:39p
Apr	Li	Li	Li S 8:39p	S	S Sg 8:47a	Sg	Sg Cp 7:23p	Cp	Cp	Cp Aq 7:47a	Aq	Aq P 7:41p	P	P	P A 5:14a	A	A T 11:49a	T	T G 4:02p	G	G C 6:52p	C	C L 9:22p	L	L	L V 12:17a	V	V Li 4:14a	Li	Li S 9:47a	
May	S	S Sg 5:30p	Sg	Sg	Sg Cp 3:42a	Cp	Cp Aq 3:49p	Aq	Aq	Aq P 4:07a	P	P A 2:18p	A	A T 9:03p	T	T	T G 12:31a	G	G C 2:03a	C	C L 3:18a	L	L V 5:40a	V	V Li 10:00a	Li	Li S 4:26p	S	S	S Sg 12:54a	Sg
Jn	Sg Cp 11:17a	Cp	Cp Aq 11:18p	Aq	Aq	Aq P 11:54a	P	P A 11:01p	A	A	A T 6:46a	T	T G 10:31a	G	G C 11:23a	C	C L 11:15a	L	L V 12:09p	V	V Li 3:33p	Li	Li S 9:57p	S	S	S Sg 6:57a	Sg	Sg Cp 5:49p	Cp	Cp	
Jly	Cp Aq 5:57a	Aq	Aq P 6:39p	P	P	P A 6:29a	A	A T 3:31p	T	T G 8:33p	G	G C 9:53p	C	C L 9:15p	L	L V 8:49p	V	V Li 10:37p	Li	Li	Li S 3:52a	S	S Sg 10:21a	Sg	Sg Cp 11:41p	Cp	Cp	Cp Aq 12:00n	Aq	Aq	Aq P 12:39a
Aug	P	P A 12:38p	A	A T 10:35p	T	T	T G 5:08a	G	G C 7:56a	C	C L 7:59a	L	L V 7:13a	V	V Li 7:48a	Li	Li S 11:28a	S	S Sg 6:58p	Sg	Sg	Sg Cp 5:42a	Cp	Cp Aq 6:06p	Aq	Aq	Aq P 6:39a	P	P A 6:20p	A	A
Sep	A T 4:18a	T	T G 11:43a	G	G C 4:04p	C	C L 5:42p	L	L V 5:50p	V	V Li 6:17p	Li	Li S 8:54p	S	S	S Sg 2:59a	Sg	Sg Cp 12:43p	Cp	Cp	Cp Aq 12:51a	Aq	Aq P 1:24p	P	P	P A 12:43a	A	A T 10:03a	T	T G 5:11p	
Oct	G	G C 10:08p	C	C	C L 1:10a	L	L V 2:54a	V	V Li 4:24a	Li	Li S 7:04a	S	S Sg 12:19p	Sg	Sg Cp 8:56p	Cp	Cp	Cp Aq 8:30a	Aq	Aq P 9:07p	P	P	P A 8:28a	A	A T 5:13p	T	T G 11:21p	G	G	G C 3:34a	C
Nov	C L 6:45a	L	L V 9:33a	V	V Li 12:31p	Li	Li S 4:12p	S	S Sg 9:44p	Sg	Sg	Sg Cp 5:47a	Cp	Cp Aq 4:45p	Aq	Aq	Aq P 5:32a	P	P A 5:16p	A	A	A T 2:11a	T	T G 7:39a	G	G C 10:35a	C	C L 12:33p	L	L V 2:54p	
Dec	V	V Li 6:25p	Li	Li S 11:21p	S	S	S Sg 5:48a	Sg	Sg Cp 2:10p	Cp	Cp	Cp Aq 12:51a	Aq	Aq P 1:25p	P	P	P A 1:58a	A	A T 11:54a	T	T G 5:49p	G	G C 8:10p	C	C L 8:43p	L	L V 9:27p	V	V Li 11:55p	Li	Li

MOON SIGNS 1910 – 1969

1913

	1	2	3	4	5	6	7	8	9	10	11	12	13	14	15	16
Jan	Li S 4:49a	S	S 12:01p	S Sg	Sg Cp 9:10p	Cp	Cp	Cp Aq 9:13a	Aq	Aq P 8:38p	P	P	P A 9:35a	A	A T 8:45p	T
Feb	Sg	Sg Cp 2:59a	Cp	Cp Aq 2:25p	Aq	Aq	Aq P 3:02a	P	P A 3:58p	A	A	A T 2:54a	T	T G 12:36p	G	G C 5:27p
Mar	Sg Cp 8:52a	Cp	Cp Aq 8:21p	Aq	Aq	Aq P 9:09a	P	P A 9:56p	A	A	A T 9:34a	T	T G 6:59p	G	G	G C 1:18a
Apr	Aq	Aq P 3:38p	P	P	P A 4:21a	A	A T 3:20p	T	T	T G 12:29a	G	G C 7:09a	C	C L 11:23a	L	L V 1:52p
May	P	P A 11:37a	A	A T 10:33p	T	T	T G 6:49a	G	G C 12:41p	C	C L 4:56p	L	L V 8:09p	V	V Li 10:43p	Li
Jn	A T 6:45a	T	T G 2:41p	G	G C 7:39p	C	C L 10:50p	L	L	L V 1:31a	V	V Li 4:27a	Li	Li S 8:00a	S	S Sg 12:31p
Jly	G	G	G C 4:28a	C	C L 6:39a	L	L V 8:00a	V	V Li 9:59	Li	Li S 1:26p	S	S Sg 6:36p	Sg	Sg	Sg Cp 1:39a
Aug	C L 4:23p	L	L V 4:43p	V	V Li 5:12p	Li	Li S 7:21p	S	S	S Sg 12:03a	Sg	Sg Cp 7:24a	Cp	Cp Aq 5:09p	Aq	Aq
Sep	V	V Li 2:46a	Li	Li S 3:21a	S	S Sg 6:30a	Sg	Sg Cp 1:08p	Cp	Cp Aq 10:56p	Aq	Aq	Aq P 10:37a	P	P A 11:54p	A
Oct	Li S 1:31p	S	S Sg 3:08p	Sg	Sg Cp 8:12p	Cp	Cp	Cp Aq 5:09a	Aq	Aq P 5:06p	P	P	P A 6:08a	A	A T 6:30p	T
Nov	Sg	Sg Cp 5:08a	Cp	Cp Aq 12:44p	Aq	Aq	Aq P 12:01a	P	P A 1:01p	A	A	A T 1:15a	T	T G 11:23a	G	G C 7:16p
Dec	Cp Aq 9:42p	Aq	Aq	Aq P 8:00a	P	P A 8:45p	A	A	A T 9:10a	T	T G 7:08p	G	G	G C 2:10a	C	C L 7:08a

	17	18	19	20	21	22	23	24	25	26	27	28	29	30	31
Jan	T	T G 4:05a	G	G C 7:13a	C	C L 7:25a	L	L V 6:47a	V	V Li 7:25a	Li	Li S 10:50a	S	S Sg 5:10p	Sg
Feb	C	C L 6:46p	L	L V 6:07p	V	V Li 5:37p	Li	Li S 7:10p	S	S	S Sg 12:11a	Sg			
Mar	C	C L 4:26a	L	L V 5:07a	V	V Li 4:54a	Li	Li S 5:36a	S	S Sg 8:59a	Sg	Sg Cp 4:09	Cp	Cp	Cp Aq 2:53a
Apr	V	V Li 3:02p	Li	Li S 4:14p	S	S Sg 7:02p	Sg	Sg	Sg Cp 12:57a	Cp	Cp Aq 10:33a	Aq	Aq P 10:53p	P	
May	Li	Li S 1:14a	S	S Sg 4:38	Sg	Sg Cp 10:13a	Cp	Cp Aq 6:59p	Aq	Aq	Aq P 6:46a	P	P A 7:35p	A	A
Jn	Sg	Sg Cp 6:40p	Cp	Cp	Cp Aq 3:21a	Aq	Aq P 2:45p	P	P	P A 3:37a	A	A T 3:21p	T	T G 11:45p	
Jly	Cp	Cp Aq 10:48a	Aq	Aq P 10:12p	P	P	P A 11:06a	A	A T 11:28p	T	T	T G 8:56a	G	G C 2:21p	C
Aug	Aq P 4:51a	P	P A 5:47p	A	A	A T 6:29a	T	T G 5:01p	G	G C 11:52p	C	C	C L 2:53a	L	L V 3:15a
Sep	A	A T 12:32p	T	T G 11:33p	G	G C 7:44a	C	C	C L 12:24p	L	L V 2:00	V	V Li 1:46	Li	
Oct	T	T G 5:12a	G	G C 1:43p	C	C L 7:44p	L	L V 11:05p	V	V	V Li 12:16a	Li	Li S 12:30a	S	S Sg 1:30a
Nov	C	C	C L 1:15a	L	L V 5:39a	V	V Li 8:29a	Li	Li S 10:12a	S	S Sg 11:54a	Sg	Sg Cp 3:12p	Cp	
Dec	L	L V 10:59a	V	V Li 2:18p	Li	Li S 5:20p	S	S Sg 8:27p	Sg	Sg	Sg Cp 12:36a	Cp	Cp Aq 7:00a	Aq	Aq P 4:38p

1914

	1	2	3	4	5	6	7	8	9	10	11	12	13	14	15	16
Jan	P	P	P A 4:57a	A	A T 5:42p	T	T	T G 4:11a	G	G C 11:13a	C	C L 5:39p	L	L V 5:39p	V	V Li 7:52p
Feb	A	A T 1:53a	T	T G 1:18p	G	G C 9:14p	C	C	C L 1:25a	L	L V 2:58a	V	V Li 3:36a	Li	Li S 4:54a	S
Mar	A T 9:49a	T	T G 9:13p	G	G	G C 6:33a	C	C L 12:01p	L	L V 2:01p	V	V Li 1:56p	Li	Li S 1:39p	S	S Sg 3:01p
Apr	G	G C 1:57p	C	C L 9:04p	L	L	L V 12:34a	V	V Li 1:11a	Li	Li S 12:26a	S	S Sg 12:38a	Sg	Sg Cp 2:59a	Cp
May	C	C L 3:52a	L	L V 9:01a	V	V Li 11:12a	Li	Li S 11:19a	S	S Sg 11:04a	Sg	Sg Cp 12:31a	Cp	Cp Aq 5:29a	Aq	Aq
Jn	V	V Li 6:50p	Li	Li S 8:29p	S	S Sg 9:12p	Sg	Sg Cp 10:40p	Cp	Cp	Cp Aq 2:47a	Aq	Aq P 10:45a	P	P A 10:21p	A
Jly	Li	Li S 3:18a	S	S Sg 5:25a	Sg	Sg Cp 7:53a	Cp	Cp Aq 12:11p	Aq	Aq P 7:32p	P	P	P A 6:14a	A	A T 6:48p	T
Aug	Sg	Sg Cp 3:14p	Cp	Cp Aq 8:26p	Aq	Aq	Aq P 4:03a	P	P A 2:25p	A	A	A T 2:45a	T	T G 3:05p	G	G
Sep	Cp Aq 3:03a	Aq	Aq P 11:26a	P	P A 10:10p	A	A	A T 10:14a	T	T G 10:52p	G	G	G C 9:55a	C	C L 5:40p	L
Oct	P	P	P A 4:37a	A	A T 4:59p	T	T	T G 5:39a	G	G C 5:25p	C	C	C L 2:34a	L	L V 8:00a	V
Nov	A T 11:09p	T	T	T G 11:43a	G	G C 11:32p	C	C L 9:35a	L	L	L V 4:40p	V	V Li 8:09p	Li	Li S 8:35p	S
Dec	T G 5:52p	G	G	G C 5:18a	C	C L 3:12p	L	L V 11:01p	V	V	V Li 4:07a	Li	Li S 6:22a	S	S Sg 6:39a	Sg

	17	18	19	20	21	22	23	24	25	26	27	28	29	30	31
Jan	Li	Li S 10:45p	S	S	S Sg 2:39a	Sg	Sg Cp 7:58a	Cp	Cp Aq 3:13p	Aq	Aq	Aq P 12:58a	P	P A 12:56p	A
Feb	S Sg 8:03a	Sg	Sg Cp 1:38p	Cp	Cp Aq 9:41p	Aq	Aq	Aq P 8:00a	P	P A 8:08p	A	A			
Mar	Sg	Sg Cp 7:22p	Cp	Cp	Cp Aq 3:15a	Aq	Aq P 2:01p	P	P	P A 2:29a	A	A T 3:26p	T	T	T G 3:41a
Apr	Cp Aq 9:17a	Aq	Aq P 7:52p	P	P	P A 8:29a	A	A T 9:29p	T	T	T G 9:28a	G	G C 7:49p	C	
May	Aq P 2:40a	P	P A 2:53p	A	A	A T 3:50a	T	T G 3:48p	G	G	G C 1:27a	C	C L 9:20a	L	L V 3:11p
Jn	A	A T 10:58a	T	T G 10:43p	G	G	G C 8:06a	C	C L 3:12p	L	L V 8:34p	V	V	V Li 12:31a	
Jly	T	T G 6:46a	G	G C 4:10p	C	C L 10:41p	L	L	L V 2:59a	V	V Li 6:04a	Li	Li S 8:44a	S	S Sg 11:35a
Aug	G C 1:09a	C	C L 7:51a	L	L V 11:29a	V	V Li 1:17p	Li	Li S 2:20p	S	S Sg 4:59p	Sg	Sg Cp 8:57p	Cp	Cp
Sep	L V 9:40p	V	V Li 10:56p	Li	Li S 10:52p	S	S Sg 11:36p	Sg	Sg	Sg Cp 2:35a	Cp	Cp Aq 8:36a	Aq	Aq P 5:32p	
Oct	V Li 9:48a	Li	Li S 9:20a	S	S Sg 8:40a	Sg	Sg Cp 9:55a	Cp	Cp Aq 2:40p	Aq	Aq P 11:13p	P	P	P A 10:34a	A
Nov	S Sg 7:42p	Sg	Sg Cp 7:42p	Cp	Cp Aq 10:43p	Aq	Aq	Aq P 5:52a	P	P A 4:43p	A	A	A T 5:21a	T	
Dec	Sg Cp 6:45a	Cp	Cp Aq 8:47a	Aq	Aq P 2:25p	P	P	P A 12:03a	A	A T 12:18p	T	T	T G 12:52a	G	G C 12:00n

1915

	1	2	3	4	5	6	7	8	9	10	11	12	13	14	15	16
Jan	C	C L 9:12p	L	L	L V 4:28a	V	V Li 9:52a	Li	Li S 1:24p	S	S Sg 3:25p	Sg	Sg Cp 4:52p	Cp	Cp Aq 7:17p	Aq
Feb	L V 11:09a	V	V Li 3:32p	Li	Li S 6:48p	S	S Sg 9:33p	Sg	Sg	Sg Cp 12:26a	Cp	Cp Aq 4:10a	Aq	Aq P 9:41a	P	P A 5:47p
Mar	V	V Li 11:15p	Li	Li	Li S 1:05a	S	S Sg 2:59a	Sg	Sg Cp 5:59a	Cp	Cp Aq 10:41a	Aq	Aq P 5:17p	P	P	P A 1:56a
Apr	Li S 9:49a	S	S Sg 10:06a	Sg	Sg Cp 11:48a	Cp	Cp Aq 4:04p	Aq	Aq P 11:09p	P	P	P A 8:32a	A	A T 7:38p	T	T
May	Sg	Sg Cp 7:40p	Cp	Cp Aq 10:24p	Aq	Aq	Aq P 4:42a	P	P A 2:12p	A	A	A T 1:41a	T	T G 2:09p	G	G
Jn	Cp Aq 6:49a	Aq	Aq P 11:33a	P	P A 8:07p	A	A	A T 7:31a	T	T G 8:07p	G	G	G C 8:38a	C	C L 8:12p	L
Jly	P	P	P A 3:25a	A	A T 2:02p	T	T	T G 2:20a	G	G C 2:56p	C	C	C L 2:06a	L	L V 11:22a	V
Aug	A T 9:40p	T	T	T G 9:43a	G	G C 10:11p	C	C	C L 9:08a	L	L V 5:42p	V	V Li 11:55p	Li	Li	Li S 4:16a
Sep	G	G	G C 6:12a	C	C L 5:24p	L	L	L V 1:41a	V	V Li 7:00a	Li	Li S 10:15a	S	S Sg 12:41p	Sg	Sg Cp 3:21p
Oct	C	C	C L 2:13a	L	L V 11:04a	V	V Li 4:08p	Li	Li S 6:20p	S	S Sg 7:21p	Sg	Sg Cp 8:57p	Cp	Cp	Cp Aq 12:16a
Nov	L V 8:30p	V	V	V Li 2:28a	Li	Li S 4:37a	S	S Sg 4:36a	Sg	Sg Cp 4:34a	Cp	Cp Aq 6:23a	Aq	Aq P 11:06a	P	P A 6:40p
Dec	V Li 12:10p	Li	Li S 3:32p	S	S Sg 3:47p	Sg	Sg Cp 2:53p	Cp	Cp Aq 3:02p	Aq	Aq P 5:58p	P	P	P A 12:31a	A	A T 10:15a

	17	18	19	20	21	22	23	24	25	26	27	28	29	30	31
Jan	Aq	Aq P 1:16a	P	P A 8:43a	A	A T 8:13p	T	T	T G 8:48a	G	G C 8:08a	C	C	C L 4:55a	L
Feb	A	A	A T 4:38a	T	T G 5:06p	G	G	G C 4:57a	C	C L 2:10p	L	L V 8:03p			
Mar	A	A T 12:39p	T	T	T G 12:58a	G	G C 1:21p	C	C L 11:37p	L	L	L V 6:13a	V	V Li 9:09a	Li
Apr	T G 7:57a	G	G C 8:37p	C	C	C L 7:53a	L	L V 3:52p	V	V Li 7:47p	Li	Li S 8:23p	S	S Sg 7:37p	
May	G C 2:48a	C	C L 2:31p	L	L V 11:46p	V	V	V Li 5:16a	Li	Li S 7:02a	S	S Sg 6:27a	Sg	Sg Cp 3:40a	Cp
Jn	L	L V 5:53a	V	V Li 12:38p	Li	Li S 4:03p	S	S Sg 4:46p	Sg	Sg Cp 4:22p	Cp	Cp Aq 4:56p	Aq	Aq P 8:15p	
Jly	V Li 6:21p	Li	Li S 10:50p	S	S	S Sg 1:06a	Sg	Sg Cp 1:04a	Cp	Cp Aq 3:11a	Aq	Aq P 6:05a	P	P A 12:08p	A
Aug	S	S Sg 7:19a	Sg	Sg Cp 9:38a	Cp	Cp Aq 12:04p	Aq	Aq P 3:36p	P	P A 9:23p	A	A	A T 6:08a	T	T G 5:39p
Sep	Cp	Cp Aq 6:50p	Aq	Aq P 11:33p	P	P	P A 5:56a	A	A T 2:36p	T	T	T G 1:43a	G	G C 2:20p	
Oct	Aq	Aq P 5:38a	P	P A 12:58p	A	A T 10:09p	T	T	T G 9:16a	G	G C 9:53p	C	C	C L 10:26a	L
Nov	A	A	A T 4:30a	T	T G 3:57p	G	G	G C 4:34a	C	C L 5:23p	L	L	L V 4:33a	V	
Dec	T	T G 10:03p	G	G	G C 10:45a	C	C L 11:23p	L	L	L V 10:50a	V	V Li 7:42p	Li	Li	Li S 12:54a

MOON SIGNS 1910 – 1969

1916

	1	2	3	4	5	6	7	8	9	10	11	12	13	14	15	16	17	18	19	20	21	22	23	24	25	26	27	28	29	20	31
Jan	S	S Sg 2:43a	Sg	Sg Cp 2:26a	Cp	Cp Aq 1:59a	Aq	Aq P 3:23a	P	P A 8:08a	A	A T 4:44p	T	T	T G 4:19a	G	G C 5:07p	C	C	C L 5:33a	L	L V 4:32p	V	V	V Li 1:25a	Li	Li S 7:43a	S	S Sg 11:17a	Sg	Sg Cp 12:42p
Feb	Cp	Cp Aq 1:10a	Aq	Aq P 2:17p	P	P A 5:46p	A	A	A T 12:51a	T	T F 11:31a	G	G	G C 12:13a	C	C L 12:38p	L	L V 11:08p	V	V	V Li 7:14a	Li	Li S 1:08p	S	S Sg 5:20p	Sg	Sg Cp 8:13p	Cp	Cp Aq 10:18p		
Mar	Aq	Aq	Aq P 12:28a	P	P A 3:57a	A	A T 10:09a	T	T G 7:46p	G	G	G C 8:04a	C	C L 8:41p	L	L	L V 7:12a	V	V Li 2:37p	Li	Li S 7:27p	S	S Sg 10:48p	Sg	Sg	Sg Cp 1:44a	Cp	Cp Aq 4:47a	Aq	Aq P 8:36a	P
Apr	P A 12:49p	A	A T 7:11p	T	T	T G 4:20a	G	G C 4:11p	C	C	C L 5:01a	L	L V 4:06p	V	V Li 11:40p	Li	Li	Li S 3:47a	S	S Sg 5:53a	Sg	Sg Cp 7:34a	Cp	Cp Aq 10:08p	Aq	Aq P 2:06p	P	P A 7:35p	A	A	
May	A T 2:50a	T	T G 12:13p	G	G C 11:54a	C	C	C L 12:51p	L	L	L V 12:44a	V	V Li 9:14a	Li	Li S 1:41p	S	S Sg 3:09p	Sg	Sg Cp 3:31p	Cp	Cp Aq 4:34p	Aq	Aq P 7:35p	P	P	P A 1:04a	A	A T 8:55a	T	T G 6:54p	G
Jn	G	G C 6:46a	C	C L 7:47p	L	L	L V 8:15a	V	V Li 5:59p	Li	Li S 11:38p	S	S	S Sg 1:39a	Sg	Sg Cp 1:33a	Cp	Cp Aq 1:17a	Aq	Aq P 2:41a	P	P A 6:55a	A	A T 2:27p	T	T	T G 12:44a	G	G C 12:56p	C	
Jly	C	C L 1:57a	L	L V 2:32p	V	V	V Li 1:05a	Li	Li S 8:16a	S	S Sg 11:43a	Sg	Sg Cp 12:20p	Cp	Cp Aq 11:47a	Aq	Aq P 11:56a	P	P A 2:34p	A	A T 8:47p	T	T	T G 6:36a	G	G C 6:53p	C	C	C L 7:56a	L	L V 8:18p
Aug	V	V	V Li 6:54a	Li	Li S 2:55p	S	S Sg 7:57p	Sg	Sg Cp 10:08p	Cp	Cp Aq 10:28p	Aq	Aq P 10:30p	P	P	P A 12:03a	A	A T 4:46a	T	T G 1:28p	G	G C 1:22a	C	C	C L 2:24p	L	L	L V 2:29a	V	V Li 12:43p	Li
Sep	Li S 8:24p	S	S	S Sg 2:05a	Sg	Sg Cp 5:44a	Cp	Cp Aq 7:39a	Aq	Aq P 8:42a	P	P A 10:19a	A	A T 2:11p	T	T G 9:39p	G	G	G C 8:46a	C	C L 9:41p	L	L	L V 9:46a	V	V Li 7:22p	Li	Li	Li S 2:21a	S	
Oct	S Sg 7:28a	Sg	Sg Cp 11:23a	Cp	Cp Aq 2:28p	Aq	Aq P 5:00p	P	P A 7:41p	A	A T 11:46p	T	T	T G 6:38a	G	G C 4:59p	C	C	C L 3:38a	L	L V 6:04p	V	V	V Li 3:45a	Li	Li S 10:08a	S	S Sg 2:07p	Sg	Sg Cp 5:01p	Cp
Nov	Cp Aq 7:50p	Aq	Aq P 11:05p	P	P	P A 3:00a	A	A T 8:07a	T	T G 3:20p	G	G	G C 1:20a	C	C L 1:45p	L	L	L V 2:33a	V	V Li 1:02p	Li	Li S 7:48p	S	S Sg 11:11p	Sg	Sg	Sg Cp 12:45a	Cp	Cp Aq 2:07a	Aq	
Dec	Aq P 4:30a	P	P A 8:35a	A	A T 2:36p	T	T G 10:41p	G	G	G C 9:00a	C	C L 9:18p	L	L	L V 10:19a	V	V Li 9:49p	Li	Li	Li S 5:52a	S	S Sg 9:57a	Sg	Sg Cp 11:07a	Cp	Cp Aq 11:05a	Aq	Aq P 11:43a	P	P A 2:27p	A

1917

	1	2	3	4	5	6	7	8	9	10	11	12	13	14	15	16	17	18	19	20	21	22	23	24	25	26	27	28	29	30	31
Jan	A T 8:05p	T	T	T G 4:40a	G	G C 3:36p	C	C	C L 4:03a	L	L V 5:02p	V	V	V Li 5:04a	Li	Li S 2:31p	S	S Sg 8:17p	Sg	Sg Cp 10:28p	Cp	Cp Aq 10:19p	Aq	Aq P 9:42p	P	P A 10:35p	A	A	A T 2:36a	T	T G 10:27a
Feb	G	G C 9:31p	C	C L 10:16a	L	L	L V 11:09p	V	V	V Li 11:04a	Li	Li S 9:06p	S	S	S Sg 4:22a	Sg	Sg Cp 8:24a	Cp	Cp Aq 9:32a	Aq	Aq P 9:06a	P	P A 9:01a	A	A T 11:21a	T	T G 5:35p	G			
Mar	G	G C 3:53a	C	C L 4:36p	L	L 5:29a	V	V	V Li 5:01p	Li	Li	Li S 2:40a	S	S Sg 10:18a	Sg	Sg Cp 3:38p	Cp	Cp Aq 6:33p	Aq	Aq P 7:31	P	P A 7:54p	A	A T 9:36p	T	T	T G 2:30a	G	G C 11:29a	C	C L 11:39p
Apr	L	L	L V 12:32p	V	V Li 11:53p	Li	Li	Li S 8:54a	S	S Sg 3:50p	Sg	Sg Cp 9:08p	Cp	Cp	Cp Aq 12:56a	Aq	Aq P 3:25a	P	P A 5:11a	A	A T 7:31a	T	T G 12:06p	G	G C 8:08p	C	C	C L 7:32a	L	L V 8:19p	
May	V	V	V Li 7:52a	Li	Li S 4:39p	S	S Sg 10:44p	Sg	Sg	Sg Cp 2:59a	Cp	Cp Aq 6:18a	Aq	Aq P 9:11a	P	P A 12:05p	A	A T 3:39p	T	T G 8:54p	G	G	G C 4:50a	C	C L 3:43p	L	L	L V 4:21a	V	V Li 4:20p	Li
Jn	Li	Li S 1:34a	S	S Sg 7:28a	Sg	Sg Cp 10:45a	Cp	Cp Aq 12:46p	Aq	Aq P 2:43p	P	P A 5:31p	A	A T 9:49p	T	T	T G 4:03a	G	G C 12:34p	C	C L 11:28p	L	L	L V 12:00n	V	V	V Li 12:26a	Li	Li S 10:37a	S	
Jly	S Sg 5:14p	Sg	Sg Cp 8:25p	Cp	Cp Aq 9:25p	Aq	Aq P 9:54p	P	P A 11:26p	A	A	A T 3:14a	T	T G 9:48a	G	G C 7:00p	C	C	C L 6:17a	L	L V 6:52p	V	V	V Li 7:33a	Li	Li S 6:41p	S	S	S Sg 2:37a	Sg	Sg Cp 6:48a
Aug	Cp	Cp Aq 7:50a	Aq	Aq P 7:20a	P	P A 7:19a	A	A T 9:38a	T	T G 3:25p	G	G	G C 12:40a	C	C L 12:20p	L	L	L V 1:02a	V	V Li 1:42p	Li	Li	Li S 1:15a	S	S Sg 10:27a	Sg	Sg Cp 4:14p	Cp	Cp Aq 6:28p	Aq	Aq P 6:11p
Sep	P	P A 5:21p	A	A T 6:07p	T	T G 10:21p	G	G	G C 6:40a	C	C L 6:13p	L	L	L V 7:03a	V	V Li 7:33p	Li	Li	Li S 6:55a	S	S Sg 4:32p	Sg	Sg	Sg Cp 11:36p	Cp	Cp Aq 3:33a	Aq	Aq P 4:39a	P	P A 4:16a	
Oct	A	A T 4:26a	T	T G 7:14a	G	G C 2:08p	C	C	C L 12:51a	L	L V 1:32p	V	V	V Li 1:58a	Li	Li S 12:53p	S	S Sg 10:00p	Sg	Sg	Sg Cp 5:13a	Cp	Cp Aq 10:16a	Aq	Aq P 1:07p	P	P A 2:09p	A	A T 3:00p	T	T G 5:27p
Nov	G	G C 11:10p	C	C	C L 8:43a	L	L	L V 8:57p	V	V Li 9:26a	Li	Li S 8:13p	S	S	S Sg 4:36a	Sg	Sg Cp 10:55a	Cp	Cp Aq 3:38p	Aq	Aq P 7:04p	P	P A 9:36p	A	A T 11:56p	T	T	T G 3:14a	G	G C 8:49a	
Dec	C	C L 5:33p	L	L	L V 5:07a	V	V Li 5:42p	Li	Li	Li S 4:52a	S	S Sg 1:10p	Sg	Sg Cp 6:35p	Cp	Cp Aq 10:00p	Aq	Aq	Aq P 12:32a	P	P A 3:07a	A	A T 6:26a	T	T G 11:04a	G	G C 5:30p	C	C	C L 2:16a	L

1918

	1	2	3	4	5	6	7	8	9	10	11	12	13	14	15	16	17	18	19	20	21	22	23	24	25	26	27	28	29	30	31
Jan	L V 1:24p	V	V	V Li 1:56a	Li	Li S 1:49p	S	S Sg 10:57p	Sg	Sg	Sg Cp 4:26a	Cp	Cp Aq 6:56a	Aq	Aq P 7:54a	P	P A 9:04a	A	A T 11:50a	T	T G 4:53p	G	G	G C 12:18a	C	C L 9:46a	L	L V 8:59p	V	V	V Li 9:27a
Feb	Li	Li S 9:51p	S	S	S Sg 8:15a	Sg	Sg Cp 2:56p	Cp	Cp Aq 5:46p	Aq	Aq P 5:57p	P	P A 5:31p	A	A T 6:32p	T	T G 10:31p	G	G	G C 5:51a	C	C L 3:53p	L	L	L V 3:33a	V	V Li 4:02a	Li			
Mar	Li	Li S 4:32a	S	S Sg 3:47p	Sg	Sg	Sg Cp 12:03a	Cp	Cp Aq 4:22a	Aq	Aq P 5:12a	P	P A 4:16a	A	A T 3:49a	T	T G 5:58a	G	G C 12:00n	C	C L 9:38p	L	L	L V 9:31a	V	V Li 10:07p	Li	Li	Li S 10:29a	S	S Sg 9:47p
Apr	Sg	Sg	Sg Cp 6:57a	Cp	Cp Aq 12:55p	Aq	Aq P 3:22p	P	P A 3:19p	A	A T 2:41p	T	T G 3:39p	G	G C 7:58p	C	C	C L 4:20a	L	L V 3:47p	V	V	V Li 4:25a	Li	Li S 4:37p	S	S	S Sg 3:30a	Sg	Sg Cp 12:33p	
May	Cp	Cp Aq 7:13p	Aq	Aq P 11:07p	P	P	P A 12:40a	A	A T 1:05a	T	T G 2:07a	G	G C 5:32a	C	C L 12:33p	L	L V 11:01p	V	V	V Li 11:26a	Li	Li S 11:38p	S	S	S Sg 10:08a	Sg	Sg Cp 6:27p	Cp	Cp	Cp Aq 12:37a	Aq
Jn	Aq P 4:53a	P	P A 7:37a	A	A T 9:30a	T	T G 11:37a	G	G C 3:13p	C	C L 9:37p	L	L	L V 7:11a	V	V Li 7:10p	Li	Li	Li S 7:30a	S	S Sg 6:04p	Sg	Sg	Sg Cp 1:50a	Cp	Cp Aq 7:01a	Aq	Aq P 10:26a	P	P A 7:05a	
Jly	A	A T 3:44p	T	T G 7:04p	G	G C 11:43p	C	C	C L 6:21a	L	L V 3:34p	V	V	V Li 3:10a	Li	Li S 3:41p	S	S	S Sg 2:48a	Sg	Sg Cp 10:45a	Cp	Cp Aq 5:14p	Aq	Aq P 5:32p	P	P A 6:59p	A	A T 9:07p	T	T
Aug	T G 12:49a	G	G C 6:22a	C	C L 1:50p	L	L V 11:18p	V	V	V Li 10:46a	Li	Li S 11:27p	S	S	S Sg 11:22a	Sg	Sg Cp 8:17p	Cp	Cp	Cp Aq 1:10a	Aq	Aq P 2:48a	P	P A 2:56a	A	A T 3:36a	T	T G 6:20a	G	G C 11:51a	C
Sep	C L 7:53p	L	L	L V 5:57a	V	V Li 5:35p	Li	Li	Li S 6:20a	S	S Sg 6:49p	Sg	Sg 5:02a	Sg Cp	Cp	Cp Aq 11:14a	Aq	Aq P 1:26p	P	P A 1:07p	A	A T 12:28p	T	T G 1:32p	G	G C 5:46p	C	C	C L 1:26a	L	
Oct	L V 11:46a	V	V Li 11:44p	Li	Li	Li S 12:28p	S	S	S Sg 1:04a	Sg	Sg Cp 1:04p	Cp	Cp Aq 7:54p	Aq	Aq P 11:41p	P	P	P A 12:14a	A T 11:21p	T	T G 11:12p	G	G	G C 1:42a	C	C L 7:55a	L	L V 5:43p	V	V	V Li 5:46a
Nov	Li	Li S 6:32p	S	S	S Sg 6:52a	Sg	Sg Cp 5:50p	Cp	Cp	Cp Aq 2:25a	Aq	Aq P 7:52a	P	P A 10:11a	A	A T 10:27a	T	T G 10:21a	G	G C 11:48a	C	C L 4:24p	L	L	L V 12:52a	V	V Li 12:26p	Li	Li	Li S 1:13a	
Dec	S	S Sg 1:20p	Sg	Sg Cp 11:41p	Cp	Cp	Cp Aq 7:52a	Aq	Aq P 1:47p	P	P A 5:33p	A	A T 7:36p	T	T G 8:49p	G	G C 10:36p	C	C	C L 2:28a	L	L V 9:34a	V	V Li 8:10p	Li	Li	Li S 8:49a	S	S Sg 9:03p	Sg	Sg

MOON SIGNS 1910 – 1969

1919

	1	2	3	4	5	6	7	8	9	10	11	12	13	14	15	16
Jan	Sg Cp 7:02a	Cp	Cp Aq 2:15p	Aq	Aq P 7:19p	P A	9:41p	A	A	A T 2:02a	T	T G 4:49a	G	G C 7:56a	C	C L 12:18p
Feb	Aq	Aq P 2:37a	P	P A 5:02a	A	A T 7:22a	T	T G 10:31a	G	G C 2:47p	C	C L 8:18p	L	L	L V 3:33a	V
Mar	Aq P 12:14p	P	P A 1:28p	A	A T 2:15p	T	T G 4:11p	G	G C 8:10p	C	C	C L 2:19a	L	L V 10:27a	V	V Li 8:29p
Apr	A T 11:41p	T	T G 11:57p	G	G	G C 2:24a	C	C L 7:49a	L	L V 4:08p	V	V	V Li 2:43a	Li	Li S 2:55p	S
May	T G 10:01a	G	G C 10:52a	C	C L 2:39p	L	L V 10:02p	V	V	V Li 8:33a	Li	Li S 8:58p	S	S	S Sg 9:54a	Sg
Jn	C L 11:28p	L	L	L V 5:19a	V	V Li 2:59p	Li	Li	Li S 3:16a	S	S Sg 4:12p	Sg	Sg	Sg Cp 4:04a	Cp	Cp Aq 1:58p
Jly	L V 2:08p	V	V Li 10:36p	Li	Li	Li S 10:19a	S	S Sg 11:13p	Sg	Sg	Sg Cp 10:56a	Cp	Cp Aq 8:14p	Aq	Aq	Aq P 3:06a
Aug	Li	Li S 6:08p	S	S	S Sg 6:58a	Sg	Sg Cp 6:52p	Cp	Cp	Cp Aq 3:56a	Aq	Aq P 9:59a	P	P A 1:59p	A	A T 5:05p
Sep	S Sg 2:58p	Sg	Sg	Sg Cp 3:20a	Cp	Cp Aq 12:53p	Aq	Aq P 6:46p	P	P A 9:48p	A	A T 11:36p	T	T	T G 1:36a	G
Oct	Sg Cp 6:28a	Cp	Cp Aq 10:02p	Aq	Aq	Aq P 4:42a	P	P A 7:44a	A	A T 8:33a	T	T G 9:00a	G	G C 10:40a	C	C L 2:33p
Nov	Aq	Aq P 2:18p	P	P A 6:30p	A	A T 7:31p	T	T G 7:03p	G	G C 7:03p	C	C L 9:15p	L	L	L V 2:42a	V
Dec	P	P A 4:02a	A	A T 6:34a	T	T G 6:36a	G	G C 5:55a	C	C L 6:28a	L	L V 10:08a	V	V Li 5:48p	Li	Li

	17	18	19	20	21	22	23	24	25	26	27	28	29	30	31
Jan	L	L V 6:57p	V	V	V Li 4:43a	Li	Li S 5:00p	S	S	S Sg 5:35a	Sg	Sg Cp 3:53p	Cp	Cp Aq 10:43p	Aq
Feb	V Li 11:08p	Li	Li	Li S 1:04a	S	S Sg 1:57p	Sg	Sg	Sg Cp 1:02a	Cp	Cp Aq 8:36a	Aq			
Mar	Li	Li	Li S 8:25a	S	S Sg 9:24p	Sg	Sg	Sg Cp 9:25a	Cp	Cp Aq 6:11p	Aq	Aq P 10:45p	P	P A 10:31p	A
Apr	S	S Sg 3:52a	Sg	Sg Cp 4:13p	Cp	Cp	Cp Aq 2:08a	Aq	Aq P 8:17a	P	P A 10:39a	A	A T 10:36a	T	
May	Sg Cp 10:06p	Cp	Cp	Cp Aq 8:23a	Aq	Aq P 3:44p	P	P A 7:47p	A	A T 9:03p	T	T G 8:53p	G	G C 9:06p	C
Jn	Aq	Aq P 9:31p	P	P	P A 2:37a	A	A T 5:29a	T	T G 6:42a	G	G C 7:29a	C	C L 9:25a	L	
Jly	P	P A 8:06a	A	A T 11:43a	T	T G 2:19p	G	G C 4:25p	C	C L 7:04p	L	L V 11:29p	V	V	V Li 9:07a
Aug	T	T G 8:03p	G	G C 11:14p	C	C	C L 3:00a	L	L V 8:09a	V	V Li 3:42p	Li	Li	Li S 2:16a	S
Sep	G C 4:39a	C	C L 9:08a	L	L V 3:16p	V	V Li 11:25p	Li	Li	Li S 10:00a	S	S Sg 10:37p	Sg	Sg	
Oct	L	L V 8:59p	V	V	V Li 5:51a	Li	Li S 4:53p	S	S	S Sg 5:31a	Sg	Sg Cp 6:35p	Cp	Cp	Cp Aq 6:08a
Nov	V Li 11:27a	Li	Li S 10:59p	S	S	S Sg 11:48a	Sg	Sg	Sg Cp 12:45a	Cp	Cp Aq 12:37p	Aq	Aq P 10:02p	P	
Dec	Li S 5:01a	S	S Sg 5:59p	Sg	Sg	Sg Cp 6:49a	Cp	Cp Aq 6:20p	Aq	Aq	Aq P 3:55a	P	P A 11:05a	A	A T 2:02p

1920

	1	2	3	4	5	6	7	8	9	10	11	12	13	14	15	16
Jan	T	T G 5:13p	G	G C 5:19p	C	C L 5:31p	L	L V 7:46p	V	V	V Li 1:50a	Li	Li S 11:58a	S	S	S Sg 12:44a
Feb	G C 2:54a	C	C L 3:33a	L	L V 6:19a	V	V Li 11:21a	Li	Li S 8:14p	S	S	S Sg 8:25a	Sg	Sg Cp 9:14p	Cp	Cp
Mar	C L 12:23p	L	L V 3:41p	V	V Li 8:54p	Li	Li	Li S 5:11a	S	S Sg 4:36p	Sg	Sg	Sg Cp 5:25a	Cp	Cp Aq 4:58p	Aq
Apr	V	V Li 6:00a	Li	Li S 1:35p	S	S	S Sg 12:42a	Sg	Sg Cp 1:25p	Cp	Cp	Cp Aq 1:31a	Aq	Aq P 10:49a	P	P A 4:29p
May	Li S 8:38p	S	S	S Sg 8:00a	Sg	Sg Cp 8:39p	Cp	Cp	Cp Aq 9:09a	Aq	Aq P 7:32p	P	P	P A 2:22a	A	A T 5:35a
Jn	Sg	Sg	Sg Cp 3:05a	Cp	Cp Aq 3:38p	Aq	Aq	Aq P 2:42a	P	P A 10:56a	A	A T 3:34p	T	T G 4:57p	G	G C 4:27p
Jly	Cp	Cp Aq 9:31p	Aq	Aq	Aq P 8:37a	P	P A 5:38p	A	A T 11:44p	T	T	T G 2:39a	G	G C 3:03a	C	C L 2:23a
Aug	Aq P 2:18p	P	P A 11:09p	A	A	A T 5:56a	T	T G 10:14a	G	G C 12:11p	C	C L 12:42p	L	L V 1:28p	V	V Li 4:29p
Sep	A	A T 11:19a	T	T G 3:57p	G	G C 7:04p	C	C L 9:02p	L	L V 10:55p	V	V	V Li 2:12a	Li	Li S 8:20a	S
Oct	T G 9:32p	G	G	G C 12:29a	C	C L 3:14a	L	L V 6:23a	V	V Li 10:45a	Li	Li S 5:14p	S	S	S Sg 2:31a	Sg
Nov	C	C L 8:38a	L	L V 12:04p	V	V Li 5:25p	Li	Li	Li S 12:51a	S	S Sg 10:27a	Sg	Sg Cp 10:03p	Cp	Cp	Cp Aq 10:46a
Dec	L V 5:45p	V	V Li 10:51p	Li	Li	Li S 6:51a	S	S Sg 5:10p	Sg	Sg	Sg Cp 5:00a	Cp	Cp Aq 5:39p	Aq	Aq	Aq P 6:03a

	17	18	19	20	21	22	23	24	25	26	27	28	29	30	31
Jan	Sg	Sg Cp 1:33p	Cp	Cp	Cp Aq 12:39a	Aq	Aq P 9:34a	P	P A 4:32p	A	A T 9:43p	T	T	T G 1:04a	G
Feb	Cp Aq 8:20a	Aq	Aq P 4:38p	P	P A 11:13p	A	A	A T 3:05a	T	T G 6:42a	G	G C 9:41a	C		
Mar	Aq	Aq P 1:24a	P	P A 6:43a	A	A T 9:58a	T	T G 3:26p	G	G C 3:02p	C	C L 6:21p	L	L V 10:49p	V
Apr	A	A T 7:08p	T	T G 8:15p	G	G C 9:23p	C	C L 11:50p	L	L	L V 4:22a	V	V Li 11:19a	Li	
May	T	T G 6:13a	G	G C 6:01a	C	C L 6:50a	L V 10:12p	V	V	V Li 4:51p	Li	Li	Li S 2:33a	S	S Sg 2:21p
Jn	C	C L 4:02p	L	L V 5:45p	V	V Li 11:07p	Li	Li	Li S 8:20a	S	S Sg 8:15p	Sg	Sg	Sg Cp 9:06a	
Jly	L	L V 3:14a	V	V Li 7:03a	Li	Li S 3:04p	S	S	S Sg 2:32a	Sg	Sg Cp 3:22p	Cp	Cp	Cp Aq 3:36a	Aq
Aug	Li	Li S 11:14p	S	S	S Sg 9:46a	Sg	Sg Cp 10:22p	Cp	Cp	Cp Aq 10:36a	Aq	Aq P 8:55p	P	P	P A 5:03a
Sep	S Sg 5:58p	Sg	Sg	Sg Cp 6:09a	Cp	Cp Aq 6:33p	Aq	Aq	Aq P 4:57a	P	P A 12:34p	A	A T 5:49p	T	
Oct	Sg Cp 2:17p	Cp	Cp	Cp Aq 2:52a	Aq	Aq P 1:56p	P	P A 9:52p	A	A	A T 2:33a	T	T G 4:59a	G	G C 6:35a
Nov	Aq	Aq P 10:37p	P	P	P A 7:45a	A	A T 1:01p	T	T G 2:59p	G	G C 3:12p	C	C L 3:33p	L	
Dec	P	P A 4:29p	A	A T 11:21p	T	T	T G 2:14a	G	G C 2:13a	C	C L 1:17a	L	L V 1:39a	V	V Li 5:07a

1921

	1	2	3	4	5	6	7	8	9	10	11	12	13	14	15	16
Jan	L	L S 12:28p	S	S Sg 7:24p	Sg	Sg	Sg Cp 11:10a	Cp	Cp Aq 11:50p	Aq	Aq	Aq P 12:10p	P	P A 11:14p	A	A
Feb	S Sg 5:04a	Sg	Sg Cp 5:14p	Cp	Cp	Cp Aq 5:59a	Aq	Aq P 6:04p	P	P	P A 4:51a	A	A T 1:44p	T	T G 8:04p	G
Mar	Sg	Sg	Sg Cp 12:04a	Cp	Cp Aq 12:46p	Aq	Aq	Aq P 12:44a	P	P A 10:58a	A	A T 7:15p	T	T	T G 1:26a	G
Apr	Cp Aq 8:22p	Aq	Aq	Aq P 8:28a	P	P A 6:31p	A	A	A T 1:59a	T	T G 7:16a	G	G C 10:59a	C	C L 1:48p	L
May	Aq P 4:46p	P	P	P A 3:13a	A	A T 10:31a	T	T G 2:51p	G	G C 5:19p	C	C L 7:17p	L	L V 9:52p	V	V
Jn	A	A T 8:03p	T	T	T G 12:16a	G	G C 1:46a	C	C L 2:19a	L	L V 3:42	V	V L 7:10a	L	L S 12:22p	S
Jly	T	T G 10:22a	G	G C 11:55a	C	C L 11:34a	L	L V 11:27a	V	V L 1:30p	L	L S 6:43p	S	S	S Sg 3:06a	Sg
Aug	C	C L 10:11p	L	L V 9:19p	V	V L 9:53p	L	L S 1:35a	S	S	S Sg 9:00a	Sg	Sg Cp 7:30p	Cp	Cp	Cp Aq 7:42a
Sep	L V 8:07a	V	V L 8:06a	L	L S 10:25a	S	S Sg 4:22p	Sg	Sg	Sg Cp 1:59a	Cp	Cp Aq 2:01p	Aq	Aq	Aq P 2:39a	P
Oct	L	L S 8:38p	S	S	S Sg 1:24a	Sg	Sg Cp 9:46a	Cp	Cp Aq 7:13p	Aq	Aq	Aq P 9:51a	P	P A 9:34p	A	A
Nov	S Sg 11:09a	Sg	Sg Cp 6:38p	Cp	Cp	Cp Aq 5:18a	Aq	Aq P 5:51p	P	P	P A 5:52a	A	A T 3:19p	T	T G 9:40p	G
Dec	Sg Cp 3:33a	Cp	Cp Aq 1:42p	Aq	Aq	Aq P 2:04a	P	P A 2:36p	A	A	A T 12:45a	T	T G 7:08a	G	G C 10:11a	C

	17	18	19	20	21	22	23	24	25	26	27	28	29	30	31
Jan	A T 7:40a	T	T G 12:22p	G	G C 1:35p	C	C L 12:45p	L	L V 12:05p	V	V L 7:41a	L	L S 7:26p	S	S
Feb	G C 10:57p	C	C L 11:34p	L	L V 11:21p	V	V	V L 12:22a	L	L S 4:29a	S	S Sg 12:38p			
Mar	G C 6:36a	C	C L 7:52a	L	L V 9:08a	V	V L 10:50a	L	L S 7:35p	S	S Sg 9:35p	Sg	Sg	Sg Cp 7:58p	Cp
Apr	L V 4:21p	V	V L 7:25p	L	L S 11:56p	S	S	S Sg 6:45a	Sg	Sg Cp 4:28p	Cp	Cp	Cp Aq 4:26a	Aq	
May	V L 1:47a	L	L S 7:22a	S	S Sg 2:54p	Sg	Sg	Sg Cp 12:35a	Cp	Cp Aq 12:18p	Aq	Aq	Aq P 12:50a	P	P A 12:04p
Jn	S Sg 9:08p	Sg	Sg Cp 7:34a	Cp	Cp	Cp Aq 7:24p	Aq	Aq	Aq P 8:04a	P	P A 8:02p	A	A	A T 5:13a	
Jly	Sg Cp 1:44p	Cp	Cp	Cp Aq 1:44a	Aq	Aq P 2:23p	P	P	P A 2:41a	A	A T 12:57p	T	T G 7:37p	G	G C 10:17p
Aug	Aq	Aq P 8:20p	P	P	P A 8:30a	A	A T 7:07p	T	T	T G 2:57a	G	G C 7:18a	C	C L 8:31a	L
Sep	P A 2:29p	A	A	A T 12:40a	T	T G 8:41a	G	G C 2:06p	C	C L 4:56p	L	L V 6:02p	V	V L 6:41p	
Oct	A T 7:08a	T	T G 2:20p	G	G C 7:32p	C	C L 11:08p	L	L	L V 1:40a	V	V L 3:49	L	L S 6:34a	S
Nov	G	G C 1:41a	C	C L 4:32a	L	L V 7:17a	V	V L 10:32a	L	L S 2:38p	S	S Sg 8:03p	Sg	Sg	
Dec	C L 11:41a	L	L V 1:03p	V	V L 3:53p	L	L S 8:33p	S	S	S Sg 3:02a	Sg	Sg Cp 3:02a	Cp	Cp Aq 9:32p	Aq

MOON SIGNS 1910 – 1969

1922

	1	2	3	4	5	6	7	8	9	10	11	12	13	14	15	16	17	18	19	20	21	22	23	24	25	26	27	28	29	30	31
Jan	Aq	Aq P 9:45a	P	P A 10:42p	A	A	A T 9:58a	T	T G 5:26p	G	G C 6:47p	C	C L 9:21p	L	L V 9:13p	V	V Li 10:23p	Li	Li	Li S 2:03a	S	S Sg 8:34a	Sg	Sg Cp 5:29p	Cp	Cp	Cp Aq 4:17a	Aq	Aq P 4:34p	P	P
Feb	P A 5:36a	A	A T 5:42p	T	T	T G 2:41a	G	G C 7:30a	C	C L 8:40a	L	L V 7:58a	V	V Li 7:35a	Li	Li S 9:24a	S	S Sg 2:33p	Sg	Sg Cp 11:06p	Cp	Cp	Cp Aq 10:13a	Aq	Aq P 10:45p	P	P	P A 11:41a			
Mar	A	A T 11:51p	T	T	T G 9:48a	G	G C 4:18a	C	C L 7:10p	L	L V 7:23p	V	V Li 6:44p	Li	Li S 7:15p	S	S Sg 10:36p	Sg	Sg	Sg Cp 5:42a	Cp	Cp Aq 4:18p	Aq	Aq	Aq P 4:56a	P	P A 5:49p	A	A	A T 5:38a	T
Apr	T G 3:29p	G	G C 10:46p	C	C	C L 3:12a	L	L V 5:09a	V	V Li 5:36a	Li	Li S 6:07a	S	S Sg 8:26a	Sg	Sg Cp 2:03p	Cp	Cp Aq 11:29p	Aq	Aq	Aq P 11:44a	P	P	P A 12:37a	A	A T 12:07a	T	G	G	G	
May	G C 4:12a	C	C L 9:05a	L	L V 12:19p	V	V Li 2:22p	Li	Li S 4:01p	S	S Sg 6:33p	Sg	Sg	Sg Cp 11:27p	Cp	Cp Aq 7:46a	Aq	Aq P 7:21p	P	P	P A 7:13a	A	A T 7:46p	T	T	T G 4:28a	G	G C 10:26a	C	C L 2:34p	L
Jn	L V 5:48p	V	V Li 8:44p	Li	Li S 11:43p	S	S	S Sg 3:19a	Sg	Sg Cp 8:31a	Cp	Cp Aq 4:26p	Aq	Aq	Aq P 3:26a	P	P A 4:12p	A	A	A T 4:08a	T	T G 1:01p	G	G C 6:27p	C	C L 9:28p	L	L V 11:37p	V	V	
Jly	V Li 2:05a	Li	Li S 2:05a	S	S Sg 10:06a	Sg	Sg Cp 4:13p	Cp	Cp	Cp Aq 12:28a	Aq	Aq P 11:17a	P	P A 11:59p	A	A	A T 12:27p	T	T G 10:09p	G	G	G C 3:55a	C	C L 6:27a	L	L V 7:22a	V	V Li 7:09a	Li	Li S 11:00a	S
Aug	S Sg 3:36p	Sg	Sg Cp 10:23p	Cp	Cp	Cp Aq 7:19a	Aq	Aq P 6:23p	P	P	P A 7:06a	A	A T 7:57p	T	T	T G 6:43a	G	G C 1:39p	C	C L 4:45p	L	L V 5:16p	V	V Li 5:06p	Li	Li S 6:02p	S	S Sg 9:27p	Sg	Sg	Sg Cp 11:00a
Sep	Cp	Cp Aq 1:13p	Aq	Aq	Aq P 12:42a	P	P A 1:29p	A	A	A T 2:24a	T	T G 1:50p	G	G C 10:12p	C	C	C L 2:47a	L	L V 4:08a	V	V Li 3:44a	Li	Li S 3:28a	S	S Sg 5:12a	Sg	Sg Cp 10:17a	Cp	Cp Aq 7:03p	Aq	
Oct	Aq	Aq P 6:41a	P	P A 7:36p	A	A	A T 8:20a	T	T G 7:44p	G	G	G C 4:52a	C	C L 11:01a	L	L V 2:03p	V	V Li 2:43p	Li	Li S 2:27p	S	S Sg 3:07p	Sg	Sg Cp 6:34p	Cp	Cp	Cp Aq 2:01a	Aq	Aq P 1:08p	P	P
Nov	P A 2:04a	A	A T 2:39p	T	T	T G 1:33a	G	G C 10:23a	C	C L 5:05p	L	L V 9:36	V	V	V Li 12:01a	Li	Li S 12:59a	S	S Sg 1:52a	Sg	Sg Cp 3:20a	Cp	Cp Aq 10:37p	Aq	Aq P 8:40p	P	P	P A 9:21a	A	A T 10:00p	
Dec	T	T	T G 8:34a	G	G C 4:33p	C	C L 10:32p	L	L	L V 3:09a	V	V Li 6:40a	Li	Li S 9:14a	S	S Sg 11:28a	Sg	Sg Cp 2:36p	Cp	Cp Aq 8:10p	Aq	Aq	Aq P 5:14a	P	P A 5:23p	A	A	A T 6:13a	T	T G 5:02p	G

1923

	1	2	3	4	5	6	7	8	9	10	11	12	13	14	15	16	17	18	19	20	21	22	23	24	25	26	27	28	29	30	31
Jan	G	G C 12:39a	C	C L 5:34a	L	L V 8:59a	V	V Li 11:59a	Li	Li S 3:05p	S	S Sg 6:34p	Sg	Sg Cp 10:57p	Cp	Cp	Cp Aq 5:08a	Aq	Aq P 1:58p	P	P	P A 1:38a	A	A T 2:33p	T	T	T G 2:06a	G	G C 10:18a	C	C L 2:56p
Feb	L	L V 5:12p	V	V Li 6:38p	Li	Li S 8:37p	S	S	S Sg 12:00a	Sg	Sg Cp 5:08a	Cp	Cp Aq 12:19p	Aq	Aq P 9:44p	P	P	P A 9:20a	A	A T 10:15p	T	T	T G 10:30a	G	G C 7:57p	C	C	C L 1:29a			
Mar	L	L V 3:41a	V	V Li 4:01a	Li	Li S 4:17a	S	S Sg 6:06a	Sg	Sg Cp 10:35a	Cp	Cp Aq 6:02p	Aq	Aq	Aq P 4:08a	P	P A 4:06p	A	A	A T 5:00a	T	T G 5:33p	G	G	G C 4:05a	C	C L 11:12a	L	L V 2:35p	V	V Li 3:06p
Apr	Li	Li S 2:26p	S	S Sg 2:35p	Sg	Sg Cp 5:20p	Cp	Cp Aq 11:50p	Aq	Aq	Aq P 9:51a	P	P A 10:09p	A	A	A T 11:07a	T	T G 11:33p	G	G	G C 10:27a	C	C L 6:51p	L	L V 11:55p	V	V	V Li 1:48a	Li	Li S 1:33a	
May	S	S Sg 1:00a	Sg	Sg Cp 2:16a	Cp	Cp Aq 7:05a	Aq	Aq P 4:00p	P	P	P A 4:13a	A	A T 5:13p	T	T	T G 5:27a	G	G C 4:03p	C	C	C L 12:40a	L	L V 6:54a	V	V P 10:24a	Li	Li S 11:23a	S	S Sg 11:38a	Sg	Sg Cp 12:28p
Jn	Cp	Cp Aq 4:05p	Aq	Aq P 11:44p	P	P	P 11:03a	A	A T 11:56p	T	T	T G 12:03p	G	G C 10:09p	C	C	C L 6:12a	L	L V 12:22p	V	V Li 4:44p	Li	Li S 7:21p	S	S Sg 8:47p	Sg	Sg Cp 10:20p	Cp	Cp	Cp Aq 1:45a	
Jly	Aq	Aq P 8:28a	P	P A 6:51p	A	A	A T 7:25a	T	T G 7:37p	G	G	G C 5:33a	C	C L 12:53p	L	L V 6:10p	V	V Li 10:06p	Li	Li	Li S 1:08a	S	S Sg 3:43a	Sg	Sg Cp 6:33a	Cp	Cp Aq 10:43a	Aq	Aq P 5:24p	P	P
Aug	P A 3:12a	A	A T 3:22p	T	T	T G 3:47a	G	G C 2:07p	C	C L 9:19p	L	L	L V 1:43a	V	V Li 4:27a	Li	Li S 6:38a	S	S Sg 9:12a	Sg	Sg Cp 12:50p	Cp	Cp Aq 6:03p	Aq	Aq	Aq P 1:26a	P	P A 11:15a	A	A T 11:12p	T
Sep	T	T G 11:50a	G	G C 10:58p	C	C	C L 6:56a	L	L V 11:16a	V	V Li 1:02p	Li	Li S 1:47p	S	S Sg 3:04p	Sg	Sg Cp 6:14p	Cp	Cp Aq 11:54p	Aq	Aq	Aq P 8:03p	P	P A 6:24p	A	A	A T 6:23a	T	T G 7:06p	G	
Oct	G	G C 7:00a	C	C L 4:14p	L	L V 9:40p	V	V Li 11:35p	Li	Li S 11:25p	S	S Sg 11:09p	Sg	Sg	Sg Cp 12:44a	Cp	Cp Aq 5:30a	Aq	Aq P 1:44p	P	P	P A 12:34a	A	A T 12:48p	T	T	T G 1:29a	G	G C 1:39p	C	C L 11:59p
Nov	L	L	L V 7:07a	V	V Li 10:23a	Li	Li S 10:37a	S	S Sg 9:37a	Sg	Sg Cp 9:38a	Cp	Cp Aq 12:41p	Aq	Aq P 7:47p	P	P	P A 6:25a	A	A T 6:53p	T	T	T G 7:32a	G	G C 7:28p	C	C	C L 6:01a	L	L V 2:17p	
Dec	V	V Li 7:24p	Li	Li S 9:14p	S	S Sg 8:57p	Sg	Sg Cp 8:32p	Cp	Cp Aq 10:11p	Aq	Aq	Aq P 3:37a	P	P A 1:09p	A	A	A T 1:22a	T	T G 2:03p	G	G	G C 1:39a	C	C L 11:39a	L	L V 7:51p	V	V	V Li 1:50a	Li

1924

	1	2	3	4	5	6	7	8	9	10	11	12	13	14	15	16	17	18	19	20	21	22	23	24	25	26	27	28	29	30	31
Jan	Li S 5:22a	S	S Sg 6:48a	Sg Cp 7:22a	Cp	Cp	Cp Aq 8:55a	Aq	Aq P 1:15p	P	P A 9:23p	A	A	A T 8:49a	T	T G 9:28p	G	G	G C 9:05a	C	C L 6:33p	L	L	L V 1:48a	V	V Li 7:14a	Li	Li S 11:08a	S	S Sg 1:52p	Sg
Feb	Sg Cp 4:03a	Cp	Cp Aq 6:43p	Aq	Aq P 11:13p	P	P	P A 6:37a	A	A T 5:10p	T	T	T G 5:35a	G	G C 5:33p	C	C	C L 3:08a	L	L V 9:45a	V	V Li 1:57p	Li	Li S 4:47p	S	S Sg 7:16p	Sg	Sg Cp 10:13p	Cp		
Mar	Cp	Cp Aq 2:12a	Aq	Aq P 7:45a	P	P A 3:27p	A	A	A T 1:36a	T	T G 1:44p	G	G	G C 2:07a	C	C L 12:30p	L	L V 7:27p	V	V Li 11:00p	Li	Li	Li S 12:27a	S	S Sg 1:30a	Sg	Sg Cp 3:38a	Cp	Cp Aq 7:47a	Aq	Ap P 2:14p
Apr	P	P A 10:46p	A	A	A T 9:12a	T	T G 9:13p	G	G	G C 9:53a	C	C L 9:15p	L	L	L V 5:21a	V	V Li 9:26a	Li	Li S 10:24a	S	S Sg 10:05a	Sg	Sg Cp 10:34a	Cp	Cp Aq 1:31p	Aq	Aq P 7:39p	P	P	P A 4:40a	
May	A	A T 3:37p	T	T	T G 3:48a	G	G C 4:31a	C	C	C L 4:30a	L	L V 1:56p	V	V Li 7:28p	Li	Li S 9:10p	S	S Sg 8:34p	Sg	Sg Cp 7:49p	Cp	Cp Aq 9:05p	Aq	Aq	Aq P 1:51a	P	P A 10:37a	A	A T 9:23p	T	T
Jn	T G 9:48a	G	G C 10:27p	C	C	C L 10:29a	L	L V 8:40p	V	V	V Li 3:40a	Li	Li S 6:57a	S	S Sg 7:17a	Sg	Sg Cp 6:29a	Cp	Cp Aq 6:42a	Aq	Aq P 9:53a	P	P A 4:57p	A	A	A T 3:28a	T	T G 3:51a	G	G	
Jly	G C 4:28a	C	C L 4:11a	L	L	L V 2:15a	V	V Li 9:54a	Li	Li S 2:35p	S	S Sg 4:31p	Sg	Sg Cp 4:49p	Cp	Cp Aq 5:12p	Aq	Aq P 7:31p	P	P	P A 1:14a	A	A T 10:37a	T	T G 10:37p	G	G	G C 11:11a	C	C L 10:38p	L
Aug	L	L V 8:06a	V	V Li 3:19p	Li	Li S 8:24p	S	S Sg 11:31p	Sg	Sg	Sg Cp 1:20a	Cp	Cp Aq 2:52a	Aq	Aq P 5:29a	P	P A 10:33a	A	A T 6:54p	T	T	T G 6:15a	G	G C 6:48p	C	C	C L 6:19a	L	L V 3:18p	V	V Li 9:37p
Sep	Li	Li	Li S 1:54a	S	S Sg 5:00a	Sg	Sg Cp 7:41a	Cp	Cp Aq 10:33a	Aq	Aq P 2:17p	P	P A 7:42p	A	A	A T 3:40a	T	T G 2:25p	G	G	G C 2:54a	C	C L 2:52p	L	L	L V 12:05a	V	V Li 5:56a	Li	Li S 9:00a	
Oct	S	S Sg 10:54a	Sg	Sg Cp 1:03p	Cp	Cp Aq 4:20p	Aq	Aq P 9:07p	P	P	P A 3:31a	A	A T 11:51a	T	T G 10:23p	G	G	G C 10:48a	C	C L 11:21p	L	L	L V 9:32a	V	V Li 3:48p	Li	Li S 6:26p	S	S Sg 7:03p	Sg	Sg Cp 7:39p
Nov	Cp	Cp Aq 9:54p	Aq	Aq	Aq P 2:35a	P	P A 9:40a	A	A T 6:44p	T	T	T G 5:35a	G	G C 5:57p	C	C	C L 6:51a	L	L V 6:11p	V	V	V Li 1:50a	Li	Li S 5:17a	S	S Sg 5:38a	Sg	Sg Cp 4:57a	Cp	Cp Aq 5:26a	
Dec	Aq	Aq P 8:39a	P	P A 3:12p	A	A	A T 12:34a	T	T G 11:53a	G	G	G C 12:21a	C	C L 1:13p	L	L	L V 1:06a	V	V Li 10:14a	Li	Li S 3:24p	S	S Sg 4:55p	Sg	Sg Cp 4:18p	Cp	Cp Aq 3:42p	Aq	Aq P 5:07p	P	P A 9:58p

MOON SIGNS 1910 – 1969

1925

	1	2	3	4	5	6	7	8	9	10	11	12	13	14	15	16	17	18	19	20	21	22	23	24	25	26	27	28	29	30	31
Jan	A	A	A T 6:31a	T	T G 5:53p	G	G	G C 6:33a	C	C L 7:14p	L	L	L V 6:55a	V	V Li 4:32p	Li	Li S 11:10p	S	S	S Sg 2:33a	Sg	Sg Cp 3:22a	Cp	Cp Aq 3:09a	Aq	Aq P 3:47a	P	P A 6:59a	A	A T 1:59p	T
Feb	T	T G 12:33a	G	G C 1:11p	C	C	C L 1:49a	L	L V 1:00p	V	V Li 10:06p	Li	Li	Li S 4:54a	S	S Sg 9:27a	Sg	Sg Cp 12:02a	Cp	Cp Aq 1:21p	Aq	Aq P 2:37p	P	P A 5:22p	A	A T 11:05p	T	T			
Mar	T G 8:27a	G	G C 8:38p	C	C	C L 9:22a	L	L V 8:24p	V	V	V Li 4:43a	Li	Li S 10:37a	S	S Sg 2:51p	Sg	Sg Cp 6:07p	Cp	Cp Aq 8:51p	Aq	Aq P 11:34p	P	P	P A 3:05a	A	A T 8:35a	T	T G 5:08p	G	G	G C 4:43a
Apr	C	C L 5:32p	L	L	L V 4:54a	V	V Li 1:03p	Li	Li S 6:04p	S	S Sg 9:05p	Sg	Sg Cp 11:32p	Cp	Cp	Cp Aq 2:08a	Aq	Aq P 6:03a	P	P A 10:45a	A	A T 5:00p	T	T	T G 1:34a	G	G C 12:46p	C	C	C L 1:36a	
May	L	L V 1:37p	V	V Li 10:25p	Li	Li	Li S 3:21a	S	S Sg 5:27a	Sg	Sg Cp 6:30a	Cp	Cp Aq 8:09a	Aq	Aq P 11:24a	P	P A 4:35p	A	A T 11:42p	T	T	T G 8:51a	G	G C 8:08p	C	C	C L 8:58a	L	L V 9:35p	V	V
Jn	V Li 7:30a	Li	Li S 1:20p	S	S Sg 3:33p	Sg	Sg Cp 3:45p	Cp	Cp Aq 3:54p	Aq	Aq P 5:41p	P	P A 10:04p	A	A	A T 5:16a	T	T G 2:58p	G	G	G C 2:37a	C	C L 3:31p	L	L	L V 4:21a	V	V Li 3:14p	Li	Li S 10:31p	
Jly	S	S	S Sg 1:54a	Sg	Sg Cp 2:24a	Cp	Cp Aq 1:50a	Aq	Aq P 2:07a	P	P A 4:54a	A	A T 11:06a	T	T G 8:38p	G	G	G C 8:33a	C	C L 9:32p	L	L	L V 10:17a	V	V Li 9:29p	Li	Li	Li S 5:56a	S	S Sg 10:55a	Sg
Aug	Sg Cp 12:46a	Cp	Cp Aq 12:41a	Aq	Aq P 12:24p	P	P A 1:48p	A	A T 6:25p	T	T	T G 2:58a	G	G C 2:39p	C	C	C L 3:41a	L	L V 4:12p	V	V	V Li 3:05a	Li	Li S 11:44a	S	S Sg 5:50p	Sg	Sg Cp 9:19p	Cp	Cp Aq 10:41p	Aq
Sep	Aq P 11:03p	P	P	P A 12:03a	A	A T 3:29a	T	T G 10:40a	G	G C 9:35p	C	C	C L 8:30a	L	L V 10:56p	V	V	V Li 9:18a	Li	Li S 5:18p	S	S Sg 11:17p	Sg	Sg	Sg Cp 3:36a	Cp	Cp Aq 6:29a	Aq	Aq P 8:19a	P	
Oct	P A 10:06a	A	A T 1:21p	T	T G 7:35p	G	G	G C 5:33a	C	C L 6:09p	L	L	L V 6:44a	V	V Li 4:57p	Li	Li	Li S 12:12a	S	S Sg 5:11a	Sg	Sg Cp 8:57a	Cp	Cp Aq 12:12p	Aq	Aq P 3:14p	P	P A 6:24p	A	A T 10:30p	T
Nov	T	T G 4:45a	G	G C 2:07p	C	C	C L 2:16a	L	L V 3:06p	V	V	V Li 1:51a	Li	Li S 9:05a	S	S Sg 1:12p	Sg	Sg Cp 3:38p	Cp	Cp Aq 5:46p	Aq	Aq P 8:38p	P	P	P A 12:32a	A	A T 5:46a	T	T G 12:51p	G	
Dec	G C 10:19p	C	C	C L 10:13a	L	L V 11:13p	V	V	V Li 10:51a	Li	Li S 7:04p	S	S Sg 11:22p	Sg	Sg	Sg Cp 12:59a	Cp	Cp Aq 1:36a	Aq	Aq P 2:52a	P	P A 5:58a	A	A T 11:26a	T	T G 7:19p	G	G	G C 5:27a	C	C L 5:27p

1926

	1	2	3	4	5	6	7	8	9	10	11	12	13	14	15	16	17	18	19	20	21	22	23	24	25	26	27	28	29	30	31
Jan	L	L	L V 6:26a	V	V Li 6:44p	Li	Li	Li S 4:18a	S	S Sg 10:01a	Sg	Sg Cp 12:08p	Cp	Cp Aq 12:07p	Aq	Aq P 11:49a	P	P A 1:05p	A	A T 5:16p	T	T	T G 12:56a	G	G C 11:31a	C	C L 11:52p	L	L	L V 12:49p	V
Feb	V	V Li 1:10a	Li	Li S 11:38a	S	S Sg 7:02p	Sg	Sg Cp 10:48p	Cp	Cp Aq 11:37p	Aq	Aq P 10:57p	P	P A 10:49p	A	A	A T 1:10p	T	T G 7:22a	G	G C 5:28p	C	C	C L 6:00a	L	L V 6:59p	V	V			
Mar	V Li 7:03a	Li	Li S 5:28p	S	S	S Sg 1:39a	Sg	Sg Cp 7:07a	Cp	Cp Aq 9:39a	Aq	Aq P 10:03a	P	P A 9:52a	A	A T 11:08a	T	T G 3:43p	G	G	G C 12:31a	C	C L 12:36p	L	L	L V 1:36a	V	V Li 1:26p	Li	Li	Li S 12:17a
Apr	S	S Sg 7:08a	Sg	Sg Cp 1:04p	Cp	Cp Aq 5:00p	Aq	Aq P 7:04p	P	P A 8:03p	A	A T 9:32p	T	T	T G 1:22a	G	G C 8:55a	C	C L 8:07p	L	L	L V 8:59a	V	V Li 8:52p	Li	Li	Li S 6:19a	S	S Sg 1:18p	Sg	
May	Sg Cp 6:32p	Cp	Cp Aq 10:31p	Aq	Aq	Aq P 1:32a	P	P A 3:55a	A	A T 6:33a	T	T G 10:47a	G	G C 5:53p	C	C	C L 4:21a	L	L V 7:54a	V	V	V Li 5:04a	Li	Li S 2:41p	S	S Sg 9:14p	Sg	Sg	Sg Cp 1:24a	Cp	Cp Aq 4:19a
Jn	Aq	Aq P 6:53a	P	P A 9:46a	A	A T 1:29p	T	T G 6:43p	G	G	G C 2:16a	C	C L 12:30p	L	L	L V 12:49a	V	V Li 1:18p	Li	Li S 11:39p	S	S	S Sg 6:35a	Sg	Sg Cp 10:17a	Cp	Cp Aq 12:01p	Aq	Aq P 1:14p	P	
Jly	P A 3:15p	A	A T 6:59p	T	T	T G 12:58a	G	G C 9:17a	C	C L 7:51p	L	L	L V 8:08a	V	V Li 8:52p	Li	Li	Li S 8:07a	S	S Sg 4:10p	Sg	Sg Cp 8:28p	Cp	Cp Aq 9:48p	Aq	Aq P 9:46p	P	P A 10:14p	A	A	A T 12:48a
Aug	T	T G 6:25a	G	G C 3:09p	C	C	C L 2:13a	L	L V 2:39p	V	V	V Li 3:26a	Li	Li S 3:17p	S	S	S Sg 12:38a	Sg	Sg Cp 6:23a	Cp	Cp Aq 8:30a	Aq	Aq P 8:14a	P	P A 7:30a	A	A T 8:25a	T	T G 12:41p	G	G C 8:49p
Sep	C	C	C L 8:01a	L	L V 8:40p	V	V	V Li 9:23a	Li	Li S 9:15p	S	S	S Sg 7:21a	Sg	Sg Cp 2:36p	Cp	Cp Aq 6:23p	Aq	Aq P 7:07p	P	P A 6:20p	A	A T 6:13p	T	T G 8:51p	G	G	G C 3:36a	C	C L 2:11p	
Oct	L	L	L V 2:49a	V	V Li 3:28p	Li	Li	Li S 2:58a	S	S Sg 12:53p	Sg	Sg Cp 8:46p	Cp	Cp	Cp Aq 2:01a	Aq	Aq P 4:29a	P	P A 4:56a	A	A T 5:02a	T	T G 6:50a	G	G C 12:10p	C	C L 9:31p	L	L	L V 9:43a	V
Nov	V Li 10:22p	Li	Li	Li S 9:37a	S	S Sg 6:51p	Sg	Sg	Sg Cp 2:10a	Cp	Cp Aq 7:42a	Aq	Aq P 11:21a	P	P A 1:28p	A	A T 2:54p	T	T G 5:11p	G	G C 9:55p	C	C	C L 6:11a	L	L V 5:36p	V	V	V Li 6:14a	Li	
Dec	Li S 5:39p	S	S	S Sg 2:31a	Sg	Sg Cp 8:52a	Cp	Cp Aq 1:21p	Aq	Aq P 4:44p	P	P A 7:33p	A	A T 10:23p	T	T	T G 2:00a	G	G C 7:20a	C	C L 3:18p	L	L	L V 2:03a	V	V Li 2:31p	Li	Li	Li S 2:28a	S	S Sg 11:49a

1927

	1	2	3	4	5	6	7	8	9	10	11	12	13	14	15	16	17	18	19	20	21	22	23	24	25	26	27	28	29	30	31
Jan	Sg	Sg Cp 5:51p	Cp	Cp Aq 9:10p	Aq	Aq P 11:06p	P	P	P A 1:00a	A	A T 3:56a	T	T G 8:31a	G	G C 3:00p	C	C L 11:32p	L	L	L V 10:10a	V	V Aq 10:27p	Aq	Aq	Aq S 10:54a	S	S Sg 9:20p	Sg	Sg	Sg Cp 4:11a	
Feb	Cp Aq 7:22a	Aq	Aq P 8:07a	P	P A 8:20a	A	A T 9:51a	T	T G 1:56p	G	G C 8:51p	C	C	C L 6:12a	L	L V 5:16p	V	V	V Li 5:31a	Li	Li S 6:09p	S	S	S Sg 5:34a	Sg	Sg Cp 1:54p	Cp	Cp Aq 6:13p			
Mar	Aq	Aq P 7:06p	P	P A 6:19p	A	A T 6:07p	T	T G 8:30p	G	G	G C 2:31a	C	C L 11:52a	L	L V 11:23p	V	V	V Li 11:48a	Li	Li	Li S 12:21a	S	S Sg 12:06p	Sg	Sg Cp 9:38p	Cp	Cp	Cp Aq 3:38a	Aq	Aq P 5:52a	P
Apr	P A 5:30a	A	A T 4:37a	T	T G 5:26a	G	G C 9:43a	C	C L 6:00p	L	L	L V 5:19a	V	V Li 5:54p	Li	Li	Li S 6:20a	S	S Sg 5:49p	Sg	Sg	Sg Cp 3:35a	Cp	Cp Aq 10:42a	Aq	Aq P 2:36p	P	P A 3:43p	A	A T 3:29p	
May	T	T G 3:53p	G	G C 6:52p	C	C	C L 1:40a	L	L V 12:04p	V	V	V Li 12:27a	Li	Li S 12:52p	S	S Sg 11:57p	Sg	Sg	Sg Cp 9:11a	Cp	Cp Aq 4:15p	Aq	Aq P 9:01p	P	P A 11:37p	A	A	A T 12:51a	T	T G 2:03a	G
Jn	G C 4:51a	C	C L 10:38a	L	L V 7:56p	V	V	V Li 7:50a	Li	Li S 8:16p	S	S	S Sg 7:16a	Sg	Sg Cp 3:51p	Cp	Cp Aq 10:04p	Aq	Aq	Aq P 2:25a	P	P A 5:29a	A	A T 7:54a	T	T G 10:27a	G	G C 2:04p	C	C L 7:49p	
Jly	L	L	L V 4:28a	V	V Li 3:48p	Li	Li	Li S 4:17a	S	S Sg 3:36p	Sg	Sg	Sg Cp 12:05a	Cp	Cp Aq 5:31a	Aq	Aq P 8:43a	P	P A 10:58a	A	A T 1:24p	T	T G 4:47p	G	G C 9:31p	C	C	C L 4:01a	L	L V 12:43p	V
Aug	V Li 11:44p	Li	Li	Li S 12:16p	S	S	S Sg 12:13a	Sg	Sg Cp 9:22a	Cp	Cp Aq 2:45p	Aq	Aq P 5:04p	P	P A 5:57p	A	A T 7:12p	T	T G 10:09p	G	G	G C 3:20a	C	C L 10:40a	L	L V 7:56p	V	V	V Li 7:02a	Li	Li S 7:36p
Sep	S	S	S Sg 8:10a	Sg	Sg Cp 6:28p	Cp	Cp	Cp Aq 12:48a	Aq	Aq P 3:15a	P	P A 3:18a	A	A T 3:04a	T	T G 4:30a	G	G C 8:50a	C	C L 4:14p	L	L	L V 2:02a	V	V Li 1:31p	Li	Li	Li S 2:06a	S	S Sg 2:54p	
Oct	Sg	Sg	Sg Cp 2:12a	Cp	Cp Aq 10:06a	Aq	Aq P 1:49p	P	P A 2:14p	A	A T 1:18p	T	T G 1:13p	G	G C 3:51p	C	C	C L 10:08a	L	L V 7:44a	V	V Li 7:28p	Li	Li	Li S 8:08a	S	S Sg 8:48a	Sg	Sg	Sg Cp 8:22a	Cp
Nov	Cp Aq 5:26p	Aq	Aq P 10:55p	P	P	P A 12:53a	A	A T 12:37a	T	T G 12:04a	G	G C 1:17a	C	C L 5:49a	L	L V 2:15p	V	V	V Li 1:41a	Li	Li S 2:27p	S	S	S Sg 2:53a	Sg	Sg Cp 2:00p	Cp	Cp Aq 11:06p	Aq	Aq	
Dec	Aq P 5:36a	P	P A 9:20a	A	A T 10:46a	T	T G 11:11a	G	G C 12:12p	C	C L 3:33p	L	L V 10:26p	V	V	V Li 8:55a	Li	Li S 9:31p	S	S	S Sg 9:59a	Sg	Sg Cp 8:37p	Cp	Cp	Cp Aq 4:54a	Aq	Aq P 11:00a	P	P A 3:18p	A

MOON SIGNS 1910 – 1969

1928

	1	2	3	4	5	6	7	8	9	10	11	12	13	14	15	16
Jan	A T 6:15p	T	T G 8:20p	G	G C 10:28p	C	C	C L 1:53a	L	L V 7:54a	V	V Li 5:18p	Li	Li	Li S 5:27a	S
Feb	G	G C 6:22a	C	C L 10:53a	L	L S 5:10p	S	S	S Li 2:04a	Li	Li S 1:42p	S	S	S Sg 2:32a	Sg	Sg Cp 1:53p
Mar	C	C L 5:39p	L	L	L V 12:52a	V	V Li 10:05a	Li	Li S 9:31p	S	S	S Sg 10:24a	Sg	Sg Cp 10:32p	Cp	Cp
Apr	L V 6:54a	V	V Li 4:47p	Li	Li	Li S 4:28a	S	S Sg 5:20p	Sg	Sg	Sg Cp 5:56a	Cp	Cp Aq 4:06p	Aq	Aq P 10:18p	P
May	Li	Li	Li S 10:38a	S	S Sg 11:32p	Sg	Sg	Sg Cp 12:08p	Cp	Cp Aq 10:57p	Aq	Aq	Aq P 6:37a	P	P A 10:29a	A
Jn	S	S Sg 5:38a	Sg	Sg Cp 6:00p	Cp	Cp	Cp A 4:40a	Aq	Aq P 12:53p	P	P A 6:13p	A	A T 8:46p	T	T G 9:24p	G
Jly	Sg	Sg Cp 12:27a	Cp	Cp Aq 10:32a	Aq	Aq P 6:23p	P	P	P A 12:03a	A	A T 3:49a	T	T G 6:00a	G	G C 7:36a	C
Aug	Aq	Aq	Aq P 12:34a	P	P A 5:33a	A	A T 9:18a	T	T G 12:22p	G	G C 3:03p	C	C L 5:57p	L	L V 10:08p	V
Sep	P A 12:26p	A	A T 3:07p	T	T G 5:43p	G	G C 8:51p	C	C	C L 12:50a	L	L V 6:02a	V	V Li 1:13p	Li	Li S 11:05p
Oct	T	T	T 12:10a	G	G C 2:22a	C	C L 6:18a	L	L V 12:14p	V	V Li 8:15p	Li	Li	Li S 6:29a	S	S Sg 6:44p
Nov	G C 9:41a	C	C L 12:15p	L	L V 5:42p	V	V	V Li 2:06a	Li	Li S 12:54p	S	S	S Sg 1:20a	Sg	Sg Cp 2:25p	Cp
Dec	L	L	L 12:18a	V	V Li 7:53a	Li	Li S 6:46p	S	S	S Sg 7:29a	Sg	Sg Cp 8:26p	Cp	Cp	Cp Aq 8:35a	Aq

	17	18	19	20	21	22	23	24	25	26	27	28	29	30	31
Jan	S Sg 6:06p	Sg	Sg	Sg Cp 4:49a	Cp	Cp Aq 12:27p	Aq	Aq P 5:24p	P	P A 8:48p	A	A T 11:43p	T	T	T G 2:47a
Feb	Cp	Cp Aq 9:46a	Aq	Aq	Aq P 2:05a	P	P A 4:09a	A	A T 5:42a	T	T G 8:08a	G	G C 12:05p		
Mar	Cp Aq 7:31a	Aq	Aq P 12:19p	P	P A 1:53p	A	A T 2:06p	T	T G 2:56p	G	G C 5:42p	C	C L 11:05p	L	L
Apr	P	P A 12:39a	A	A T 12:36a	T	T G 12:10a	G	G C 1:15a	C	C L 5:12a	L	L V 12:29p	V	V Li 10:36p	
May	A T 11:25a	T	T G 10:57a	G	G C 10:58a	C	C L 1:18p	L	L V 7:07p	V	V	V Li 4:37a	Li	Li S 4:41p	S
Jn	G C 9:35p	C	C L 11:03p	L	L	L V 3:28a	V	V Li 11:44a	Li	Li S 11:17p	S	S	S Sg 12:13p	Sg	
Jly	C L 9:06a	L	L V 12:54p	V	V Li 8:03p	Li	Li	Li S 6:48a	S	S Sg 7:34p	Sg	Sg	Sg Cp 7:47a	Cp	Cp Aq 5:33p
Aug	V	V Li 4:54a	Li	Li S 2:58p	S	S	S Sg 3:29a	Sg	Sg Cp 3:58p	Cp	Cp	Cp Aq 1:56a	Aq	Aq P 8:30a	P
Sep	S	S	S Sg 11:23a	Sg	Sg	Sg Cp 12:15a	Cp	Cp Aq 11:00a	Aq	Aq P 6:01p	P	P A 9:31p	A	A T 11:00p	
Oct	Sg	Sg	Sg Cp 7:50a	Cp	Cp Aq 7:33p	Aq	Aq	Aq P 3:49a	P	P 8:04a	A	A T 9:16a	T	T G 9:11a	
Nov	Cp	Cp Aq 2:39a	Aq	Aq P 12:18p	P	P A 6:14p	A	A T 8:30p	T	T G 8:23p	G	G C 7:44p	C	C L 8:29p	
Dec	Aq P 6:49p	P	P	P A 2:14a	A	A T 6:25a	T	T G 7:40a	G	G C 7:17a	C	C L 7:07a	L	L V 9:13a	V

1929

	1	2	3	4	5	6	7	8	9	10	11	12	13	14	15	16
Jan	V Li 3:09p	Li	Li	Li S 1:10a	S	S Sg 1:50p	Sg	Sg	Sg Cp 2:51a	Cp	Cp Aq 2:32p	Aq	Aq	Aq P 12:21a	P	P A 8:07a
Feb	S	S Sg 8:59p	Sg	Sg	Sg Cp 10:00a	Cp	Cp Aq 9:34p	Aq	Aq	Aq P 6:43a	P	P 1:41p	A	A T 7:02p	T	T G 11:02p
Mar	S	S Sg 5:03a	Sg	Sg Cp 5:55p	Cp	Cp	Cp Aq 5:44a	Aq	Aq P 2:44p	P	P A 8:51p	A	A	A T 1:05a	T	T G 4:23a
Apr	Sg Cp 2:03a	Cp	Cp Aq 2:18p	Aq	Aq P 11:52p	P	P	P A 5:58a	A	A T 9:17a	T	T G 11:13a	G	G C 1:05p	C	C L 3:51p
May	Aq	Aq	Aq P 8:51a	P	P A 3:51p	A	A T 7:18p	T	T G 8:22p	G	G C 8:44p	C	C L 10:03p	L	L	L V 1:34a
Jn	P	P A 12:58a	A	A T 5:34a	T	T G 6:57a	G	G C 6:35a	C	C L 6:25a	L	L V 8:20a	V	V Li 1:39p	Li	Li S 10:33p
Jly	A T 2:32p	T	T G 5:14p	G	G C 5:21p	C	C L 4:37p	L	L V 5:10p	V	V Li 8:54p	Li	Li	Li S 4:45a	S	S Sg 4:00p
Aug	G	G C 3:15a	C	C L 3:11a	L	L V 3:23a	V	V Li 5:56a	Li	Li S 12:22p	S	S Sg 10:45p	Sg	Sg	Sg Cp 11:21a	Cp
Sep	L	L V 1:27p	V	V Li 3:51p	Li	Li S 9:21p	S	S	S Sg 6:39a	Sg	Sg Cp 6:45p	Cp	Cp	Cp Aq 7:17a	Aq	Aq P 6:07p
Oct	V	V Li 1:10a	Li	L S 6:40a	S	S Sg 3:19p	Sg	Sg	Sg Cp 2:49a	Cp	Cp Aq 3:25p	Aq	Aq	Aq P 2:40a	P	P A 11:02a
Nov	S	S Sg 11:47p	Sg	Sg	Sg Cp 10:57a	Cp	Cp Aq 11:33p	Aq	Aq	Aq P 11:30a	P	P A 8:43p	A	A	A T 2:19a	T
Dec	Sg	Sg Cp 6:25p	Cp	Cp	Cp Aq 6:58a	Aq	Aq P 7:27p	P	P	P A 5:57a	A	A T 12:50p	T	T G 3:49p	G	G C 4:05p

	17	18	19	20	21	22	23	24	25	26	27	28	29	30	31
Jan	A	A T 1:37p	T	T G 4:43p	G	G C 5:52p	C	C L 6:17	L	L V 7:47p	V	V	V Li 12:19a	Li	Li S 8:57a
Feb	G	G	G C 1:45a	C	C L 3:41a	L	L V 5:59a	V	V Li 10:15a	Li	Li S 5:54p	S			
Mar	G	G C 7:24a	C	C L 10:27a	L	L V 2:05p	V	V Li 7:12p	Li	Li	Li S 2:50a	S	S Sg 1:26p	Sg	Sg
Apr	L	L V 8:06p	V	V	V Li 2:14a	Li	Li S 10:35a	S	S Sg 9:16p	Sg	Sg	Sg Cp 9:43a	Cp	Cp Aq 10:19p	
May	V	V Li 7:53a	Li	Li S 4:54p	S	S	S Sg 4:04a	Sg	Sg Cp 4:34p	Cp	Cp	Cp Aq 5:17a	Aq	Aq P 4:37p	P
Jn	S	S	S Sg 10:03a	Sg	Sg Cp 10:45p	Cp	Cp	Cp Aq 11:24a	Aq	A P 10:59p	P	P	P A 8:21a	A	
Jly	Sg	Sg	Sg Cp 4:48a	Cp	Cp Aq 5:20p	Aq	Aq	Aq P 4:39a	P	P A 2:13p	A	A T 9:25p	T	T	T G 1:43a
Aug	Cp Aq 11:50p	Aq	Aq	Aq P 10:46a	P	P A 7:47p	A	A	A T 2:55a	T	T G 8:03a	G	G C 11:04a	C	C L 12:57p
Sep	P	P	P A 2:30a	A	A T 8:45a	T	T G 1:25p	G	G C 4:52p	C	C L 7:28p	L	L V 8:52p	V	
Oct	A	A T 4:29p	T	T G 7:54p	G	G C 10:24p	C	C	C L 12:55a	L	L V 4:09a	V	V Li 8:39a	Li	Li S 3:02p
Nov	T G 4:53a	G	G C 5:53a	C	C L 6:58a	L	L V 9:32a	V	V Li 2:23p	Li	Li S 9:40p	S	S	S Sg 7:08a	
Dec	C	C L 3:35p	L	L V 4:22p	V	V Li 8:03p	Li	Li	Li S 3:12a	S	S Sg 1:12p	Sg	Sg	Sg Cp 12:56a	Cp

1930

	1	2	3	4	5	6	7	8	9	10	11	12	13	14	15	16
Jan	Cp Aq 1:30p	Aq	Aq	Aq P 2:04a	P	P A 1:27p	A	A T 9:58p	T	T	T G 2:47a	G	G C 3:34a	C	C L 2:37a	L
Feb	P	P A 7:23p	A	A	A T 4:48a	T	T G 11:07a	G	G C 1:54p	C	C L 2:00p	L	L V 1:15p	V	V Li 1:52p	Li
Mar	P	P A 1:08a	A	A T 10:18a	T	T G 5:16p	G	G C 9:34p	C	C L 11:25p	L	L V 11:54p	V	V	V Li 12:44a	Li
Apr	T	T G 10:42p	G	G	G C 3:11a	C	C L 6:09a	L	L V 8:11a	V	V Li 10:17a	Li	Li S 1:46p	S	S Sg 7:50p	Sg
May	G	G C 8:54a	C	C L 11:32a	L	L V 2:11p	V	V Li 5:30p	Li	Li S 10:07p	S	S	S Sg 4:39a	Sg	Sg Cp 1:40p	Cp
Jn	L	L V 7:37p	V	V Li 11:05p	Li	Li	Li S 4:31a	S	S Sg 11:57a	Sg	Sg Cp 9:21p	Cp	Cp	Cp Aq 8:39a	Aq	Aq P 9:12p
Jly	V	V Li 4:48a	Li	Li S 9:57a	S	S Sg 5:50p	Sg	Sg	Sg Cp 3:50a	Cp	Cp Aq 3:23p	Aq	Aq	Aq P 3:57a	P	P A 4:26p
Aug	S	S Sg 11:25p	Sg	Sg	Sg Cp 9:35a	Cp	Cp Aq 9:27p	Aq	Aq	Aq P 10:03a	P	P A 10:32p	A	A	A T 9:37a	T
Sep	Sg Cp 3:36p	Cp	Cp	Cp Aq 3:28a	Aq	Aq P 4:08p	P	P	P A 4:21a	A	A T 3:18p	T	T	T G 12:00a	G	G C 5:42a
Oct	Cp Aq 10:10a	Aq	Aq P 10:48p	P	P	P A 10:51a	A	A T 9:14p	T	T	T G 5:29a	G	G C 11:29a	C	C L 3:19p	L
Nov	P	P A 6:35p	A	A	A T 4:37a	T	T G 11:58a	G	G C 5:05p	C	C L 8:45p	L	L V 11:41p	V	V	V Li 2:27a
Dec	A	A T 1:31p	T	T G 8:32p	G	G	G C 12:31a	C	C L 2:53a	L	L V 5:04a	V	V Li 8:05a	Li	Li S 12:20p	S

	17	18	19	20	21	22	23	24	25	26	27	28	29	30	31
Jan	L V 1:58a	V	V Li 3:46a	Li	Li S 9:26a	S	S Sg 6:56p	Sg	Sg	Sg Cp 6:53a	Cp	Cp Aq 7:33p	Aq	Aq	Aq P 7:59a
Feb	Li S 5:45p	S	S	S Sg 1:50a	Sg	Sg Cp 1:13p	Cp	Cp	Cp Aq 1:57a	Aq	Aq P 2:13p	P			
Mar	Li S 3:47a	S	S Sg 10:25a	Sg	Sg Cp 8:41p	Cp	Cp	Cp Aq 9:05a	Aq	Aq P 9:23p	P	P	P A 8:00a	A	A T 4:23p
Apr	Sg	Sg Cp 5:08a	Cp	Cp Aq 4:59p	Aq	Aq	Aq P 5:23a	P	P A 4:09p	A	A	A T 12:07a	T	T G 5:26a	
May	Cp	Cp Aq 1:04a	Aq	Aq P 1:34p	P	P	P A 12:55a	A	A T 9:15a	T	T G 2:06p	G	G C 4:25p	C	C L 5:45p
Jn	P	P	P A 9:14a	A	A T 6:35p	T	T G 11:59p	G	G	G C 1:57a	C	C L 2:06a	L	L V 2:29a	
Jly	A	A	A T 2:53a	T	T G 9:38a	G	G C 12:21p	C	C L 12:19p	L	L V 11:35a	V	V Li 12:19p	Li	Li S 4:08p
Aug	T G 5:46p	G	G C 10:01p	C	C L 10:57p	L	L V 10:14p	V	V Li 9:59p	Li	Li	Li S 12:12a	S	S Sg 6:05a	Sg
Sep	C	C L 8:18a	L	L V 8:45a	V	V Li 8:44a	Li	Li S 10:08a	S	S Sg 2:36p	Sg	Sg Cp 10:49p	Cp	Cp	
Oct	L V 5:26p	V	V Li 6:43p	Li	Li S 8:33p	S	S	S Sg 12:25a	Sg	Sg Cp 7:27a	Cp	Cp Aq 5:54p	Aq	Aq	Aq P 6:23a
Nov	Li	Li S 5:37a	S	S Sg 10:01a	Sg	Sg Cp 4:43p	Cp	Cp	Cp Aq 2:24a	Aq	Aq P 2:33p	P	P	P A 3:06a	
Dec	S Sg 5:55p	Sg	Sg	Sg Cp 1:12a	Cp	Cp Aq 10:44a	Aq	Aq P 10:36p	P	P	P A 11:29a	A	A T 10:51p	T	T

MOON SIGNS 1910 – 1969

1931

	1	2	3	4	5	6	7	8	9	10	11	12	13	14	15	16
Jan	T G 6:34a	G	G C 10:20a	C	C L 11:32a	L	L V 12:07p	V	V Li 1:49p	Li	Li S 5:41p	S	S Sg 11:51p	Sg	Sg	Sg Cp 8:02a
Feb	C L 10:24p	L	L V 9:57p	V	V Li 9:56p	Li	Li	Li S 12:06a	S	S Sg 5:22a	Sg	Sg Cp 1:40p	Cp	Cp	Cp Aq 12:15a	Aq
Mar	C L 9:24a	L	L V 9:21a	V	V Li 8:33a	Li	Li S 9:03a	S	S Sg 12:32p	Sg	Sg Cp 7:39p	Cp	Cp	Cp Aq 6:04a	Aq	Aq P 6:27p
Apr	V Li 7:49p	Li	Li S 7:51p	S	S Sg 9:53p	Sg	Sg	Sg Cp 3:22a	Cp	Cp Aq 12:43p	Aq	Aq	Aq P 12:49a	P	P A 1:48p	A
May	Li S 6:26a	S	S Sg 8:14a	Sg	Sg Cp 12:37p	Cp	Cp Aq 8:37p	Aq	Aq	Aq P 8:02a	P	P A 8:57p	A	A	A T 8:54a	T
Jn	Sg Cp 10:08p	Cp	Cp	Cp Aq 5:24a	Aq	Aq P 4:01p	P	P	P A 4:44a	A	A T 4:54p	T	T	T G 2:21a	G	G C 8:38a
Jly	Cp Aq 1:57p	Aq	Aq	Aq P 12:10a	P	P A 12:40p	A	A	A T 1:13a	T	T G 11:13a	G	G C 5:30p	C	C L 8:41p	L
Aug	P	P A 8:10p	A	A	A T 9:05a	T	T G 8:01p	G	G ,	G C 3:09a	C	C L 6:31a	L	L V 7:25a	V	V Li 7:45a
Sep	A T 3:59p	T	T	T G 3:43a	G	G C 12:13p	C	C L 4:47p	L	L V 6:04p	V	V Li 5:43p	Li	Li S 5:41p	S	S Sg 7:40p
Oct	G 10:03a	G	G C 7:37p	C	C	C L 1:48a	L	L V 4:34a	V	V Li 4:50a	Li	Li S 4:19a	S	S Sg 4:52a	Sg	Sg Cp 8:19a
Nov	C	C L 8:38a	L	L V 1:07p	V	V Li 3:02p	Li	Li S 3:21p	S	S Sg 3:39p	Sg	Sg Cp 5:53p	Cp	Cp Aq 11:42p	Aq	Aq
Dec	L V 7:17p	V	V Li 10:44p	Li	Li	Li S 12:43a	S	S Sg 2:04a	Sg	Sg Cp 4:18a	Cp	Cp Aq 9:11a	Aq	Aq P 5:51p	P	P

	17	18	19	20	21	22	23	24	25	26	27	28	29	30	31
Jan	Cp	Cp Aq 6:04p	Aq	Aq	Aq P 5:55a	P	P A 6:55p	A	A T 7:10p	T	T	T G 4:17p	G	G C 9:09p	C
Feb	Aq P 12:24p	P	P	P A 1:21a	A	A T 1:53p	T	T	T G 12:12a	G	G C 6:47a	C			
Mar	P	P	P A 7:24a	A	A T 7:44p	T	T	T G 6:19a	G	G C 2:03p	C	C L 6:29p	L	L V 7:58p	V
Apr	A	A T 1:50a	T	T G 11:55a	G	G C 7:42p	C	C	C L 1:03a	L	L V 4:09a	V	V Li 5:35a	Li	
May	T G 6:26p	G	G	G C 1:25a	C	C L 6:27a	L	L V 10:07a	V	V Li 12:51p	Li	Li S 3:08p	S	S Sg 5:48p	Sg
Jn	C	C L 12:36p	L	L V 3:32p	V	V Li 6:23p	Li	Li S 9:35p	S	S	S Sg 1:27a	Sg	Sg Cp 6:35a	Cp	
Jly	L V 10:22p	V	V	V Li 12:07a	Li	Li S 2:57a	S	S Sg 7:19a	Sg	Sg Cp 1:23p	Cp	Cp Aq 9:25p	Aq	Aq	Aq P 7:46a
Aug	Li	Li S 9:11a	S	S Sg 12:48p	Sg	Sg Cp 6:58p	Cp	Cp	Cp Aq 3:38a	Aq	Aq P 2:28p	P	P	P A 2:57a	A
Sep	Sg	Sg	Sg Cp 12:49a	Cp	Cp Aq 9:18a	Aq	Aq P 8:29p	P	P	P A 9:09a	A	A T 10:07p	T	T	
Oct	Cp	Cp Aq 3:40p	Aq	Aq	Aq P 2:33a	P	P A 3:21p	A	A	A T 4:12a	T	T G 3:47p	G	G	G C 1:26a
Nov	Aq P 9:33a	P	P A 10:09p	A	A	A T 10:59a	T	T G 10:11p	G	G	G C 7:09a	C	C L 2:05p	L	
Dec	P A 5:50a	A	A T 6:45p	T	T	T G 5:59a	G	G C 2:21p	C	C L 8:16p	L	L	L V 12:40a	V	V Li 4:17a

1932

	1	2	3	4	5	6	7	8	9	10	11	12	13	14	15	16
Jan	Li	Li S 7:24a	S	S Sg 10:16a	Sg	Sg Cp 1:37p	Cp	Cp Aq 6:44p	Aq	Aq	Aq P 2:50a	P	P A 2:07p	A	A	A T 3:02a
Feb	Sg	Sg Cp 8:39p	Cp	Cp	Cp Aq 2:49a	Aq	Aq P 11:15a	P	P A 10:17p	A	A	A T 11:05a	T	T G 11:27p	G	G
Mar	Sg Cp 2:07a	Cp	Cp Aq 9:00a	Aq	Aq P 6:16p	P	P	P A 5:35a	A	A T 6:20p	T	T	T G 7:03a	G	G C 5:46p	C
Apr	Aq	Aq P 12:05a	P	P A 11:52a	A	A	A T 12:44a	T	T G 1:27p	G	G	G C 12:47a	C	C L 9:22a	L	L V 2:22p
May	P A 5:46p	A	A	A T 6:46a	T	T G 7:20p	G	G	G C 6:34a	C	C L 3:46p	L	L V 10:13p	V	V	V Li 1:32a
Jn	T	T	T G 1:32a	G	G C 12:21p	C	C L 9:14p	L	L	L V 4:06a	V	V Li 8:41a	Li	Li S 11:00a	S	S Sg 11:55a
Jly	G	G C 7:07p	C	C	C L 3:18a	L	L V 9:33a	V	V Li 2:12p	Li	Li S 5:28p	S	S Sg 7:38p	Sg	Sg Cp 9:36p	Cp
Aug	C L 10:57a	L	L V 4:15p	V	V Li 7:56p	Li	Li S 10:49p	S	S	S Sg 1:32a	Sg	Sg Cp 4:38a	Cp	Cp Aq 8:54a	Aq	Aq P 3:14p
Sep	V	V Li 3:32a	Li	Li S 5:06a	S	S Sg 12:00p	Sg	Sg Cp 10:12a	Cp	Cp Aq 3:16p	Aq	Aq P 10:31p	P	P	P A 8:01a	A
Oct	Li S 1:44p	S	S Sg 2:02p	Sg	Sg Cp 4:00p	Cp	Cp Aq 8:44p	Aq	Aq	Aq P 4:27a	P	P A 2:36p	A	A	A T 2:24a	T
Nov	Sg Cp 11:55p	Cp	Cp	Cp Aq 3:06a	Aq	Aq P 10:07a	P	P A 8:25p	A	A	A T 8:34a	T	T G 9:13p	G	G	G C 9:32a
Dec	Cp Aq 11:47a	Aq	Aq P 5:08p	P	P	P A 2:36a	A	A T 2:42p	T	T	T G 3:26a	G	G C 3:28p	C	C	C L 2:13a

	17	18	19	20	21	22	23	24	25	26	27	28	29	30	31
Jan	T	T G 2:47p	G	G C 11:22p	C	C	C L 4:39a	L	L V 7:47a	V	V Li 10:07a	Li	Li S 12:43p	S	S Sg 4:07p
Feb	G C 9:02a	C	C L 2:49p	L	L V 5:25p	V	V Li 6:22p	Li	Li S 7:20p	S	S Sg 9:39p	Sg	Sg		
Mar	C	C L 12:56a	L	L V 4:18a	V	V Li 4:56a	Li	Li S 4:35a	S	S Sg 5:07a	Sg	Sg Cp 8:08a	Cp	Cp Aq 2:31p	Aq
Apr	V	V Li 4:00p	Li	Li S 3:33p	S	S Sg 2:57p	Sg	Sg Cp 4:15p	Cp	Cp Aq 9:05p	Aq	Aq	Aq P 5:55a	P	
May	Li	Li S 2:15a	S	S Sg 1:48a	Sg	Sg Cp 2:13a	Cp	Cp Aq 5:31a	Aq	Aq P 12:58p	P	P	P A 12:09a	A	A T 1:05p
Jn	Sg	Sg Cp 12:31p	Cp	Cp Aq 3:12p	Aq	Aq P 9:26p	P	P	P A 7:34a	A	A T 8:08p	T	T	T G 8:35a	
Jly	Cp	Cp Aq 12:45a	Aq	Aq P 6:34a	P	P A 3:52p	A	A	A T 3:54a	T	T G 4:26p	G	G	G C 3:07a	C
Aug	P	P	P A 12:18a	A	A T 11:56a	T	T	T G 12:33a	G	G C 11:50a	C	C L 8:03p	L	L	L V 12:58a
Sep	A T 7:34p	T	T	T G 8:14a	G	G C 8:13p	C	C	C L 5:32a	L	L V 11:07a	V	V Li 1:22p	Li	
Oct	T G 3:03p	G	G	G C 3:26a	C	C L 1:57p	L	L V 9:03p	V	V	V Li 12:16a	Li	Li S 12:31a	S Sg 11:40p	Sg
Nov	C	C L 8:35p	L	L	L V 5:08a	V	V Li 10:08a	Li	Li S 11:38a	S	S Sg 10:58a	Sg	Sg Cp 10:16a	Cp	
Dec	L	L V 11:09a	V	V Li 5:31p	Li	Li S 8:53p	S	S Sg 9:42p	Sg	Sg Cp 9:31p	Cp	Cp Aq 10:23p	Aq	Aq	Aq P 2:17a

1933

	1	2	3	4	5	6	7	8	9	10	11	12	13	14	15	16
Jan	P	P A 10:14a	A	A T 9:37p	T	T	T G 10:19a	G	G C 10:16p	C	C	C L 8:26a	L	L V 4:41p	V	V Li 11:02p
Feb	A T 5:40a	T	T G 6:06p	G	G	G C 6:13a	C	C L 4:16p	L	L V 11:42p	V	V	V Li 4:59a	Li	Li S 8:46a	S
Mar	T	T	T G 2:18a	G	G C 2:43p	C	C	C L 1:17a	L	L V 8:41a	V	V Li 1:02p	Li	Li S 3:27p	S	S Sg 5:18p
Apr	G C 10:50p	C	C	C L 10:16a	L	L V 6:33p	V	V Li 10:59p	Li	Li	Li S 12:32a	S	S Sg 12:52a	Sg	Sg Cp 1:54a	Cp
May	C L 6:06p	L	L	L V 3:40a	V	V Li 9:16a	Li	Li S 11:06a	S	S Sg 10:43a	Sg	Sg Cp 10:16a	Cp	Cp Aq 11:47a	Aq	Aq P 4:34p
Jn	V	V Li 6:14p	Li	Li S 9:24p	S	S Sg 9:32p	Sg	Sg Cp 8:33p	Cp	Cp Aq 8:42p	Aq	Aq P 11:51p	P	P	P A 6:51a	A
Jly	Li	Li S 5:56a	S	S Sg 7:32a	Sg	Sg Cp 7:15a	Cp	Cp Aq 7:05a	Aq	Aq P 9:02a	P	P A 2:32p	A	A T 11:50p	T	T
Aug	Sg	Sg Cp 4:40p	Cp	Cp Aq 5:22p	Aq	Aq P 7:11p	P	P A 11:42p	A	A	A T 7:45a	T	T G 6:57p	G	G	G C 7:32a
Sep	Cp Aq 2:00a	Aq	Aq P 4:44a	P	P A 9:15a	A	A T 4:36p	T	T	T G 3:01a	G	G C 3:25p	C	C	C L 3:30a	L
Oct	P	P A 5:51p	A	A	A T 1:19a	T	T G 11:19a	G	G C 11:29p	C	C	C L 12:01p	L	L V 10:24p	V	V
Nov	A T 8:53a	T	T G 7:02p	G	G	G C 7:06a	C	C L 7:58p	L	L	L V 7:24a	V	V Li 3:11p	Li	Li S 6:52p	S
Dec	T G 1:46a	G	G C 1:53p	C	C	C L 2:49a	L	L V 2:59p	V	V	V Li 12:17a	Li	Li S 5:26a	S	S Sg 6:49a	Sg

	17	18	19	20	21	22	23	24	25	26	27	28	29	30	31
Jan	Li	Li	Li S 3:24a	S	S Sg 5:54a	Sg	Sg Cp 7:18a	Cp	Cp Aq 8:57a	A	A P 12:32p	P	P A 7:21p	A	A
Feb	S Sg 11:42a	Sg	Sg Cp 2:23p	Cp	Cp Aq 5:29p	Aq	Aq P 9:57p	P	P	P A 4:43a	A	A T 2:21p			
Mar	Sg	Sg Cp 7:47p	Cp	Cp Aq 11:40p	Aq	Aq	Aq P 5:16a	P	P A 12:50p	A	A T 10:32p	T	T	T G 10:14a	G
Apr	Cp Aq 5:03a	Aq	Aq P 10:55a	P	P A 7:14p	A	A	A T 5:31a	T	T G 5:18p	G	G	G C 5:58a	C	
May	P	P	P A 12:46a	A	A T 11:27a	T	T G 11:32p	G	G	G C 12:12p	C	C	C L 12:33a	L	L V 11:05a
Jn	A T 5:12p	T	T	T G 5:06a	G	G C 6:07p	C	C	C L 6:17a	L	L V 5:01p	V	V	V Li 1:10a	
Jly	T G 11:44a	G	G	G C 12:24a	C	C L 12:18p	L	L V 10:35p	V	V	V Li 6:44a	Li	Li S 12:20p	S	S Sg 3:26p
Aug	C	C L 7:23p	L	L	L V 5:07a	V	V Li 12:29p	Li	Li S 5:44p	S	S Sg 9:21p	Sg	Sg Cp 11:52p	Cp	Cp
Sep	L V 1:12p	V	V Li 7:51p	Li	Li S 11:59p	S	S	S Sg 2:49a	Sg	Sg Cp 5:23a	Cp	Cp Aq 8:27a	Aq	Aq P 12:27p	
Oct	V Li 5:07a	Li	Li S 8:27a	S	S Sg 9:54a	Sg	Sg Cp 11:14a	Cp	Cp Aq 1:49p	Aq	Aq P 6:17p	P	P	P A 12:41a	A
Nov	S Sg 7:35p	Sg	Sg Cp 7:24p	Cp	Cp Aq 8:21p	Aq	Aq P 11:51p	P	P	P A 6:13a	A	A T 3:04p	T	T	
Dec	Sg Cp 6:08a	Cp	Cp Aq 5:38a	Aq	Aq P 5:34p	P	P A 12:17p	A	A T 8:43p	T	T	T G 7:43a	G	G C 8:07p	C

MOON SIGNS 1910 – 1969

1934

	1	2	3	4	5	6	7	8	9	10	11	12	13	14	15	16	17	18	19	20	21	22	23	24	25	26	27	28	29	30	31
Jan	C	C L 8:56a	L	L V 9:08p	V	V	V Li 7:20a	Li	Li S 2:11p	S	S Sg 5:17p	Sg	Sg Cp 5:37p	Cp	Cp Aq 4:56p	Aq	Aq P 5:17p	P	P A 8:28p	A	A	A T 3:26a	T	T G 1:54p	G	G	G C 2:24a	C	C L 3:11p	L	L
Feb	L V 3:01a	V	V Li 1:00p	Li	Li S 8:30p	S	S	S Sg 1:14a	Sg	Sg Cp 3:23a	Cp	Cp Aq 3:57a	Aq	Aq P 4:28a	P	P A 6:39a	A	A T 12:04p	T	T G 9:17p	G	G	G C 9:23a	C	C L 10:13p	L	L	L V 9:46a			
Mar	V	V Li 7:02p	Li	Li	Li S 1:59a	S	S Sg 6:58a	Sg	Sg Cp 10:22a	Cp	Cp Aq 12:36p	Aq	Aq P 2:25p	P	P A 5:00p	A	A T 9:46p	T	T	T G 5:52a	G	G C 5:13p	C	C	C L 6:03a	L	L S 5:44p	S	S	S Li 2:37a	
Apr	Li S 8:36a	S	S Sg 12:37p	Sg	Sg Cp 3:45p	Cp	Cp Aq 6:43p	Aq	Aq P 9:52p	P	P	P A 1:40a	A	A T 6:56a	T	T G 2:41p	G	G	G C 1:26a	C	C L 2:10p	L	L	L V 2:20a	V	V Li 11:32a	Li	Li S 5:07p	S	S Sg 8:02p	
May	Sg	Sg Cp 9:53p	Cp	Cp	Cp Aq 12:06a	Aq	Aq P 3:26a	P	P A 8:09a	A	A T 2:24p	T	T G 10:38p	G	G	G C 9:17a	C	C L 9:54p	L	L	L V 10:35a	V	V Li 8:43p	Li	Li	Li S 2:52a	S	S Sg 5:28a	Sg	Sg Cp 6:12a	Cp
Jn	Cp Aq 6:55a	Aq	Aq P 9:07a	P	P A 1:32p	A	A T 8:17p	T	T	T G 5:14a	G	G C 4:14p	C	C	C L 4:53a	L	L V 5:51p	V	V	V Li 4:59a	Li	Li S 12:25p	S	S Sg 3:49p	Sg	Sg Cp 4:24p	Cp	Cp Aq 4:02p	Aq	Aq P 4:28p	
Jly	P	P A 7:39p	A	A	A T 1:47a	T	T G 10:55a	G	G C 10:20p	C	C	C L 11:07a	L	L	L V 12:07a	V	V Li 11:47a	Li	Li S 8:31p	S	S	S Sg 1:28a	Sg	Sg Cp 3:04a	Cp	Cp Aq 2:43a	Aq	Aq P 2:20a	P	P A 3:46a	A
Aug	A T 8:25a	T	T G 4:49p	G	G	G C 4:13a	C	C L 5:08p	L	L	L V 5:59a	V	V Li 5:32p	Li	Li	Li S 2:51a	S	S Sg 9:11a	Sg	Sg Cp 12:27p	Cp	Cp Aq 1:18p	Aq	Aq P 1:08p	P	P A 1:44p	A	A T 4:55p	T	T G 11:56p	G
Sep	G	G C 10:40a	C	C L 11:32p	L	L	L V 12:16p	V	V Li 11:23p	Li	Li	Li S 8:19a	S	S Sg 3:03p	Sg	Sg Cp 7:35p	Cp	Cp Aq 10:07p	Aq	Aq P 11:14p	P	P	P A 12:13a	A	A T 2:47a	T	T G 8:34a	G	G C 6:14p	C	
Oct	C	C L 6:44a	L	L V 7:31p	V	V	V Li 6:20a	Li	Li S 2:31p	S	S Sg 8:32p	Sg	Sg	Sg Cp 1:04a	Cp	Cp Aq 4:32a	Aq	Aq P 7:10a	P	P A 9:28a	A	A T 12:34p	T	T G 5:58p	G	G	G C 2:46a	C	C L 2:43p	L	L
Nov	L V 3:36a	V	V Li 2:41p	Li	Li S 10:32p	S	S	S Sg 3:33a	Sg	Sg Cp 6:56a	Cp	Cp Aq 9:52a	Aq	Aq P 12:56p	P	P A 4:26p	A	A T 8:47p	T	T	T G 2:47a	G	G C 11:25a	C	C L 10:54a	L	L	L V 11:52a	V	V Li 11:39p	
Dec	Li	Li	Li S 8:06a	S	S Sg 12:53p	Sg	Sg Cp 3:09p	Cp	Cp Aq 4:34p	Aq	Aq P 6:31p	P	P A 9:52p	A	A	A T 2:56a	T	T G 9:58a	G	G C 7:11p	C	C	C L 6:37a	L	L V 7:32p	V	V	V Li 7:59a	Li	Li S 5:41p	

1935

	1	2	3	4	5	6	7	8	9	10	11	12	13	14	15	16	17	18	19	20	21	22	23	24	25	26	27	28	29	30	31
Jan	S Sg 11:27p	Sg	Sg	Sg Cp 1:44a	Cp	Cp Aq 2:04a	Aq	Aq P 2:17a	P	P A 4:03a	A	A T 8:25a	T	T G 3:43p	G	G	G C 1:37a	C	C L 1:27p	L	L	L V 2:20a	V	V Li 2:59p	Li	Li	Li S 1:46a	S	S Sg 9:10a	Sg	Sg Cp 12:48p
Feb	Cp	Cp Aq 1:26p	Aq	Aq P 12:46p	P	P A 12:49p	A	A T 3:22p	T	T G 9:35p	G	G	G C 7:24a	C	C L 7:35p	L	L	L V 8:33a	V	V Li 9:02p	Li	Li	Li S 8:04a	S	S Sg 4:40p	Sg	Sg Cp 10:04p	Cp	Cp		
Mar	Cp	Cp Aq 12:16a	Aq	Aq P 12:13a	P A 11:41p	A	A	A T 12:43a	T	T G 5:12a	G	G C 1:52p	C	C	C L 1:48a	L	L V 2:51p	V	V	V Li 3:08a	Li	Li S 1:46p	S	S Sg 10:23p	Sg	Sg	Sg Cp 4:48a	Cp	Cp Aq 8:41a	Aq	Aq P 10:14a
Apr	P	P A 10:31a	A	A T 11:18a	T	T G 2:36p	G	G C 9:46p	C	C	C L 8:52a	L	L V 9:47p	V	V	V Li 10:01a	Li	Li S 8:09p	S	S	S Sg 4:06a	Sg	Sg Cp 10:13a	Cp	Cp Aq 2:43p	Aq	Aq P 5:39a	P	P A 7:26p	A	
May	A T 9:09p	T	T	T G 12:26a	G	G C 6:50a	C	C L 4:55p	L	L	L V 5:26a	V	V Li 5:48p	Li	Li	Li S 3:53a	S	S Sg 11:12a	Sg	Sg Cp 4:20p	Cp	Cp Aq 8:08p	Aq	Aq P 11:13p	P	P	P A 1:59a	A	A T 4:58a	T	T G 9:11a
Jn	G	G C 3:44p	C	C	C L 1:19a	L	L V 1:26p	V	V	V Li 1:59a	Li	Li S 12:35p	S	S Sg 7:57p	Sg	Sg	Sg Cp 12:21a	Cp	Cp Aq 2:56a	Aq	Aq P 4:57a	P	P A 7:21a	A	A T 10:54a	T	T G 4:06p	G	G C 11:27p	C	
Jly	C	C L 7:13a	L	L V 9:08p	V	V	V Li 9:52a	Li	Li S 9:14p	S	S	S Sg 5:27a	Sg	Sg Cp 10:03a	Cp	Cp Aq 11:53a	Aq	Aq P 12:31p	P	P A 1:34p	A	A T 4:21p	T	T G 9:42p	G	G	G C 5:43a	C	C L 4:04p	L	
Aug	L V 4:06a	V	V Li 4:54p	Li	Li	Li S 4:57a	S	S Sg 2:24p	Sg	Sg Cp 8:10p	Cp	Cp Aq 10:21p	Aq	Aq P 10:18p	P	P A 9:55p	A	A T 11:08p	T	T	T G 3:25a	G	G C 11:17a	C	C L 10:00p	L	L	L V 10:20a	V	V Li 11:08p	Li
Sep	Li	Li S 11:22a	S	S Sg 9:48p	Sg	Sg	Sg Cp 5:08a	Cp	Cp Aq 8:44a	Aq	Aq P 9:15a	P	P A 8:21a	A	A T 8:10a	T	T G 10:48a	G	G C 5:27p	C	C	C L 3:50a	L	L V 4:18p	V	V	V Li 5:06a	Li	Li S 5:06p	S	
Oct	S	S Sg 3:40a	Sg	Sg Cp 12:02p	Cp	Cp Aq 5:20p	Aq	Aq P 7:26p	P	P A 7:20p	A	A T 6:53p	T	T G 8:14p	G	G	G C 1:21a	C	C L 10:36a	L	L V 10:44p	V	V	V Li 11:31a	Li	Li S 11:14p	S	S	S Sg 9:17a	Sg	Sg Cp 5:31p
Nov	Cp	Cp Aq 11:38p	Aq	Aq	Aq P 3:20a	P	P A 4:54a	A	A T 5:59a	T	T G 6:52a	G	G C 10:56a	C	C L 6:51p	L	L	L V 6:10a	V	V Li 6:52p	Li	Li	Li S 6:36a	S	S Sg 4:10p	Sg	Sg Cp 11:28p	Cp	Cp	Cp Aq 5:00a	
Dec	Aq	Aq P 9:02a	P	P A 11:52a	A	A T 2:02p	T	T G 4:37p	G	G C 8:54p	C	C	C L 4:07a	L	L V 2:33p	V	V	V Li 2:58a	Li	Li S 3:00p	S	S	S Sg 12:44a	Sg	Sg Cp 7:27a	Cp	Cp Aq 11:46a	Aq	Aq P 2:42p	P	P A 5:16p

1936

	1	2	3	4	5	6	7	8	9	10	11	12	13	14	15	16	17	18	19	20	21	22	23	24	25	26	27	28	29	30	31
Jan	A	A T 8:11p	T	T	T G 12:04a	G	G C 5:29a	C	C L 1:02p	L	L V 11:05p	V	V	V Li 11:10a	Li	Li S 11:38p	S	S	S Sg 10:12a	Sg	Sg Cp 5:18p	Cp	Cp Aq 9:02p	Aq	Aq P 10:35p	P	P A 11:36p	A	A	A T 1:37a	
Feb	T G 5:38a	G	G C 11:58a	C	C L 8:26p	L	L	L V 6:48a	V	V Li 6:46p	Li	Li	Li S 7:24a	S	S Sg 6:56p	Sg	Sg	Sg Cp 3:21a	Cp	Cp Aq 7:46a	Aq	Aq P 8:55a	P	P A 8:35a	A	A T 8:51a	T	T G 11:30a	G		
Mar	G C 5:26p	C	C	C L 2:20a	L	L V 1:18p	V	V	V Li 1:27a	Li	Li S 2:03p	S	S	S Sg 2:06a	Sg	Sg Cp 11:51a	Cp	Cp Aq 5:52p	Aq	Aq P 7:59p	P	P A 7:31p	A	A T 6:37p	T	T G 7:31p	G	G C 11:52p	C	C	C L 8:04a
Apr	L	L V 7:07p	V	V	V Li 7:31a	Li	Li S 8:05p	S	S	S Sg 8:03a	Sg	Sg Cp 6:23p	Cp	Cp	Cp Aq 1:49a	Aq	Aq P 5:37a	P	P A 6:20a	A	A T 5:37a	T	T G 5:38a	G	G C 8:23a	C	C L 3:03p	L	L	L V 1:22a	
May	V	V Li 1:43p	Li	Li	Li S 2:16a	S	S Sg 1:54p	Sg	Sg Cp 11:56p	Cp	Cp	Cp Aq 7:47a	Aq	Aq P 12:53p	P	P A 3:14p	A	A T 3:47p	T	T G 4:12p	G	G C 6:19p	C	C L 11:42p	L	L	L V 8:48a	V	V Li 8:38p	Li	Li
Jn	Li S 9:13a	S	S Sg 8:37p	Sg	Sg	Sg Cp 6:02a	Cp	Cp Aq 1:17p	Aq	Aq P 6:26p	P	P A 9:47p	A	A T 11:48p	T	T	T G 1:30a	G	G C 4:09a	C	C L 9:06a	L	L V 5:15p	V	V	V Li 4:24a	Li	Li S 4:52p	S	S	
Jly	S Sg 4:27a	Sg	Sg Cp 1:34p	Cp	Cp Aq 7:56p	Aq	Aq	Aq P 12:10a	P	P A 3:10a	A	A T 5:46a	T	T G 8:38a	G	G C 12:28p	C	C L 5:58p	L	L	L V 1:54a	V	V Li 12:31p	Li	Li	Li S 12:54a	S	S Sg 12:36p	Sg	Sg Cp 10:23p	Cp
Aug	Cp	Cp Aq 4:25a	Aq	Aq P 7:36a	P	P A 9:21a	A	A T 11:12a	T	T G 2:12p	G C	C 6:52p	C	C	C L 1:20a	L	L V 9:45a	V	V Li 8:17p	Li	Li	Li S 8:36a	S	S Sg 9:09p	Sg	Sg	Sg Cp 7:16a	Cp	Cp Aq 2:12p	Aq	Aq P 5:05p
Sep	P	P A 5:43p	A	A T 6:04p	T	T G 7:55p	G	G	G C 12:16a	C	C L 7:13a	L	L V 4:20p	V	V	V Li 3:12a	Li	Li S 3:32p	S	S	S Sg 4:24	Sg	Sg Cp 3:52p	Cp	Cp Aq 11:53p	Aq	Aq	Aq P 3:38a	P	P A 4:10a	
Oct	A	A T 3:25a	T	T G 3:37a	G	G C 6:28a	C	C L 12:45p	L	L V 10:01p	V	V	V Li 9:19a	Li	Li S 9:47p	S	S	S Sg 10:38a	Sg	Sg Cp 10:37p	Cp	Cp	Cp Aq 8:00a	Aq	Aq P 1:28p	P	P A 3:09p	A	A T 2:34p	T	T G 1:49p
Nov	G	G C 3:00p	C	C L 7:37p	L	L	L V 4:00a	V	V Li 3:15p	Li	Li	Li S 3:52a	S	S Sg 4:34p	Sg	Sg	Sg Cp 4:20a	Cp	Cp Aq 2:11p	Aq	Aq P 9:04p	P	P	P A 12:37a	A	A T 1:29a	T	T G 1:11a	G	G C 1:40a	
Dec	C	C L 4:34a	L	L V 11:31a	V	V Li 9:55p	Li	Li	Li S 10:28a	S	S Sg 11:07p	Sg	Sg	Sg Cp 10:25a	Cp	Cp Aq 7:42p	Aq	Aq	Aq P 2:43a	P	P A 7:26a	A	A T 10:05a	T	T G 11:24a	G	G C 12:20p	C	C L 3:14p	L	L V 8:50p

MOON SIGNS 1910 – 1969

1937

	1	2	3	4	5	6	7	8	9	10	11	12	13	14	15	16	17	18	19	20	21	22	23	24	25	26	27	28	29	30	31
Jan	V	V	V Li 5:56a	Li	Li S 5:59p	S	S	S Sg 6:42a	Sg	Sg Cp 5:50p	Cp	Cp	Cp Aq 2:23a	Aq	Aq P 8:28a	P	P A 12:48	A	A T 4:07	T	T G 6:53p	G	G C 9:39p	C	C	C L 1:10a	L	L V 6:31a	V	V Li 2:53p	Li
Feb	Li	Li S 2:11a	S	S Sg 2:58p	Sg	Sg	Sg Cp 2:32a	Cp	Cp Aq 10:57p	Aq	Aq P 4:07p	P	P A 7:11p	A	A T 9:35p	T	T	T G 12:23a	G	G C 4:05a	C	C L 8:51p	L	L V 3:07p	V	V Li 11:30p	Li	Li			
Mar	S Sg 10:23a	Sg	Sg Cp 11:08p	Cp	Cp	Cp Aq 11:20a	Aq	Aq P 8:29p	P	P	P A 1:48a	A	A T 3:59a	T	T G 4:55a	G	G C 6:19a	C	C L 9:27a	L	V	V	V Li 9:43p	Li	Li	Li S 6:46a	S	S Sg 5:53p	Sg	Sg	Sg Cp
Apr	Cp	Cp Aq 7:13a	Aq	Aq	Aq P	P	P A 11:45a	A	A T 2:25p	T	T G 2:39p	G	G C 2:36p	C	C L 4:07p	L	L V 8:16p	V	V	V Li 3:38a	Li	Li S 12:53p	S	S	S Sg 12:21a	Sg	Sg Cp 1:05p	Cp	Cp	Cp Aq 1:56a	
May	Aq	Aq P 1:05p	P	P A 8:51p	A	A	A T 12:43a	T	T G 1:29a	G	G C 12:57a	C	C L 1:03a	L	L V 3:30a	V	V Li 9:21a	Li	Li S 6:38p	S	S	S Sg 6:18a	Sg	Sg Cp 7:10a	Cp	Cp	Cp Aq 7:54a	Aq	Aq P 7:10p	P	P
Jn	P A 9:11a	A	A T 11:25p	T	T	T G 4:37a	G	G C 1:04p	C	C L 11:58p	L	L	L V 12:20p	V	V	V Li 1:06a	Li	Li S 1:01p	S	S Sg 10:35p	Sg	Sg	Sg Cp 1:56p	Cp	Cp	Cp Aq 12:52a	Aq	Aq P 9:36a	P	P A 3:46p	
Jly	A	A T 7:31p	T	T G 9:13a	G	G C 9:54p	C	C L 11:02p	L	L	L V 2:19a	V	V Li 9:06a	Li	Li S 7:39p	S	S	S Sg 8:18a	Sg	Sg Cp 8:48p	Cp	Cp	Cp Aq 7:19a	Aq	Aq P 3:18p	P	P A 9:13p	A	A	A T 1:29a	T
Aug	T G 4:28a	G	G C 6:33a	C	C L 8:36a	L	L V 11:56a	V	V Li 6:03p	Li	Li	Li S 3:38a	S	S Sg 3:59p	Sg	Sg	Sg Cp 4:36a	Cp	Cp Aq 3:02p	Aq	Aq P 10:25p	P	P	P A 3:22a	A	A T 6:56a	T	T G 10:02a	G	G C 1:03p	C
Sep	C L 4:23p	L	L V 8:37p	V	V	V Li 2:50a	Li	Li S 12:01p	S	S	S Sg 12:00a	Sg	Sg Cp 12:49p	Cp	Cp Aq 11:47p	Aq	Aq	Aq P 7:19a	P	P A 11:29a	A	A T 1:49p	T	T G 3:48p	G	G C 6:26p	C	C L 10:16p	L	L	
Oct	L V 3:30a	V	V Li 10:33a	Li	Li S 7:58p	S	S	S Sg 7:45a	Sg	Sg Cp 8:45p	Cp	Cp	Cp Aq 8:36a	Aq	Aq P 4:57p	P	P A 9:28p	A	A T 11:08p	T	T G 11:40p	G	G	G C 12:49a	C	C L 3:44a	L	L V 9:03a	V	V Li 4:50p	Li
Nov	Li	Li S 2:49a	S	S Sg 2:48p	Sg	Sg	Sg Cp 3:35a	Cp	Cp Aq 4:16p	Aq	Aq P 2:03a	P	P	P 7:58a	A	A T 10:10a	T	T G 10:10a	G	G C 9:48a	C	C L 10:57a	L	L V 3:01p	V	V Li 10:26p	Li	Li	Li S 8:46a	S	
Dec	S Sg 9:06p	Sg	Sg	Sg Cp 10:07a	Cp	Cp Aq 10:38p	Aq	Aq	Aq P 9:20a	P	P A 4:50p	A	A T 8:43p	T	T G 9:40p	G	G C 9:03p	C	C L 8:53p	L	L V 11:02p	V	V	V Li 4:55a	Li	Li S 2:47p	S	S	S Sg 3:12a	Sg	Sg Cp 4:16p

1938

	1	2	3	4	5	6	7	8	9	10	11	12	13	14	15	16	17	18	19	20	21	22	23	24	25	26	27	28	29	30	31
Jan	Cp	Cp	Cp Aq 4:30a	Aq	Aq P 3:04p	P	P A 11:48p	A	A	A T 5:04a	T	T G 7:49a	G	G C 8:21a	C	C L 8:09a	L	L V 9:14a	V	V Li 1:32p	Li	Li S 10:00p	S	S	S Sg 9:51p	Sg	Sg Cp 10:57p	Cp	Cp	Cp Aq 10:59a	Aq
Feb	Aq P 8:56p	P	P	P A 4:53a	A	A T 10:56a	T	T G 3:05p	G	G C 5:23p	C	C L 6:34p	L	L V 8:00p	V	V Li 11:32p	Li	Li	Li S 6:37a	S	S Sg 5:36p	Sg	Sg	Sg Cp 6:27a	Cp	Cp Aq 6:32p	Aq	Aq			
Mar	Aq P 4:12a	P	P A 11:14a	A	A T 4:28p	T	T G 8:32p	G	G C 11:45p	C	C	C L 2:22a	L	L V 5:06a	V	V Li 9:06a	Li	Li S 3:58p	S	S	S Sg 2:03a	Sg	Sg Cp 2:31p	Cp	Cp	Cp Aq 2:55a	Aq	Aq P 12:48p	P	P A 7:29a	A
Apr	A T 11:41p	T	T	T G 2:33a	G	G C 5:07a	C	C L 5:51p	L	L V 11:53a	V	V Li 5:05p	Li	Li	Li S 12:24a	S	S Sg 10:21a	Sg	Sg Cp 10:32p	Cp	Cp	Cp Aq 11:09a	Aq	Aq P 9:49p	P	P	P A 5:06a	A	A T 9:00a	T	
May	T G 10:44a	G	G C 11:52a	C	C L 1:44p	L	L V 5:21p	V	V Li 11:08p	Li	Li	Li S 7:17a	S	S Sg 5:43p	Sg	Sg	Sg Cp 5:51a	Cp	Cp Aq 6:36p	Aq	Aq	Aq P 6:07a	P	P A 2:31p	A	A T 7:21p	T	T G 8:49p	G	G C 7:52p	C
Jn	C L 9:11p	L	L 11:25p	V	V	V Li 4:37a	Li	Li S 1:04p	S	S Sg 11:58p	Sg	Sg	Sg Cp 12:20p	Cp	Cp	Cp Aq 1:06a	Aq	Aq P 1:01p	P	P A 10:35p	A	A	A T 4:48a	T	T G 11:02a	G	G C 7:27a	C	C L 6:46a	L	
Jly	L V 10:57a	V	V Li 11:12a	Li	Li S 6:53p	S	S	S Sg 5:46a	Sg	Sg Cp 6:21p	Cp	Cp	Cp Aq 7:06a	Aq	Aq P 6:53p	P	P	P A 5:01a	A	A T 12:28p	T	T G 4:42p	G	G C 5:54a	C	C L 5:25p	L	L V 5:18p	V	V Li 7:42p	Li
Aug	Li	Li S 1:53a	S	S Sg 12:04p	Sg	Sg	Sg Cp 12:34a	Cp	Cp Aq 1:15p	Aq	Aq	Aq P 12:43a	P	P A 10:33a	A	A T 6:22p	T	T G 11:47p	G	G	G C 2:37a	C	C L 3:26a	L	L V 3:43a	V	V Li 5:28a	Li	Li S 10:29a	S	S Sg 7:32p
Sep	Sg	Sg	Sg Cp 12:30a	Cp	Cp Aq 7:09p	Aq	Aq	Aq P 7:29a	P	P A 4:38p	A	A T 11:51p	T	T	T G 5:23a	G	G C 9:08a	C	C L 11:25a	L	L V 1:02p	V	V Li 3:22p	Li	Li S 8:02p	S	S	S Sg 4:04a	Sg	Sg Cp 3:21p	
Oct	Cp	Cp	Cp Aq 3:56a	Aq	Aq P 3:24p	P	P	P A 12:20a	A	A T 6:42a	T	T G 11:09a	G	G C 2:30p	C	C L 5:19p	L	L V 8:10p	V	V Li 11:46p	Li	Li	Li S 5:01a	S	S Sg 12:58p	Sg	Sg Cp 11:40p	Cp	Cp	Cp Aq 12:07p	Aq
Nov	Aq	Aq P 12:05a	P	P A 9:33a	A	A T 3:37p	T	T G 7:01p	G	G C 8:59p	C	C L 10:51p	L	L	L V 1:40a	V	V Li 6:03a	Li	Li S 12:28p	S	S Sg 9:00p	Sg	Sg	Sg Cp 7:38a	Cp	Cp Aq 7:59p	Aq	Aq	Aq P 8:29a	P	
Dec	P A 6:57p	A	A	A T 1:57a	T	T G 5:18a	G	G C 6:07a	C	C L 6:18a	L	L V 7:37a	V	V Li 11:30p	Li	Li S 6:16p	S	S	S Sg 3:33a	Sg	Sg Cp 2:39p	Cp	Cp	Cp Aq 2:59p	Aq	Aq P 3:40p	P	P	P A 1:15a	A	A T 11:43a

1939

	1	2	3	4	5	6	7	8	9	10	11	12	13	14	15	16	17	18	19	20	21	22	23	24	25	26	27	28	29	30	31
Jan	T	T G 4:14p	G	G C 5:17p	C	C L 4:32p	L	L V 4:28p	V	V Li 6:16p	Li	Li S 11:58p	S	S	S Sg 9:10a	Sg	Sg Cp 8:44p	Cp	Cp Aq 9:16p	Aq	Aq	Aq P 9:50p	P	P	P A 9:40a	A	A T 7:24p	T	T	T G 1:46a	G
Feb	G C 3:57a	C	C L 4:05a	L	L V 2:35a	V	V Li 3:33a	Li	Li S 7:22a	S	S Sg 3:28p	Sg	Sg	Sg Cp 2:42a	Cp	Cp Aq 3:22p	Aq	Aq	Aq P 3:52a	P	P A 3:21p	A	A	A T 1:17a	T G 8:47p	G	G	G C 1:03p			
Mar	C	C L 2:28p	L	L V 2:20p	V	V Li 2:35p	Li	Li S 5:05p	S	S Sg 11:28p	Sg	Sg	Sg Cp 9:36a	Cp	Cp Aq 10:01p	Aq	Aq	Aq P 10:31a	P	P A 9:38p	A	A	A T 7:02a	T	T G 2:12p	G	G C 7:16p	C	C L 10:12p	L	L V 11:38p
Apr	V	V	V Li 12:51a	Li	Li S 3:24a	S	S Sg 8:48a	Sg	Sg Cp 5:51p	Cp	Cp	Cp Aq 5:34a	Aq	Aq P 6:03p	P	P	P A 5:13a	A	A T 1:54p	T	T G 8:13p	G	G	G C 12:41a	C	C L 3:54a	L	L V 1:37a	V	V Li 9:03a	
May	Li	Li S 12:39p	S	S g 6:15p	Sg	Sg	Sg Cp 2:36a	Cp	Cp Aq 1:42p	Aq	Aq	Aq P 2:01a	P	P A 1:43p	A	A T 10:24p	T	T	T G 6:04a	G	G C 7:24a	C	C L 10:14a	L	L V 11:52a	V	V Li 3:09p	Li	Li S 7:46p	S	S
Jn	S Sg 2:17a	Sg	Sg Cp 10:52p	Cp	Cp Aq 9:42p	Aq	Aq	Aq P 10:04a	P	P A 9:58p	A	A	A T 7:42a	T	T G 1:29p	G	G C 4:04p	C	C L 4:58p	L	L V 5:57p	V	V Li 8:34p	Li	Li	Li S 1:54a	S	S Sg 8:40a	Sg	Sg Cp 5:56p	
Jly	Cp	Cp	Cp Aq 4:55a	Aq	Aq P 5:18p	P	P	P A 5:50a	A	A T 4:22p	T	T G 11:14p	G	G	G C 1:47a	C	C L 2:29a	L	L V 2:08a	V	V Li 3:14a	Li	Li S 7:04a	S	S Sg 2:13p	Sg	Sg Cp 11:53p	Cp	Cp	Cp Aq 11:15a	Aq
Aug	Aq P 11:41p	P	P	P A 12:21p	A	A	A T 4:04a	T	T G 8:04a	G	G C 12:18a	C	C L 1:07p	L	L V 12:20p	V	V Li 12:05p	Li	Li S 2:25p	S	S Sg 8:18p	Sg	Sg	Sg Cp 5:35a	Cp	Cp Aq 1:10p	Aq	Aq	Aq P 5:43a	P	P A 6:14p
Sep	A	A	A T 5:47a	T	T G 2:58p	G	G C 8:47p	C	C L 11:07p	L	L V 11:08p	V	V Li 10:41p	Li	Li S 11:48p	S	S	S Sg 4:05a	Sg	Sg Cp 12:13p	Cp	Cp Aq 11:25p	Aq	Aq	Aq P 11:59a	P	P	P A 12:20a	A	A T 11:28a	
Oct	T	T G 8:34p	G	G	G C 3:16a	C	C L 7:20a	L	L V 8:45a	V	V Li 9:16a	Li	Li S 10:44a	S	S Sg 1:39p	Sg	Sg Cp 8:27p	Cp	Cp	Cp Aq 6:40a	Aq	Aq P 7:05p	P	P	P A 7:28a	A	A T 6:05p	T	T	T G 2:30a	G
Nov	G C 8:47a	C	C L 2:00p	L	L V 3:55p	V	V Li 6:03p	Li	Li S 8:16p	S	S Sg 11:44p	Sg	Sg	Sg Cp 5:43a	Cp	Cp Aq 3:03p	Aq	Aq	Aq P 5:00a	P	P A 3:33p	A	A	A T 2:21a	T	T G 10:07a	G	G C 3:09p	C	C L 6:33p	
Dec	L	L V 9:23p	V	V	V Li 12:23a	Li	Li S 3:57a	S	S Sg 8:33a	Sg	Sg Cp 2:55p	Cp	Cp Aq 11:45p	Aq	Aq	Aq P 11:19a	P	P	P A 12:01a	A	A T 11:28a	T	T G 7:32p	G	G	G C 12:00a	C	C L 2:07a	L	L V 3:31a	V

MOON SIGNS 1910 – 1969

1940

	1	2	3	4	5	6	7	8	9	10	11	12	13	14	15	16	17	18	19	20	21	22	23	24	25	26	27	28	29	30	31
Jan	V Li 5:44a	Li	Li S 9:37a	S	S Sg 3:14p	Sg	Sg Cp 10:32p	Cp	Cp	Cp Aq 7:43a	Aq	Aq P 7:05p	P	P	P A 7:55a	A	A T 8:11p	T	T	T G 5:30a	G	G C 10:32a	C	C L 12:09p	L	L V 12:12p	V	V Li 12:46p	Li	Li S 3:22p	S
Feb	S Sg 8:39p	Sg	Sg	Sg Cp 4:27a	Cp	Cp Aq 2:24p	Aq	Aq	Aq P 1:59a	P	P A 2:49p	A	A	A T 3:35a	T	T G 2:05p	G	G C 8:40p	C	C L 11:15p	L	L V 11:10p	V	V Li 10:31p	Li	Li S 11:18p	S	S	S Sg 2:57a		
Mar	Sg	Sg Cp 9:46a	Cp	Cp	Cp Aq 8:09a	Aq	Aq P 11:07p	P	P A 9:00p	A	A	A T 9:44a	T	T G 8:48p	G	G	G C 4:56a	C	C L 9:13a	L	L V 10:19a	V	V Li 9:48a	Li	Li S 9:35a	S	S Sg 11:34a	Sg	Sg Cp 5:05p	Cp	Cp
Apr	Cp Aq 2:16a	Aq	Aq P 2:12p	P	P	P A 3:10a	A	A T 3:37	T	T	T G 2:31a	G	G C 11:01a	C	C L 4:39p	L	L V 7:31p	V	V Li 8:21p	Li	Li S 8:34p	S	S Sg 9:52p	Sg	Sg	Sg Cp 1:54a	Cp	Cp Aq 9:41a	Aq	Aq P 8:58p	
May	P	P	P A 9:50a	A	A T 10:10p	T	T	T G 8:33a	G	G C 4:31p	C	C L 10:19p	L	L V 2:16a	V	V	V Li 4:40a	Li	Li S 6:12a	S	S Sg 8:01a	Sg	Sg Cp 11:38a	Cp	Cp Aq 6:23p	Aq	Aq	Aq P 4:39a	P	P A 5:17p	A
Jn	A	A T 5:42a	T	T G 3:45p	G	G C 10:59p	C	C	C L 4:00a	L	L V 7:41a	V	V Li 10:44a	Li	Li S 1:32p	S	S Sg 4:34p	Sg	Sg Cp 8:48p	Cp	Cp	Cp Aq 3:18a	Aq	Aq P 12:57p	P	P	P A 1:13a	A	A T 1:50p	T	
Jly	T	T G 12:12a	G	G C 7:11a	C	C L 11:11a	L	L V 1:44p	V	V Li 4:08p	Li	Li S 7:08p	S	S Sg 11:06p	Sg	Sg	Sg Cp 4:19a	Cp	Cp Aq 11:24a	Aq	Aq P 9:02p	P	P	P A 9:02a	A	A T 9:53p	T	T G 9:03a	G	G	G C 4:27p
Aug	C	C L 8:16p	L	L V 9:49p	V	V Li 10:51p	Li	Li	Li S 12:48a	S	S Sg 4:30a	Sg	Sg Cp 10:17a	Cp	Cp Aq 6:11p	Aq	Aq	Aq P 4:11a	P	P A 4:16p	A	A T 5:16a	T	T	T G 5:08p	G	G	G C 1:49a	C	C L 6:31a	L
Sep	L V 7:56a	V	V Li 7:54a	Li	Li S 8:18a	S	S Sg 10:39a	Sg	Sg Cp 3:50p	Cp	Cp Aq 11:55p	Aq	Aq	Aq P 10:25a	P	P A 10:44p	A	A	A T 11:44a	T	T	T G 10:03a	G	G C 9:56a	C	C L 4:03p	L	L V 6:36p	V	V Li 6:45p	
Oct	Li	Li S 6:15p	S	S Sg 6:59p	Sg	Sg Cp 10:34p	Cp	Cp	Cp Aq 5:45a	Aq	Aq P 4:19p	P	P	P A 4:50a	A	A T 5:48p	T	T	T G 5:58a	G	G C 4:14p	C	C L 11:46p	L	L	L V 4:07a	V	V Li 5:36a	Li	Li S 5:25a	S
Nov	S Sg 5:22a	Sg	Sg Cp 7:23a	Cp	Cp Aq 1:07p	Aq	Aq P 10:49p	P	P A 11:13a	A	A	A T 12:11a	T	T	T G 11:59a	G	G C 9:50p	C	C L 5:37a	L	L	L V 11:08a	V	V Li 8:22p	Li	Li S 3:44p	S	S Sg 4:20p	Sg	Sg Cp 5:55p	
Dec	Cp	Cp Aq 10:18p	Aq	Aq	Aq P 6:35a	P	P A 6:28p	A	A	A T 7:26a	T	T G 7:05p	G	G	G C 4:18a	C	C L 11:15a	L	L V 4:33p	V	V Li 8:35p	Li	Li S 11:29p	S	S	S Sg 1:37a	Sg	Sg Cp 3:59a	Cp	Cp Aq 8:09a	Aq

1941

	1	2	3	4	5	6	7	8	9	10	11	12	13	14	15	16	17	18	19	20	21	22	23	24	25	26	27	28	29	30	31
Jan	Aq P 3:40p	P	P	P A 2:36a	A	A T 3:27p	T	T	T G 3:25a	G	G C 12:31p	C	C L 6:36p	L	L V 10:45p	V	V	V L 2:00a	L	L S 5:04a	S	S Sg 8:17a	Sg	Sg Cp 12:02p	Cp	Cp Aq 5:09p	Aq	Aq	Aq P 12:37a	P	P A 11:03a
Feb	A	A T 11:41p	T	T	T G 12:07p	G	G C 9:53p	C	C	C L 4:05a	L	L V 7:22a	V	V Li 9:07a	Li	Li S 10:36a	S	S Sg 1:39p	Sg	Sg Cp 5:56p	Cp	Cp	Cp Aq 1:04a	Aq	Aq P 8:19a	P	P	P A 6:56p			
Mar	A	A T 7:22a	T	T G 8:09p	G	G	G C 7:04a	C	C L 2:14p	L	L V 5:47p	V	V Li 6:50p	Li	Li S 7:04p	S	S Sg 8:12p	Sg	Sg Cp 11:29p	Cp	Cp	Cp Aq 5:36a	Aq	Aq P 2:33p	P	P	P A 1:41a	A	A T 2:13p	T	T
Apr	T G 3:05a	G	G C 2:40p	C	C L 11:21p	L	L	L V 4:18a	V	V Li 5:53p	Li	Li S 5:32a	S	S Sg 5:08a	Sg	Sg Cp 6:38a	Cp	Cp Aq 11:34a	Aq	Aq P 8:11p	P	P	P A 7:34a	A	A T 8:22p	T	T	T G 9:11a	G	G C 8:53p	
May	C	C	C L 6:33a	L	L V 1:01p	V	V Li 4:06p	Li	Li S 4:31p	S	S Sg 3:52p	Sg	Sg Cp 4:09p	Cp	Cp Aq 7:21p	Aq	Aq	Aq P 2:37a	P	P A 1:35p	A	A	A T 2:25a	T	T G 3:09p	G	G	G C 2:35a	C	C L 12:14p	L
Jn	L V 7:34p	V	V	V Li 12:13a	Li	Li S 2:12a	S	S Sg 2:24a	Sg	Sg Cp 2:33a	Cp	Cp Aq 4:44a	Aq	Aq P 10:37a	P	P A 8:33p	A	A	A T 9:02a	T	T G 9:42p	G	G	G C 8:50a	C	C L 5:52	L	L	L V 1:01a	V	
Jly	V Li 6:16a	Li	Li S 9:32a	S	S Sg 11:12a	Sg	Sg Cp 12:22p	Cp	Cp Aq 2:40p	Aq	Aq P 7:47p	P	P	P A 4:37a	A	A T 4:31p	T	T	T G 5:09a	G	G C 4:12p	C	C	C L 12:46a	L	L V 7:04a	V	V Li 11:40a	Li	Li S 3:07p	S
Aug	S Sg 5:49p	Sg	Sg Cp 9:27p	Cp	Cp Aq 11:35p	Aq	Aq	Aq P 4:52a	P	P A 1:15p	A	A	A T 12:33a	T	T G 1:08p	G	G	G C 12:34a	C	C L 9:14a	L	L V 2:50p	V	V Li 6:19p	Li	Li S 8:48p	S	S Sg 11:14p	Sg	Sg	Sg Cp 2:19a
Sep	Cp	Cp Aq 6:39a	Aq	Aq P 12:54p	P	P A 9:31a	A	A	A T 7:32a	T	T G 9:05p	G	G	G C 9:09a	C	C L 6:30p	L	L	L V 12:25a	V	V Li 3:15a	Li	Li S 4:24a	S	S Sg 6:25a	Sg	Sg Cp 7:46a	Cp	Cp Aq 12:19p	Aq	
Oct	Aq P 7:30p	P	P	P A 4:39a	A	A T 3:53p	T	T	T G 4:22a	G	G C 4:50p	C	C	C L 3:27a	L	L V 10:34a	V	V Li 1:50p	Li	Li S 2:25p	S	S Sg 2:02p	Sg	Sg Cp 2:44p	Cp	Cp Aq 6:08p	Aq	Aq	Aq P 12:53a	P	P A 10:39a
Nov	A	A T 10:20p	T	T	T G 10:53a	G	G C 11:24p	C	C	C L 10:47a	L	L V 7:23p	V	V	V Li 12:16a	Li	Li S 1:37a	S	S Sg 12:53a	Sg	Sg Cp 12:14a	Cp	Cp Aq 1:50a	Aq	Aq P 7:09a	P	P A 4:30p	A	A	A T 4:19a	
Dec	T	T G 5:00p	G	G	G C 5:22a	C	C L 4:41p	L	L	L V 2:10a	V	V Li 8:44a	Li	Li S 11:48a	S	S Sg 12:09p	Sg	Sg Cp 11:27a	Cp	Cp Aq 11:57a	Aq	Aq P 3:38p	P	P A 11:27p	A	A	A T 10:44a	T	T G 11:26p	G	G

1942

	1	2	3	4	5	6	7	8	9	10	11	12	13	14	15	16	17	18	19	20	21	22	23	24	25	26	27	28	29	30	31
Jan	G C 11:41a	C	C L 10:30p	L	L	L V 7:41a	V	V Li 2:45p	Li	Li S 7:20p	S	S Sg 9:29p	Sg	Sg Cp 10:07p	Cp	Cp Aq 10:55p	Aq	Aq	Aq P 1:46a	P	P A 8:09a	A	A T 6:21p	T	T	T G 6:44a	G	G C 7:01p	C	C	C L 5:37a
Feb	L	L V 1:55p	V	V Li 8:15p	Li	Li	Li S 12:54	S	S Sg 4:05a	Sg	Sg Cp 6:18a	Cp	Cp Aq 8:28a	Aq	Aq P 11:53a	P	P A 5:50p	A	A	A T 2:59a	T	T G 2:49p	G	G	G C 3:43a	C	C L 2:02p	L			
Mar	L V 10:02p	V	V	V Li 3:21a	Li	Li S 6:50a	S	S Sg 9:28a	Sg	Sg Cp 12:09p	Cp	Cp Aq 3:33p	Aq	Aq P 8:11p	P	P	P A 2:43a	A	A T 11:41a	T	T G 11:01p	G	G	G C 11:32a	C	C L 11:01p	L	L	L V 7:36a	V	V Li 12:09a
Apr	Li	Li S 2:52p	S	S Sg 4:05p	Sg	Sg Cp 5:45p	Cp	Cp Aq 9:00a	Aq	Aq	Aq P 2:22a	P	P A 9:51a	A	A T 7:20p	T	T	T G 6:36a	G	G C 7:09p	C	C	C L 7:22a	L	L V 4:58p	V	V Li 10:45p	Li	Li	Li S 12:56a	
May	S	S Sg 1:02a	Sg	Sg Cp 1:05a	Cp	Cp Aq 2:58a	Aq	Aq P 7:44a	p	P A 3:55p	A	A	A T 1:39a	T	T G 1:16p	G	G	G C 1:50a	C	C L 2:19p	L	L	L V 1:05a	V	V Li 8:20a	Li	Li S 12:11p	S	S Sg 11:38a	Sg	Sg Cp 10:45a
Jn	Cp	Cp Aq 11:02a	Aq	Aq P 2:18p	P	P A 9:15p	A	A	A T 7:16a	T	T G 7:13p	G	G	G C 7:51a	C	C L 8:18p	L	L	L V 7:33a	V	V Li 3:59p	Li	Li S 8:45a	S	S Sg 10:05p	Sg	Sg Cp 9:30p	Cp	Cp Aq 9:05p	Aq	
Jly	Aq P 10:51p	P	P A 4:12a	A	A	A T 1:26p	T	T	T G 1:11a	G	G C 1:51p	C	C	C L 2:06a	L	L V 1:06p	V	V Li 9:58p	Li	Li	Li S 4:00a	S	S Sg 6:58a	Sg	Sg Cp 7:38a	Cp	Cp Aq 7:37a	Aq	Aq P 8:51a	P	P A 12:59p
Aug	A	A	A T 12:26a	T	T G 7:55a	G	G C 8:29p	C	C	C L 8:39a	L	L V 7:06p	V	V	V Li 3:29a	Li	Li S 9:36a	S	S Sg 1:33a	Sg	Sg Cp 3:45p	Cp	Cp Aq 5:07p	Aq	Aq P 6:58p	P	P A 10:43p	A	A	A T 5:30a	T
Sep	T G 3:43p	G	G	G C 4:00a	C	C L 4:12p	L	L	L V 2:29a	V	V Li 10:03a	Li	Li S 3:16p	S	S Sg 6:57p	Sg	Sg Cp 9:48p	Cp	Cp	Cp Aq 12:28a	Aq	Aq P 3:34a	P	P A 7:57a	A	A T 2:37p	T	T	T G 12:07a	G	
Oct	G C 12:03p	C	C	C L 12:33a	L	L V 11:11a	V	V Li 6:28p	Li	Li S 10:43p	S	S	S Sg 1:09a	Sg	Sg Cp 3:14a	Cp	Cp Aq 6:02a	Aq	Aq P 10:05a	P	P A 3:39p	A	A T 10:55p	T	T	T G 8:19a	G	G C 8:02p	C	C	C L 8:48a
Nov	L	L V 8:15p	V	V Li 4:19p	Li	Li	Li S 8:26a	S	S Sg 9:46a	Sg	Sg Cp 10:19a	Cp	Cp Aq 11:51a	Aq	Aq P 3:31a	P	P A 9:33p	A	A	A T 5:39a	T	T G 3:37p	G	G	G C 3:17a	C	C L 4:08p	L	L	L V 4:28a	
Dec	V	V Li 1:50p	Li	Li S 7:00p	S	S Sg 8:30p	Sg	Sg Cp 8:07p	Cp	Cp Aq 9:38p	Aq	Aq P 10:01p	P	P	P A 3:07a	A	A T 11:18a	T	T G 9:48p	G	G	G C 9:46a	C	C L 10:35p	L	L	L V 11:08a	V	V Li 9:40p	Li	Li

MOON SIGNS 1910 – 1969

1943

	1	2	3	4	5	6	7	8	9	10	11	12	13	14	15	16	17	18	19	20	21	22	23	24	25	26	27	28	29	30	31
Jan	Li S 4:37a	S	S Sg 7:34a	Sg	Sg Cp 7:35a	Cp	Cp Aq 6:41a	Aq	Aq P 7:03a	P	P A 10:23a	A	A T 5:26p	T	T	T G 3:40a	G	G C 3:55p	C	C	C L 4:44a	L	L V 5:01p	V	V	V Li 3:45a	Li	Li S 11:48a	S	S Sg 4:29p	Sg
Feb	Sg Cp 6:11p	Cp	Cp Aq 6:10p	Aq	Aq P 6:11p	P	P A 8:06p	A	A	A T 1:21a	T	T G 10:27a	G	G C 10:26p	C	C	C L 11:18a	L	L V 11:17p	V	V	V Li 9:29a	Li	Li S 6:13p	S	S Sg 10:56p	Sg	Sg			
Mar	Sg Cp 2:17a	Cp	Cp Aq 3:56	Aq	Aq P 4:54a	P	P A 6:42a	A	A T 10:56a	T	T G 6:44	G	G	G C 5:52a	C	C L 6:40p	L	L	L V 6:42a	V	V Li 4:17p	Li	Li S 11:20	S	S	S Sg 4:22a	Sg	Sg Cp 8:06a	Cp	Cp Aq 10:57a	Aq
Apr	Aq P 1:27p	P	P A 4:20p	A	A T 8:41p	T	T	T G 3:43a	G	G C 2:06p	C	C	C L 2:40a	L	L V 2:56p	V	V	V Li 2:37a	Li	Li S 7:04a	S	S Sg 10:56a	Sg	Sg Cp 1:40p	Cp	Cp Aq 4:26p	Aq	Aq P 7:37a	P	P A 11:41p	
May	A	A	A T 4:58a	T	T G 12:19a	G	G C 10:19p	C	C	C L 10:39a	L	L V 11:19p	V	V	V Li 9:42a	Li	Li S 4:14p	S	S Sg 7:29p	Sg	Sg Cp 9:02p	Cp	Cp Aq 10:25p	Aq	Aq	Aq P 1:00a	P	P A 5:18a	A	A T 11:26a	T
Jn	T G 7:32p	G	G	G C 5:45a	C	C L 6:04p	L	L	L V 7:04a	V	V Li 6:17p	Li	Li	Li S 1:54a	S	S Sg 5:36a	Sg	Sg Cp 6:29a	Cp	Cp Aq 6:33a	Aq	Aq P 7:37a	P	P A 10:55a	A	A T 4:55p	T	T	T G 1:28a	G	
Jly	G C 12:15p	C	C	C L 12:40a	L	L V 1:43p	V	V	V Li 1:15a	Li	Li S 10:37a	S	S Sg 3:31p	Sg	Sg Cp 5:03p	Cp	Cp Aq 4:46p	Aq	Aq P 4:34p	P	P A 6:13p	A	A T 10:57p	T	T	T G 7:04a	G	G C 6:05p	C	C	C L 6:43a
Aug	L	L V 7:44p	V	V	V Li 7:51a	Li	Li S 5:35p	S	S	S Sg 12:03a	Sg	Sg Cp 3:06a	Cp	Cp Aq 3:36a	Aq	Aq P 3:07a	P	P A 3:34a	A	A T 6:39a	T	T G 1:39p	G	G	G C 12:10a	C	C L 12:49p	L	L	L V 1:46a	V
Sep	V Li 1:31p	Li	Li S 11:18p	S	S	S Sg 6:38a	Sg	Sg Cp 11:11a	Cp	Cp Aq 1:16p	Aq	Aq P 1:46p	P	P A 2:11p	A	A T 4:19p	T	T	T G 9:48p	G	G C 7:10a	C	C L 7:34p	L	L	L V 8:30a	V	V Li 7:53p	Li	Li	
Oct	Li S 4:04a	S	S Sg 12:01p	Sg	Sg Cp 5:08p	Cp	Cp Aq 8:37p	Aq	Aq P 10:43p	P	P	P A 12:12a	A	A T 2:29a	T	T G 7:07a	G	G C 3:22p	C	C	C L 3:14a	L	L V 4:09p	V	V	V Li 3:35a	Li	Li S 12:12p	S	S Sg 6:11p	Sg
Nov	Sg Cp 10:34p	Cp	Cp	Cp Aq 2:09a	Aq	Aq P 5:16a	P	P A 8:10a	A	A T 11:33a	T	T G 4:35p	G	G	G C 12:26a	C	C L 11:29a	L	L	L V 12:20a	V	V Li 12:16p	Li	Li S 9:04p	S	S	S Sg 2:33a	Sg	Sg Cp 5:42a	Cp	
Dec	Cp Aq 8:01a	Aq	Aq P 10:36a	P	P A 2:01p	A	A T 6:32p	T	T	T G 12:34a	G	G C 8:46a	C	C L 7:39p	L	L	L V 8:21a	V	V Li 8:52p	Li	Li	Li S 6:45a	S	S Sg 12:40p	Sg	Sg Cp 3:21p	Cp	Cp Aq 4:21p	Aq	Aq P 5:19p	P

1944

	1	2	3	4	5	6	7	8	9	10	11	12	13	14	15	16	17	18	19	20	21	22	23	24	25	26	27	28	29	30	31
Jan	P A 7:37p	A	A T 11:08p	T	T	T G 6:45a	G	G C 3:50p	C	C	C L 2:59a	L	L V 3:39p	V	V	V Li 4:29a	Li	Li S 3:23p	S	S Sg 10:47p	Sg	Sg	Sg Cp 2:23a	Cp	Cp Aq 3:08a	Aq	Aq P 2:48a	P	P A 3:16a	A	A T 6:08a
Feb	T	T G 12:22p	G	G C 9:43p	C	C	C L 9:19a	L	L V 10:08p	V	V	V Li 10:53p	Li	Li S 10:21p	S	S	S Sg 7:15a	Sg	Sg Cp 12:29p	Cp	Cp Aq 2:23p	Aq	Aq P 2:08p	P	P A 1:33p	A	A T 2:41p	T	T G 7:12p		
Mar	G	G	G C 3:40a	C	C L 3:20p	L	L	L V 4:17a	V	V Li 4:54p	Li	Li	Li S 4:12a	S	S Sg 1:27p	Sg	Sg Cp 8:08p	Cp	Cp Aq 11:50p	Aq	Aq	Aq P 12:56a	P	P A 12:42a	A	A T 1:04a	T	T G 4:01a	G	G C 11:02a	C
Apr	C L 9:56p	L	L	L V 10:48a	V	V Li 11:20p	Li	Li	Li S 10:10a	S	S Sg 6:58p	Sg	Sg	Sg Cp 1:53a	Cp	Cp Aq 6:46a	Aq	Aq P 9:27a	P	P A 10:43a	A	A T 11:30a	T	T G 2:03p	G	G C 7:54p	C	C	C L 5:37a	L	
May	L V 6:04p	V	V	V Li 6:40a	Li	Li S 5:15p	S	S	S Sg 1:25a	Sg	Sg Cp 7:33a	Cp	Cp Aq 12:09p	Aq	Aq P 3:33p	P	P A 6:02p	A	A T 8:17p	T	T G 11:30p	G	G	G C 5:05a	C	C L 2:08p	L	L	L V 1:59a	V	V Li 2:35p
Jn	Li	Li	Li S 1:28a	S	S Sg 9:26p	Sg	Sg Cp 2:38p	Cp	Cp Aq 6:11p	Aq	Aq P 8:58p	P	P A 11:41p	A	A	A T 2:53a	T	T G 7:11a	G	G C 1:31p	C	C L 10:28p	L	L	L V 9:58a	V	V Li 10:39p	Li	Li	Li S 10:08a	
Jly	S	S Sg 6:33p	Sg	Sg Cp 11:38p	Cp	Cp	Cp Aq 2:12a	Aq	Aq P 3:40a	P	P A 5:18a	A	A T 8:17a	T	T G 1:14p	G	G C 8:24p	C	C	C L 5:52a	L	L V 5:26p	V	V	V Li 6:07a	Li	Li S 6:14p	S	S	S Sg 3:48a	Sg
Aug	Sg Cp 9:38a	Cp	Cp Aq 12:09p	Aq	Aq P 10:02a	P	P A 12:46	A	A T 2:23p	T	T G 6:43p	G	G	G C 2:06a	C	C L 12:09p	L	L	L V 12:01a	V	V Li 12:44p	Li	Li	Li S 1:12a	S	S Sg 11:49a	Sg	Sg Cp 7:06p	Cp	Cp Aq 10:39p	Aq
Sep	Aq P 11:12p	P	P A 10:28p	A	A T 10:33p	T	T	T G 1:18a	G	G C 7:47a	C	C L 5:54p	L	L	L V 6:02a	V	V Li 5:52p	Li	Li	Li S 7:12a	S	S Sg 6:14p	Sg	Sg	Sg Cp 2:52a	Cp	Cp Aq 8:09a	Aq	Aq P 9:56a	P	
Oct	P A 9:29a	A	A T 8:46a	T	T G 10:02a	G	G C 3:02p	C	C	C L 12:06a	L	L V 12:04p	V	V	V Li 12:54a	Li	Li S 1:02p	S	S Sg 11:48p	Sg	Sg Cp 8:47a	Cp	Cp	Cp Aq 3:15p	Aq	Aq P 6:48p	P	P A 7:52p	A	A T 7:47p	T
Nov	T G 8:33p	G	G	G C 12:09a	C	C L 7:45a	L	L V 7:01p	V	V	V Li 7:44a	Li	Li S 7:45p	S	S	S Sg 6:00a	Sg	Sg Cp 2:48p	Cp	Cp Aq 8:44p	Aq	Aq	Aq P 1:16a	P	P A 3:56a	A	A T 5:22a	T	T G 6:55a	G	
Dec	G C 10:19a	C	C L 4:58p	L	L V 3:06a	V	V	V Li 3:28p	Li	Li	Li S 3:41a	S	S Sg 1:47p	Sg	Sg Cp 9:19p	Cp	Cp	Cp Aq 2:43a	Aq	Aq P 6:39a	P	P A 9:42a	A	A T 12:25p	T	T G 3:28p	G	G C 7:47p	C	C	C L 2:22a

1945

	1	2	3	4	5	6	7	8	9	10	11	12	13	14	15	16	17	18	19	20	21	22	23	24	25	26	27	28	29	30	31
Jan	L	L V 11:52a	V	V Li 11:45p	Li	Li	Li S 12:11p	S	S Sg 10:52p	Sg	Sg	Sg Cp 6:27a	Cp	Cp Aq 10:55a	Aq	Aq P 1:26p	P	P A 3:22p	A	A T 5:50p	T	T G 9:37p	G	G	G C 3:07a	C	C L 10:34a	L	L V 8:11p	V	V
Feb	V Li 7:46a	Li	Li S 8:21p	S	S	S Sg 7:58a	Sg	Sg Cp 4:24p	Cp	Cp Aq 9:07p	Aq	Aq P 10:50p	P	P A 11:13p	A	A	A T 12:08a	T	T G 3:03a	G	G C 8:44a	C	C L 5:01p	L	L	L V 3:15a	V	V Li 2:57p			
Mar	Li	Li	Li S 3:32a	S	S Sg 3:41p	Sg	Sg	Sg Cp 1:34a	Cp	Cp Aq 7:39a	Aq	Aq P 9:49a	P	P A 9:32a	A	A T 8:56a	T	T G 10:06a	G	G C 2:36p	C	C	C L 10:36a	L	L V 9:11a	V	V Li 9:16p	Li	Li	Li S 9:50a	S
Apr	S Sg 10:05p	Sg	Sg	Sg Cp 8:50a	Cp	Cp Aq 4:22a	Aq	Aq P 8:04p	P	P A 8:35p	A	A T 7:41p	T	T G 7:36p	G	G C 10:20p	C	C	C L 4:53a	L	L V 3:05p	V	V	V Li 3:14a	Li	Li S 3:52p	S	S	S Sg 3:55a	Sg	
May	Sg Cp 2:37p	Cp	Cp Aq 11:02p	Aq	Aq	Aq P 4:18a	P	P A 6:24a	A	A T 6:24a	T	T G 6:12a	G	G C 7:52a	C	C L 1:01p	L	L V 10:00p	V	V	V Li 9:44a	Li	Li S 10:20p	S	S	S Sg 10:10a	Sg	Sg Cp 8:22p	Cp	Cp	Cp Aq 4:34a
Jn	Aq	Aq P 10:23a	P	P A 1:48p	A	A T 3:22p	T	T G 4:16p	G	G C 6:07p	C	C L 10:24p	L	L	L V 6:07a	V	V Li 5:08p	Li	Li	Li S 5:35a	S	S Sg 5:25p	Sg	Sg	Sg Cp 3:12a	Cp	Cp Aq 10:35a	Aq	Aq P 3:49p	P	
Jly	P A 7:27p	A	A T 10:04p	T	T	T G 12:20a	G	G C 3:11a	C	C L 7:43a	L	L V 3:01p	V	V	V Li 1:14a	Li	Li S 1:28p	S	S	S Sg 1:35a	Sg	Sg Cp 11:26a	Cp	Cp Aq 6:12p	Aq	Aq P 10:25p	P	P	P A 1:07a	A	A T 3:30a
Aug	T	T G 6:22a	G	G C 10:23a	C	C L 3:54p	L	L V 11:26p	V	V	V Li 9:23a	Li	Li S 9:26p	S	S	S Sg 9:55a	Sg	Sg Cp 8:25p	Cp	Cp	Cp Aq 3:29a	Aq	Aq P 7:05a	P	P A 8:30a	A	A T 9:34a	T	T G 11:48a	G	G C 4:03p
Sep	C	C L 10:23p	L	L	L V 6:37a	V	V Li 4:51p	Li	Li	Li S 4:49a	S	S Sg 5:28p	Sg	Sg	Sg Cp 5:11a	Cp	Cp Aq 1:15p	Aq	Aq P 5:14p	P	P A 6:08p	A	A T 5:55p	T	T G 6:36p	G	G C 9:42p	C	C	C L 3:49a	
Oct	L	L V 12:36p	V	V Li 11:18p	Li	Li	Li S 11:25a	S	S	S Sg 12:18a	Sg	Sg Cp 12:30p	Cp	Cp Aq 10:00p	Aq	Aq	Aq P 3:30a	P	P A 5:08a	A	A T 4:29a	T	T G 3:47a	G	G C 5:13a	C	C L 9:57a	L	L V 6:15p	V	V
Nov	V Li 5:09a	Li	Li S 5:30p	S	S Sg 6:18a	Sg	Sg	Sg Cp 6:33p	Cp	Cp	Cp Aq 4:57a	Aq	Aq P 12:00p	P	P A 3:19p	A	A T 3:46p	T	T G 3:04p	G	G C 3:19p	C	C L 6:18p	L	L	L V 1:03a	V	V Li 11:20a	Li	Li S 11:44p	
Dec	S	S	S Sg 12:28p	Sg	Sg	Sg Cp 12:22a	Cp	Cp Aq 10:32a	Aq	Aq P 6:16p	P	P A 11:11p	A	A	A T 1:27a	T	T G 2:02a	G	G C 2:29a	C	C L 4:33a	L	L V 9:46a	V	V Li 6:49p	Li	Li	Li S 6:42a	S	S Sg 7:30p	Sg

MOON SIGNS 1910 – 1969

1946	1	2	3	4	5	6	7	8	9	10	11	12	13	14	15	16	17	18	19	20	21	22	23	24	25	26	27	28	29	30	31
Jan	Sg	Sg Cp 7:10a	Cp	Cp Aq 4:32p	Aq	Aq P 11:42p	P	P	P A 4:52a	A	A T 8:23a	T	T G 10:43a	G	G C 12:34p	C	C L 3:11p	L	L V 7:50p	V	V	V Li 3:38a	Li	Li S 2:43p	S	S	S Sg 3:25a	Sg	Sg Cp 3:11p	Cp	Cp
Feb	Cp Aq 12:16a	Aq	Aq P 6:30a	P	P A 10:36a	A	A T 1:48p	T	T G 4:47p	G	G C 8:01p	C	C L 11:55p	L	L	L V 5:07a	V	V Li 12:44p	Li	Li S 11:11p	S	S	S Sg 11:42a	Sg	Sg Cp 11:54p	Cp	Cp	Cp Aq 9:29a			
Mar	Aq	Aq P 3:17p	P	P A 6:20p	A	A T 8:10p	T	T G 10:16p	G	G	G C 1:34a	C	C L 6:18a	L	L V 12:38p	V	V Li 8:47p	Li	Li S 7:08a	S	S	S Sg 7:31p	Sg	Sg	Sg Cp 8:15a	Cp	Cp Aq 6:40p	Aq	Aq	Aq P 1:17a	P
Apr	P A 4:10a	A	A T 4:57a	T	T G 5:29a	G	G C 7:26a	C	C L 11:44a	L	L V 6:28p	V	V	V Li 3:17a	Li	Li S 2:07p	S	S	S Sg 2:30a	Sg	Sg Cp 3:26p	Cp	Cp	Cp Aq 2:51a	Aq	Aq P 10:45a	P	P A 2:35p	A	A T 3:27p	
May	T	T G 3:07p	G	G C 3:31p	C	C L 6:15p	L	L	L V 12:04a	V	V Li 8:57a	Li	Li S 8:12p	S	S	S Sg 8:48a	Sg	Sg Cp 9:40p	Cp	Cp	Cp Aq 9:27a	Aq	Aq P 6:30p	P	P A 11:55p	A	A	A T 1:58a	T	T G 1:54a	G
Jn	G C 2:12a	C	C L 2:48a	L	L V 7:02a	V	V Li 3:05p	Li	Li	Li S 2:08a	S	S Sg 2:51p	Sg	Sg	Sg Cp 3:38a	Cp	Cp Aq 3:11p	Aq	Aq	Aq P 12:36a	P	P A 7:16a	A	A T 10:49a	T	T G 12:04p	G	G C 12:12p	C	C L 12:56p	
Jly	L	L V 3:56p	V	V Li 10:31p	Li	Li	Li S 8:46a	S	S Sg 9:21p	Sg	Sg	Sg Cp 10:03a	Cp	Cp Aq 9:12p	Aq	Aq	Aq P 6:11a	P	P A 12:54p	A	A T 5:25p	T	T G 8:15p	G	G C 9:43p	C	C L 11:01p	L	L	L V 1:41a	V
Aug	V Li 7:09a	Li	Li S 4:30p	S	S	S Sg 4:38a	Sg	Sg Cp 5:19p	Cp	Cp	Cp Aq 4:19a	Aq	Aq P 12:36p	P	P A 6:33p	A	A T 10:56p	T	T	T G 2:20a	G	G C 5:07	C	C L 7:39a	L	L V 11:00a	V	V Li 4:25p	Li	Li	Li S 12:57a
Sep	S	S Sg 1:19p	Sg	Sg	Sg Cp 1:21a	Cp	Cp Aq 12:35p	Aq	Aq P 8:37p	P	P	P A 1:41a	A	A T 5:03a	T	T G 7:47a	G	G C 10:44a	C	C L 2:16p	L	L V 7:36p	V	V	V Li 12:47a	Li	Li S 9:16a	S	S Sg 8:32p	Sg	
Oct	Sg	Sg Cp 9:28a	Cp	Cp Aq 9:19p	Aq	Aq	Aq P 6:03a	P	P A 10:58a	A	A T 1:18p	T	T G 2:39p	G	G C 4:29p	C	C L 7:42p	L	L	L V 12:42a	V	V Li 7:36a	Li	Li S 4:47p	S	S	S Sg 4:05a	Sg	Sg Cp 4:59p	Cp	Cp
Nov	Cp Aq 5:32a	Aq	Aq P 3:22p	P	P A 9:18p	A	A T 11:42p	T	T	T G 12:07a	G	G C 12:20a	C	C L 2:01a	L	L V 6:10a	V	V Li 1:18p	Li	Li S 11:03p	S	S	S Sg 10:46a	Sg	Sg Cp 11:40p	Cp	Cp	Cp Aq 12:26p	Aq	Aq P 11:22p	
Dec	P	P	P A 6:44a	A	A T 10:41a	T	T G 11:26a	G	G C 10:48a	C	C L 10:54a	L	L V 1:20p	V	V Li 7:18p	Li	Li	Li S 4:47a	S	S Sg 4:51p	Sg	Sg Cp 5:51a	Cp	Cp	Cp Aq 6:27p	Aq	Aq	Aq P 5:40a	P	P A 2:23p	A

1947	1	2	3	4	5	6	7	8	9	10	11	12	13	14	15	16	17	18	19	20	21	22	23	24	25	26	27	28	29	30	31
Jan	A T 8:02p	T	T G 10:22p	G	G C 10:27p	C	C L 9:56p	L	L V 10:50p	V	V	V Li 2:59a	Li	Li S 11:19a	S	S Sg 11:06p	Sg	Sg	Sg Cp 12:11p	Cp	Cp	Cp Aq 12:37a	Aq	Aq P 11:23a	P	P A 8:08p	A	A	A T 2:44a	T	T G 6:53a
Feb	G	G C 8:39a	C	C L 9:02a	L	L V 9:45a	V	V Li 12:44p	Li	Li S 7:35p	S	S	S Sg 6:16a	Sg	Sg Cp 7:12p	Cp	Cp	Cp Aq 7:39a	Aq	Aq P 5:54p	P	P	P A 1:56a	A	A T 8:07a	T	T G 12:47p	G			
Mar	G C 12:36p	C	C L 6:00p	L	L V 7:49p	V	V Li 10:55p	Li	Li	Li S 4:53a	S	S Sg 2:37p	Sg	Sg	Sg Cp 3:02a	Cp	Cp Aq 3:33p	Aq	Aq	Aq P 1:56a	P	P A 10:17a	A	A T 3:21p	T	T G 6:15p	G	G C 9:26p	C	C	C L 12:23a
Apr	L	L V 3:31a	V	V Li 7:41a	Li	Li S 10:46a	S	S Sg 11:16p	Sg	Sg	Sg Cp 11:09a	Cp	Cp Aq 11:50p	Aq	Aq	Aq P 9:22a	P	P A 6:21p	A	A T 10:53p	T	T	T G 1:28a	G	G C 3:24a	C	C L 5:46a	L	L V 9:17a	V	
May	V Li 2:27p	Li	Li S 9:39p	S	S	S Sg 7:10a	Sg	Sg Cp 6:53p	Cp	Cp	Cp Aq 7:42a	Aq	Aq P 7:18p	P	P A 3:55a	A	A	A T 8:52a	T	T G 10:49a	G	G C 11:29a	C	C L 12:21p	L	L V 2:54p	V	V Li 7:58p	Li	Li	Li S 3:45a
Jn	S	S Sg 1:57p	Sg	Sg	Sg Cp 1:52a	Cp	Cp Aq 2:37p	Aq	Aq	Aq P 2:46a	P	P A 12:30p	A	A T 6:40p	T	T G 9:19p	G	G C 9:32p	C	C L 9:09p	L	L V 10:07p	V	V	V Li 1:31a	Li	Li S 9:18a	S	S Sg 7:49p	Sg	
Jly	Sg	Sg Cp 8:03a	Cp	Cp Aq 8:49p	Aq	Aq	Aq P 9:03a	P	P A 7:32p	A	A	A T 3:10a	T	T G 7:17a	G	G C 8:14a	C	C L 7:35a	L	L V 7:20a	V	V Li 9:36a	Li	Li S 3:46p	S	S	S Sg 1:44a	Sg	Sg Cp 2:02p	Cp	Cp
Aug	Cp Aq 2:50a	Aq	Aq P 2:48p	P	P	P A 1:19a	A	A T 10:37a	T	T G 3:14p	G	G C 5:45p	C	C L 6:06p	L	L V 5:53p	V	V Li 7:10p	Li	Li S 11:40p	S	S	S Sg 8:36a	Sg	Sg Cp 8:32p	Cp	Cp	Cp Aq 9:19a	Aq	Aq P 9:02p	P
Sep	P	P A 7:04a	A	A T 3:08p	T	T G 9:15p	G	G	G C 1:10a	C	C L 3:10a	L	L V 3:52a	V	V Li 5:18a	Li	Li S 9:14a	S	S Sg 4:55p	Sg	Sg	Sg Cp 4:00a	Cp	Cp Aq 4:37p	Aq	Aq	Aq P 4:24a	P	P A 1:57p	A	
Oct	A T 9:13p	T	T	T G 2:43a	G	G C 6:48a	C	C L 9:41a	L	L V 11:58a	V	V Li 3:26p	Li	Li S 6:50p	S	S	S Sg 1:57a	Sg	Sg Cp 12:16p	Cp	Cp	Cp Aq 12:40a	Aq	Aq P 12:44p	P	P A 10:28p	A	A	A T 5:16a	T	T G 9:36a
Nov	G	G C 12:32p	C	C L 3:04p	L	L V 5:58p	V	V Li 9:45p	Li	Li	Li S 3:06a	S	S Sg 10:35a	Sg	Sg Cp 8:41p	Cp	Cp	Cp Aq 8:45a	Aq	Aq P 9:15p	P	P	P A 7:53a	A	A T 3:02p	T	T G 6:35p	G	G C 7:31p	C	
Dec	C L 9:32p	L	L V 11:26p	V	V	V Li 3:17a	Li	Li S 9:27a	S	S Sg 5:53a	Sg	Sg	Sg Cp 4:16a	Cp	Cp Aq 4:17p	Aq	Aq	Aq P 4:59a	P	P A 4:34p	A	A	A T 1:08a	T	T G 5:46a	G	G C 7:03p	C	C L 6:43a	L	L V 6:47a

1948	1	2	3	4	5	6	7	8	9	10	11	12	13	14	15	16	17	18	19	20	21	22	23	24	25	26	27	28	29	30	31
Jan	V	V Li 10:12a	Li	Li S 2:54p	S	S Sg 11:44p	Sg	Sg	Sg Cp 10:42a	Cp	Cp Aq 10:54p	Aq	Aq	Aq P 11:39a	P	P A 11:41p	A	A	A T 9:53a	T	T G 3:55p	G	G C 6:18p	C	C L 5:58p	L	L V 5:00p	V	V Li 5:35p	Li	Li S
Feb	S	S	S Sg 5:26a	Sg	Sg Cp 4:31p	Cp	Cp	Cp Aq 4:59a	Aq	Aq P 5:36p	P	P	P A 5:36a	A	A T 4:05p	T	T G 11:52p	G	G	G C 4:06a	C	C L 5:06a	L	L V 4:21a	V	V Li 4:07a	Li	Li S 6:24a	S		
Mar	S Sg 12:45	Sg	Sg Cp 10:53p	Cp	Cp	Cp Aq 11:15a	Aq	Aq P 11:52p	P	P	P A 11:32a	A	A T 9:39p	T	T	T G 5:44a	G	G C 10:54a	C	C L 1:55p	L	L V 2:41p	V	V Li 3:04p	Li	Li S 4:55p	S	S Sg 9:50p	Sg	Sg	Sg Cp 6:33a
Apr	Cp	Cp Aq 6:20p	Aq	Aq	Aq P 6:56a	P	P A 6:10p	A	A	A T 3:57a	T	T G 11:18a	G	G C 4:39p	C	C L 8:14p	L	L V 10:29p	V	V	V Li 12:17a	Li	Li S 2:51a	S	S Sg 7:31a	Sg	Sg Cp 3:26p	Cp	Cp	Cp Aq 2:17a	
May	Aq	Aq P 2:43p	P	P	P A 2:26a	A	A T 11:45a	T	T G 6:16p	G	G C 10:36p	C	C	C L 1:38a	L	L V 4:15a	V	V Li 7:07a	Li	Li S 10:57a	S	S Sg 12:46p	Sg	Sg	Sg Cp 12:10a	Cp	Cp Aq 10:31a	Aq	Aq P 10:45p	P	P
Jn	P A 10:53a	A	A T 8:39p	T	T	T G 3:04a	G	G C 6:28a	C	C L 8:11p	L	L V 9:49a	V	V Li 12:35p	Li	Li S 5:07p	S	S Sg 11:31p	Sg	Sg	Sg Cp 7:52a	Cp	Cp Aq 6:17p	Aq	Aq	Aq P 6:24a	P	P A 6:54p	A	A	
Jly	A T 5:39a	T	T G 12:44p	G	G C 4:02p	C	C L 4:52p	L	L V 5:06p	V	V Li 6:35p	Li	Li S 10:32p	S	S	S Sg 5:12a	Sg	Sg Cp 2:15p	Cp	Cp	Cp Aq 1:03a	Aq	Aq P 1:14p	P	P	P A 1:57a	A	A T 1:30p	T	T G 9:56a	G
Aug	G	G C 2:17a	C	C L 3:11a	L	L V 2:26a	V	V Li 2:33a	Li	Li S 4:58a	S	S Sg 10:52a	Sg	Sg Cp 7:54p	Cp	Cp	Cp Aq 7:02a	Aq	Aq P 7:23p	P	P	P A 8:04a	A	A T 8:00p	T	T	T G 5:39a	G	G C 11:30a	C	C L 1:11p
Sep	L	L V 1:20p	V	V Li 12:38p	Li	Li S 1:38p	S	S Sg 5:57p	Sg	Sg	Sg Cp 1:59a	Cp	Cp Aq 12:59p	Aq	Aq	Aq P 1:26a	P	P A 2:01p	A	A	A T 1:44a	T	T G 11:37a	G	G C 6:40p	C	C L 10:30p	L	L V 11:38p	V	
Oct	V Li 11:31p	Li	Li	Li S 12:51a	S	S Sg 2:58a	Sg	Sg Cp 9:32a	Cp	Cp Aq 7:45p	Aq	Aq P 8:03a	P	P	P A 7:34p	A	A	A T 7:54a	T	T G 5:12p	G	G	G C 1:13a	C	C L 5:09a	L	L V 7:53a	V	V Li 7:51a	Li	Li S 10:33a
Nov	S	S Sg 1:50p	Sg	Sg Cp 6:46p	Cp	Cp	Cp Aq 2:10a	Aq	Aq P 3:34p	P	P	P A 4:11a	A	A T 3:21p	T	T G 11:59p	G	G	G C 6:10a	C	C L 10:31a	L	L V 1:47p	V	V Li 4:32p	Li	Li S 7:03p	S	S Sg 10:55p	Sg	
Dec	Sg	Sg Cp 4:17a	Cp	Cp Aq 12:35p	Aq	Aq P 11:48p	P	P	P A 12:29p	A	A	A T 12:06a	T	T G 8:43a	G	G C 1:57p	C	C L 5:02p	L	L V 7:03p	V	V Li 10:00p	Li	Li	Li S 1:40a	S	S Sg 6:28a	Sg	Sg Cp 12:49p	Cp	Cp

MOON SIGNS 1910 – 1969

1949	1	2	3	4	5	6	7	8	9	10	11	12	13	14	15	16	17	18	19	20	21	22	23	24	25	26	27	28	29	30	31
Jan	Cp Aq 9:10p	Aq	A P 7:58a	P	P A 8:39p	A	A	A T	T	T G 6:25p	G	G C 11:52p	C	C	C L 2:06a	L	L V 2:52a	V	V Li 4:04a	Li	Li S 7:00a	S	S Sg 12:10p	Sg	Sg Cp 7:24p	Cp	Cp	Cp Aq 4:28a	Aq	Aq P 3:28p	P
Feb	P	P A 4:05a	A	A T 4:55p	T	T	T G 3:37a	G	G C 10:19a	C	C L 12:58p	L	L V 1:06p	V	V Li 12:46p	Li	Li S 1:57p	S	S Sg 5:54p	Sg	Sg	Sg Cp 12:53a	Cp	Cp Aq 10:26a	Aq	Aq P 9:55p	P	P			
Mar	P A 10:36a	A	A T 11:31p	T	T	T G 11:02a	G	G C 7:15p	C	C L 11:28p	L	L	L V 12:21a	V Li 11:40p	Li	Li S 11:29p	S	S	S Sg 1:35a	Sg	Sg Cp 7:37a	Cp	Cp Aq 4:14p	Aq	Aq	Aq P 3:51a	P	P A 4:42p	A	A	A T 5:29a
Apr	T	T G 5:00p	G	G	G C	C	C L 7:58a	L	L V 10:30a	V	V Li 10:55a	Li	Li S 10:29a	S	S Sg 11:27a	Sg	Sg Cp 2:46p	Cp	Cp Aq 11:40p	Aq	Aq	Aq P 10:08a	P	P A 11:00p	A	A	A T 11:39a	T	T G 10:45p	G	
May	G	G C 7:42a	C	C L 2:08p	L	L V 6:07p	V	V Li 8:05p	Li	Li S 8:53p	S	S Sg 10:00p	Sg	Sg	Sg Cp 1:00a	Cp	Cp Aq 7:19a	Aq	Aq P 5:29p	P	P	P A 6:01a	A	A T 6:39p	T	T	T G 5:25a	G	G C 1:36p	C	C L 7:34p
Jn	L	L V 11:52p	V	V	V Li 2:58a	Li	Li S 5:14a	S	S Sg 7:24	Sg	Sg Cp 10:42a	Cp	Cp Aq 4:31p	Aq	Aq	Aq P 1:42a	P	P A 1:45p	A	A	A T 2:28a	T	T G 1:16p	G	G C 8:58p	C	C	C L 1:59a	L	L V 5:26a	
Jly	V	V Li 8:22a	Li	Li S 11:23a	S	S Sg 2:46a	Sg	Sg Cp 7:04p	Cp	Cp	Cp Aq 1:11a	Aq	Aq P 10:02a	P	P A 9:45p	A	A	A T 10:36a	T	T G 9:53p	G	G	G C 5:51a	C	C	L	L V 12:35p	V	V Li 2:21p	Li	Li S 4:46p
Aug	S	S Sg 8:26p	Sg	Sg	Sg Cp 1:37a	Cp	Cp Aq 8:34a	Aq	Aq P 5:49p	P	P	P A 5:20a	A	A T 6:18p	T	T	T G 6:22a	G	G C 3:09p	C	C L 8:02p	L	L V 9:54p	V	V Li 10:25p	Li	Li S 11:21p	S	S	S Sg 2:03a	Sg
Sep	Sg Cp 7:06a	Cp	Cp Aq 2:39p	Aq	Aq	Aq P 12:29a	P	P A 12:13p	A	A	A T 1:11a	T	T G 1:44p	G	G C 11:47p	C	C	C L 6:03a	L	L V 8:32a	V	V Li 8:41a	Li	Li S 8:21a	S	S Sg 9:22a	Sg	Sg Cp 1:11a	Cp	Cp Aq 8:18p	
Oct	Aq	Aq	Aq P 6:21a	P	P A 6:29p	A	A	A T 7:26a	T	T G 8:00p	G	G	G C 6:50a	C	C L 2:30p	L	L V 6:37p	V	V Li 7:44p	Li	Li S 7:19p	S	S Sg 7:11p	Sg	Sg Cp 9:16p	Cp	Cp	Cp Aq 2:54a	Aq	Aq P 12:23p	P
Nov	P	P A 12:34a	A	A T 1:36p	T	T	T G 1:53a	G	G C 12:33p	C	C L 8:56p	L	L	L V 2:40a	V	V Li 5:35a	Li	Li S 6:18a	S	S Sg 6:15a	Sg	Sg Cp 7:20a	Cp	Cp Aq 11:28a	Aq	Aq P 7:40p	P	P	P A 7:18a	A	
Dec	A	A T 8:20p	T	T G 8:28a	G	G C 6:29p	C	C	C L 2:26a	L	L V 8:30a	V	V Li 12:42p	Li	Li S 3:12p	S	S Sg 4:32p	Sg	Sg Cp 6:03p	Cp	Cp Aq 9:30p	Aq	Aq	Aq P 4:22a	P	P A 3:07p	A	A	A T 3:59a	T	T G 4:13p

1950	1	2	3	4	5	6	7	8	9	10	11	12	13	14	15	16	17	18	19	20	21	22	23	24	25	26	27	28	29	30	31
Jan	G	G	G C 1:54a	C	C L 8:56a	L	L V 2:05p	V	V Li 6:07p	Li	Li S 9:26p	S	S	S Sg 12:16a	Sg	Sg Cp 3:07a	Cp	Cp Aq 7:07a	Aq	Aq P 1:46p	P	P A 11:41p	A	A	A T 12:07p	T	T	T G 12:40a	G	G C 10:47a	C
Feb	C L 5:30p	L	L V 9:34p	V	V	V Li 12:18a	Li	Li S 2:50a	S	S Sg 5:52a	Sg	Sg Cp 9:45a	Cp	Cp Aq 2:59p	Aq	Aq P 10:14p	P	P	P A 8:02a	A	A T 8:12p	T	T	T G 9:02a	G	G C 7:58p	C	C			
Mar	C L 3:27a	L	L V 7:23a	V	V Li 8:59a	Li	Li S 8:17a	S	S Sg 11:39a	Sg	Sg Cp 3:11p	Cp	Cp Aq 8:55p	Aq	Aq	Aq P 5:01a	P	P A 3:23p	A	A	A T 3:32a	T	T G 4:26p	G	G	G C 4:15a	C	C L 1:00p	L	L V 5:55p	V
Apr	V Li 7:37p	Li	Li S 7:36p	S	S Sg 7:40p	Sg	Sg Cp 9:34p	Cp	Cp	Cp Aq 2:28p	Aq	Aq P 10:39a	P	P A 9:33p	A	A	A T 9:59a	T	T G 10:54p	G	G	G C 10:59a	C	C L 8:52p	L	L	L V 3:27a	V	V Li 6:25a	Li	
May	Li S 6:38a	S	S Sg 5:51a	Sg	Sg Cp 6:08a	Cp	Cp Aq 9:24a	Aq	Aq P 4:39p	P	P	P A 3:47a	A	A T 3:59p	T	T	T G 4:52a	G	G C 4:48p	C	C	C L 3:04a	L	L V 10:47a	V	V Li 3:21p	Li	Li S 4:58p	S	S Sg 4:43p	Sg
Jn	Sg Cp 4:30p	Cp	Cp Aq 6:25p	Aq	Aq	Aq P 12:02a	P	P A 9:46a	A	A T 10:13p	T	T	T G 11:03a	G	G C 10:43p	C	C	C L 8:36a	L	L V 4:28p	V	V Li 10:06a	Li	Li	Li S 1:16a	S	S Sg 2:25a	Sg	Sg Cp 2:49a	Cp	
Jly	Cp Aq 4:21a	Aq	Aq P 8:52a	P	P A 5:28p	A	A	A T 5:13a	T	T G 6:01p	G	G	G C 5:34a	C	C L 2:50p	L	L V 10:03p	V	V	V Li 3:32a	Li	Li S 7:27a	S	S Sg 9:54a	Sg	Sg Cp 11:39a	Cp	Cp Aq 1:58p	Aq	Aq P 6:24p	P
Aug	P	P A 2:05a	A	A T 1:07p	T	T	T G 1:43a	G	G C 11:28a	C	C L 10:33p	L	L	L V 5:02a	V	V Li 9:30a	Li	Li S 12:48p	S	S Sg 3:35p	Sg	Sg Cp 6:23p	Cp	Cp Aq 9:55p	Aq	Aq	Aq P 3:04a	P	P A 10:47a	A	A T 9:21p
Sep	T	T	T G 9:47a	G	G C 9:51p	C	C	C L 7:33a	L	L V 1:51p	V	V Li 5:25p	Li	Li S 7:26p	S	S Sg 9:13p	Sg	Sg Cp 11:50p	Cp	Cp	Cp Aq 4:01a	Aq	Aq P 10:11a	P	P A 6:34p	A	A	A T 5:09a	T	T G 5:27p	
Oct	G	G	G C 5:58a	C	C L 4:36p	L	L V 11:49p	V	V	V Li 3:26a	Li	Li S 4:44a	S	S Sg 4:45a	Sg	Sg Cp 5:55a	Cp	Cp Aq 9:28a	Aq	Aq P 3:56p	P	P	P A 1:00a	A	A T 12:04p	T	T	T G 12:22a	G	G C 1:02p	C
Nov	C	C L 12:34a	L	L V 9:19a	V	V Li 2:05p	Li	Li S 3:26p	S	S Sg 2:52p	Sg	Sg Cp 2:29p	Cp	Cp Aq 4:20p	Aq	Aq P 9:44p	P	P	P A 6:39a	A	A T 6:09p	T	T	T G 6:38a	G	G C 7:12p	C	C	C L 7:02a	L	
Dec	L V 4:36p	V	V Li 11:36p	Li	Li	Li S 2:29a	S	S Sg 2:15a	Sg	Sg Cp 1:18a	Cp	Cp Aq 1:38a	Aq	Aq P 5:12a	P	P A 1:02p	A	A	A T 12:11a	T	T G 12:48p	G	G	G C 1:17a	C	C L 12:44p	L	L V 10:38p	V	V	V Li 6:20a

1951	1	2	3	4	5	6	7	8	9	10	11	12	13	14	15	16	17	18	19	20	21	22	23	24	25	26	27	28	29	30	31
Jan	Li	Li S 11:00a	S	S Sg 12:36p	Sg	Sg Cp 12:32p	Cp	Cp Aq 12:38p	Aq	Aq P 3:02p	P	P A 8:24p	A	A	A T 7:10a	T	T G 7:36p	G	G	G C 8:06a	C	C	C L 10:17p	L	L V 4:25a	V	V Li 11:45a	Li	Li S 5:47p	S	S Sg 8:13p
Feb	Sg	Sg	Sg Cp 12:13a	Cp Aq 11:05p	Aq	Aq	Aq P 1:32a	P	P A 6:42a	A	A T 3:36p	T	T	T G 3:19a	G	G C 3:49p	C	C	C L 2:59a	L	L V 11:41a	V	V Li 5:54p	Li	Li S 10:29p	S	S	S Sg 1:49a			
Mar	Sg	Sg Cp 4:30a	Cp	Cp Aq 7:10a	Aq	Aq P 10:46a	P	P A 4:20p	A	A	A T 12:35a	T	T G 11:37a	G	G	G C 12:05a	C	C L 11:43a	L	L V 8:34p	V	V	V Li 2:18a	Li	Li S 5:35a	S	S Sg 7:40a	Sg	Sg Cp 9:51a	Cp	Cp Aq 1:04p
Apr	Aq	Aq P 5:47p	P	P	P A 12:18a	A	A T 8:53a	T	T G 7:43p	G	G	G C 8:05a	C	C L 8:14p	L	L	L V 6:07a	V	V Li 12:09p	Li	Li S 2:52p	S	S Sg 3:40p	Sg	Sg Cp 4:22p	Cp	Cp Aq 6:36p	Aq	Aq P 11:16p	P	
May	P	P A 6:27a	A	A T 3:48p	T	T	T G 2:51a	G	G C 2:02p	C	C	C L 3:49a	L	L V 2:40p	V	V Li 9:59p	Li	Li	Li S 1:19a	S	S Sg 1:42a	Sg	Sg Cp 1:08a	Cp	Cp Aq 1:45	Aq	Aq P 5:10a	P	P A 11:55a	A	A T 9:35p
Jn	T	T	T G 9:03a	G	G	G C 9:31a	C	C L 10:11a	L	L V 9:43p	V	V	V Li 6:30a	Li	Li S 11:13a	S	S Sg 12:24p	Sg	Sg Cp 11:38a	Cp	Cp Aq 11:07a	Aq	Aq P 12:53p	P	P A 6:17p	A	A	A T 3:19a	T	T G 2:53p	
Jly	G	G	G C	C	C L 4:00p	L	L	L V 3:35a	V	V Li 1:01p	Li	Li S 7:12p	S	S Sg 9:59p	Sg	Sg Cp 10:13p	Cp	Cp Aq 9:43p	Aq	Aq P 10:33p	P	P	P A 2:24a	A	A T 10:08a	T	T G 9:09p	G	G	G C 9:42a	C
Aug	C L 10:06p	L	L	L V 9:17a	V	V Li 6:30p	Li	Li	Li S 1:21a	S	S Sg 5:29a	Sg	Sg Cp 7:18a	Cp	Cp Aq 7:54a	Aq	Aq P 9:20a	P	P A 12:01p	A	A T 6:31p	T	T	T G 4:28a	G	G C 4:44p	C	C	C L 5:10a	L	L V 3:58p
Sep	V	V	V Li 12:29a	Li	Li S 2:05p	S	S Sg 11:10a	Sg	Sg Cp 2:05p	Cp	Cp Aq 4:12p	Aq	Aq P 6:24p	P	P A 9:50p	A	A	A T 3:44a	T	T G 12:50p	G	G	G C 12:35a	C	C L 1:05p	L	L	L V 12:01a	V	V Li 8:08a	
Oct	Li	Li S 1:21p	S	S Sg 4:47p	Sg	Sg Cp 7:30p	Cp	Cp Aq 10:20p	Aq	Aq	Aq P 1:47a	P	P A 6:19a	A	A T 12:40p	T	T G 9:26p	G	G	G C 8:43a	C	C L 9:23p	L	L	L V 8:59a	V	V Li 5:20p	Li	Li S 10:06p	S	S
Nov	S Sg 12:18a	Sg	Sg Cp 1:40a	Cp	Cp Aq 12:54p	Aq	Aq P 7:23a	P	P A 12:54p	A	A T 8:09p	T	T	T G 5:16a	G	G C 4:30p	C	C	C L 5:12a	L	L V 5:32p	V	V	V Li 3:06a	Li	Li S 7:31a	S	S Sg 10:18a	Sg	Sg Cp 10:23a	
Dec	Cp	Cp Aq 10:46a	Aq	Aq P 1:21p	P	P A 6:22p	A	A	A T 2:05a	T	T G 11:55a	G	G C 11:23p	C	C	C L 12:05p	L	L	L V 12:50a	V	V Li 11:37a	Li	Li S 6:31p	S	S Sg 9:22p	Sg	Sg Cp 9:22p	Cp	Cp Aq 8:38p	Aq	Aq P 9:26p

MOON SIGNS 1910 – 1969

1952

	1	2	3	4	5	6	7	8	9	10	11	12	13	14	15
Jan	P	P	P A 12:47a	A	A T 7:57a	T	T G 6:13p	G	G	G C 6:00a	C	C L 6:42p	L	L	L V 7:12a
Feb	A T 3:06p	T	T	T G 12:19a	G	G C 12:18p	C	C	C L 1:13a	L	L V 1:10p	V	V Li 11:59p	Li	Li
Mar	T	T G 7:36a	G	G C 7:06p	C	C	C L 8:57a	L	L V 8:02p	V	V	V Li 6:27a	Li	Li S 2:25p	S
Apr	G C 2:48a	C	C L 3:45p	L	L	L V 3:50a	V	V Li 1:53p	Li	Li S 9:12p	S	S	S Sg 2:16a	Sg	Sg Cp 6:29a
May	L	L	L V 12:07p	V	V Li 10:27p	Li	Li	Li S 5:32a	S	S Sg 9:45a	Sg	Sg Cp 12:24p	Cp	Cp Aq 2:44p	Aq
Jn	V	V Li 7:34a	Li	Li S 3:15p	S	S Sg 7:20p	Sg	Sg Cp 8:53p	Cp	Cp Aq 9:58p	Aq	Aq	Aq P 11:17p	P	P A 2:48a
Jly	Li	Li S 12:18a	S	S Sg 5:38a	Sg	Sg Cp 7:20a	Cp	Cp Aq 7:10a	Aq	Aq P 7:00a	P	P A 9:05a	A	A T 3:37p	T
Aug	Sg	Sg Cp 5:52p	Cp	Cp Aq 6:20p	Aq	Aq P 5:42p	P	P A 6:08p	A	A T 9:01p	T	T	T G 3:36a	G	G C 2:24p
Sep	Cp Aq 4:25a	Aq	Aq P 4:10a	P	P A 4:10a	A	A T 6:10a	T	T	T G 11:27a	G	G C 8:42p	C	C	C L 9:15a
Oct	P	P A 2:45p	A	A T 4:45p	T	T G 8:42p	G	G	G C 4:34a	C	C L 4:10p	L	L	L V 5:00a	V
Nov	A T 2:14a	T	T G 6:39a	G	G C 1:28p	C	C	C L 12:24a	L	L V 10:42a	V	V Li 10:53p	Li	Li	Li S 8:37a
Dec	G	G C 10:30p	C	C	C L 8:35a	L	L V 9:02p	V	V	V Li 9:36a	Li	Li S 7:56p	S	S	S Sg 2:30a

	16	17	18	19	20	21	22	23	24	25	26	27	28	29	30	31
Jan	V	V Li 6:14p	Li	Li	Li S 2:28a	S	S Sg 7:20a	Sg	Sg Cp 8:38a	Cp	Cp Aq 8:07a	Aq	Aq P 7:59a	P	P A 9:45a	A
Feb	Li S 8:59a	S	S Sg 2:52p	Sg	Sg Cp 5:57p	Cp	Cp Aq 6:49p	Aq	Aq P 6:51p	P	P A 8:05p	A	A T 11:54p	T		
Mar	S Sg 8:30p	Sg	Sg	Sg Cp 12:30a	Cp	Cp Aq 3:20a	Aq	Aq P 4:37a	P	P A 6:21a	A	A T 9:43a	T	T G 4:22p	G	G
Apr	Cp	Cp Aq 9:21a	Aq	Aq P 11:53a	P	P A 3:12p	A	A T 7:21p	T	T	T G 1:49a	G	G C 11:23a	C	C L 11:24p	
May	Aq P 5:26p	P	P A 9:20p	A	A	A T 2:33a	T	T G 9:51a	G	G C 7:29p	C	C	C L 7:12a	L	L V 8:02p	V
Jn	A	A T 8:18a	T	T G 4:31p	G	G	G C 2:41a	C	C L 2:30p	L	L	L V 3:09a	V	V Li 3:21p	Li	
Jly	T G 10:03p	G	G	G C 8:37a	C	C L 8:37p	L	L	L V 9:26a	V	V Li 9:36p	Li	Li	Li S 8:08a	S	S Sg 2:57p
Aug	C	C	C L 2:23a	L	L V 3:04p	V	V	V Li 3:01a	Li	Li S 1:21p	S	S Sg 9:45p	Sg	Sg	Sg Cp 2:41a	Cp
Sep	L V 9:44p	V	V	V Li 9:11a	Li	Li S 7:28p	S	S	S Sg 3:28a	Sg	Sg Cp 9:15a	Cp	Cp Aq 12:48p	Aq	Aq P 1:49p	
Oct	V Li 4:52p	Li	Li	Li S 2:02a	S	S Sg 9:20a	Sg	Sg Cp 2:41p	Cp	Cp Aq 7:17p	Aq	Aq P 9:12p	P	P A 11:27p	A	A
Nov	S	S Sg 4:53p	Sg	Sg Cp 8:55p	Cp	Cp	Cp Aq 12:15a	Aq	Aq P 2:57a	P	P A 5:48a	A	A T 9:49a	T	T G 3:13p	
Dec	Sg	Sg Cp 5:41a	Cp	Cp Aq 7:20a	Aq	Aq P 9:00a	P	P A 11:21a	A	A T 3:53p	T	T G 9:58p	G	G	G C 6:15a	C

1953

	1	2	3	4	5	6	7	8	9	10	11	12	13	14	15
Jan	C L 4:34p	L	L	L V 4:36a	V	V Li 5:30p	Li	Li	Li S 4:53a	S	S Sg 12:29p	Sg	Sg Cp 4:11p	Cp	Cp Aq 5:10p
Feb	V	V	V Li 12:24a	Li	Li S 12:19p	S	S Sg 9:36p	Sg	Sg	Sg Cp 2:23a	Cp	Cp Aq 4:08a	Aq	Aq P 3:53a	P
Mar	V	V Li 6:24a	Li	Li S 6:31p	S	S	S Sg 4:53a	Sg	Sg Cp 11:12a	Cp	Cp Aq 2:38p	Aq	Aq P 2:54p	P	P A 2:14p
Apr	Li S 12:27a	S	S Sg 10:33a	Sg	Sg Cp 5:56p	Cp	Cp Aq 10:46p	Aq	Aq	Aq P 12:38a	P	P A 1:00a	A	A T 1:33a	T
May	Sg	Sg Cp 11:11p	Cp	Cp	Cp Aq 4:30a	Aq	Aq P 7:51a	P	P A 9:48a	A	A T 11:18a	T	T G 1:44p	G	G C 6:36p
Jn	Cp Aq 9:45a	Aq	Aq P 1:25p	P	P A 3:58p	A	A T 5:43p	T	T G 9:22p	G	G	G C 2:30a	C	C L 10:30a	L
Jly	P	P A 9:12p	A	A	A T 1:29a	T	T G 5:04a	G	G C 11:25a	C	C L 7:52p	L	L	L V 6:14a	V
Aug	A T 5:50a	T	T G 10:26a	G	G C 5:14p	C	C	C L 2:23a	L	L V 1:19p	V	V	V Li 1:45a	Li	Li S 2:33p
Sep	G C 10:38p	C	C	C L 8:11a	L	L V 8:00p	V	V	V Li 8:00a	Li	Li S 8:44p	S	S	S Sg 8:22a	Sg
Oct	C L 2:02p	L	L	L V 1:39a	V	V Li 2:20p	Li	Li	Li S 2:48a	S	S Sg 2:24p	Sg	Sg Cp 11:41p	Cp	Cp
Nov	V	V Li 9:02p	Li	Li	Li S 9:22a	S	S Sg 8:15p	Sg	Sg	Sg Cp 5:29a	Cp	Cp Aq 12:23p	Aq	Aq P 2:53p	P
Dec	Li	Li S 4:53p	S	S	S Sg 3:33a	Sg	Sg Cp 12:06p	Cp	Cp Aq 6:01p	Aq	Aq P 10:36p	P	P	P A 1:54a	A

	16	17	18	19	20	21	22	23	24	25	26	27	28	29	30	31
Jan	Aq	Aq P 5:19p	P	P A 6:17p	A	A T 9:27p	T	T	T G 3:32a	G	G C 12:25p	C	C L 11:28p	L	L	L V 11:27a
Feb	P A 3:32a	A	A T 4:52a	T	T G 9:47a	G	G C 6:09p	C	C	C L 5:37a	L	L V 5:59p	V			
Mar	A	A T 2:44p	T	T G 5:51p	G	G	G C 12:42a	C	C L 11:59a	L	L	L V 12:18a	V	V Li 12:51p	Li	Li
Apr	T G 3:47a	G	G C 9:04a	C	C L 6:53p	L	L	L V 7:12a	V	V Li 8:00p	Li	Li	Li S 7:12a	S	S Sg 4:09a	
May	C	C	C L 2:57a	L	L V 2:36p	V	V	V Li 3:12a	Li	Li S 2:36p	S	S Sg 11:26p	Sg	Sg	Sg Cp 5:32a	Cp
Jn	L V 10:32p	V	V	V Li 11:06a	Li	Li S 11:15p	S	S	S Sg 8:17a	Sg	Sg Cp 1:37p	Cp	Cp Aq 5:03p	Aq	Aq P 7:12p	
Jly	V Li 6:48p	Li	Li	Li S 7:12a	S	S Sg 3:19p	Sg	Sg Cp 11:28p	Cp	Cp	Cp Aq 2:13a	Aq	Aq P 3:15a	P	P A 4:07a	A
Aug	S	S	S Sg 1:38a	Sg	Sg Cp 9:16a	Cp	Cp Aq 12:21p	Aq	Aq P 1:22p	P	P A 12:53p	A	A T 1:28p	T	T G 4:30p	G
Sep	Sg Cp 5:33p	Cp	Cp Aq 10:10p	Aq	Aq P 11:57p	P	P	P A 3:31a	A T 11:41p	T	T	T G 12:35a	G	G C 5:13a	C	
Oct	Cp Aq 6:18a	Aq	Aq P 9:39a	P	P A 10:27a	A	A T 10:04a	T	T G 10:52a	G	G C 1:55p	C	C L 9:14p	L	L	L V 8:01a
Nov	P A 7:19p	A	A T 8:25p	T	T G 9:18p	G	G C 11:59p	C	C	C L 5:53a	L	L V 3:48p	V	V	V Li 4:22a	
Dec	A T 4:25a	T	T G 6:40a	G	G C 10:00a	C	C L 3:37p	L	L	L V 12:15a	V	V Li 12:18p	Li	Li	Li S 1:07a	S

1954

	1	2	3	4	5	6	7	8	9	10	11	12	13	14	15
Jan	S Sg 12:18p	Sg	Sg Cp 8:06p	Cp	Cp	Cp Aq 1:01a	Aq	Aq P 4:59a	P	P A 7:31a	A	A T 10:15a	T	T G 1:40p	G
Feb	Cp	Cp Aq 10:26a	Aq	Aq P 12:59p	P	P A 2:25p	A	A T 4:11p	T	T G 7:21p	G	G	G C 12:36a	C	C L 7:30a
Mar	Cp Aq 8:44p	Aq	Aq P 11:01p	P	P A 11:26p	A	A T 11:50p	T	T	T G 1:30a	G	G C 6:08a	C	C L 1:25p	L
Apr	P	P A 10:13a	A	A T 9:51a	T	T G 9:59a	G	G C 12:52p	C	C L 7:22p	L	L	L V 5:14a	V	V Li 5:23p
May	A T 8:35p	T	T 8:15p	G	G C 9:43p	C	C	C L 2:28a	L	L V 11:11a	V	V Li 11:20p	Li	Li	Li S 12:12p
Jn	G	G C 7:51a	C	C L 11:31a	L	L V 6:55p	V	V	V Li 6:00a	Li	Li S 7:06p	S	S	S Sg 7:00a	Sg
Jly	C L 9:20p	L	L	L V 3:32a	V	V Li 1:45p	Li	Li	Li S 2:23a	S	S Sg 2:39p	Sg	Sg	Sg Cp 12:54a	Cp
Aug	V	V Li 9:57p	Li	Li	Li S 10:01a	S	S Sg 10:52p	Sg	Sg	Sg Cp 9:27a	Cp	Cp Aq 4:44p	Aq	Aq P 9:10p	P
Sep	Li S 5:41p	S	S	S Sg 6:23a	Sg	Sg Cp 6:08p	Cp	Cp	Cp Aq 2:28a	Aq	Aq P 7:00a	P	P A 8:27a	A	A T 9:17a
Oct	S Sg 1:31p	Sg	Sg	Sg Cp 1:53a	Cp	Cp Aq 11:25a	Aq	Aq P 5:08p	P	P A 7:01p	A	A T 7:17p	T	T G 6:51p	G
Nov	Cp Aq 7:00p	Aq	Aq	Aq	Aq P 2:24a	P	P A 5:58a	A	A T 6:04a	T	T G 5:36a	G	G C 5:36a	C	C L 8:45a
Dec	Aq	Aq P 9:21a	P	P A 2:25p	A	A T 4:32p	T	T G 4:29p	G	G C 4:28p	C	C L 6:20p	L	L V 11:07p	V

	16	17	18	19	20	21	22	23	24	25	26	27	28	29	30	31
Jan	G C 6:22p	C	C	C L 12:20a	L	L V 8:57a	V	V Li 8:30p	Li	Li	Li S 9:03a	S	S Sg 8:50p	Sg	Sg	Sg Cp 5:33a
Feb	L	L V 4:50p	V	V	V Li 4:11a	Li	Li S 4:34p	S	S	S Sg 5:00a	Sg	Sg Cp 2:49p	Cp			
Mar	L V 11:31p	V	V	V Li 11:02a	Li	Li S 11:29p	S	S	S Sg 12:09p	Sg	Sg Cp 11:01p	Cp	Cp	Cp Aq 6:18a	Aq	Aq P 9:50a
Apr	Li	Li	Li S 5:59a	S	S Sg 6:18p	Sg	Sg	Sg Cp 5:38a	Cp	Cp Aq 2:14p	Aq	Aq P 7:21p	P	P A 8:53p	A	
May	S	S	S Sg 12:12a	Sg	Sg Cp 11:03a	Cp	Cp Aq 7:55p	Aq	Aq	Aq P 2:12a	P	P A 5:31a	A	A T 7:00a	T	T G 6:50a
Jn	Sg Cp 5:19p	Cp	Cp	Cp Aq 1:28a	Aq	Aq P 7:43a	P	P A 11:50a	A	A T 2:46p	T	T G 4:17p	G	G C 6:10p	C	
Jly	Cp Aq 8:15a	Aq	Aq P 1:16p	P	P A 7:13p	A	A T 11:53p	T	T	T G 2:36a	G	G C 5:48a	C	C L 10:10a	L	L V 3:09p
Aug	P A 11:34p	A	A	A T 1:33a	T	T G 4:13a	G	G C 8:04a	C	C L 1:31p	L	L 8:41p	V	V	V Li 6:03a	Li
Sep	T	T G 10:21a	G	G C 1:25p	C	C L 7:05p	L	L	L V 3:12a	V	V Li 1:07p	Li	Li	Li S 12:57a	S	
Oct	G C 8:21p	C	C	C L 12:44a	L	L V 8:55a	V	V Li 7:13p	Li	Li	Li S 7:24a	S	S Sg 7:55p	Sg	Sg	Sg Cp 8:12a
Nov	L	L V 2:50p	V	V	V Li 1:13a	Li	Li S 1:40p	S	S	S Sg 2:23a	Sg	Sg Cp 2:04p	Cp	Cp	Cp Aq 1:00a	
Dec	V	V Li 8:11a	Li	Li S 8:20p	S	S	S Sg 8:48a	Sg	Sg Cp 8:46p	Cp	Cp	Cp Aq 6:49a	Aq	Aq P 2:56p	P	P

MOON SIGNS 1910 – 1969

1955

	1	2	3	4	5	6	7	8	9	10	11	12	13	14	15	16	17	18	19	20	21	22	23	24	25	26	27	28	29	30	31
Jan	A	A	A T 12:29a	T	T G 1:59a	G	G C 3:06a	C	C L 4:43a	L	L V 8:49a	V	V Li 4:12p	Li	Li	Li S 3:48a	S	S Sg 4:24p	Sg	Sg	Sg Cp 4:25a	Cp	Cp Aq 1:41p	Aq	Aq P 8:53p	P	P	P A 2:32a	A	A T	T
Feb	T G 9:09a	G	G C 11:34a	C	C L 2:20p	L	L V 6:31p	V	V	V Li 1:14a	Li	Li S 11:48a	S	S	S Sg 12:35a	Sg	Sg Cp 12:43p	Cp	Cp Aq 10:23p	Aq	Aq	Aq P 5:00a	P	P A 9:04a	A	A T 12:05p	T	T G 2:52p			
Mar	G	G C 5:47p	C	C L 9:43p	L	L	L V 3:02a	V	V Li 10:13a	Li	Li S 8:17a	S	S	S Sg 8:02a	Sg	Sg Cp 9:00p	Cp	Cp	Cp Aq 7:34a	Aq	Aq P 2:30p	P	P A 5:48p	A	A T 7:39p	T	T G 9:04p	G	G C 11:18p	C	C
Apr	C L 3:29a	L	L V 9:37a	V	V Li 5:47p	Li	Li	Li S 4:04a	S	S Sg 3:57p	Sg	Sg	Sg Cp 4:59a	Cp	Cp Aq 4:30p	Aq	Aq	Aq P 12:19a	P	P A 4:25a	A	A T 5:23a	T	T G 5:43a	G	G C 6:22a	C	C L 9:08a	L	L V 3:03p	
May	V	V Li 11:39p	Li	Li	Li S 10:21a	S	S Sg 10:36p	Sg	Sg	Sg Cp 11:17a	Cp	Cp Aq 11:24p	Aq	Aq	Aq P 9:11a	P	P A 2:16p	A	A T 4:15p	T	T G 3:59p	G	G C 3:40p	C	C L 4:53p	L	L V 9:11p	V	V	V Li 5:07a	Li
Jn	Li S 4:24p	S	S	S Sg 4:49a	Sg	Sg Cp 5:18p	Cp	Cp	Cp Aq 5:13a	Aq	Aq P 3:35p	P	P A 10:35p	A	A	A T 2:18a	T	T G 2:43a	G	G C 2:25a	C	C L 2:38a	L	L V 5:29a	V	V Li 11:56a	Li	Li S 10:32p	S	S	
Jly	S Sg 10:51a	Sg	Sg Cp 11:24p	Cp	Cp	Cp Aq 10:49a	Aq	Aq P 8:55p	P	P	P A 4:49a	A	A T 9:53a	T	T G 12:05p	G	G C 12:43p	C	C L 1:06p	L	L V 3:11p	V	V Li 8:18p	Li	Li	Li S 5:28a	S	S Sg 5:41p	Sg	Sg	Sg Cp 6:36a
Aug	Cp	Cp Aq 5:19p	Aq	Aq	Aq P 2:33a	P	P A 10:03a	A	A T 3:04p	T	T G 6:51p	G	G C 8:50p	C	C L 10:44p	L	L	L V 1:11a	V	V Li 5:32a	Li	Li S 1:38p	S	S	S Sg 1:19a	Sg	Sg Cp 1:55p	Cp	Cp	Cp Aq 1:23a	Aq
Sep	Aq P 10:09a	P	P A 4:23p	A	A T 8:49p	T	T	T G 12:12a	G	G C 2:50a	C	C L 5:50a	L	L V 9:38a	V	V Li 2:49p	Li	Li S 10:33p	S	S	S Sg 9:01a	Sg	Sg Cp 10:22p	Cp	Cp	Cp Aq 10:08a	Aq	Aq P 7:16p	P	P	
Oct	P A 12:53a	A	A T 4:18a	T	T G 6:21a	G	G C 8:21a	C	C L 11:23a	L	L V 4:04p	V	V Li 10:26p	Li	Li	Li S 6:49a	S	S Sg 5:07p	Sg	Sg	Sg Cp 5:36a	Cp	Cp Aq 6:18p	Aq	Aq	Aq P 4:42a	P	P A 11:07a	A	A T 1:50p	T
Nov	T G 2:53p	G	G C 3:39p	C	C L 5:21p	L	L V 9:39p	V	V	V Li 4:27a	Li	Li S 1:28p	S	S	S Sg 12:37a	Sg	Sg Cp 12:48p	Cp	Cp	Cp Aq 1:21a	Aq	Aq P 12:54p	P	P A 8:47p	A	A	A T 12:35a	T	T G 1:26a	G	
Dec	G C 1:10a	C	C L 1:26a	L	L V 4:05a	V	V Li 10:02a	Li	Li S 7:24p	S	S	S Sg 7:00a	Sg	Sg Cp 7:19p	Cp	Cp	Cp Aq 8:00a	Aq	Aq P 7:47p	P	P	P A 5:08a	A	A T 10:26a	T	T G 12:27p	G	G C 12:11p	C	C L 11:41a	L

1956

	1	2	3	4	5	6	7	8	9	10	11	12	13	14	15	16	17	18	19	20	21	22	23	24	25	26	27	28	29	30	31
Jan	L V 1:00p	V	V Li 5:11p	Li	Li	Li S 1:38a	S	S Sg 1:16p	Sg	Sg	Sg Cp 1:55a	Cp	Cp Aq 2:33p	Aq	Aq	Aq P 1:53a	P	P A 11:19a	A	A T 6:17p	T	T G 9:50p	G	G C 10:58p	C	C L 10:58p	L	L V 11:20p	V	V	V Li 2:14a
Feb	Li	Li S 9:06a	S	S Sg 7:49p	Sg	Sg	Sg Cp 8:38a	Cp	Cp Aq 9:00p	Aq	Aq	Aq P 8:09a	P	P A 4:57p	A	A	A T 12:12a	T	T G 4:45a	G	G C 7:47a	C	C L 8:38a	L	L V 9:50a	V	V Li 12:32p	Li	Li S 6:11p		
Mar	S	S	S Sg 3:37a	Sg	Sg Cp 3:49p	Cp	Cp	Cp Aq 4:36a	Aq	Aq P 3:23p	P	P A 11:48p	A	A	A T 5:57a	T	T G 10:37a	G	G C 1:39p	C	C L 4:21p	L	L V 6:51p	V	V Li 10:08p	Li	Li	Li S 3:42a	S	S Sg 12:04p	Sg
Apr	Sg Cp 11:44p	Cp	Cp	Cp Aq 12:48p	Aq	Aq P 11:59p	P	P	P A 7:55a	A	A T 1:28p	T	T G 4:42p	G	G C 7:31p	C	C L 10:03p	L	L	L V 1:28a	V	V Li 6:08a	Li	Li S 12:24p	S	S Sg 8:44p	Sg	Sg	Sg Cp 8:00a	Cp	
May	Cp Aq 8:19p	Aq	Aq	Aq P 8:33a	P	P A 5:14p	A	A T 10:24p	T	T	T G 1:01a	G	G C 2:12a	C	C L 3:38a	L	L V 6:39a	V	V Li 11:45a	Li	Li S 7:00a	S	S	S Sg 4:16a	Sg	Sg Cp 3:17p	Cp	Cp	Cp Aq 3:46a	Aq	Aq P 4:15p
Jn	P	P	P A 2:37a	A	A T 8:33a	T	T G 11:21a	G	G C 11:38a	C	C L 11:34a	L	L V 1:13p	V	V Li 5:24p	Li	Li	Li S 12:27a	S	S Sg 10:33a	Sg	Sg Cp 9:50p	Cp	Cp	Cp Aq 10:16a	Aq	Aq P 11:12p	P	P	P A 10:15a	
Jly	A	A T 5:39p	T	T G 9:24p	G	G C 10:25p	C	C L 9:45p	L	L V 9:41p	V	V	V Li 12:10a	Li	Li S 6:16a	S	S Sg 3:57p	Sg	Sg	Sg Cp 3:48a	Cp	Cp Aq 4:29p	Aq	Aq	Aq P 4:49a	P	P A 4:12p	A	A	A T 1:09a	T
Aug	T G 6:29a	G	G C 8:27a	C	C L 8:25a	L	L V 8:08a	V	V Li 9:13a	Li	Li S 1:45p	S	S Sg 9:54p	Sg	Sg	Sg Cp 9:51a	Cp	Cp Aq 10:44p	Aq	Aq	Aq P 10:56a	P	P A 9:38p	A	A	A T 6:38a	T	T G 1:08p	G	G L 4:51p	L
Sep	C L 6:18p	L	L V 6:41p	V	V Li 7:38p	Li	Li S 11:01p	S	S	S Sg 5:43a	Sg	Sg Cp 4:48p	Cp	Cp	Cp Aq 5:50a	Aq	Aq P 5:44p	P	P	P A 4:17a	A	A T 12:19p	T	T G 6:27p	G	G C 10:46p	C	C	C L 1:50a	L	
Oct	L V 3:41a	V	V Li 5:41a	Li	Li S 8:46a	S	S Sg 3:00p	Sg	Sg	Sg Cp 12:46a	Cp	Cp Aq 1:16p	Aq	Aq	Aq P 1:55a	P	P A 12:14p	A	A T 7:26p	T	T	T G 12:31a	G	G C 4:31a	C	C L 7:21a	L	L V 10:14a	V	V Li 1:26p	Li
Nov	Li S 5:56p	S	S	S Sg 12:14a	Sg	Sg Cp 9:33a	Cp	Cp Aq 9:08p	Aq	Aq	Aq P 10:11a	P	P A 9:06p	A	A	A T 4:50a	T	T G 9:02a	G	G C 11:36a	C	C L 1:11p	L	L V 3:51p	V	V Li 7:33p	Li	Li	Li S 12:56p	S	
Dec	S Sg 8:08a	Sg	Sg Cp 5:44p	Cp	Cp	Cp Aq 5:00a	Aq	Aq P 5:53p	P	P	P A 6:00a	A	A T 2:27p	T	T G 7:06p	G	G C 8:58p	C	C L 9:21p	L	L V 10:27p	V	V	V Li 1:16a	Li	Li S 6:29a	S	S Sg 2:38p	Sg	Sg	Sg Cp 12:43a

1957

	1	2	3	4	5	6	7	8	9	10	11	12	13	14	15	16	17	18	19	20	21	22	23	24	25	26	27	28	29	30	31
Jan	Cp	Cp Aq 12:18p	Aq	Aq	Aq P 12:57a	P	P A 1:01p	A	A T 11:23p	T	T	T G 5:27a	G	G C 7:58a	C	C L 7:48a	L	L V 7:29a	V	V Li 8:22a	Li	Li S 12:44p	S	S Sg 8:20p	Sg	Sg	Sg Cp 6:37a	Cp	Cp Aq 6:48p	Aq	Aq
Feb	Aq P 7:29a	P	P A 7:49p	A	A	A T 6:37a	T	T G 2:25p	G	G C 5:59p	C	C L 6:58p	L	L V 6:27p	V	V Li 6:20p	Li	Li S 8:45p	S	S	S Sg 2:45a	Sg	Sg Cp 12:48p	Cp	Cp	Cp Aq 1:16a	Aq	Aq P 1:43p			
Mar	P	P	P A 1:51a	A	A T 12:44p	T	T G 9:06p	G	G	G C 2:31a	C	C L 5:02a	L	L V 4:55a	V	V Li 5:05a	Li	Li S 6:31a	S	S Sg 11:04a	Sg	Sg Cp 7:47	Cp	Cp	Cp Aq 7:49a	Aq	Aq P 8:30p	P	P	P A 8:22a	A
Apr	A T 6:24p	T	T	T G 2:44a	G	G C 8:35a	C	C L 12:26p	L	L V 12:14p	V	V Li 3:17p	Li	Li S 5:00p	S	S Sg 8:52p	Sg	Sg	Sg Cp 4:00a	Cp	Cp Aq 3:24p	Aq	Aq	Aq P 3:59a	P	P A 3:59p	A	A	A T 1:42a	T	
May	T G 8:37a	G	G C 2:00p	C	C L 5:52p	L	L V 8:46p	V	V Li 11:11p	Li	Li	Li S 2:17a	S	S Sg 6:08a	Sg	Sg Cp 1:05p	Cp	Cp Aq 11:03p	Aq	Aq	Aq P 11:39a	P	P	P A 12:08a	A	A T 9:56a	T	T G 4:47p	G	G C 8:44p	C
Jn	C L 11:37p	L	L	L V 2:17a	V	V Li 5:10a	Li	Li S 9:08a	S	S Sg 2:18p	Sg	Sg Cp 9:42p	Cp	Cp	Cp Aq 7:24a	Aq	Aq P 7:19p	P	P	P A 8:23a	A	A T 7:00p	T	T	T G 2:24a	G	G C 5:41a	C	C L 7:30a	L	
Jly	L V 8:28a	V	V Li 10:35a	Li	Li S 2:25p	S	S Sg 8:29p	Sg	Sg	Sg Cp 4:23a	Cp	Cp Aq 2:53p	Aq	Aq	Aq P 2:46a	P	P A 3:28p	A	A	A T 3:14a	T	T G 11:50a	G	G C 3:58p	C	C L 5:24p	L	L V 5:24p	V	V Li 5:54p	Li
Aug	Li S 8:02p	S	S	S Sg 1:44a	Sg	Sg Cp 10:08a	Cp	Cp Aq 9:10p	Aq	Aq	Aq P 9:02a	P	P A 9:46p	A	A	A T 10:08a	T	T G 7:50p	G	G	G C 1:45a	C	C L 3:52a	L	L V 3:51a	V	V Li 3:15a	Li	Li S 4:24a	S	S Sg 8:06a
Sep	Sg	Sg Cp 3:51p	Cp	Cp	Cp Aq 2:59a	Aq	Aq P 3:28p	P	P	P A 3:46a	A	A T 3:57p	T	T	T G 2:22a	G	G C 9:40a	C	C L 1:40p	L	L V 2:22p	V	V Li 2:05p	Li	Li S 2:14p	S	S Sg 4:48p	Sg	Sg Cp 10:56p	Cp	
Oct	Cp	Cp Aq 9:01a	Aq	Aq P 9:44p	P	P	P A 10:14a	A	A T 9:45p	T	T	T G 7:56a	G	G C 3:37p	C	C L 8:55p	L	L V 11:34p	V	V	V Li 12:31a	Li	Li S 12:56a	S	S Sg 2:50a	Sg	Sg Cp 7:34a	Cp	Cp Aq 4:31p	Aq	Aq
Nov	Aq P 4:45a	P	P A 5:30p	A	A	A T 4:44a	T	T G 2:05p	G	G C 9:23p	C	C	C L 2:39a	L	L V 6:40a	V	V Li 8:31a	Li	Li S 10:31a	S	S Sg 1:11p	Sg	Sg Cp 5:29p	Cp	Cp	Cp Aq 1:08a	Aq	Aq P 12:30p	P	P	
Dec	P A 1:25a	A	A T 1:00p	T	T G 10:06p	G	G	G C 4:12a	C	C L 8:44a	L	L V 12:05p	V	V Li 2:32p	Li	Li S 5:48p	S	S Sg 9:37p	Sg	Sg	Sg Cp 2:42a	Cp	Cp Aq 10:07a	Aq	Aq P 8:53p	P	P	P A 9:27a	A	A T 9:38p	T

MOON SIGNS 1910 – 1969

1958

	1	2	3	4	5	6	7	8	9	10	11	12	13	14	15	16
Jan	T	T G 7:33a	G	G C 1:16p	C	C L 4:37p	L	L V 6:35p	V	V Li 8:35p	Li	Li S 11:28p	S	S	S Sg 3:56a	Sg
Feb	C	C	C L 2:29a	L	L V 3:32a	V	V Li 4:17a	Li	Li S 5:31a	S	S Sg 9:41a	Sg	Sg Cp 4:17p	Cp	Cp	Cp Aq 1:05a
Mar	C	C L 1:03p	L	L V 2:14p	V	V Li 1:43p	Li	Li S 1:56p	S	S Sg 4:19p	Sg	Sg Cp 9:51p	Cp	Cp	Cp Aq 6:49a	Aq
Apr	L V 12:49a	V	V Li 12:56a	Li	Li S 12:20a	S	S Sg 1:20a	Sg	Sg Cp 4:55a	Cp	Cp Aq 1:05p	Aq	Aq	Aq P 12:27a	P	P A 1:04p
May	Li	Li S 10:53a	S	S Sg 11:34a	Sg	Sg Cp 2:14p	Cp	Cp Aq 8:29p	Aq	Aq	Aq P 7:00a	P	P	P A 7:37p	A	A T 8:00a
Jn	Sg	Sg	Sg Cp 12:19a	Cp	Cp Aq 5:33a	Aq	Aq P 2:43p	P	P	P A 2:46a	A	A T 3:28p	T	T	T G 2:33a	G
Jly	Cp	Cp Aq 2:54p	Aq	Aq P 11:08p	P	P	P A 10:39a	A	A T 11:25p	T	T	T G 10:53a	G	G C 7:11p	C	C
Aug	Aq P 7:24a	P	P A 6:24p	A	A	A T 6:48a	T	T G 7:07p	G	G	G C 4:45a	C	C L 9:45a	L	L V 12:27p	V
Sep	A	A T 2:11p	T	T	T G 2:51a	G	G C 1:22p	C	C L 7:57p	L	L V 10:47p	V	V Li 11:14p	Li	Li S 11:04p	S
Oct	T	T G 9:36a	G	G C 8:50p	C	C	C L 5:10a	L	L V 9:09a	V	V Li 10:18a	Li	Li S 9:40a	S	S Sg 9:37a	Sg
Nov	G C 2:43a	C	C L 12:19p	L	L V 5:47p	V	V Li 8:33p	Li	Li S 8:39p	S	S Sg 8:22p	Sg	Sg Cp 9:16p	Cp	Cp	Cp Aq 1:18a
Dec	L	L	L V 12:30a	V	V Li 4:41a	Li	Li S 6:22a	S	S Sg 7:00a	Sg	Sg Cp 8:00a	Cp	Cp Aq 11:04a	Aq	Aq P 5:35p	P

	17	18	19	20	21	22	23	24	25	26	27	28	29	30	31
Jan	Sg Cp 10:10a	Cp	Cp Aq 6:18p	Aq	Aq	Aq P 4:39a	P	P A 5:05p	A	A	A T 5:59a	T	T G 4:27p	G	G C 11:21p
Feb	Aq	Aq P 11:57a	P	P	P A 12:09a	A	A T 12:54p	T	T	T G 12:43a	G	G C 9:08a			
Mar	Aq P 6:18p	P	P	P A 6:48a	A	A T 7:06p	T	T	T G 7:12a	G	G C 4:38p	C	C L 10:40p	L	L
Apr	A	A	A T 1:33a	T	T G 12:54p	G	G C 10:49p	C	C	C L 6:05a	L	L V 10:00a	V	V Li 11:24a	
May	T	T G 6:55p	G	G	G C 4:11a	C	C L 11:10a	L	L V 4:20p	V	V Li 7:26p	Li	Li S 8:33p	S	S Sg 10:01p
Jn	G C 10:44a	C	C L 5:02p	L	L V 9:41p	V	V	V Li 1:11a	Li	Li S 3:27a	S	S Sg 6:31a	Sg	Sg Cp 9:47a	
Jly	C L 12:37a	L	L V 3:56a	V	V Li 6:21a	Li	Li S 8:45a	S	S Sg 12:22p	Sg	Sg Cp 5:02p	Cp	Cp Aq 11:15p	Aq	Aq
Aug	V Li 1:41p	Li	Li S 2:44p	S	S Sg 5:34p	Sg	Sg Cp 10:30p	Cp	Cp	Cp Aq 5:32a	Aq	Aq P 2:50p	P	P	P A 1:51a
Sep	S	S Sg 12:21a	Sg	Sg Cp 4:04a	Cp	Cp Aq 10:59a	Aq	Aq P 8:57p	P	P	P A 8:13a	A	A T 8:44p	T	
Oct	Sg Cp 11:31a	Cp	Cp Aq 5:08p	Aq	Aq	Aq P 2:22a	P	P A 2:30p	A	A	A T 3:09a	T	T G 3:20p	G	G
Nov	Aq	Aq P 8:57a	P	P A 8:49p	A	A	A T 9:27a	T	T G 9:53p	G	G	G C 8:44a	C	C L 5:53p	
Dec	P	P A 4:02a	A	A T 4:53p	T	T	T G 5:12a	G	G C 3:35p	C	C L 11:47p	L	L	L V 5:57a	V

1959

	1	2	3	4	5	6	7	8	9	10	11	12	13	14	15	16
Jan	V Li 10:39a	Li	Li S 1:47p	S	S Sg 3:41p	Sg	Sg Cp 5:48p	Cp	Cp Aq 9:07p	Aq	Aq	Aq P 2:56a	P	P A 12:21p	A	A
Feb	S Sg 10:10p	Sg	Sg	Sg Cp 1:30a	Cp	Cp Aq 5:48a	Aq	Aq P 12:11p	P	P A 9:14p	A	A	A T 8:37a	T	T G 9:32p	G
Mar	S Sg 3:40a	Sg	Sg Cp 7:11a	Cp	Cp Aq 12:36p	Aq	Aq P 6:59p	P	P	P A 5:14a	A	A T 4:29p	T	T	T G 5:12a	G
Apr	Cp Aq 6:11p	Aq	Aq	Aq P 2:16a	P	P A 12:09p	A	A T 11:44p	T	T	T G 12:27p	G	G	G C 12:45a	C	C L 11:08a
May	Aq P 7:12a	P	P A 5:54p	A	A	A T 6:00a	T	T G 6:36p	G	G	G C 7:00a	C	C L 5:52p	L	L	L V 1:47a
Jn	A	A T 11:56a	T	T	T G 12:37a	G	G C 12:45p	C	C L 11:18p	L	L	L V 8:06a	V	V Li 1:47p	Li	Li S 4:32p
Jly	T	T G 7:12a	G	G C 7:07a	C	C	C L 5:17a	L	L V 1:19p	V	V Li 7:21p	Li	Li S 11:24p	S	S	S Sg 1:42a
Aug	G C 2:31a	C	C L 12:21p	L	L V 7:26p	V	V	V Li 12:53a	Li	Li S 4:35a	S	S Sg 7:41a	Sg	Sg Cp 10:14a	Cp	Cp Aq 1:13p
Sep	L	L V 3:44a	V	V Li 8:01a	Li	Li S 10:42a	S	S Sg 1:03p	Sg	Sg Cp 4:07p	Cp	Cp Aq 7:47p	Aq	Aq	Aq P 1:17a	P
Oct	V Li 5:03p	Li	Li S 6:56p	S	S Sg 9:03p	Sg	Sg Cp 9:43p	Cp	Cp	Cp Aq 1:14a	Aq	Aq P 7:22a	P	P A 3:21p	A	A
Nov	S	S Sg 5:05a	Sg	Sg Cp 5:23a	Cp	Cp Aq 7:32a	Aq	Aq P 1:01p	P	P A 9:18p	A	A	A T 8:11a	T	T G 8:07p	G
Dec	Sg Cp 3:37p	Cp	Cp Aq 4:21p	Aq	Aq P 7:49p	P	P	P A 3:23a	A	A	A T 2:08p	T	T G 2:33a	G	G C 3:04p	C

	17	18	19	20	21	22	23	24	25	26	27	28	29	30	31
Jan	A T 12:45a	T	T G 1:16p	G	G C 11:46p	C	C	C L 7:33a	L	L V 12:27p	V	V Li 4:23p	Li	Li S 7:06p	S
Feb	G	G C 8:54a	C	C L 4:42p	L	L V 9:04p	V	V Li 11:44p	Li	Li	Li S 1:22a	S			
Mar	G C 5:28p	C	C	C L 2:21a	L	L V 10:30a	V	V Li 9:25a	Li	Li S 9:36a	S	S Sg 10:39a	Sg	Sg Cp 12:54p	Cp
Apr	L	L V 5:20p	V	V Li 8:03p	Li	Li S 8:16p	S	S Sg 7:49p	Sg	Sg Cp 8:35p	Cp	Cp	Cp Aq 12:28a	Aq	
May	V	V Li 6:00a	Li	Li S 7:10a	S	S Sg 6:24a	Sg	Sg Cp 6:22a	Cp	Cp Aq 8:45a	Aq	Aq P 2:27p	P	P	P A 12:08a
Jn	S	S Sg 4:59p	Sg	Sg Cp 5:07p	Cp	Cp Aq 6:20p	Aq	Aq P 10:42p	P	P	P A 6:37a	A	A T 6:36p	T	
Jly	Sg	Sg Cp 2:54a	Cp	Cp Aq 4:41a	Aq	Aq P 8:05a	P	P A 3:12p	A	A	A T 1:51a	T	T G 2:37p	G	G
Aug	Aq	Aq P 5:19p	P	P	P A 12:09a	A	A T 9:38a	T	T G 10:13p	G	G	G C 11:07a	C	C L 8:59p	L
Sep	P A 8:31a	A	A T 6:03p	T	T	T G 6:00a	G	G C 6:48p	C	C	C L 5:50a	L	L V 1:32p	V	
Oct	A T 1:42a	T	T G 1:28p	G	G	G C 2:10a	C	C L 2:10p	L	L V 10:57p	V	V	V Li 3:44a	Li	Li S 5:13a
Nov	G	G C 8:38a	C	C L 9:10p	L	L	L V 7:11a	V	V Li 1:26p	Li	Li S 4:04p	S	S Sg 4:06p	Sg	
Dec	C	C L 3:00a	L	L V 1:31p	V	V Li 9:13p	Li	Li	Li S 1:44a	S	S Sg 2:48a	Sg	Sg Cp 2:30a	Cp	Cp Aq 2:40a

1960

	1	2	3	4	5	6	7	8	9	10	11	12	13	14	15	16
Jan	Aq	Aq P 5:00a	P	P A 10:57a	A	A T 8:42p	T	T	T G 9:14a	G	G C 9:52p	C	C	C L 9:33a	L	L V 7:34p
Feb	A	A	A T 4:28a	T	T G 4:22p	G	G	G C 5:12a	C	C L 4:30p	L	L	L V 1:55a	V	V Li 9:11a	Li
Mar	A T 1:10p	T	T	T G 12:09a	G	G C 12:54p	C	C	C L 12:53a	L	L V 10:07a	V	V Li 4:19p	Li	Li S 9:35p	S
Apr	G	G C 9:02p	C	C L 9:22a	L	L	L V 7:22p	V	V	V Li 1:27a	Li	Li S 4:59a	S	S Sg 6:41a	Sg	Sg Cp 8:31a
May	C	C L 5:05p	L	L	L V 4:17a	V	V Li 11:23a	Li	Li S 2:36p	S	S Sg 3:43p	Sg	Sg Cp 3:59p	Cp	Cp Aq 5:25p	Aq
Jn	L V 12:00n	V	V Li 8:34p	Li	Li	Li S 12:53a	S	S Sg 2:25a	Sg	Sg Cp 1:57a	Cp	Cp Aq 1:59a	Aq	Aq P 3:47a	P	P A 9:02a
Jly	V Li 3:49a	Li	Li S 9:40a	S	S Sg 12:31p	Sg	Sg Cp 12:51p	Cp	Cp Aq 12:08p	Aq	Aq P 1:03p	P	P A 4:27p	A	A T 11:54p	T
Aug	S Sg 8:52p	Sg	Sg Cp 10:51p	Cp	Cp Aq 10:42p	Aq	Aq P 11:20p	P	P	P A 1:30a	A	A T 7:45a	T	T G 5:41p	G	G
Sep	Cp	Cp Aq 7:50a	Aq	Aq P 9:21a	P	P A 11:48a	A	A T 4:49p	T	T	T G 1:32a	G	G C 1:31p	C	C	C L 2:12a
Oct	Aq P 5:34p	P	P A 9:10p	A	A	A T 2:17a	T	T G 10:37a	G	G C 9:34p	C	C	C L 10:05a	L	L V 10:01p	V
Nov	A	A T 10:22a	T	T G 6:50p	G	G	G C 5:37a	C	C L 6:05p	L	L	L V 6:37a	V	V Li 4:17p	Li	Li S 9:52p
Dec	T	T G 2:02a	G	G C 1:00p	C	C	C L 1:31a	L	L V 2:16p	V	V	V Li 1:05a	Li	Li S 8:03a	S	S Sg 11:07a

	17	18	19	20	21	22	23	24	25	26	27	28	29	30	31
Jan	V	V	V Li 3:32a	Li	Li S 9:05a	S	S Sg 11:47a	Sg	Sg Cp 12:53p	Cp	Cp Aq 1:22p	Aq	Aq P 3:20p	P	P A 7:49p
Feb	Li S 2:38p	S	S Sg 6:15p	Sg	Sg Cp 8:45p	Cp	Cp Aq 10:41p	Aq	Aq	Aq P 1:23a	P	P A 3:58a	A		
Mar	S Sg 11:07p	Sg	Sg Cp 11:30p	Cp	Cp	Cp Aq 12:58a	Aq	Aq P 5:13a	P	P A 12:16p	A	A T 9:38p	T	T	T G 8:35a
Apr	Cp	Cp Aq 11:17a	Aq	Aq P 3:48p	P	P A 9:45p	A	A	A T 5:53a	T	T G 4:24p	G	G	G C 4:36a	
May	Aq P 9:03p	P	P	P A 3:16a	A	A T 12:15p	T	T G 11:08p	G	G	G C 11:06a	C	C	C L 12:09a	L
Jn	A	A T 5:44p	T	T	T G 5:12a	G	G C 5:35p	C	C	C L 6:12a	L	L V 6:13p	V	V	
Jly	T	T G 11:00a	G	G C 11:41p	C	C	C L 12:03p	L	L V 11:44p	V	V	V Li 9:38a	Li	Li S 5:02p	S
Aug	G C 6:23a	C	C L 6:42p	L	L	L V 5:50a	V	V Li 3:10p	Li	Li S 9:59a	S	S	S Sg 3:29a	Sg	Sg Cp 6:31a
Sep	L	L V 1:28p	V	V Li 9:51p	Li	Li	Li S 3:58a	S	S Sg 8:53a	Sg	Sg Cp 12:15p	Cp	Cp Aq 2:36p	Aq	
Oct	V	V Li 6:39a	Li	Li S 12:03p	S	S Sg 3:17p	Sg	Sg Cp 5:52p	Cp	Cp Aq 8:06p	Aq	Aq P 11:31p	P	P	P A 4:04a
Nov	S	S	S Sg 12:27a	Sg	Sg Cp 1:38a	Cp	Cp Aq 2:38a	Aq	Aq P 5:10a	P	P A 9:55a	A	A T 4:57p	T	
Dec	Sg	Sg Cp 11:39a	Cp	Cp Aq 11:35a	Aq	Aq P 12:21p	P	P A 4:00p	A	A T 10:38p	T	T	T G 8:11a	G	G C 7:49p

MOON SIGNS 1910 – 1969

1961

	1	2	3	4	5	6	7	8	9	10	11	12	13	14	15	16	17	18	19	20	21	22	23	24	25	26	27	28	29	30	31
Jan	C	C	C L 8:24a	L	L V 8:49p	V	V	V Li 8:22a	Li	Li S 5:05p	S	S Sg 9:32p	Sg	Sg Cp 10:57p	Cp	Cp Aq 10:20p	Aq	Aq P 9:59p	P	P A 11:53p	A	A	A T 4:49a	T	T G 1:54p	G	G	G C 2:02a	C	C L 2:30p	L
Feb	L	L V 2:58a	V	V Li 2:32p	Li	Li	Li S 12:04a	S	S Sg 5:58a	Sg	Sg Cp 9:06a	Cp	Cp Aq 9:14a	Aq	Aq P 9:04a	P	P A 9:43a	A	A T 1:22p	T	T G 8:55p	G	G	G C 8:26a	C	C L 9:00p	L	L			
Mar	L V 9:34a	V	V Li 8:26p	Li	Li	Li S 5:29a	S	S Sg 12:13p	Sg	Sg Cp 4:46p	Cp	Cp Aq 6:41p	Aq	Aq P 7:20p	P	P A 8:25p	A	A T 11:10p	T	T	T G 5:23a	G	G C 3:48p	C	C	C L 4:22a	L	L V 4:55p	V	V	V Li 3:09a
Apr	Li	Li S 11:37a	S	S Sg 5:56p	Sg	Sg Cp 10:29p	Cp	Cp	Cp Aq 2:08a	Aq	Aq P 3:53a	P	P A 6:00a	A	A T 9:27a	T	T G 2:49p	G	G	G C 12:16a	C	C L 12:08p	L	L	L V 12:57a	V	V Li 11:09a	Li	Li S 7:26p	S	
May	S	S Sg 12:14a	Sg	Sg Cp 3:56a	Cp	Cp Aq 7:00a	Aq	Aq P 9:35a	P	P A 1:05p	A	A T 5:30p	T	T G 11:48p	G	G	G C 8:34a	C	C L 8:08p	L	L	L V 8:38a	V	V Li 8:21p	Li	Li	Li S 4:30a	S	S Sg 9:30a	Sg	Sg Cp 11:36a
Jn	Cp	Cp Aq 1:11p	Aq	Aq P 3:11p	P	P A 6:51p	A	A T 11:58p	T	T	T G 7:11a	G	G C 4:22p	C	C	C L 3:36a	L	L V 4:17p	V	V	V Li 4:25a	Li	Li S 1:51p	S	S Sg 7:16p	Sg	Sg Cp 9:28p	Cp	Cp Aq 9:43p	Aq	
Jly	Aq P 10:02p	P	P	P A 12:04a	A	A T 5:00a	T	T G 12:29p	G	G C 10:25p	C	C	C L 9:50a	L	L V 11:04p	V	V	V Li 11:15a	Li	Li S 10:00p	S	S Sg 4:53a	Sg	Sg	Sg Cp 7:49a	Cp	Cp Aq 8:17a	Aq	Aq P 7:38a	P	P A 8:10a
Aug	A	A T 11:08a	T	T G 5:53p	G	G	G C 4:02a	C	C L 4:17p	L	L	L V 4:48a	V	V Li 5:05p	Li	Li	Li S 4:30a	S	S Sg 12:47p	Sg	Sg Cp 5:28p	Cp	Cp Aq 5:28p	Aq	Aq P 6:23p	P	P A 6:08p	A	A T 7:55p	T	T
Sep	T G 12:58a	G	G C 10:01a	C	C L 10:13p	L	L	L V 11:00a	V	V Li 10:56p	Li	Li	Li S 9:41a	S	S Sg 5:39p	Sg	Sg	Sg Cp 12:53a	Cp	Cp Aq 3:58a	Aq	Aq P 4:46a	P	P A 4:54a	A	A T 6:00a	T	T G 9:55a	G	G C 5:39p	
Oct	C	C	C L 4:49a	L	L V 5:53p	V	V	V Li 6:00a	Li	Li S 3:54p	S	S	S Sg 12:18a	Sg	Sg Cp 6:18a	Cp	Cp Aq 10:42a	Aq	Aq P 1:01p	P	P A 2:34p	A	A T 4:23p	T	T G 7:43p	G	G	G C 2:21a	C	C L 12:48p	L
Nov	L	L V 1:33a	V	V Li 1:38p	Li	Li S 11:37p	S	S	S Sg 7:00a	Sg	Sg Cp 12:15p	Cp	Cp Aq 4:03p	Aq	Aq P 2:11p	P	P A 10:03p	A	A	A T 12:58a	T	T G 5:06a	G	G C 11:43a	C	C L 9:07p	L	L	L V 9:27a	V	
Dec	V Li 10:13p	Li	Li	Li S 8:41a	S	S Sg 3:30p	Sg	Sg Cp 9:32p	Cp	Cp	Cp Aq 12:18a	Aq	Aq P 2:52a	P	P A 5:29a	A	A T 7:32a	T	T G 12:51p	G	G C 8:14p	C	C	C L 5:39a	L	L V 5:30p	V	V	V Li 6:24a	Li	Li S 539p

1962

	1	2	3	4	5	6	7	8	9	10	11	12	13	14	15	16	17	18	19	20	21	22	23	24	25	26	27	28	29	30	31
Jan	S	S	S Sg 1:53a	Sg	Sg Cp 5:38a	Cp	Cp Aq 7:20a	Aq	Aq P 8:09a	P	P A 9:23a	A	A T 12:50p	T	T G 7:04p	G	G	G C 2:53a	C	C L 1:10p	L	L	L V 12:55a	V	V Li 1:31p	Li	Li	Li S 2:01a	S	S Sg 11:00a	Sg
Feb	Sg Cp 4:13p	Cp	Cp Aq 6:02p	Aq	Aq P 5:57p	P	P A 5:24p	A	A T 7:26p	T	T	T G 12:30a	G	G C 8:46a	C	C L 7:42p	L	L	L V 7:37a	V	V Li 8:02p	Li	Li	Li S 8:46a	S	S Sg 6:54p	Sg	Sg			
Mar	Sg Cp 1:42a	Cp	Cp Aq 4:52a	Aq	Aq P 4:47a	P	P A 4:07a	A	A T 4:37a	T	T G 7:54a	G	G C 2:56p	C	C	C L 1:39a	L	L V 1:43p	V	V	V Li 2:33a	Li	Li S 2:27p	S	S	S Sg 12:54a	Sg	Sg Cp 9:18a	Cp	Cp Aq 1:45p	Aq
Apr	Aq P 3:27p	P	P A 3:27p	A	A T 3:09p	T	T G 5:08p	G	G C 10:23p	C	C	C L 7:48a	L	L V 8:20p	V	V	V Li 9:13a	Li	Li	Li S 8:49p	S	S Sg 5:49a	Sg	Sg Cp 2:56p	Cp	Cp Aq 8:40p	Aq	Aq P 11:52p	P	P	
May	P A 1:00a	A	A T 1:40a	T	T G 3:20a	G C 7:22a	C	C	C L 3:29p	L	L	L V 3:10a	V	V Li 4:05p	Li	Li	Li S 3:53a	S	S Sg 1:12p	Sg	Sg Cp 8:32p	Cp	Cp	Cp Aq 1:50a	Aq	Aq P 5:38a	P	P A 8:36a	A	A T 12:07p	T
Jn	T G 1:00p	G	G C 5:24p	C	C	C L 12:27a	L	L V 10:51a	V	V Li 11:49p	Li	Li	Li S 11:53a	S	S Sg 9:21p	Sg	Sg	Sg Cp 3:47a	Cp	Cp Aq 8:02a	Aq	Aq P 11:03a	P	P A 2:03p	A	A T 4:53p	T	T G 8:45p	G	G	
Jly	G C 1:50a	C	C L 9:06a	L	L V 7:54p	V	V	V Li 7:25a	Li	Li S 8:00p	S	S	S Sg 6:27a	Sg	Sg Cp 12:48p	Cp	Cp Aq 4:09p	Aq	Aq P 6:06p	P	P A 7:28p	A	A T 10:13p	T	T	T G 2:24a	G	G C 8:40a	C	C L 4:43p	L
Aug	L	L V 2:43a	V	V Li 2:52p	Li	Li	Li S 3:33a	S	S Sg 2:50p	Sg	Sg Cp 10:24p	Cp	Cp	Cp Aq 1:59a	Aq	Aq P 3:16a	P	P A 3:16a	A	A T 4:43a	T	T G 7:43a	G	G C 2:01p	C	C L 10:53p	L	L	L V 9:35a	V	V Li 9:36p
Sep	Li	Li	Li S 10:37a	S	S Sg 10:21p	Sg	Sg	Sg Cp 7:33a	Cp	Cp Aq 12:28p	Aq	Aq P 2:02p	P	P A 1:48p	A	A T 1:22p	T	T G 2:55p	G	G C 7:55p	C	C	C L 4:17a	L	L V 3:32p	V	V	V Li 4:10a	Li	Li S 4:34p	
Oct	S	S	S Sg 4:36a	Sg	Sg Cp 2:40p	Cp	Cp Aq 9:07p	Aq	Aq	Aq P 12:00n	P	P A 12:33a	A T 11:55p	T	T	T G 12:36a	G	G C 3:39a	C	C L 10:50a	L	L V 9:44p	V	V	V Li 10:26a	Li	Li S 10:52p	S	S	S Sg 10:10a	Sg
Nov	Sg Cp 8:20p	Cp	Cp	Cp Aq 4:02a	Aq	Aq P 8:40a	P	P A 10:27a	A	A T 10:51a	T	T G 11:00a	G	G C 1:23p	C	C L 7:10p	L	L	L V 4:49a	V	V Li 5:11p	Li	Li	Li S 5:48a	S	S Sg 4:57p	Sg	Sg	Sg Cp 2:16a	Cp	
Dec	Cp Aq 9:31a	Aq	Aq P 2:52p	P	P A 6:00p	A	A T 7:54p	T	T G 9:14p	G	G C 11:47p	C	C	C L 4:30a	L	L V 12:57p	V	V	V Li 12:46a	Li	Li	Li S 1:40p	S	S Sg 1:03a	Sg	Sg Cp 9:34a	Cp	Cp Aq 3:53p	Aq	Aq P 8:29p	P

1963

	1	2	3	4	5	6	7	8	9	10	11	12	13	14	15	16	17	18	19	20	21	22	23	24	25	26	27	28	29	30	31
Jan	P A 11:41p	A	A	A T 2:43a	T	T G 5:19a	G	G C 9:15a	C	C L 2:07p	L	L V 10:03p	V	V	V Li 8:37a	Li	Li S 9:27p	S	S	S Sg 9:21a	Sg	Sg Cp 6:11p	Cp	Cp Aq 11:49p	Aq	Aq	Aq P 3:05a	P	P A 5:18a	A	A T 7:52a
Feb	T	T G 11:14a	G	G C 4:04p	C	C L 10:09p	L	L	L V 6:38a	V	V Li 5:13p	Li	Li	Li S 5:24a	S	S Sg 6:08p	Sg	Sg	Sg Cp 3:59a	Cp	Cp Aq 10:24a	Aq	Aq P 12:50p	P	P A 1:52p	A	A T 2:57p	T			
Mar	T G 5:08p	G	G C 9:42p	C	C	C L 4:27a	L	L V 1:35p	V	V	V Li 12:30a	Li	Li S 12:51p	S	S	S Sg 6:45a	Sg	Sg Cp 12:44p	Cp	Cp Aq 8:03p	Aq	Aq P 11:27p	P	P	P A 12:16a	A T 11:57p	T	T	T G 12:36a	G	G C 3:32a
Apr	C	C L 9:54a	L	L V 7:35p	V	V	V Li 7:00a	Li	Li S 7:25p	S	S	S Sg 8:12a	Sg	Sg Cp 7:53p	Cp	Cp	Cp Aq 4:57a	Aq	Aq P 9:32a	P	P A 11:12a	A	A T 10:40a	T	T G 10:31a	G	G C 11:50a	C	C L 4:36a	L	
May	L	L V 1:12a	V	V Li 12:51p	Li	Li	Li S 1:33a	S	S Sg 1:57p	Sg	Sg	Sg Cp 1:18a	Cp	Cp Aq 10:59a	Aq	Aq P 5:25p	P	P A 8:40p	A	A T 9:26p	T	T G 9:04p	G	G C 9:44p	C	C	C L 1:03a	L	L V 8:21a	V	V Li 7:13p
Jn	Li	Li	Li S 8:12a	S	S Sg 8:18p	Sg	Sg	Sg Cp 7:24a	Cp	Cp Aq 4:22p	Aq	Aq P 11:26p	P	P	P A 4:03a	A	A T 6:22a	T	T G 7:10a	G	G C 8:11a	C	C L 11:00a	L	L V 4:54p	V	V	V Li 2:48a	Li	Li S 3:04p	
Jly	S	S	S Sg 4:00a	Sg	Sg Cp 2:03p	Cp	Cp Aq 10:34p	Aq	Aq	Aq P 4:40a	P	P A 9:15a	A	A T 12:28p	T	T G 2:48p	G	G C 5:13p	C	C L 8:35p	L	L	L V 2:07a	V	V Li 10:56a	Li	Li S 10:44p	S	S	S Sg 11:39a	Sg
Aug	Sg Cp 10:25p	Cp	Cp	Cp Aq 6:18a	Aq	Aq P 11:23a	P	P A 3:04p	A	A T 5:41p	T	T G 8:31p	G	G C 11:56p	C	C	C L 4:21a	L	L V 10:44a	V	V Li 7:18p	Li	Li	Li S 6:24a	S	S Sg 7:19p	Sg	Sg	Sg Cp 7:12a	Cp	Cp Aq 3:33p
Sep	Aq	Aq P 8:23p	P	P A 10:54p	A	A	A T 12:23a	T	T G 2:03a	G	G C 5:08a	C	C L 10:36a	L	L V 5:53p	V	V	V Li 2:57a	Li	Li S 2:13p	S	S	S Sg 2:45a	Sg	Sg Cp 3:09p	Cp	Cp	Cp Aq 12:57a	Aq	Aq P 6:29a	
Oct	P	P A 8:49a	A	A T 9:33a	T	T G 9:29a	G	G C 11:29a	C	C L 3:55p	L	L V 11:37p	V	V	V Li 9:23a	Li	Li S 8:56p	S	S	S Sg 9:38a	Sg	Sg Cp 9:53p	Cp	Cp	Cp Aq 9:05a	Aq	Aq P 4:19p	P	P A 7:38p	A	A T 7:57p
Nov	T	T G 7:43p	G	G C 7:58p	C	C L 10:46p	L	L	L V 5:10a	V	V Li 3:13p	Li	Li	Li S 3:23a	S	S Sg 3:48p	Sg	Sg	Sg Cp 4:11a	Cp	Cp Aq 3:37p	Aq	Aq	Aq P 12:09a	P	P A 5:17a	A	A T 7:00a	T	T G 6:32a	
Dec	G	G C 6:31a	C	C L 7:52a	L	L V 12:36p	V	V Li 9:24p	Li	Li	Li S 9:26a	S	S Sg 10:07p	Sg	Sg	Sg Cp 10:43a	Cp	Cp Aq 9:18p	Aq	Aq	Aq P 6:16a	P	P A 12:29p	A	A T 3:50p	T	T G 4:58p	G	G C 5:16p	C	C L 6:20p

MOON SIGNS 1910 – 1969

1964

	1	2	3	4	5	6	7	8	9	10	11	12	13	14	15
Jan	L	L V 9:50p	V	V	V Li 5:19a	Li	Li S 4:29p	S	S	S Sg 5:24a	Sg	Sg Cp 5:34p	Cp	Cp	Cp Aq 3:35a
Feb	V Li 2:21p	Li	Li	Li S 12:24a	S	S Sg 12:54p	Sg	Sg	Sg Cp 1:30a	Cp	Cp Aq 11:41a	Aq	Aq P 6:54p	P	P
Mar	Li	Li S 8:48a	S	S Sg 8:56p	Sg	Sg	Sg Cp 9:58a	Cp	Cp Aq 8:20p	Aq	Aq	Aq P 3:47a	P	P A 8:12a	A
Apr	S Sg 4:59a	Sg	Sg Cp 5:47p	Cp	Cp	Cp Aq 5:26a	Aq	Aq P 1:38p	P	P A 5:59p	A	A T 7:34p	T	T G 8:33p	G
May	Sg Cp 12:37a	Cp	Cp Aq 1:04p	Aq	Aq P 10:34p	P	P	P A 4:05a	A	A T 6:10a	T	T G 6:16a	G	G C 5:43a	C
Jn	Aq	Aq P 5:52a	P	P A 1:20p	A	A T 4:17p	T	T G 4:59p	G	G C 4:22p	C	C L 4:38p	L	L V 7:14p	V
Jly	P A 8:00p	A	A	A T 1:06a	T	T G 2:55a	G	G C 3:02a	C	C L 2:58a	L	L V 4:43a	V	V Li 9:36a	Li
Aug	T	T G 10:42a	G	G C 12:14p	C	C L 1:06p	L	L V 2:51p	V	V Li 6:50p	Li	Li	Li S 2:24a	S	S Sg 1:52p
Sep	C	C L 8:50p	L	L	L V 12:15a	V	V Li 4:33a	Li	Li S 11:14a	S	S Sg 9:50p	Sg	Sg	Sg Cp 10:17a	Cp
Oct	L	L V 7:22a	V	V Li 12:51p	Li	Li S 8:08p	S	S	S Sg 6:14a	Sg	Sg Cp 6:18p	Cp	Cp	Cp Aq 7:12a	Aq
Nov	Li	Li	Li S 3:46a	S	S Sg 1:54p	Sg	Sg	Sg Cp 2:02a	Cp	Cp Aq 2:47p	Aq	Aq	Aq P 2:18a	P	P A 10:24a
Dec	S	S Sg 9:13p	Sg	Sg	Sg Cp 8:49a	Cp	Cp Aq 9:39p	Aq	Aq	Aq P 9:46a	P	P A 7:10p	A	A	A T 12:34a

	16	17	18	19	20	21	22	23	24	25	26	27	28	29	30	31
Jan	Aq	Aq P 11:54a	P	P A 6:08p	A	A T 10:26p	T	T	T G 12:52a	G	G C 2:45a	C	C L 4:32a	L	L V 7:43a	V
Feb	P A 12:11a	A	A T 3:56a	T	T G 7:00a	G	G C 9:53a	C	C L 12:48p	L	L V 5:14p	V	V Li 11:35p	Li		
Mar	A T 10:41a	T	T G 12:50p	G	G C 3:20p	C	C L 7:08p	L	L	L V 12:33a	V	V Li 7:46a	Li	Li S 5:17p	S	S
Apr	G C 9:34p	C	C L 12:39p	L	L	L V 6:29a	V	V Li 2:25p	Li	Li	Li S 12:27a	S	S Sg 12:18p	Sg	Sg	
May	C L 7:21a	L	L V 11:50a	V	V Li 7:58p	Li	Li	Li S 6:36a	S	S Sg 6:30p	Sg	Sg	Sg Cp 7:00a	Cp Aq 7:30p	Aq	Aq
Jn	V	V Li 1:57a	Li	Li S 12:12p	S	S	S Sg 12:31a	Sg	Sg Cp 1:14p	Cp	Cp	Cp Aq 1:15a	Aq	Aq P 10:47a	P	
Jly	Li S 6:41p	S	S	S Sg 6:48a	Sg	Sg Cp 7:43p	Cp	Cp	Cp Aq 7:24a	Aq	Aq P 5:18p	P	P	P A 1:31a	A	A T 7:31a
Aug	Sg	Sg	Sg Cp 2:46a	Cp	Cp Aq 2:46a	Aq	Aq P 11:53p	P	P	P A 7:22a	A	A T 12:29p	T	T G 4:23p	G	Gl C 7:06p
Sep	Cp Aq 10:44p	Aq	Aq	Aq P 8:18a	P	P A 2:56p	A	A T 6:55p	T	T G 10:03p	G	G	G C 12:45a	C	C L 3:44a	
Oct	Aq P 5:43p	P	P	P A 12:19a	A	A T 3:40a	T	T G 5:29a	G	G C 6:41a	C	C L 9:04a	L	L V 1:16p	V	V Li
Nov	A	A T 2:14p	T	T G 3:27p	G	G C 3:21p	C	C L 4:15p	L	L V 7:05p	V	V	V Li 1:02a	Li	Li S 9:45a	
Dec	T	T G 2:26a	G	G C 2:06a	C	C L 1:46a	L	L V 2:54a	V	V Li 7:22a	Li	Li S 3:37p	S	S	S Sg 2:51a	Sg

1965

	1	2	3	4	5	6	7	8	9	10	11	12	13	14	15
Jan	Sg Cp 3:21p	Cp	Cp	Cp Aq 3:59a	Aq	Aq P 4:02p	P	P	P A 2:23a	A	A T 9:18a	T	T G 12:43p	G	G C 1:32p
Feb	Aq	Aq P 9:53p	P	P	P A 7:53a	A	A T 3:51p	T	T G 8:44p	G	G C 11:04p	C	C L 11:32p	L	L V 11:55p
Mar	Aq	Aq P 4:34a	P	P A 2:08p	A	A T 9:15p	T	T	T G 2:39a	G	G C 5:41a	C	C L 8:00a	L	L V 9:50a
Apr	A	A	A T 3:55a	T	T G 8:14a	G	G C 11:53a	C	C L 2:25p	L	L V 5:26p	V	V Li 9:07p	Li	Li
May	T	T G 4:33p	G	G C 5:27p	C	C L 7:49p	L	L V 10:54p	V	V	V Li 3:35a	Li	Li S 9:37a	S	S Sg 6:03p
Jn	G C 1:47a	C	C L 2:47a	L	L V 4:41a	V	V Li 8:58a	Li	Li S 3:31p	S	S	S Sg 12:40a	Sg	Sg Cp 11:37a	Cp
Jly	L	L V 12:10p	V	V Li 2:59p	Li	Li S 3:53p	S	S	S Sg 6:03a	Sg	Sg Cp 5:54p	Cp	Cp	Cp Aq 5:48a	Aq
Aug	Li	Li	Li S 3:35a	S	S Sg 11:44a	Sg	Sg Cp 11:24p	Cp	Cp	Cp Aq 12:06p	Aq	Aq	Aq P 12:04p	P	P A 12:04p
Sep	S Sg 7:11p	Sg	Sg	Sg Cp 5:49a	Cp	Cp Aq 6:42p	Aq	Aq	Aq P 7:00a	P	P A 9:46a	A	A	A T 3:02a	T
Oct	Sg Cp 1:33p	Cp	Cp	Cp Aq 1:55a	Aq	Aq P 2:33p	P	P	P A 1:23a	A	A T 9:46a	T	T G 3:48p	G	G C 8:22p
Nov	Aq	Aq P 10:48p	P	P	P A 9:51a	A	A T 5:59p	T	T G 11:10p	G	G	G C 2:43a	C	C L 5:29a	L
Dec	P	P A 6:41p	A	A	A T 3:32a	T	T G 8:52a	G	G C 11:07a	C	C L 12:33	L	L V 2:03p	V	V Li 5:13p

	16	17	18	19	20	21	22	23	24	25	26	27	28	29	30	31
Jan	C	C L 12:25p	L	L V 1:03p	V	V Li 3:56p	Li	Li S 10:40p	S	S	S Sg 9:13a	Sg	Sg Cp 9:52p	Cp	Cp	Cp Aq 10:16a
Feb	V	V	V Li 1:56a	Li	Li S 7:11a	S	S Sg 4:27p	Sg	Sg	Sg Cp 4:45a	Cp	Cp Aq 5:30p	Aq			
Mar	V	V Li 12:10p	Li	Li S 4:49p	S	S	S Sg 12:52a	Sg	Sg Cp 12:30p	Cp	Cp	Cp Aq 1:01a	Aq	Aq P 12:37p	P	P A 9:31p
Apr	Li S 2:10a	S	S Sg 9:54a	Sg	Sg Cp 8:24p	Cp	Cp	Cp Aq 9:15a	Aq	Aq P 9:25p	P	P	P A 6:28a	A	A T 12:20p	
May	Sg	Sg	Sg Cp 4:17a	Cp	Cp Aq 4:46p	Aq	Aq	Aq P 5:24a	P	P A 3:47p	A	A T 10:11p	T	T	T G 1:08a	G
Jn	Cp Aq 11:53p	Aq	Aq	Aq P 12:40p	P	P A 11:58p	A	A	A T 8:03a	T	T G 11:28a	G	G C 12:27p	C	C L 12:05p	
Jly	Aq P 6:36p	P	P	P A 6:37a	A	A T 3:49p	T	T G 9:10p	G	G C 10:58p	C	C L 10:55p	L	L V 10:16p	V	V Li 11:14p
Aug	A	A T 9:44p	T	T G 4:39p	G	G	G C 8:10a	C	C L 9:13a	L	L V 8:47a	V	V Li 9:39a	Li	Li S 12:29p	S
Sep	T G 10:13a	G	G C 3:01p	C	C L 5:43p	L	L V 6:45p	V	V Li 7:54p	Li	Li S 10:20p	S	S	S Sg 4:00a	Sg	
Oct	C	C L 11:41p	L	L	L V 2:17a	V	V Li 4:52a	Li	Li S 8:14a	S	S Sg 1:34p	Sg	Sg Cp 10:07p	Cp	Cp	Cp Aq 9:40a
Nov	L V 8:02a	V	V Li 11:21a	Li	Li S 4:04p	S	S Sg 10:18p	Sg	Sg	Sg Cp 6:38a	Cp	Cp Aq 5:47p	Aq	Aq	Aq P 6:36a	
Dec	Li	Li S 10:21p	S	S	S Sg 5:19a	Sg	Sg Cp 2:24p	Cp	Cp	Cp Aq 1:37a	Aq	Aq P 1:58p	P	P	P A 2:46a	A

1966

	1	2	3	4	5	6	7	8	9	10	11	12	13	14	15
Jan	A T 1:15p	T	T G 7:05p	G	G C 9:28p	C	C L 10:03p	L	L V 10:03p	V	V Li 11:37p	Li	Li	Li S 3:38a	S
Feb	G	G C 8:11a	C	C L 8:56a	L	L V 8:25a	V	V Li 8:29a	Li	Li S 10:55a	S	S Sg 5:08p	Sg	Sg	Sg Cp 2:41a
Mar	G C 5:26p	C	C L 7:24p	L	L V 7:24p	V	V Li 6:58p	Li	Li S 8:26p	S	S	S Sg 12:33a	Sg	Sg Cp 9:00a	Cp
Apr	L	L V 5:31a	V	V Li 5:52a	Li	Li S 6:30a	S	S Sg 10:04a	Sg	Sg Cp 5:13p	Cp	Cp	Cp Aq 4:02a	Aq	Aq P 4:58p
May	V Li 2:40p	Li	Li S 4:48p	S	S Sg 7:57p	Sg	Sg	Sg Cp 2:04a	Cp	Cp Aq 11:46a	Aq	Aq	Aq P 12:18a	P	P A 12:54p
Jn	S	S Sg 4:55a	Sg	Sg Cp 11:06a	Cp	Cp Aq 8:17p	Aq	Aq	Aq P 8:01a	P	P A 9:02p	A	A	A T 7:57a	T
Jly	Sg Cp 6:48p	Cp	Cp	Cp Aq 4:28a	Aq	Aq P 3:45p	P	P	P A 4:23a	A	A T 4:27p	T	T	T G 1:06a	G
Aug	Aq	Aq P 10:40p	P	P	P A 11:17a	A	A T 11:50p	T	T	T G 9:37a	G	G C 3:38p	C	C L 5:51p	L
Sep	P A 5:23p	A	A	A T 6:00a	T	T G 4:48p	G	G	G C 12:23a	C	C L 4:07a	L	L V 4:46a	V	V Li 4:16a
Oct	A T 11:46a	T	T G 10:33p	G	G	G C 7:00a	C	C L 12:20p	L	L V 2:49p	V	V Li 3:03p	Li	Li S 2:59p	S
Nov	G	G C 12:41p	C	C L 6:39p	L	L V 10:26p	V	V	V Li 12:12a	Li	Li S 1:22a	S	S Sg 2:52a	Sg	Sg Cp 6:49a
Dec	C	C L 12:11a	L	L V 4:04a	V	V Li 7:10a	Li	Li S 9:31a	S	S Sg 12:30p	Sg	Sg Cp 4:36p	Cp	Cp Aq 11:19p	Aq

	16	17	18	19	20	21	22	23	24	25	26	27	28	29	30	31
Jan	S Sg 11:03a	Sg	Sg Cp 8:50p	Cp	Cp	Cp Aq 8:36a	Aq	Aq P 8:51p	P	P	P A 9:25a	A	A T 8:44p	T	T	T G 4:19a
Feb	Cp	Cp Aq 2:41p	Aq	Aq	Aq P 3:20a	P	P A 3:20a	A	A	A T 3:06a	T	T G 11:57a	G			
Mar	Cp Aq 9:12p	Aq	Aq	Aq P 9:50a	P	P A 9:53p	A	A	A T 8:44a	T	T G 5:48p	G	G	G C 12:25a	C	C L 3:58a
Apr	P	P	P A 5:02a	A	A T 3:29p	T	T G 11:38p	G	G	G C 5:57a	C	C L 10:07a	L	L V 1:13p	V	
May	A	A T 11:01p	T	T	T G 5:39a	G	G C 11:42a	C	C L 3:35p	L	L V 6:40p	V	V Li 9:22p	Li	Li	Li S 12:29a
Jn	T G 3:40p	G	G C 7:47p	C	C L 10:24p	L	L	L V 12:21a	V	V Li 2:43a	Li	Li S 6:29a	S	S Sg 11:33a	Sg	
Jly	G C 5:38a	C	C L 7:20a	L	L V 8:09a	V	V Li 9:00a	Li	Li S 11:44a	S	S Sg 5:18p	Sg	Sg	Sg Cp 1:08a	Cp	Cp Aq 11:06a
Aug	L V 6:02p	V	V Li 5:36p	Li	Li S 6:51p	S	S Sg 10:54p	Sg	Sg	Sg Cp 6:38a	Cp	Cp Aq 5:05p	Aq	Aq	Aq P 5:12a	P
Sep	Li	Li S 4:18a	S	S Sg 6:31a	Sg	Sg Cp 12:41p	Cp	Cp Aq 10:48p	Aq	Aq	Aq P 11:04a	P	P A 11:57p	A	A	
Oct	S Sg 4:34p	Sg	Sg Cp 9:01p	Cp	Cp	Cp Aq 5:39a	Aq	Aq P 5:28p	P	P	P A 6:36a	A	A T 6:13p	T	T	T G 4:23a
Nov	Cp	Cp Aq 1:59p	Aq	Aq	Aq P 1:13a	P	P A 2:00p	A	A	A T 1:53a	T	T G 11:30a	G	G C 6:45p	C	
Dec	Aq	Aq P 9:23a	P	P A 10:04p	A	A	A T 10:21a	T	T G 8:19p	G	G	G C 2:52a	C	C L 7:00a	L	L V 10:03a

MOON SIGNS 1910 – 1969

1967

	1	2	3	4	5	6	7	8	9	10	11	12	13	14	15	16	17	18	19	20	21	22	23	24	25	26	27	28	29	30	31
Jan	C	C L 12:42p	L	L V 3:35p	V	V Li 7:37p	Li	Li	Li S 12:51a	S	S Sg 8:08a	Sg	Sg Cp 5:49p	Cp	Cp	Cp Aq 6:00a	Aq	Aq P 6:36p	P	P	P A 5:39a	A	A T 12:40p	T	T G 4:11p	G	G C 6:01p	C	C L 7:04p	L	L
Feb	L	L	L V 1:18a	V	V Li 7:11a	Li	Li S 3:29p	S	S	S Sg 1:30a	Sg	Sg Cp 1:28p	Cp	Cp	Cp Aq 2:29a	Aq	Aq P 2:02p	P	P A 10:18p	A	A	A T 2:52a	T	T G 4:07a	G	G C 4:10a	C	C L 4:43a			
Mar	L V 7:11a	V	V	V Li 12:54p	Li	Li S 10:36p	S	S	S Sg 8:12a	Sg	Sg Cp 8:19p	Cp	Cp	Cp Aq 9:02a	Aq	Aq P 9:05p	P	P	P A 6:49a	A	A T 12:40p	T	T G 2:56p	G	G C 2:47p	C	C L 2:25p	L	L V 3:13p	V	V Li 7:20p
Apr	Li	Li	Li S 3:12a	S	S Sg 2:24p	Sg	Sg	Sg Cp 2:46a	Cp	Cp Aq 3:17p	Aq	Aq	Aq P 3:23a	P	P A 1:49p	A	A T 8:52p	T	T	T G 12:54a	G	G C 1:47a	C	C L 1:18a	L	L V 1:18a	V	V Li 4:05a	Li	Li S 10:20a	S
May	S	S Sg 8:19p	Sg	Sg	Sg Cp 8:49a	Cp	Cp Aq 9:24p	Aq	Aq	Aq P 8:58a	P	P A 6:54p	A	A	A T 2:59a	T	T G 8:12a	G	G C 10:47a	C	C L 11:32a	L	L V 11:50a	V	V Li 1:51p	Li	Li S 6:48p	S	S	S Sg 3:40a	Sg
Jn	Sg Cp 3:39p	Cp	Cp	Cp Aq 4:14a	Aq	Aq P 3:42p	P	P	P A 1:20a	A	A T 8:48a	T	T G 2:15p	G	G C 5:48p	C	C L 7:35p	L	L V 9:20p	V	V	V Li 12:02a	Li	Li S 4:21a	S	S Sg 12:04p	Sg	Sg Cp 11:20p	Cp	Cp	
Jly	Cp Aq 12:00n	Aq	Aq P 11:34p	P	P	P A 8:39a	A	A T 2:56p	T	T G 7:14p	G	G C 10:40p	C	C	C L 1:25a	L	L V 4:15a	V	V Li 8:04a	Li	Li S 1:11p	S	S Sg 9:01p	Sg	Sg	Sg Cp 7:12a	Cp	Cp Aq 7:55p	Aq	Aq	Aq P 8:11a
Aug	P	P A 5:29p	A	A T 11:21p	T	T	T G 2:52a	G	G C 4:43a	C	C L 6:41a	L	L V 9:45a	V	V Li 2:17p	Li	Li S 8:29p	S	S	S Sg 4:33a	Sg	Sg Cp 2:56p	Cp	Cp	Cp Aq 3:33a	Aq	Aq P 4:00p	P	P A 2:39a	A	A
Sep	A T 9:25a	T	T G 12:33p	G	G C 1:19p	C	C L 2:08p	L	L V 3:34p	V	V Li 7:37p	Li	Li	Li S 2:09a	S	S Sg 11:07a	Sg	Sg Cp 9:53p	Cp	Cp Aq 10:26a	Aq	Aq	Aq P 11:04p	P	P	P A 10:37a	A	A T 7:00p	T	T G 11:04p	
Oct	G	G	G C 12:02a	C L 11:31p	L	L V 11:47p	V	V Li 2:10a	Li	Li	Li S 7:45a	S	S Sg 4:02	Sg	Sg	Sg Cp 4:24a	Cp	Cp	Cp Aq 4:29p	Aq	Aq P 5:24a	P	P A 5:15p	A	A	A T 2:41a	T	T G 8:33a	G	G C 10:44a	C
Nov	C L 10:40a	L	L V 10:14a	V	V Li 11:04a	Li	Li S 4:15p	S	S Sg 10:56p	Sg	Sg	Sg Cp 10:25a	Cp	Cp Aq 11:04p	Aq	Aq	Aq P 11:37a	P	P A 11:00p	A	A	A T 8:52a	T	T G 4:33p	G	G C 7:50p	C	C L 9:10p	L	L V 9:04p	
Dec	V	V Li 9:44p	Li	Li	Li S 12:22a	S	S Sg 6:49a	Sg	Sg Cp 5:15p	Cp	Cp	Cp Aq 5:59a	Aq	Aq P 6:18p	P	P	P A 5:26a	A	A T 2:25p	T	T G 9:42p	G	G	G C 2:39a	C	C L 5:41a	L	L V 6:50a	V	V Li 8:00a	Li

1968

	1	2	3	4	5	6	7	8	9	10	11	12	13	14	15	16	17	18	19	20	21	22	23	24	25	26	27	28	29	30	31
Jan	Li S 10:47a	S	S Sg 5:55p	Sg	Sg	Sg Cp 1:15a	Cp	Cp Aq 3:22p	Aq	Aq	Aq P 3:51a	P	P A 12:58p	A	A T 9:21p	T	T	T G 3:29a	G	G C 8:13a	C	C L 11:32a	L	L V 2:06p	V	V Li 4:42p	Li	Li S 8:06p	S	S	S Sg 1:32a
Feb	Sg	Sg Cp 9:46a	Cp	Cp Aq 9:15p	Aq	Aq	Aq P 10:14a	P	P A 9:31p	A	A	A T 5:54a	T	T G 11:29	G	G C 12:39p	C	C Li 10:17p	Li	Li S 7:47p	S	S Sg 11:14p	Sg	Sg	Sg	Sg Cp 3:47p	Cp	Cp	Cp Aq 6:24p		
Mar	Aq	Aq	Aq P 5:24a	P	P A 5:53p	A	A	A T 6:24a	T	T G 3:30p	G	G C 8:53p	C	C L 11:24p	L	L	L V 12:38a	V	V Li 1:54a	Li	Li S 4:47a	S	S Sg 9:35a	Sg	Sg Cp 4:42p	Cp	Cp	Cp Aq 1:55a	Aq	Aq P 1:00p	P
Apr	P	P A 1:21a	A	A T 2:00p	T	T	T G 12:40a	G	G C 7:11a	C	C L 9:56a	L	L V 8:14a	V	V Li 10:16a	Li	Li S 11:34a	S	S Sg 3:19p	Sg	Sg Cp 10:23p	Cp	Cp	Cp Aq 8:23a	Aq	Aq P 7:42p	P	P	P A 8:00a	A	
May	A T 8:37p	T	T	T G 8:09a	G	G C 3:57p	C	C L 8:06p	L	L V 9:10p	V	V Li 8:34p	Li	Li S 8:28p	S	S Sg 10:40p	Sg	Sg	Sg Cp 3:02a	Cp	Cp Aq 1:33p	Aq	Aq	Aq P 1:33a	P	P A 2:13p	A	A	A T 2:36a	T	T G 1:51p
Jn	G	G C 10:08p	C	C	C L 4:53a	L	L V 8:29a	V	V Li 8:19a	Li	Li S 8:19a	S	S Sg 9:12a	Sg	Sg Cp 12:08p	Cp	Cp Aq 8:04p	Aq	Aq	Aq P 8:49a	P	P A 8:30p	A	A	A T 8:47a	T	T G 7:41p	G	G	G C 4:45a	
Jly	C	C L 10:56a	L	L V 3:13p	V	V Li 4:52p	Li	Li S 5:31p	S	S Sg 6:35p	Sg	Sg Cp 10:26p	Cp	Cp	Cp Aq 4:11a	Aq	Aq P 2:37p	P	P	P A 3:10a	A	A T 3:41p	T	T	T G 2:11a	G	G C 10:20a	C	C L 4:34p	L	L V 8:53p
Aug	V	V Li 11:52p	Li	Li	Li S 2:02a	S	S Sg 3:53a	Sg	Sg Cp 7:21a	Cp	Cp Aq 1:07p	Aq	Aq P 10:25p	P	P	P A 10:52a	A	A T 11:24p	T	T	T G 10:02a	G	G C 7:19p	C	C L 10:36p	L	L	L V 2:32a	V	V Li 5:18a	Li
Sep	Li S 7:02a	S	S Sg 11:21a	Sg	Sg Cp 4:00p	Cp	Cp Aq 10:07p	Aq	Aq	Aq P 7:00a	P	P A 6:36p	A	A	A T 7:25a	T	T G 6:49p	G	G	G C 2:44a	C	C L 7:00a	L	L V 9:48a	V	V Li 11:20a	Li	Li S 1:39p	S	S S 5:16p	
Oct	Sg	Sg Cp 10:30p	Cp	Cp	Cp Aq 5:52a	Aq	Aq P 3:12p	P	P	P A 2:25a	A	A T 3:09p	T	T	T G 3:35a	G	G C 12:17p	C	C L 5:12p	L	L V 7:09p	V	V Li 7:34p	Li	Li S 8:25p	S	S Sg 10:46p	Sg	Sg	Sg Cp 3:56a	Cp
Nov	Cp Aq 11:58a	Aq	Aq P 10:05p	P	P A 9:36a	A	A	A T 10:07p	T	T	T G 10:49a	G	G C 9:04p	C	C L 3:22a	L	L	L V 6:01a	V	V Li 6:12a	Li	Li S 5:43a	S	S Sg 6:22a	Sg	Sg Cp 10:15a	Cp	Cp Aq 5:30p	Aq	Aq	
Dec	Aq P 4:02a	P	P A 4:06p	A	A	A T 4:36a	T	T G 5:00p	G	G	G C 4:06a	C	C L 12:01p	L	L V 4:15p	V	V Li 5:09p	Li	Li S 4:33p	S	S Sg 4:32p	Sg	Sg Cp 6:34p	Cp	Cp	Cp Aq 12:14a	Aq	Aq P 10:01a	P	P A 10:11p	A

1969

	1	2	3	4	5	6	7	8	9	10	11	12	13	14	15	16	17	18	19	20	21	22	23	24	25	26	27	28	29	30	31
Jan	A T 11:04p	T	T	T G 11:01p	G	G C 10:06p	C	C	C L 6:32p	L	L	L V 12:23a	V	V Li 2:52a	Li	Li S 5:32a	S	S Sg 5:11a	Sg	Sg Cp 4:50a	Cp	Cp Aq 8:50a	Aq	Aq P 5:23p	P	P	P A 4:49a	A	A T 5:48p	T	T
Feb	T G 5:37a	G	G C 3:04p	C	C	C L 2:09a	L	L V 6:18a	V	V Li 10:06a	Li	Li S 12:31p	S	S Sg 1:25p	Sg	Sg Cp 3:20p	Cp	Cp Aq 6:50p	Aq	Aq	Aq P 1:40a	P	P A 12:42p	A	A	A T 1:28a	T	T G 1:38p			
Mar	G	G C 11:19p	C	C	C L 6:38a	L	L V 11:57p	V	V Li 3:56p	Li	Li S 6:51p	S	S Sg 9:16p	Sg	Sg	Sg Cp 12:29a	Cp	Cp Aq 3:22a	Aq	Aq P 10:59a	P	P A 8:57p	A	A	A T 9:16a	T	T G 9:58p	G	G	G C 8:07a	C
Apr	C V 2:59p	V	V Li 7:16p	Li	Li S 9:56p	S	S	S Sg 12:24a	Sg	Sg Cp 3:16a	Cp	Cp Aq 7:21a	Aq	Aq P 12:31p	P	P A 7:46p	A	A	A T 5:40a	T	T G 5:13p	G	G	G C 6:12a	C	C L 5:07p	L	L	L V 12:40a	V	
May	V Li 3:10a	Li	Li S 6:00a	S	S Sg 7:00a	Sg	Sg Cp 8:43a	Cp	Cp Aq 12:29p	Aq	Aq P 6:36p	P	P	P A 2:26a	A	A T 12:43p	T	T	T G 12:24a	G	G C 1:16p	C	C	C L 1:18a	L	L V 9:54a	V	V Li 2:44p	Li	Li S 4:13p	S
Jn	S Sg 4:04p	Sg	Sg Cp 4:22p	Cp	Cp Aq 6:34p	Aq	Aq P 11:55p	P	P	P A 8:10a	A	A T 7:07p	T	T	T G 7:12a	G	G C 7:37p	C	C	C L 8:00	L	L V 6:04p	V	V	V Li 12:14a	Li	Li S 2:47a	S	S Sg 3:02a	Sg	
Jly	Sg Cp 2:06a	Cp	Cp Aq 2:45a	Aq	Aq P 5:19a	P	P A 2:53p	A	A	A T 12:37a	T	T G 1:16p	G	G	G C 1:43a	C	C L 1:33p	L	L	L V 12:15a	V	V Li 7:54a	Li	Li S 12:12p	S	S Sg 1:22p	Sg	Sg Cp 1:05p	Cp	Cp Aq 1:03p	Aq
Aug	Aq P 3:01p	P	P A 8:57p	A	A	A T 5:37a	T	T G 7:19p	G	G	G C 8:00a	C	C L 7:24p	L	L	L V 5:39a	V	V Li 1:14p	Li	Li S 6:59p	S	S Sg 9:54p	Sg	Sg Cp 10:58p	Cp	Cp Aq 11:23p	Aq	Aq	Aq P 1:25a	P	P A 5:41a
Sep	A	A T 2:21p	T	T	T G 2:10a	G	G C 3:04p	C	C	C L 3:31a	L	L V 1:18p	V	V Li 7:04p	Li	Li	Li S 12:23a	S	S Sg 3:04a	Sg	Sg Cp 6:31a	Cp	Cp Aq 8:41a	Aq	Aq P 11:09a	P	P A 3:30p	A	A T 10:52p	T	
Oct	T	T G 11:41a	G	G	G C 12:24a	C	C L 11:58a	L	L V 8:00p	V	V	V Li 1:37a	Li	Li S 5:27a	S	S Sg 8:31a	Sg	Sg Cp 10:55a	Cp	Cp Aq 2:15p	Aq	Aq P 6:39p	P	P	P A 12:28a	A	A T 8:23a	T	T G 7:43p	G	G
Nov	G C 6:38a	C	C V 7:13p	V	V	V Li 5:08a	Li	Li S 11:18a	S	S Sg 2:33p	Sg	Sg Cp 4:26p	Cp	Cp Aq 6:12p	Aq	Aq P 8:58p	P	P A 1:22a	A	A 11:34a	A T	T	T G 3:42p	G	G	G C 2:02a	C	C L 2:23p	L	L	
Dec	L V 3:10a	V	V Li 2:11p	Li	Li S 9:25p	S	S	S Sg 12:48a	Sg	Sg Cp 1:47a	Cp	Cp Aq 2:04a	Aq	Aq P 3:20a	P	P A 7:11a	A	A T 9:40a	T	T G 6:43p	G	G	G C 5:37a	C	C L 9:32p	L	L	L V 10:13a	V	V Li 10:01p	Li

Table 3 BASE TIMES FOR EACH DAY OF THE YEAR

	January		*February*		*March*		*April*		*May*		*June*	
	h	**m**	**h**	**m**	**h**	**m**	**h**	**m**	**h**	**m**	**h**	**m**
1	6	40	8	42	10	33	12	35	14	33	16	35
2	6	44	8	46	10	37	12	39	14	37	16	39
3	6	48	8	50	10	41	12	43	14	41	16	43
4	6	52	8	54	10	44	12	47	14	45	16	47
5	6	56	8	58	10	48	12	51	14	49	16	51
6	7	0	9	2	10	52	12	55	14	53	16	55
7	7	4	9	6	10	56	12	59	14	57	16	59
8	7	8	9	10	11	00	13	2	15	01	17	03
9	7	12	9	14	11	04	13	6	15	05	17	07
10	7	16	9	18	11	08	13	10	15	09	17	11
11	7	19	9	22	11	12	13	14	15	13	17	15
12	7	23	9	26	11	16	13	18	15	17	17	19
13	7	27	9	30	11	20	13	22	15	20	17	23
14	7	31	9	34	11	24	13	26	15	24	17	27
15	7	35	9	37	11	28	13	30	15	28	17	31
16	7	39	9	41	11	32	13	34	15	32	17	35
17	7	43	9	45	11	36	13	38	15	36	17	38
18	7	47	9	49	11	40	13	42	15	40	17	42
19	7	51	9	53	11	44	13	46	15	44	17	46
20	7	55	9	57	11	48	13	50	15	48	17	50
21	7	59	10	1	11	52	13	54	15	52	17	54
22	8	3	10	5	11	55	13	58	15	56	17	58
23	8	7	10	9	11	59	14	02	16	00	18	02
24	8	11	10	13	12	03	14	06	16	04	18	06
25	8	15	10	17	12	07	14	10	16	08	18	10
26	8	19	10	21	12	11	14	13	16	12	18	14
27	8	23	10	25	12	15	14	17	16	16	18	18
28	8	27	10	29	12	19	14	21	16	20	18	22
29	8	30	10	31	12	23	14	25	16	24	18	26
30	8	34			12	27	14	29	16	28	18	30
31	8	38			12	31			16	31		

July		*August*		*September*		*October*		*November*		*December*	
h	**m**	**h**	**m**	**h**	**m**	**h**	**m**	**h**	**m**	**h**	**m**
18	34	20	36	22	38	0	36	2	39	4	37
18	38	20	40	22	42	0	40	2	43	4	41
18	42	20	44	22	46	0	44	2	46	4	45
18	45	20	48	22	50	0	48	2	50	4	49
18	49	20	52	22	54	0	52	2	54	4	53
18	53	20	56	22	58	0	56	2	58	4	57
18	57	21	00	23	02	1	00	3	02	5	01
19	01	21	03	23	06	1	04	3	06	5	04
19	05	21	07	23	10	1	08	3	10	5	08
19	09	21	11	23	14	1	12	3	14	5	12
19	13	21	15	23	18	1	16	3	18	5	16
19	17	21	19	23	21	1	20	3	22	5	20
19	21	21	23	23	25	1	24	3	26	5	24
19	25	21	27	23	29	1	28	3	30	5	28
19	29	21	31	23	33	1	32	3	34	5	32
19	33	21	35	23	37	1	36	3	38	5	36
19	37	21	39	23	41	1	39	3	42	5	40
19	41	21	43	23	45	1	43	3	46	5	44
19	45	21	47	23	49	1	47	3	50	5	48
19	49	21	51	23	53	1	51	3	54	5	52
19	53	21	55	23	57	1	55	3	57	5	56
19	56	21	59	0	01	1	59	4	01	6	00
20	00	22	03	0	05	1	03	4	05	6	04
20	04	22	07	0	09	2	07	4	09	6	08
20	08	22	11	0	13	2	11	4	13	6	12
20	12	22	14	0	17	2	15	4	17	6	15
20	16	22	18	0	21	2	19	4	21	6	19
20	20	22	22	0	25	2	23	4	25	6	23
20	24	22	26	0	28	2	27	4	29	6	27
20	28	22	30	0	32	2	31	4	33	6	31
20	32	22	34			2	35			6	35

ASCENDANT AND MIDHEAVEN HOUSE SIGNS FOR SIDEREAL BIRTH TIMES

Table 4

If Your Sidereal Birth Time is:	Your Ascendant is:
18:00–19:09	A
19:10–20:33	T
20:34–22:27	G
22:28–0:48	C
0:49–3:23	L
3:24–5:59	V
6:00–8:33	Li
8:34–11:07	S
11:08–13:30	Sg
13:31–15:23	Cp
15:25–16:50	Aq
16:51–17:59	P

Table 5

If Your Sidereal Birth Time is:	Your Mid-heaven House Is:
0:00–1:50	A
1:51–3:50	T
3:51–5:59	G
6:00–8:07	C
8:08–10:07	L
10:08–11:59	V
12:00–13:50	Li
13:51–15:50	S
15:51–17:59	Sg
18:00–20:07	Cp
20:08–22:07	Aq
22:08–23:59	P

G = MOON